Visual FoxPro 3 Codebook Companion CD-ROM

The Codebook companion CD contains the source code to the foundation classes as well as the CDTrak application. These can be found in the CDBK30 subdirectory path.

We have also included samples and demonstrations of various products whose creators have agreed to follow the Codebook approach with their software. These include:

- The Great Elk: A contact management package
- FoxCase: A data modeling tool
- CAPCON: A multi-developer add-on
- CTool: A CRC modeling tool
- Foxfire!: A report and query wizard

At the time of this writing, 13 companies have agreed to become compatible with the Codebook framework. Watch CompuServe (GO FOXUSER—3RD PARTY SECTION) for more information as these products and others become available.

Installation Instructions

Here's how to install the Codebook CD:

1. Copy the CDBK30 directory and all its subdirectories to your hard drive.
2. From VFP, make your default directory the directory where the Codebook project is stored (on my system the command for this would be CD \CDBK30\CD).
3. Type DO CD to run the included APP.

We have included a program which will set up the default path recommended for design time development using the Codebook framework. Using this path means that you can simply type DO MAIN from the command window instead of having to build and run the application each time a change is made. To set this path and install the following utilities (described below), type DO STARTCB.

- SUPERCLS - incredibly useful when viewing source code. Allows you to view and optionally edit superclass methods.
- FLASHSTD - Flash standard utilities, used for inserting our standard header comments, commenting code, etc. The first time you run this program you will be prompted for configuration information (i.e., company name, your initials, etc.).
- BUILDERB - A "wrapper" around the builder system included with Visual FoxPro.

You must fill in the location of the DBC files the first time you run Codebook. The local DBC is located in CD\DATA, while the remote DBC is located in CD\DATA\REMOTE. (You do not need to specify the remote DBC if you have no plans to run Codebook against SQL Server data. Note that in the sample application, the remote data text box is disabled.)

The Visual FoxPro® 3 Codebook

Yair Alan Griver

SYBEX

San Francisco • Paris • Düsseldorf • Soest

Acquisitions Manager: Kristine Plachy
Developmental Editor: Melanie Spiller
Editor: Vivian Perry
Project Editors: Lee Ann Pickrell, Emily Smith
Desktop Publisher: Scott Campbell
Production Assistant: Dave Nash
Indexer: Nancy Guenther
Cover Design and Illustration: Design Site

Library of Congress Card Number: 95-69360
ISBN: 0-7821-1648-5

Manufactured in the United States of America

10 9 8 7 6 5 4 3 2

Warranty

SYBEX warrants the enclosed CD-ROM to be free of physical defects for a period of ninety (90) days after purchase. If you discover a defect in the CD during this warranty period, you can obtain a replacement CD at no charge by sending the defective CD, postage prepaid, with proof of purchase to:

SYBEX Inc.
Customer Service Department
2021 Challenger Drive
Alameda, CA 94501
(800)227-2346
Fax: (510) 523-2373

After the 90-day period, you can obtain a replacement CD by sending us the defective CD, proof of purchase, and a check or money order for $10, payable to SYBEX.

Disclaimer

SYBEX makes no warranty or representation, either express or implied, with respect to this medium or its contents, its quality, performance, merchantability, or fitness for a particular purpose. In no event will SYBEX, its distributors, or dealers be liable for direct, indirect, special, incidental, or consequential damages arising out of the use of or inability to use the software even if advised of the possibility of such damage.

The exclusion of implied warranties is not permitted by some states. Therefore, the above exclusion may not apply to you. This warranty provides you with specific legal rights; there may be other rights that you may have that vary from state to state.

Shareware Distribution

This CD contains various programs that are distributed as shareware. Shareware is a distribution method, not a type of software. The chief advantage is that it gives you, the user, a chance to try a program before you buy it.

Copyright laws apply to both shareware and commercial software, and the copyright holder retains all rights. If you try a shareware program and continue using it, you are expected to register it. Individual programs differ on details—some request registration while others require it. Some request a payment, while others don't, and some specify a maximum trial period. With registration, you get anything from the simple right to continue using the software to program updates.

Copy Protection

None of the programs on the CD is copy-protected. However, in all cases, reselling or making copies of these programs without authorization is expressly forbidden.

Dedication

"Whew! We're not in Kansas anymore."

That was my first reaction upon seeing what was to become Visual FoxPro 3. My second reaction was a quote from Godfather 3, "They keep pulling me back in!" I had promised not to write another book (between helping to run a growing business, constantly traveling and speaking, and trying to live a home life, a book was just too much to handle). But, this product was *fun.* It answered most of the issues that I wanted in a development tool, and Sybex was on the phone. So, here I am.

For putting up with me and my efforts to write this book, I dedicate it, as I did the earlier Codebooks, to my wife, Jan.

Acknowledgments

Some friends commented to me that the last book had one of the longer acknowledgments pages that they had ever seen. Well, now they're going to see a longer one. Codebook has helped to introduce me to many friends, some of whom I've met only through CompuServe.

I'm sure that I'll forget some people, so please consider yourselves mentioned.

To begin, I want to thank my friends and coworkers at Flash Creative Management: David Blumenthal, Robert Godbey, Bryan Caplovitz, Bill Scott, Menachem Bazian, Ed and Elise Ziv, Lior Hod, Miriam Weinstein, Annie Ahn, Eric Zimmerman, Pablo Geralnik, David Lederer, Ari Neugroschl, Leslie Koorhan, Avi Greengart, Dan Freeman, Ken Levy, Paul Bienick, Noam Kaminetsky, Dovid Kosowsky, Sue Vrona, Debra Wolff, and Linda Pleyer. This book is theirs also. They all contributed ideas, code, text, and a fun place to return to when writing this book got to be too much. Thanks a lot, fellow Flashers.

To everyone on CompuServe's Foxforum and Foxuser forums: There are no better or closer forums around. I especially have to thank all of the people who made suggestions, recommendations, and just helped out with Codebook questions. These people include Maurice de Beijer, George Berotti, Steven Black, Ted Brousseau, Chaim Caron, Jose Constant, Doug Dodge, James Fisher Jr., Rick Fitch, Eldor Gemst, Dale Gilstrap, Tamar Granor, Michael Gurr, Erhard C. Gust, Adrian Humphreys, Steve Kern, Paul Moss, John Noffsinger, Joe Paquette, Robert Petruzzelli, Dan Pollak, Tony Scarpelli, George Stevenson, Bob Warzynski, and Annette Wright.

There is also a large group of Fox friends to mention: Pat Adams, Randy Brown, Norm Weil, GillyFlower Chesapeake, Doug Dodge, Chip Doolittle, Nancy Jacobsen, Tom Meeks, Jordan Powell, Tom Rettig, Ellen Sander, Alan Schwartz, John Thornton (and family), Sally Wong, and all the other Cowboys fans.

To all the folks at Microsoft who helped with creating Visual FoxPro and who help to support it: Sherri Bruhn Kennamer, Calvin Hsia, Susan Graham, Morris Sim, Roger Bischoff, Chris Pudlicki, Blaise Mitsutama, Bob Fortner, Eric Rudder, Allison Hatch, Allison Koeneke, Erik Svenson, Meng Khan Phua, Cris Wittress, Richard McAniff, Kathy Boulin, Walt Kennamer, and all the rest—way too many to mention.

To a group of friends who helped shape the thinking that went into the book: Alan Schwartz, Andy Neil, Marie Hooper, Mike and Toni Feltman, Jack Hakim, and Savannah Brentnall.

To my parents, brothers, and in-laws, who understand when I go into hibernation.

To my friend, Kory Kessel, the originator of the name YAG. You finally made it into a second book. Don't get a swelled head.

To a wonderful group of people at Sybex who put up with changing deadlines, constant e-mail messages, and early morning phone calls: Melanie Spiller, Vivian Perry, Emily Smith, Lee Ann Pickrell, Scott Campbell, and Dave Nash.

Finally, I have to mention my cat, Chushie, who has been mentioned in at least three books by two different authors. Got to keep her ahead of the pack....

Contents at a Glance

Table of Contents

Foreword

When we set out to develop Microsoft Visual FoxPro 3, we established one single, overarching goal: we wanted to build the best DBMS product ever. Planning such a sweeping new release requires visionary and forward thinking. Using Visual FoxPro to its fullest requires a similar mindset, and *The Visual FoxPro 3 Codebook* by Yair Alan Griver, affectionately known as YAG, provides developers with a roadmap to reach that promised land.

Those of us who have attended YAG's educational sessions, read his articles in *Data Based Advisor, FoxPro Advisor*, or his earlier Codebooks, have come to rely on his insight in delivering information that is meaningful and practical to the developer. Major corporations have found these methodologies invaluable in creating mission-critical, strategic applications. YAG's theories on developing maintainable, reusable applications have saved thousands of developers thousands of hours of time.

This book's discussion of a methodology for enabling business processes using Visual FoxPro 3 is both cogent and powerful. As YAG says, the combination of Visual FoxPro 3's object orientation, client-server capabilities, and a framework for analysis and development can strengthen the partnership between technology and business in reengineering efforts. I am glad to see other developers adopting the Codebook approach in their third-party tools.

I think that this book will add another dimension to every reader's development toolset. I am sure that you will come to rely on this book as we in the database development community have come to rely on YAG.

Richard McAniff
Microsoft Corporation

Introduction

Welcome to *The Visual FoxPro 3 Codebook.* This introduction discusses the purpose of the book and the differences that have occurred as FoxPro 2.6 has become Visual FoxPro 3.

The FoxPro 2.6 Codebook introduced a shift to an *approach* to developing applications. This book continues in that vein. The computer industry has matured, and with that change the job of the database professional has shifted even more to that of a business analyst and partner. In concert with this change, Visual FoxPro is a product that allows you to build applications against local, .DBF data files, and then scale them to enterprise-wide client-server databases. These changes in the business climate and in product capabilities have resulted in a book that focuses on these developments as well.

The chapters in this book that deal with business analysis, object-oriented design, and client-server development methodologies will apply to any development environment. Selecting a flexible methodology and sticking to the parts that work will improve your development approach. This book discusses the development process, while providing a methodology that will enable you to create robust FoxPro applications in a shorter timeframe with fewer bugs.

Changes and Enhancements

Unlike the previous two Codebooks, this book contains the source code on CD-ROM. This has reduced the amount of printed source code required, and has allowed me to add extra business and analysis chapters without making the book unwieldy.

Due to the changes in Visual FoxPro 3, this book contains four parts. As with the earlier Codebooks, the first part deals with "the big picture" in database application development, and the fourth part walks the reader through the sample application. New to this book is the second part, which discusses Visual FoxPro 3's new features, and the third part, which provides a detailed discussion of the Codebook framework and methodology.

How This Book Is Organized

Part One of this book discusses business process reengineering and client-server, and how the two are actually mirror images of each other. It then discusses how Visual FoxPro's combination of a local data engine, client-server capabilities, and object-oriented language provide a wonderful foundation for the client-server systems of tomorrow. It also discusses the concepts of enterprise modeling and object-oriented analysis from a reengineering perspective.

The first chapters discuss the phenomenon known as business process reengineering (BPR) or process improvement. This approach to designing a company's infrastructure and reporting structures is finding its way onto the covers of business magazines and into the minds of company presidents and CEOs around the world.

As I will discuss, business process reengineering does not mean cutting costs or personnel, although that may happen in the course of a reengineering effort. It does mean designing a corporation so that it can evolve as the business climate changes. It involves providing information to the people that need it when they need it.

At the same time as BPR has come to the forefront in the business community, client-server development has taken hold in the imagination of business and technical people everywhere. It is discussed in both technical and nontechnical magazines, and, as any good buzzword should, it means anything that a particular person wants it to mean. In fact, at the last FoxPro developer's conference, I was wearing a button that read "I'm a Client/Server" (to go with a cafe theme). Apparently client-server is not only hardware and software, it can be people, as well! This book will discuss a flexible, three-layer model for client-server development that involves solving business needs by providing for an easily scaleable solution. This model relies on an enterprise model of the business.

The part continues with chapters on object-oriented analysis and design, reviews various OOA&D methodologies, and discusses those that this book will use in detail.

Part Two discusses Visual FoxPro's approach to multiuser data access, object model, front-end capabilities, and uses for Visual FoxPro's OLE 2.0 capabilities as well as suggested naming and programming conventions. Part Three contains a complete description of the Codebook framework and class hierarchies (this is equivalent to a much enhanced version of our COMMON code).

Part Four guides the reader through the specification and development of a sample application using these techniques. Additionally, this part discusses any unique code used in the sample application, as well as a view of all of the modules that make up the application.

Finally, there are three appendices which include a list of suggested reading material, a discussion of OLE Control use in Visual FoxPro, and a step-by-step approach to developing applications using Codebook. Finally, a glossary provides definitions of important terms.

The Visual FoxPro 3 Codebook

As I mentioned earlier, this book focuses on an approach to developing applications. The hardware that we are developing on and for is becoming more powerful and less expensive. At the same time, the software tools that are available to us can accomplish more, creating larger portions of applications for us. Of course, the types of applications that we are being called on to create are also becoming more complex, as we develop applications for a user base that is comfortable with—and understands—the capabilities of computers.

When early applications were created, they tended to be monolithic applications that were geared toward solving an unchanging business problem. In order to address this business issue, a software development methodology known as the "waterfall model" came into vogue. The approach viewed software development as a waterfall. You performed and completed one phase before "falling into" the next. The typical steps in a waterfall model of software development can be seen below.

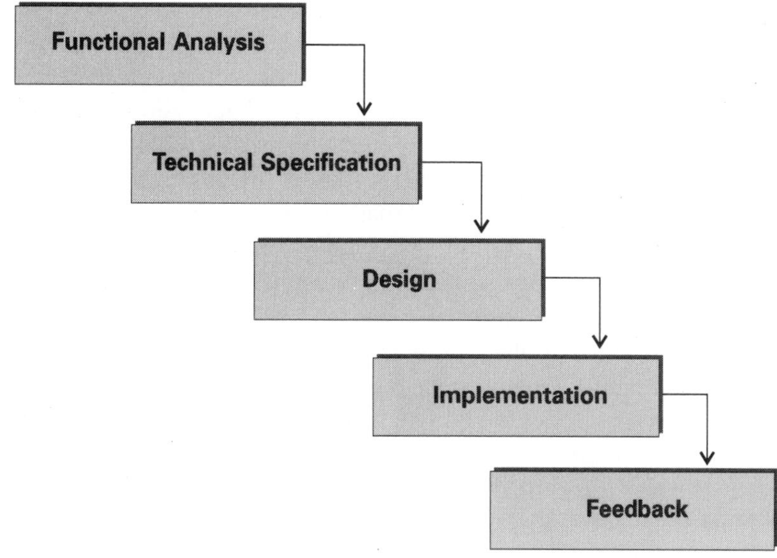

Waterfall model of software development

The development effort typically began with a functional analysis which focused on what the application had to do. The business issues were covered here. Once this phase was completed, the development group went off and developed a technical specification, including flow charts, database diagrams, etc. Upon completion of this phase, the application was developed, tested, and installed. After installation, feedback began, necessitating extensive changes to the application.

A better approach, which involved constant communication with the end-user, was needed. This one can be seen as more of a spiral approach. It involves going through the same steps of functional analysis, technical analysis, and development, but is done in "bite-sized chunks." The developer obtains a global view of the application first, then develops smaller pieces of it while keeping the user involved. This user involvement can usually be accomplished with two techniques: prototyping during analysis and the use of milestones during installation.

Prototyping moves a portion of the development section into analysis. Using tools such as form and menu designers, you can quickly develop the look of an application. Utilizing core sets of objects, you may even be able to create a working model of the application, allowing the user to become more comfortable with the "look and feel" of the proposed system. People can then relate their business needs to a sample application a lot more easily than to a paper sketch. Using a prototyping approach has two other advantages: it allows you to get to the correct design and solution *before* doing the "guts" coding, and equally important, it achieves buy-in with the end-users. They can see their recommendations coming to life and will have an investment in the success of the software that you are creating.

The use of the milestone approach in software delivery complements the prototyped analysis. This approach involves delivering working, completed sections of the application in pieces, over a span of time. Using this approach, a core set of functionality, like a section that allows the maintenance of "setup" data (client information in an accounts receivable system, for instance) is installed first, with training on that portion of the application. This allows the user to begin entry of data, become comfortable with the system, and suggest enhancements and changes to the application before it is completed (when it becomes more difficult to modify). Finally, since the user is only being trained on, and is only working with a subset of the complete application, he or she does not get overwhelmed by the enormity of the entire product. It is always easier to train someone on one task at a time than it is to train someone on an entire process. Using the milestone approach, a user learns the entire process one task at a time, and actually enters useful data throughout, ensuring proper testing of all of the application. All the test data in the world doesn't compare to real world data entry.

Once the final milestone is accomplished and the entire application is in place, the users are confident that they have a system that they understand and that meets their needs, and the developer is confident that support calls and maintenance issues have been reduced.

This book discusses the issues of keeping communication flowing between members of a development group and between a developer and a client. The code portion of the book strongly promotes the use of object-oriented techniques to enable the developer to quickly develop prototypes and finished applications, facilitating the development and delivery approaches detailed above. It also discusses the four main roles of any development project: team leader, user interface developer, database designer, and business rule modeler.

Is This Book for You?

Part One of this book will benefit any developer, because it discusses the issues that arise in application development, with a particular focus on client-server and object-oriented development issues.

Part Two and Three are geared towards the intermediate-to-advanced Visual FoxPro 3 developer. They assume that you have a basic knowledge of the command set and the use of the design tools. Part Four walks the reader through a sample application of the book. The book discusses an approach to using the commands and tools rather than telling you what each command and tool does.

By reading this book, you will gain an understanding of the issues involved in developing large-scale, robust applications. You will also gain a methodology that eases development in Visual FoxPro 3 by incorporating object-oriented and data manipulation techniques that will allow you to scale an application from a small local system to a large-scale client-server application.

Visual FoxPro 3

Visual FoxPro 3 is a generational leap in software from FoxPro 2.6. It puts FoxPro development squarely into the realm of object-oriented, client-server applications. The enhancements to Visual FoxPro 3 can be seen in four main areas: the visual design tools, object orientation, local database enhancements, and client-server capabilities.

Visual Design Tools

Visual FoxPro's design tools allow the developer to rapidly prototype and develop applications.

The form designer, which replaces the screen builder, is a modeless development tool that gives the developer easy access to Windows events and a strong visual approach to development. It works on a live instance of an object, allowing the Visual FoxPro 3 developer to access a form during design time through the language. This capability has brought about the advent of the builder technology in Visual FoxPro 3.

The report designer has added the capability of calling functions at certain points during the running of a report. The addition of the data environment to a report allows a developer great flexibility, including the ability to "bind" a form to a report to enhance the ease-of-use of that report.

The menu builder has added the capability of "negotiating" with an OLE 2.0 automation object. This capability allows the Visual FoxPro developer to combine another OLE application with his or her own, in one seamless environment.

Object Orientation

Visual FoxPro is built upon a robust object-oriented architecture with a good set of base classes to build from. The architecture provides for the common goals of object orientation: reuse and enhanced maintenance.

The class designer and class browser are the most exciting things about Visual FoxPro's object implementation. They allow a developer to design visually, enormously enhancing the ease-of-use of the product and easing a developer into this new concept.

Database Enhancements

FoxPro's local engine has been greatly enhanced through the use of the database container (.DBC). Visual FoxPro 3 developers can now take advantage of longer field names, default values, rules, triggers, null values, and primary keys. These capabilities allow the Visual FoxPro 3 developer to place the data handling and business rules where they belong: with the database, not the forms in the application.

Client-Server Capabilities

Visual FoxPro 3 has greatly enhanced the client-server capabilities of FoxPro. In addition to placing the SQL Pass Through capabilities of the FoxPro 2.6 Connectivity Kit into the base product, the new VIEW mechanism allows a developer to prototype locally and deploy globally.

The tuning capabilities in Visual FoxPro, particularly its background fetch and delayed-memo fetch abilities, allow developers to speed up their client-server applications.

PART 1

Analysis and Design Issues

Chapter 1

Business Process Reengineering

Introduction

The latest business buzzword sweeping the nation is "reengineering". This term, brought to the public eye in the best-selling *Reengineering the Corporation* by Michael Hammer and James Champy, is being touted in management seminars, making the cover of business magazines, and spawning a series of conferences. What is this movement known as "reengineering" and why has it become the rallying cry for business in the 1990s? What does it mean to us as developers, as we try to create information systems that help businesses to perform more effectively? What tools are available to us in our quest to help in reengineering?

What is Reengineering?

The traditional management structure came from the theories of Adam Smith (who created the first theories for mass production). The first major application of these theories in modern times was in the automobile manufacturing industry. According to this approach, for an industrial operation to run more efficiently, it was best to organize work into tasks, divide responsibilities, and have supervisors focused on assuring that each task was completed properly. Essentially, you had each person on the line perform one task, mindlessly. As the task list for creating an automobile grew, middle management was created to add the thinking back into the process of creating automobiles. Management boiled down to three things: enforcing business rules, allocating resources, and planning.

Coupled with the development of this approach, the world economy was expanding after World War II, and quality was not important because demand was so great. Someone, somewhere, would buy whatever was manufactured.

Suddenly though, the business world was disrupted. Competition was no longer the company down the street but was instead the company an ocean away. Customers became more sophisticated and began to expect products that worked right every time for a long time. With advances in information technology, they also expected that we would respond faster than ever before to their concerns, suggestions, and requests. Finally, our own colleagues began to value professional growth as much as any other aspect of their job.

Our business structures did not support this new world. Spreading tasks throughout an organization meant that we couldn't react quickly enough as input bubbled up and down large management structures. It also limited the professional growth and skills of our professionals. We weren't focused on the customer; we were focused on the task. We couldn't plan particularly well either and we certainly couldn't be creative in problem solving.

Enter reengineering.

According to Hammer and Champy, reengineering is defined as "the *fundamental* rethinking and *radical* redesign of business *processes* to achieve *dramatic* improvement in critical, contemporary measures of performance such as cost, quality, service and speed."

The *italicized* words in the paragraph above are key to understanding where business must focus.

By *fundamental*, we mean to ask why we do what we do. In the course of any organization's lifetime, habits develop. Sometimes, we even call them traditions. The reasons for doing things at some earlier point in time were probably sound, but as time passed and situations changed the practices often didn't.

By reexamining them, by starting over, we evaluate what makes sense for us today. This is perhaps at the core of the term *radical*. Radical means getting to the *root* of things and then beginning a process of reinvention.

Reengineering is a change in the way we approach evaluating what needs to be reviewed. We no longer look at tasks but at *processes*. Processes are a collection of activities that takes one or more kinds of inputs and creates an output that is of value to the customer.

Finally, *dramatic* is best described as a remarkable, quantifiable improvement. It's not a savings of 5 percent of time or money but a more sizable savings of, say, 50 percent. It is a reduction in defects by a large factor. It is a significant drop in the amount of time necessary to bring a product to market.

How Does Reengineering Tie Into Database Development?

To be successful at reengineering we must look at how we work in a totally new light. Can jobs be combined? What is the natural order for getting a job done? Who really needs to be involved? Where would it be most appropriate for a task to be performed? What information do workers need in order to make their own decisions?

This type of thinking changes the way we work. Jobs change from simple tasks to multidimensional work. People's roles change from controlled to empowered. Job preparation changes from training to education. The focus of performance measurement and compensation shifts from activity to results. Values change from protective to productive and managers change from supervisors to coaches. Organizational structures change from hierarchical to flat. Finally, executives change from scorekeepers to leaders.

To look back at our automotive example: In a task-oriented approach, it is very difficult to improve quality. A person responsible for adding one screw to an assembly cannot gauge overall quality. It can be statistically proven that with enough separate tasks, it is impossible to create a zero-defect automobile. When you change to having a group responsible for an entire process (for instance, creation of the suspension system), the members of the group can test the process, improve it, and build quality into that process. This allows you to ensure quality in the finished product. This is similar to quality assurance in software, which works more effectively when it is brought in during the analysis phase, rather than after the software is finished.

Interestingly, all this change creates a new set of values. We learn that the customer pays all of our salaries, so a good idea would be to please him or her. Every job is important and we all make a difference. We get paid for the value that we create. Constant learning is part of the job.

As you can see, reengineering involves decentralizing the decision making throughout the organization. Information which used to show up only in one place must appear in as many places as needed. Database applications are crucial to the information dissemination process. With decision support and online systems, now everyone can be a part of the decision-making process.

As I mentioned earlier, in the task-based approach, management was boiled down to three things: enforcing business rules, allocating resources, and planning. Database applications can now enforce business rules (preferably through a well-defined interface, but that's another chapter), and as we empower people, they can allocate their own time with the help of various computerized systems (schedulers, inventory systems, etc.). A manager's job is now predominantly one of planning. Decision support systems are used more appropriately in order to steer the corporation.

A reengineered company should have an enterprise data model that is used to consistently capture information for the online and decision support systems. As database developers, we will have to pay more attention to the big picture and not install a solution that becomes an island of information.

The first step in developing an information architecture is to look at the business processes that exist or will be put in place.

Moving into a reengineering process requires a long-term commitment to this effort by upper management. This commitment will help ensure the continued health of business. Database projects will become even more central to business, with a greater emphasis (correctly) on the development of a model that, instead of creating an island of information, supports the core needs of the business: competition, customer satisfaction, and change management.

Chapter 2

BPR and Client-Server: Two Sides of the Same Coin

Introduction

As we discussed previously, our business world has been disrupted. Competition is no longer the company down the street but the company an ocean away. Customers have become more sophisticated and now expect products that work right every time and for a long time. With advances in information technology, customers also expect that we will respond faster than ever before to their concerns, suggestions, and requests. Finally, our own colleagues value professional growth as much as any other aspect of their jobs.

Our "standard" business structures do not support this new world. Spreading tasks throughout an organization via a large organizational chart means that we can't react quickly enough as input bubbles up and down large management structures. It also limits the professional growth and skills of our professionals. Organizations aren't set up to focus on the customer; they are set up to focus on a task. We aren't able to plan particularly well because nobody has control of enough of the pieces of a problem, and we certainly can't be creative in problem solving.

Enter Business Process Reengineering. Hammer and Champy defined BPR as "the *fundamental* rethinking and *radical* redesign of business *processes* to achieve *dramatic* improvement in critical, contemporary measures of performance such as cost, quality, service and speed." Put simply, it is a change in the way we approach evaluating what needs to be reviewed. We no longer look at business tasks but look instead at *business processes*. Processes are a collection of activities that takes one or more kinds of inputs and creates an output that is of value to the customer.

As a simple example, you no longer have a person that simply screws one bolt onto an engine. You have an engine team, which is given the latitude to put together the entire engine in the most efficient way that its members deem possible. They can ensure that quality is built into the engine. It is very hard to ensure that quality is built into a bolt of an engine.

Technology has helped to drive this radical redefinition of business. In order to empower these teams, we must make sure that the information that they require is available to them when they need it. If a team that builds machinery can see the upcoming week's orders, they can reset the schedule to create similar machines in a larger batch, rather than simply filling orders in a first in/first out manner. With this power, they can actually produce more machines in a shorter span of time, since they have saved the work setup.

At the same time, American business has become a more nomadic place. "You have to be where your customers are" is a common refrain. Salespeople are going out of the office, laptops in hand, and placing orders to corporate headquarters right from their customers' offices. Software consultants are using rapid prototyping techniques to create samples of applications in client offices. This nomadic lifestyle which emphasizes strategic flexibility, in concert with the need to put information where it is most useful and an effort to reduce IS costs, has helped to push the client-server market to the forefront of the corporate mind.

The REAL Business Database Problem

Business is constantly changing. The hardware platforms of today will, in all likelihood, not be the hardware platforms of tomorrow. The business that we're in today may be very different from the business we were in yesterday and it may be different from tomorrow's business. What we need is an application development approach that allows us to change front ends, back ends, and most importantly, business rule enforcement, whenever we need to.

What does this require? Let's take a look at this issue from all three angles:

Front-End Development

To properly do front-end development, we need a prototyping tool that can lead to our finished front end. It should preferably be cross-platform so that we can leverage other hardware and software platforms. Finally, it should be extensible so that we can enhance it ourselves to provide the front ends that our users expect.

Business Rule Enforcement

This portion of our application requires that we have a language syntax that is geared towards solving business problems and that is fairly straightforward and "English-like," if at all possible. The capability to quickly understand and modify a rule is the most important need for this portion of an application. It is necessary that every front end use this layer in order to enforce the rules. It would be nice if the rules could be automatically accessed instead of the back-end data. If that capability is not possible, storing the business rules with the back-end data is the next best option.

Back-End (Database) Development

The database administration portion must have the capability of enforcing its own rules with the data. To this end, the capability of triggering a stored procedure is a must. For instance, it may be necessary to automatically create a summary view of an invoice as it is added (for use in a decision-support database). This is a database rule, and has nothing to do with the business as such. The summary view is simply used for database throughput enhancements.

What Is Client-Server Development?

According to its proponents, a server back end will:

- reduce network overhead
- enhance security of user access
- enhance data reliability
- run faster

In reality, the truth isn't so simple. Engine enhancements, like Rushmore, have been made to products, like Visual FoxPro, which drastically lower network overhead. The new Database Container has added stored procedures and triggers to the DBF format, improving its data reliability, and Visual FoxPro has been shown to be faster than various client-server DBMSs at various querying operations.

The truth also shows that *on the average,* less network overhead will take place when using a client-server back end like Microsoft SQL Server, although it is at a cost of putting more work on one process. Therefore, in many cases involving remote access, a back end like Microsoft SQL Server does make sense, but it doesn't necessarily make sense in every setting.

In actuality, client-server has nothing to do with the hardware or software that we're using. It's more of an approach to development. Client-server is a means of separating the three main portions of a business application: front end (GUI), business rules, and back end (database); so that the three can run on a combination of platforms as dictated by the business requirements. It can run on one machine, based on one product, or can run on three, based on various development languages. Each of these approaches is client-server. The main differentiator is the capability of rapidly scaling and changing the application as the business requires it.

Business Process Reengineering helps to solve one of the main issues involved in client-server distributed database systems: Where do you put the data? Creating a distributed system involves putting the data closest to the people who need them, but that is often difficult to determine. If you are creating a distributed system in concert with a reengineering effort, the answer is simple: The *process owner* also owns the data created by that process. Distribution becomes a simple process.

Client-Server—A Sample Application

Let's look at a simple example of a company that is growing and reengineering their business. For this example, we'll use Visual FoxPro as our local data engine, and Microsoft SQL Server as our back-end data engine. Visual FoxPro makes a fairly ideal client-server development environment from our three-layer model perspective. Its object orientation and visual development environment allow us to quickly create a customized front end for the client, the Xbase language syntax is English-like and has been one of the overwhelming business definition languages in use during the past 10 years, and the addition of the database container with its stored procedures and triggers has made it a wonderful local data store as well. Finally, the upsizing wizard allows one to quickly move much of an application to a remote back end, as is called for in our model.

The one piece that isn't native to Visual FoxPro (and indeed, is only beginning to be available at all) is the separate definition and implementation of a business rule layer. For now, we must use the native stored procedures in the database container, and store the name of a business rule, its description, and its associated stored procedure in our analysis documentation which should be kept up to date.

ABC Groceries—Our Example

ABC Groceries is a single grocery store that installs a point-of-sale and decision-support system based on our model. All three levels of our solution are initially installed using Visual FoxPro. The front end is prototyped and delivered using the visual development tools, the business rules are kept as stored procedures (and are documented in the analysis) and the database container is used to give the database long field names and maintain referential integrity. Data access is done through local views defined in the database container.

As the store prospers, a decision is made to move the back office and management staff to another location and open two more stores across town. These stores install the same application as the first, which has been modified to include some database rules that automatically put summaries of every transaction in a file as they are added. This summary is sent nightly to the back office location where it is used for decision support.

Joan, the manager of Store #2, decides that she wants to offer a new service: home delivery. She begins to offer this service and subclasses the data entry form to allow the addition of the customer address. Her store prospers.

Fred, the manager of Store #3, decides to offer the same service but requires that his clerks capture the local subway stop as well (he is in a more urban part of town). Joan's form is subclassed and used by Store #3.

As more stores are opened, the back office decides that they need to track people's credit better (a local con artist has been passing bad checks at different stores). They install a SQL Server application that contains the name of anyone that has passed a bad check. The individual stores' database containers have the credit check validation modified to send the check writer's name to the main office and approve the purchase if no rows are returned.

What can we learn from this simple example?

- Each local store has been given the freedom to capture the information that it needs to serve its customers better. One can capture addresses, the other subway stops. The main office doesn't care—it's given the individual stores the authority to be the best grocery stores in their neighborhood—their mandate is to do whatever it takes.
- People in the back office get the information that they require. They don't need to know that Mr. Johnson buys a dozen eggs every Wednesday (although the local stores may). They do want to know how many eggs are purchased daily so that they can do their order estimations and calculations. By standardizing what is sent to it by each store, the back office has the information that it needs.
- Visual FoxPro and SQL Server are used in concert to get the information that is required to the store, quickly and efficiently. Since credit information is the only *current* requirement for a centralized system, that is when the information is requested. If the main location decides at a later date that it wants all of the employees' IDs at its location for validation before entry into the application, that capability can be added easily.

As we can see, Visual FoxPro's object orientation, in concert with its native client-server capabilities, allows a powerful *business solution* to be crafted. If one store grows and decides that it needs a wireless capability, or wants to allow "shoppers" to go to client homes and do the ordering for them, it may scale up to a store-wide SQL Server solution without having to change the actual code base.

Chapter 3

Enterprise Modeling

Introduction

Application developers, especially those who started out with PC databases, learned to "jump right in" when developing applications. Their goal was simply to begin application coding as soon as possible.

In recent years, it has become apparent that this may not be the best way to deliver efficient and meaningful applications to clients. Our role as developers should not be just to turn out code but rather to help improve the business processes that we are automating.

To do this, we must understand the business of our clients before we can begin to improve it and have those improvements reflected in our product. The business community has tried to get this message to us for years, but today the Business Process Reengineering (BPR) and quality movements are delivering the message ever louder and clearer.

These management professionals equate understanding the business to understanding the processes the business performs, and now the information technology (IT) camp is sending the same message. We maximize the benefits of our clients' solutions and allow better information sharing by following methods that put understanding the business first. Developers of information systems on machines of all sizes use methodologies and tools that help them put the business first in their work. How do we ensure that we fully understand the business? We employ a technique called Enterprise Modeling.

The Process Map

This approach evolved from the business community and gained momentum with the publication of *Reengineering the Corporation* by Hammer and Champy. The book includes a business process map that depicts the workings of Texas Instruments' chip-making company in a single diagram. To TI and to us, this picture is worth much more than a thousand words.

This process map displays TI's major processes and how they interact. This type of picture is the goal of Enterprise Modeling: to reduce the workings of the business to a picture or map that both business and technology people can easily understand.

Let's illustrate the business process (BP) map with an example. Our example company is a mail-order house that sells compact discs. Employees take orders over the telephone and collect the money up front only by credit card, eliminating any billing and keeping overhead low. The major process is taking the customer's order and fulfilling it. The other process is developing the catalog of CDs the company sells.

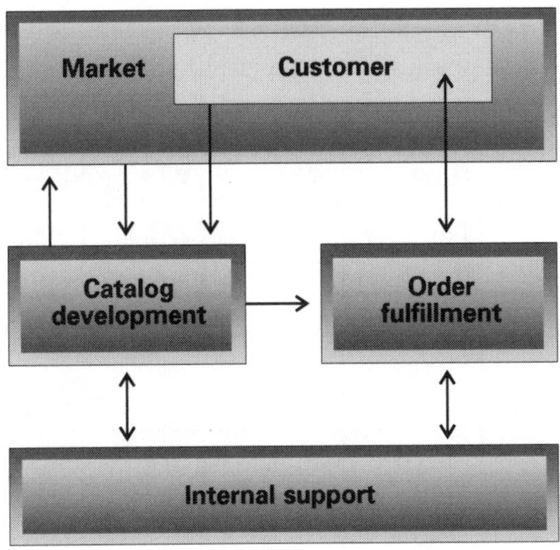

A sample business process map

The Catalog Development process group receives input (ideas for CDs) from the general market and from some customers. The output is a list (catalog) of CDs that the company sells. The group sends this list to the market (mailing list) and to the Order Fulfillment process group. The Order Fulfillment group takes a catalog and an order request, and turns it into a product delivered into the customer's hands. The Internal Support group receives employee requests and resolves problems. Payroll and other support needs could be taken care of there as well.

To understand the business well enough to develop the business process map, we need a method for talking to the "owners" of the business. By "owners" we mean the owners of the business processes, not necessarily the literal owners of the company. The method that we use is derived from another book, *Designing Quality Databases with IDEF1X Information Models* by Thomas A. Bruce. Although this is a great book for database modeling, we mention it here because it discusses the Information System Architecture (ISA) Frameworks developed by John Zachman.

The Information System Architecture

The frameworks aid data sharing and good design, and are useful to us because they start with the business. The expanded ISA Framework, in the appendix of Bruce's book, manages to ask all the business-owner questions in the first two rows of the six row framework. This abbreviated version is what we use for Enterprise Modeling and is listed below.

	What	**How**	**Where**	**Who**	**When**	**Why**
	Data	Function	Network	People	Time	Motivation
Objectives/ Scope	List of Important Business Things	List of Business Processes	List of Business Locations	List of Organi-zational Units	List of Business Events/ Cycles	List of Business Goals/ Strategies
Business Model (Example)	Entity Relation-ship Diagram	Function Flow Diagram of Process Map	Logistics Network	Org. Chart	Master Schedule, PERT Chart	Business Plan

By responding to the questions in the first row, one begins to understand the business. If the group of business owners is receptive to answering these questions, this can allow for a meaningful group discussion of the core model of the business. Even the group dynamics can help your understanding. By proceeding directly from the lists created by reviewing the first row of the table above to the representative models in the second row, you assure that the owners' ideas about the business are in the models. Whether you jump directly from the process list to a Business Process map or do a more IT-oriented function flow diagram first will probably depend on the complexity of the business. However you do it, we still think it is important to end up with a process map for later comparison. Taken all together, we call the combination of lists and models the Enterprise Model, and the activity we call Enterprise Modeling. It is the first step to success in supplying the enabling technology to make business better.

An Example

Let's use our example of a mail-order compact disc (CD) company, and go through the two rows of the framework that comprise our Enterprise Model. We need to imagine an interview with the *owners* of the CD company, by which we mean those responsible for the business processes. By going across the first row we ask all the high-level business questions and create lists on which to base our model. The order in which we ask the questions is not too important (we find most people like to start with *how*). We will start with *what* things are important to the business and continue from left to right across the row. The responses from the CD company's owners follow.

List of Things Important to the Business

Employees

Customers

Supplies

Catalogs

CDs

Sales Orders

Vendors

Business Processes

Making the catalog

Mailing the catalog

Monitoring the market

Shipping

Paying our bills

Inventory & ordering CDs

Ordering supplies

Managing relationships

Advertising

Accounting

Marketing

Business Locations

One location with one building/office

Organizational Units

Administration/Accounting

Marketing

Sales

Shipping

Business Events (Cycles)

1st Quarter—Recovery, restock, catalog by 4/1

2nd & 3rd Quarters—Sales pick up, prepare

4th Quarter—Holiday rush, catalog by 10/15, hire temp help

Business Goals

Best price/benefit for customers

Profitable and enjoyable business for employees

Reasonable growth without adding more locations

Increase revenues with automation efficiency

It is normal to spend more time on *what* and *how* than on some of the other questions. To help separate the two ideas, tell everyone that items in the Important Things list should be nouns and those in the Business Processes list should be verbs. It is a good sign for all the items to be plural (usually ending in 's') and for the processes to end in 'ing.' It is appropriate to review the obvious because what is obvious to you and to your client may be different. By discussing the number of locations *(where)*, even for a small business with only one, you may discover plans to expand or the use of a vendor for packaging and shipping that effects the business and therefore your application. The *who, when,* and *why* lists help set boundaries for the business and your application by capturing the number of employees, maximum load, and expected growth.

Try to keep ideas for changing the business separate from how it is today. If new ideas are suggested while making the lists, organize your lists into Now and Later sections. By the end of the Enterprise Modeling process you want a clear mandate on which business process you are improving and an agreement on what needs changing.

The lists taken together should give a very complete sketch of the business you are trying to improve. The next row of the framework focuses on turning that sketch into a clearer picture. Let's work backwards (from right to left) across the second row turning our lists into more organized documents that we can then discuss.

The Business Plan and Event Cycles

Row two of our framework asks us to provide a business plan as a manifestation of a business goals strategies list. If the company you are working with has a business plan, great; get it and read it. If they do not have one and are willing to create one from scratch, that could be a very worthwhile exercise. The minimum result should be an outline of between four and ten company-wide goals and supporting sub-goals for a year. In addition to having a timeframe (one year), the goals should be specific and measurable.

The minimum business plan for the CD company follows, along with some sample calendars for recording business events (cycles). To get everyone thinking in the same time frame, use some type of planner to mark the important dates. This can be as simple as monthly pages with boxes marking the dates or as complex as Gantt and PERT charts.

CD Company Business Plan, 1995	
Increase sales by 50 percent over last year	Implement marketing program Implement inventory strategy Automate order and inventory tracking
Increase profits to 20 percent of revenue	

CD Company Business Plan, 1995 *(continued)*	
Achieve 99 percent customer satisfaction	Implement quality program Liberalize return policy Automate customer service tracking
Achieve recognition as industry leader	

CD Company Monthly Planner	Events
January	Recover from holiday rush Restock inventory
February	Prepare catalog
March	Mail catalog Financial information to bank
April	Catalog orders pick up
May	ASCAP Convention
June	Financial information to bank
July	Restock inventory
August	ASCAP Convention
September	Prepare holiday catalog Financial information to bank
October	Mail catalog Hire temporary help
November	Train temporary help
December	Holiday rush Financial information to bank

The Organizational Units and Logistics Network

As we continue across row two to the left, the next two cells represent the organizational units in the company and the business locations. An "org chart" is a good way to present the business units and is commonly recognized by business people.

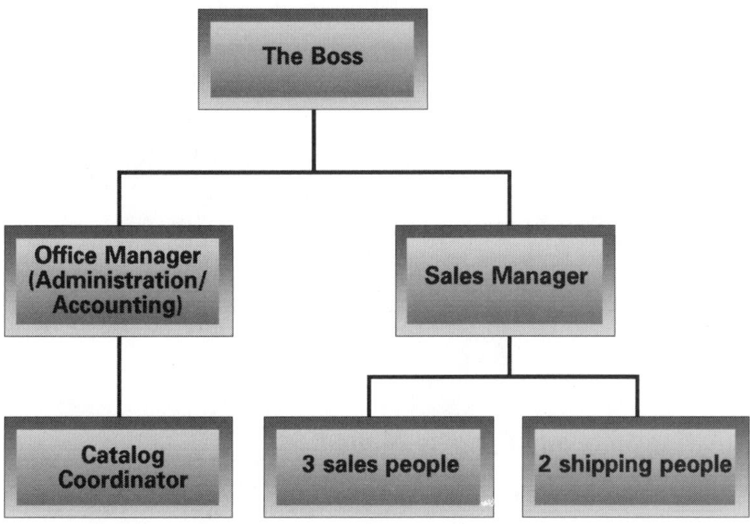

A sample organizational chart

A logistics network is a way to show required work flow by location. For a large business, manufacturing could be at one location, regional warehousing at another, and order fulfillment at a third. For our small CD company we probably do not need a logistics network. However, I will show an idealized example of CDs coming from one supplier. Traditionally, a logistics network only deals with company locations, but it may make sense today to include suppliers. Again the lesson here is to discuss even the obvious with the client, so you can uncover new issues.

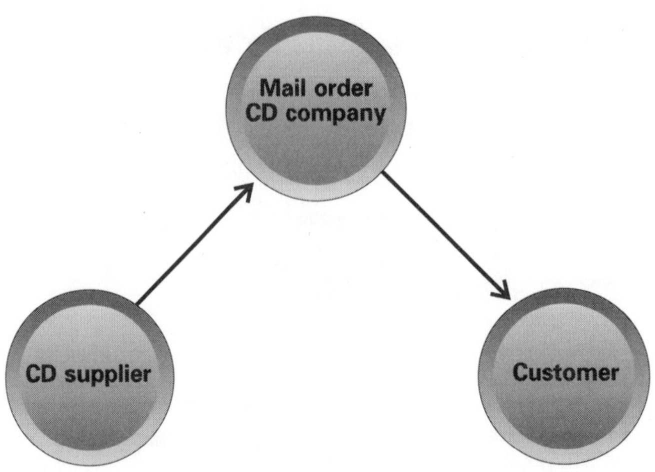

A logistics network

Entity Relationships and Process Maps

The last two cells (remember we are going right to left) can be a little more challenging. Our goal for the process cell is to create a simple picture that shows how the business works. The trick is to group the list of seemingly random processes into the fundamental processes needed to run the business. You know that you have included only the fundamental processes when removing one of the processes means the business will not run, and when any processes not explicitly listed can easily be sub-processes of the ones that are. This is the way most business people will see their business.

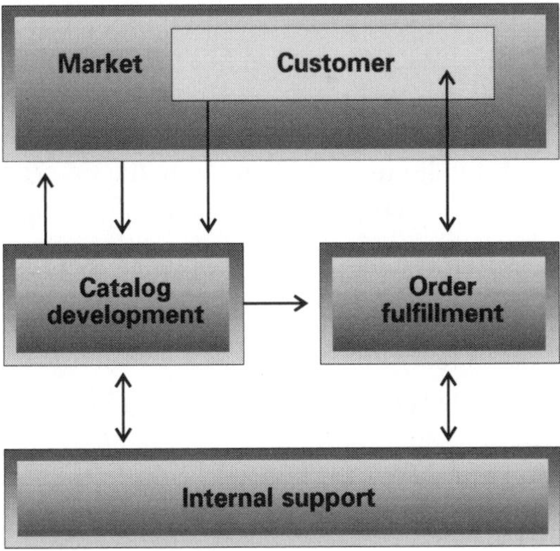

A process map

To finish the Enterprise Model we need to show the relationships between the Important Things on our last list. A high level Entity-Relationship (ER) diagram is a great way to do this. This is the way most database developers will see the business, however it should make sense to the business people after it is explained to them.

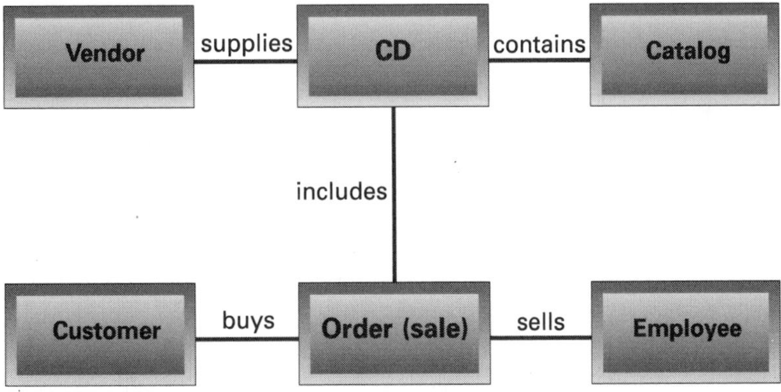

A high level Entity-Relationship diagram

By gathering this information, we have accomplished our goal of capturing the essence of the business. We turn each of our questions into lists, and each of our lists into simple models to test our understanding. The models, taken together, comprise a complete picture of the business that scales very well to the largest corporations. By discussing and refining the Enterprise Model, we improve communication between the business and information professionals. The model is technology independent, and works with single-user systems, larger client-server jobs, or new object-oriented technology. It provides a road map for us as we design and maintain applications for the company. In fact, if business owners decide to reorganize the company structure based on the process map, you are actually performing Business Process Reengineering (BPR).

Chapter 4

Object-Oriented Analysis and Design

Introduction

It has been written that when creating object-oriented software, you should spend as much as 70 percent of your time on the analysis and design of the system, with the balance devoted to actual coding and testing. What is it about object-oriented development that makes it less attractive to just jump right in and code? To understand the answer to this question, we need to take a brief look at the software development process.

In the 1980s, we witnessed the birth of the "Information Age" culminating with the explosion of the computer industry. Thousands of new programming jobs were created as companies began to bring more and more personal computers into the organization. As a result, new types of applications were required as the extent to which a personal computer could be used to accomplish common business activities quickly became apparent. The machines became more and more powerful, and the software became more and more complex and harder to create as business needs grew.

As the complexity increased, programmers looked for ways to better manage the software development process. We adopted structured programming techniques, 4GLs, CASE tools, automated testing tools—anything that would make our lives as developers easier and improve the quality of our software. Many books have been written on the subject of structured programming, and many programmers have gained useful insights from this material. For example, we've all been taught the famous "top-down" architecture, starting at the top-level menu system and working "down" from there. We've also read much about modularized code, creating small routines which serve a specific purpose that we could reuse in multiple applications.

Structured techniques have served us well for many years, but the time has come to move on to the next level. We should not, however, discard any of our existing knowledge, since many of the concepts still apply when creating object-oriented code. However, structured analysis and design techniques do not map well to object-oriented programming principles.

Using formal structured analysis and design techniques is like trying to cut a piece of beef with a fork: You might manage to do it, but a knife would have been more appropriate and more effective. The problem is that these techniques are aimed at procedural programming and a procedural way of thinking. When designing software in this fashion we first design our data structures and then create functions that support these data structures. The focus here is divided between code and functions. Because of this split, when we focus on one, we tend to lose sight of the other. Do you remember creating flow charts? Following a flow chart is like following a road map through the application:

> *Function A calls function B. If function B returns True, then loop 400 times, calling functions C & D. Function C calls functions F & G, etc....*

Which word sticks out? *Function*. Where does the data fit in? Isn't the data itself what the user of our software is most concerned about?

Object-oriented programming allows software developers to focus on data and the functions that operate on that data together as a logical unit. This is directly supported in all object-oriented programming languages with a construct known as a *class*. As we have seen, a class is really just a blueprint for creating objects of that class. Through object orientation, instead of seeing the application as a series of interconnected functions working on some externally defined data structures, we can now view our program as a collaborative collection of "intelligent" objects, all working together to achieve a common goal. You could almost look at each object as a living, breathing entity, because each object essentially "knows" how to carry out its role in the application. (In fact, we feel this concept is important when performing object-oriented analysis and design, and will therefore revisit it shortly.)

Because of this new shift in focus, and as such to a new way of thinking, we need new techniques for analyzing and designing our software systems. We need techniques that directly support object-oriented programming.

Choosing a Methodology

If you've been to the bookstore lately (maybe when you bought this book!), you may have seen one or more of the following titles:

- *Object-Oriented Software Engineering* (Jacobson)
- *Object-Oriented Analysis and Design With Applications* (Booch)
- *Designing Object-Oriented Software* (Wirfs-Brock)
- *Object-Oriented Modeling and Design* (Rumbaugh)
- *Object-Oriented Systems Design: An Integrated Approach* (Yourdan)
- *Object-Oriented Analysis and Design* (Martin and Odell)

These texts all offer what is known as an object-oriented development methodology. Each methodology comes with its own notation, i.e., shapes and constructs that are used to create various types of diagrams that represent the class hierarchy, object state transitions, etc. Each methodology also comes with its own set of terms that are different from those of other methodologies yet the concepts that the terms are describing are essentially the same. Some even have software tools that are designed to specifically support the notation used in the methodology.

How does one choose a specific methodology? There have been plenty of articles in various object-oriented publications that address this subject precisely, and even a few books as well. As a result, we won't get into a step-by-step comparison of the assorted methodologies in this book. However, we will describe what methodology we chose, why, and how we are currently using it. We'll also take a look at where this technology is headed, and where we plan on going with it.

First There Was Dark

The OOP wave started very early at our office. There were a handful of us who were really into the technology when the Visual FoxPro object model was nothing more than a twinkle in Microsoft's eye. Trip after trip was made to the local bookstore, and some of us played around with C++ and Smalltalk. We learned as much as we could about the existing methodologies, and we frequently held open discussions to share ideas and information. Object-oriented technology is addictive; the more you learn, the more it starts to make sense, and thus the more you want to learn.

As news of Visual FoxPro was released, we began to search for a methodology that would meet the following criteria:

- It should be relatively easy to learn and use. Studies have shown that simpler analysis and design techniques are more likely to be used than more complicated ones (see Alistair AR Cockburn, "In Search of a Methodology," *Object Magazine* 4, Issue 4). Furthermore, it should be simple enough for small development teams or individuals to use (one-three developers), yet scale well when more developers are needed (four-10 developers).

- It must adapt well to Visual FoxPro. The Visual FoxPro implementation is not a completely pure object-oriented programming language. Rather, it is a hybrid, allowing you to continue to write procedural code alongside object-oriented code. In this sense it is more akin to C/C++ than it is to a pure OOP language like Smalltalk, where *everything* is an object. Furthermore, because Visual FoxPro was so new, we knew that no single existing methodology would provide a seamless, perfect fit.

- It should be relatively inexpensive. Since we are essentially breaking new ground, and, perhaps more important, because Visual FoxPro is a brand new object-oriented product, it didn't seem wise to invest thousands of dollars in a methodology that didn't fit just right.

And Then There Was Light

So after reading countless books and magazine articles, we decided to adopt the use-case concept from Ivar Jacobson; the CRC card approach (Classes, Responsibilities, and Collaborations), also known as Responsibility Driven Design, from Rebecca Wirfs-Brock; and some form of planned incremental/iterative development. Let's take a brief look at each of these concepts individually.

Use Cases

One of the best ways to capture the overall system functionality is through a use-case model. The use-case model uses a concept known as *actors* (not users!) to help visualize what is outside the system, and a concept known as *use cases* to define what should be performed by the system.

The Actor

"The actors represent what interacts with the system. They represent everything that needs to exchange information with the system," according to Jacobson. Note that it is important that we differentiate between an actor and a user. This is to indicate that an actor may not necessarily be a human being sitting at a terminal interacting with the system. It could, in fact, be an external device connected to one of the computer's ports, even another computer. When an actor does represent an individual user, however, it is important for the actor to represent the *role* that the user is playing, not the individual.

We can gain the benefits of object orientation by applying object-oriented concepts to the actor/user concept. Think of an actor as a class, and individual users as instances of that class. These instances only exist when the user does something with the system. With this approach, it becomes easier to see that the same person can appear as instances of several different actors.

For example, in a very small company, one individual's job may be to input customer orders into the system. That same individual may also be responsible for going into the warehouse and filling the customer order by placing the ordered items in a shipping carton (and then mailing the order to the customer). There are two distinct actors here, the order-entry person and the shipper. Creating a use-case model with a single actor may cause us to design the system incorrectly, perhaps missing some required functionality, thereby resulting in a system that the user is not satisfied with. By using the actor concept instead of a user concept, it is easier to discover all the different ways in which the system will be used.

In the use-case model, the actor is represented by the following symbol:

The Use Case

When an actor uses the system, he or she is said to initiate "a behaviorally related sequence of transactions." We call this sequence a use case. An example of a use case would be: "Input customer order." It is important to note that at this point, we are not concerned with exactly how this use case will be implemented in the system. Instead, we will focus on what must happen for the use case to be considered complete by creating a use-case description.

We can apply object-oriented concepts to the use-case concept as well. Think of the use-case description as the class and each use case as an instance of that class. When an actor performs an action on the system, an instance of some use case is created, and the transaction belonging to that use case (defined in the use-case description) is executed. Since a use case represents some type of behavior in the system, and this behavior has a state (how far it has reached, what the status of the system is, etc.), it is useful to think of a use case as an object (an instance of a use-case description).

The use case is represented in the use-case model by the following symbol:

When discovering use cases, it is more effective to create more coarsely grained use cases than it is to create more finely grained ones. Find the answer to the question: "What is the user trying to accomplish with this sequence of actions?" or "What is the *intent* of these actions?" For example, a user may indicate that as part of his normal daily activities, he "is notified of a problem with a particular customer, calls the customer for notification, fills out a specific form, and sends the form out for approval." Just by looking at this description, we have no idea that the intent of these actions is to process overdrawn balances. Once we have determined this intent, we would create a use case for it.

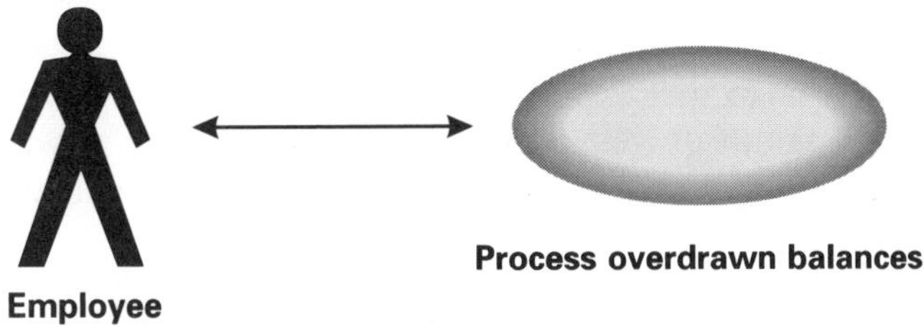

A sample use-case model

Because of the high-level nature of the "Process Overdrawn Balances" use case, it can be thought of as a kind of container, or a "use envelope," as it were. The intent of the use case is written on the outside of the envelope. The details of how the intent is accomplished, in terms of other use cases, scenarios, and even other use envelopes, are kept on the "inside," and thus can be seen in the use-case description.

It is important to capture the intent of use cases because it is less likely for the intent to change over time, even though the underlying design may. The entire set of use-case intents and use-case descriptions comprise the entire functionality of the system. As a result, the use-case model provides a simple yet effective means for communicating functional requirements to the users of the system.

Responsibility Driven Design

Once we have captured the functionality of the system, it becomes time to begin building our class hierarchy. One of the most powerful and easiest methods we've discovered of doing class hierarchy building is the CRC card method, described by Rebecca Wirfs-Brock in *Designing Object-Oriented Software.* In fact, this method has become so popular that most competing methodologists work it into their own methodology in some way.

The concept is simple: Read through the requirements specification (and use-case descriptions) for the system you are building and underline, circle, or highlight all the nouns. (You may also choose to list them on a separate sheet of paper. Whatever works best for you is the method you should choose.) These nouns represent candidate classes. The quality of our selections does not matter at this point: We are merely concerned with discovering as many candidate classes as we can. Therefore, no judgment should be made when building this list.

Once we have a list of candidate classes, we can begin to evaluate them one at a time. Note that we should use caution when selecting classes to discard since we simply do not have sufficient information yet to judge each class fairly. Duplicates and other items where another noun or phrase better expresses the concept should be removed. If there is any doubt as to whether a class should be removed, leave it in!

Undoubtedly, as this process progresses, classes that are very similar in nature are discovered. For example, a candidate class list may include both of the following phrases:

"Word processing file"

"Spreadsheet file"

Classes such as these represent a situation where a superclass that contains properties and behavior common to both types of files may be beneficial. This concept of creating a new superclass is known as *generalization.* Add these superclasses to the list.

The remaining classes will now be transferred to CRC cards. Just what is a CRC card? CRC stands for Classes, Responsibilities, and Collaborators. The card itself is really nothing more than a simple index card. Create one card per class, writing the name of the class in the upper-left corner on the front of the card. For example, for class Account:

Class: Account

Flip

Class: Account

Superclasses:

Subclasses:

A sample CRC card

Once the CRC cards are created, you can lay a subset of them (or all of them) on a large table, and begin to categorize and arrange them in a hierarchical fashion, possibly revealing new candidate classes in the process. This process may also reveal existing superclasses which need to be subclassed to suit the application's requirements. For example, our candidate class list may not include references to specific types of files, but rather, a reference to some arbitrary generic type of "file." Spotting these candidate superclasses early on may lead us to discover some interesting candidate subclasses. This process of subclassing to create a more specific form of a class is known as *specialization*.

Responsibilities

Now that the initial candidate class list is complete, it's back to the requirements specification and use-case model to begin identifying responsibilities. This time, underline, circle, highlight, or create a list of all the verbs you can find. Pay close attention to the use-case model since that is where we should have already captured the entire functionality of the system.

Once the initial list of responsibilities is complete, start assigning responsibilities to the classes. Each responsibility of a class is listed down the left-hand side of the CRC card.

Class: Account

Flip

Class: Account	
Superclasses:	
Subclasses:	
Know the account balance	
Accept deposits	
Accept withdrawals	

A completed CRC card

Sometimes it is difficult to assign responsibilities to classes that represent inanimate objects in the real world. Although this suggestion may sound silly, we've found it useful to sometimes think of inanimate objects as living, breathing entities. It is therefore helpful to ask, "If I were an account, what would I need to know about myself?" Since objects in an object-oriented program are said to contain a certain amount of built-in intelligence, this approach, in addition to being entertaining, seems to make sense.

Review for Maintenance

After discovering your classes, review them for maintenance. List a few of the main changes that could occur to the application in its lifetime. The Enterprise Model is a good place to discover these possible enhancements.

Once the enhancement list is written up, review your class hierarchy to see how many of the enhancements can be achieved within the framework of your application. If you find that most enhancements will not change the application, but can be achieved through subclassing and inheritance, you are in good shape. If you find that the enhancements require a major rethinking of your class hierarchy, go ahead and review that hierarchy and modify it so that it will be ready for maintenance. It is this iterative approach (returning to the Enterprise Model) that helps to build maintainability and reuse into your class hierarchy.

Incremental/Iterative Development

A recent study revealed that almost all successful object-oriented software projects implemented some kind of incremental development. (see Alistair AR Cockburn, "Unraveling Incremental Development," *Object Magazine* 4, Issue 8.) Incremental development is defined as "a scheduling and staging strategy that allows pieces of the system to be developed at different times or rates and integrated as they are completed."

Iterative development means not locking yourself into one phase of development at a given point in time. You analyze a little, design a little, and code a little. How better to validate your designs than through implementation? One must use caution not to take this concept too far. At Flash, where I work, we have three major deliverables to the client:

- Business needs analysis
- Software prototype and specification
- The actual system (which itself is delivered in milestones)

There are deadlines to meet at each of these phases, and therefore it is not advisable to spend most of your time coding when trying to deliver a business needs analysis! The key here is not to lock yourself into a rigid attitude that says you should not write a single line of code until you have completely analyzed and/or designed the entire system.

The Result

With the new knowledge, let's revisit the question posed at the beginning of this chapter: What is it about object-oriented development that makes it less attractive to just jump right in and code? If you've completed the use-case analysis and created your CRC cards, the next logical step would be implementation. (Incrementally and iteratively, of course). This is actually the easy part, since we already know what has to be done and where it has to go. The answer is that if we spend more time on our analysis and design, the result is a system that is more robust, easier to maintain, and easier to reuse for other applications.

Today and Tomorrow

We've given you a bird's eye view of the development methodology currently in use where I work. The third section of this book will detail each phase of our approach. I encourage you to go out and research the market for other books, tools, and other sources of information, and decide on a methodology or development approach that best suits your company's needs. Once a selection has been made, do not stop researching the market for new sources of information, as object-oriented methodologies are constantly being updated. While I do not suggest you change your methodology once a month, I feel that the industry as a whole will evolve and mature, and eventually individual methodologies will become secondary to a company-specific Software Engineering Process and Software Engineering Process Support Environment.

Chapter 5

Life Is a Feedback Loop

Introduction

In the last few chapters, we discussed the concepts of Business Process Reengineering, client-server data distribution, Enterprise Models, and object-oriented analysis. Why go through these things in a Visual FoxPro book? The answer is that the combination of these things allows us to create a model for analyzing a business problem and providing a solution (whether technological or not). This model, and indeed any analysis model, utilizes a constant pattern of checks and balances to keep us in tune with our business needs. This feedback loop is essential whenever we are to look at creating an analysis method for our use.

It All Starts Here

The approach that I espouse involves starting with the Enterprise Model. As you recall, this gives us a high-level view of our organization and a plan for its future growth. It includes descriptions of the high-level entities that the client's organization works with, a network model of locations that we interact with today and will interact with in the future, and a description of the various positions in an organization.

It is this model that we return to, over and over, as we perform the various processes required in analysis. Let's take a look at these processes and discuss how the Enterprise Model fits into the feedback loop.

Data Modeling

Many corporations wish to create an all-consuming data model for their business. They believe that if they can create one model for the company, and have all applications use this model, their job will be much easier because less duplicate data will have to be audited and corrected.

The typical procedure for achieving this data model is to have someone interview people throughout the organization, spending a year or more in the process. By the time the data model is complete, however, the organization will have changed, and the fact that new systems created during this time have not used the model compounds the problem!

I advocate using the Enterprise Model's high-level entity relationship diagram in creating the corporate data model we discussed in Chapter 3. Begin with a high-level view of what you need. As an application is created (and the Enterprise Model will help to show which applications are most important to the business), interview the appropriate people based on the organizational chart of the Enterprise Model. Create a data model for that application, and add the newly discovered information to the Entity Relationship diagram for the corporation. Any new applications should be based on this newly refined ER diagram.

This process of constantly refining the ER diagram will end with a completed data model for the company, created on an "as needed" basis, with all applications using the same model.

Object Modeling

Two of the biggest issues in object-oriented analysis and design are the concepts of reuse and maintenance. These things do not just happen because you are using an object-oriented programming language. They occur because you have developed a culture that rewards reuse and have planned maintenance into the classes that you create from the start.

How do you discover what objects will be necessary for your business, and how do you design them so that they can easily change as your business changes? The answer, once again, is to look at your Enterprise Model.

If you are lucky enough to have a team of developers whose sole job is to create classes for the corporation, they can use the Enterprise Model to focus on the issues that are most important to the corporation, and key their development to those issues. If you don't have this team of developers, the Enterprise Model allows you to select the most important candidates for business process automation. You can quickly see if any of the classes that you are creating may be useful for future automation efforts, concentrating on making these classes as complete as possible.

The Enterprise Model is also key to enhancing the maintainability of your applications. As you create your CRC cards and have a candidate class hierarchy, go back to the Enterprise Model and write down five to seven ways that your application may change based on future requirements. Check your hierarchy to see how much will have to change for each requirement. If more than half of your classes will have to change, examine whether you can restructure your classes to make your life easier in the future. You'll be glad you did.

Data Throughput and Distribution Modeling

Client-server systems rarely fail because of the software choices made. They usually fail because of a lack of analysis and design before coding begins. When designing your client-server applications, you *must* look at all of the issues that will affect your application and data throughput. Here again, the Enterprise Model comes through. The network model allows you to see how many locations will be accessing your application. You should find out how they'll be doing so. There's a big difference between 20 people working from a local 10Base-T Ethernet network and 20 people using modems to dial in at 2400 baud. Looping back to the network model allows you to take hardware concerns into your analysis process.

The process model portion of the Enterprise Model allows you to address data distribution issues. In larger systems, the question often arises, "Where should this data go?" The correct answer is usually, "Whoever owns the process needs the data most regularly." In other words, since the owner of a process is the one most likely to perform that business process, information that is changed by that process should go on his or her network and be accessed by others via dialup. For example, if your company does its sales through a catalog and has one group in New York that adds new prospects to your customer database, and has another group in Phoenix that takes the actual credit card orders, the customer data should probably be placed in New York (where it will be changed most often), while a read-only slice of it can be placed in Phoenix. If you allow the order-entry personnel to change address information, the read-only customer lookup information (name, ID number) should be placed in Phoenix, providing for quick lookup, with a dialup capability to New York for address lookups of the *one* selected customer.

Conclusion

The key thing to recall in any analysis method is to incorporate some kind of loop that takes business needs into account. You don't have to use the method that I use in this book, with the Enterprise Model driving everything, but be sure to include some kind of feedback mechanism in your analysis work.

Chapter 6

Multiuser Programming Issues

Introduction

Visual FoxPro provides a wealth of new capabilities when it comes to handling multiuser contention issues. Let's take a look at some of the basic approaches used to handle locking in the past, and then discuss what the new capabilities are and how they can be used in our applications.

FoxPro 2.6 Locking Strategies

In FoxPro 2.6, developers could natively do their GETs directly to the fields (direct READs) or to memory variables (indirect READs). As I explained in *The FoxPro 2.6 Codebook,* there was a third approach available—at a cost of doing some programming—that of a *signature field*. A signature field is a field that changed in value whenever any writing was done to a row in a table, allowing our save routines to quickly check that field in order to see if anyone else modified the data while we were working with it. I recommended using an optimistic locking scheme in which a record was only locked during a save. Let's review the three methods:

Direct READs

FoxPro will automatically attempt a lock for you when you edit a record directly, and the lock will be kept in force until the end of the edit. The advantage of this method is that little programming needs to be done. It is all automatic. A copy of the record must be saved before the edit begins (either with a SCATTER MEMVAR [MEMO], or a COPY TO <tempfile>) in case the user decides to cancel the edit.

A modeless application creates further difficulties, however. A record is *always* showing on the screen, ready to be edited. In fact, with multiple windows, many records may be showing on the screen, ready to be edited. For instance, a customer information screen may be available at the same time as the CD entry screen. As software designers, we cannot allow all of these records to be locked at all times. FoxPro 2.6 provided an enhancement to the READ command, READ NOLOCK. Issuing a READ with the NOLOCK clause allows FoxPro 2.6 to display the window without the capability of editing the fields until a lock is manually placed with a SHOW GETS LOCK. The SHOW GETS LOCK refreshes the screen and locks the record.

Indirect READs

Editing to a memory variable means that the record is never locked, and the user can do all the changes that are necessary. Canceling the edit does not require that you do anything to the record because it was never changed. When the record is saved, you must lock the record and move the changes into the record (with a GATHER MEMVAR [MEMO] or an APPEND FROM <tempfile>). The problem with this method is that another user may have modified the record, and the current user's modifications may wipe out the first user's changes.

One solution is to lock the record immediately when beginning the edit, and to hold the lock until the edit is completed. The other solution is to compare the record to a second set of memory variables that have not been changed. If there is a match, the change may take place. If the two don't match, modifications to the record have taken place and you must program accordingly.

Semaphore Locking

A third approach that can be used involves a marker that lets you check whether or not someone has modified or locked your record. The simplest form of semaphore locking allows you to know that someone else has modified the record while you were editing (to memvars), without having to check every field to see if it has been modified. This form of logical locking (called a *signature*) involves the addition of an extra field to every dbf, in which you put a unique ID. When you wish to save your modifications, simply lock the record and check whether the semaphore ID field has changed. If it has, you know that someone else has saved changes, and you can act appropriately.

A more advanced form of logical locking allows you to do edits to certain fields while other fields are being updated. For instance, if you have to globally update an inventory file with a new pricing scheme, you would normally have to lock the inventory file and change all of the records. While performing this update, nobody else could have access to the file. Using a semaphore locking scheme, however, you could let people know that you've locked the item price field, but allow them to update the on-hand field.

Concurrency Issues

The key thing to remember about multiuser programming in FoxPro is that *only the user who has the RLOCK() is viewing the current information.* FoxPro caches information at the local station, updating it as necessary. You can only assure that the user is seeing the most recent data if he or she has a lock on the record.

Accordingly, you will want to perform an RLOCK() before allowing the user to edit the data. As we'll see, Visual FoxPro allows you to request the current information from the server, which can be used during the updating of information.

Visual FoxPro 3 Locking Strategies

The addition of the data dictionary to Visual FoxPro effectively negated the use of memory variables when editing because validation rules apply to a field and users expect the validation to occur as they are entering information. Enter *buffering*.

Buffering essentially duplicates and extends the functionality of memory variable usage while implicitly binding itself to the data. When you turn buffering on, Visual FoxPro copies the current information into a buffer which you edit directly, referring to your information as if it were the actual data fields themselves. This allows column and row validation to occur. When you are satisfied with the changes, and assuming that the validation has returned a .T., the data are written which cause the appropriate triggers to fire.

There are two buffering modes: row buffering and table buffering. Each mode can be set to use optimistic or pessimistic locking. As in FoxPro 2.6, optimistic locking only locks the data at the time they are saved, while pessimistic locking locks the data when editing begins.

Buffering is set by using the CURSORSETPROP() function with the Buffering parameter and a value of one through five, which have equivalents in FOXPRO.H, as follows:

Value	Description	FOXPRO.H Named Constant
1	No buffering	DB_BUFOFF
2	Pessimistic row buffering	DB_BUFLOCKRECORD
3	Optimistic row buffering	DB_BUFOPTRECORD
4	Pessimistic table buffering	DB_BUFLOCKTABLE
5	Optimistic table buffering	DB_BUFOPTTABLE

For instance, to set the current work area to optimistically buffer the table, we would use the following line of code (assuming that we have #INCLUDEd FOXPRO.H):

```
=CURSORSETPROP("Buffering",DB_BUFOPTTABLE)
```

When working with server data in a buffered mode, Visual FoxPro forces the use of optimistic buffering. As in *The FoxPro 2.6 Codebook*, we're going to look at managing optimistic concurrency in greater detail.

Updating Our Data

In order to update our information when using table buffering, we make use of the TABLEUPDATE() function. TABLEUPDATE() takes three parameters:

- Should all rows be updated? If set to .T., all pending edits will be sent to the back-end database.
- Should failed updates be forced? If set to .T., any changes made by another user (which would normally cause the update to fail) will be lost, and the update will be forced through.
- What alias should be updated?

We can now see various approaches to multiuser contention:

The Current User Always Wins

This approach is useful for a case where we assume that the most recent user always has the most recent information. For instance, we have a table that contains contact names, addresses, and phone numbers. The assumption is that the user with the customer on the phone is keying in the correct address and phone number. In this case, we simply issue a TABLEUPDATE(.T.,.T.) to always send through our data.

The Current User Always Loses

This approach is useful for a case where a person cannot change any newly entered information. In a case like this, we issue a TABLEUPDATE(.T.) on all changed rows at once, and if the update fails, we issue a TABLEREVERT(.T.) to revert all of the rows.

The Current User Wins Some

This approach is useful for those cases where we know that the current user can never overwrite any changes to the database. For instance, we are writing a library check-out system. A patron can call up all of the books for an author and check off the ones that she wants to check out. While she is perusing the list, however, another patron has checked out some of the same books. When the update is rejected, we will check out whichever books remain, discarding the rejected updates.

In order to do this, we issue a TABLEUPDATE(.T.), attempting to update all changed rows. If the update fails, we loop through the changed rows using the GETNEXTMODIFIED() function. This function, when used in a loop, moves from modified row to modified row, with a parameter telling it what row to begin on. Passing it a zero positions us on the first modified row, passing it an existing row moves to the next modified row. As we hit a modified row, we issue a TABLEUPDATE(), attempting to update just the current row. If that fails, we issue a TABLEREVERT() for the current row. When we are finished, we've updated all possible rows and reverted those that have been changed. If we wanted to, we could keep a list of updated (or failed) rows and present them to the user.

The Current User Gets to Decide

In this situation, when an update fails, we want to present the user with as much information as possible. The basic approach for this method is similar to the previous one: We issue a TABLEUPDATE(.T.), and if it fails, do a loop with the GETNEXTMODIFIED() function.

When we encounter a row that has changed, however, we loop through the data in the row, presenting the user with the following values:

Value	Description
The field itself	This contains the information entered by the user.
OLDVAL(<field_name>)	This contains the information that the user saw before the changes were made.
CURVAL(<field_name>)	This contains the information that currently exists in the back end.

We allow the user to specify whether or not the changes he or she made should supersede the information on the back end, and we then issue a TABLEUPDATE() or TABLEREVERT() accordingly.

Conclusion

Visual FoxPro's very capable buffering scheme allows us to build robust multiuser applications. In conjunction with the updatable view support which will be discussed in the next chapter, it offers us a path to developing robust client-server applications as well.

PART 2

Visual FoxPro Capabilities

Chapter 7

Visual FoxPro and Client-Server

Introduction

With the release of Visual FoxPro 3, Microsoft has moved FoxPro into the forefront of client-server front ends. VFP includes numerous ways of accessing back-end information and, in concert with its very fast local database engine and data dictionary, becomes one of the best options for serious client-server development. This chapter will review the capabilities built into VFP, touching on when each capability may be used.

Client-Server Basics

Before we move onto Visual FoxPro's client capabilities, let's review when you should look at implementing a server back end.

Wide Area Networks	If you are using a WAN, client-server applications will, on the average, provide you with less network I/O, improving throughput.
Large databases with small result sets	One truism of client-server development is that you want to minimize the information coming over the wire; therefore you typically pre-qualify the queries that will be sent to the client. For instance, you would ask the user which customer's information a user wants, then request only that data, instead of putting up a BROWSE of all the customer's information.
Server enforced security and robust transactions	Server products have been designed to provide secure systems for your data and robust transaction handling. While non-server databases, like Visual FoxPro, can provide some transaction support and data integrity triggers, they are not comparable to the robustness built into the various server engines.

Now that we've looked at the basic reasons for going to a server, let's look at the various approaches to accessing server data that Visual FoxPro provides. They fall into two basic categories: SQL Pass Through (SPT) and View Support.

SQL Pass Through provides the same basic capabilities that the FoxPro 2.6 Connectivity Kit provided (now built into the base product with improved speed), and View Support allows you to treat back-end data as if it were native FoxPro data, though you want to keep the size of result sets in mind. Both of these approaches can use Connections, which are predefined paths to the back-end data that are given an alias.

You can set multiple properties for your back-end connection, including whether the connection is synchronous (the query completes on the back end before your application continues) or asynchronous; BatchMode (should multiple SQL statements complete on the back end before we regain control); Comment; ConnectString; ConnectTimeout; DataSource; DispLogin (when should a login dialog be displayed); DispWarnings (should non-trappable errors be displayed); IdleTimeout; PassWord; QueryTimeout; Transactions (automatic or manual); UserID; and WaitTime. All of these properties are Read-Write.

SQL Pass Through

SQL Pass Through is analogous to low-level file functions—it gives you direct access to the ODBC (Open Data Base Connectivity) functions and to your back end. SPT requires us to write code that opens the connections, passes commands, checks for errors, and more. These things are handled through a group of functions that start with the three letters, SQL.

To establish the connection we use the SQLCONNECT() or SQLSTRING-CONNECT() functions, both of which return a connection handle, a number that Visual FoxPro 3 assigns to the connection. This handle must be used in subsequent SPT function calls. There are no required arguments for these functions. If used by themselves, the functions automatically call up a connection or login window. Optionally you can pass arguments including a defined data source name, user ID, and password; or a connect string can be issued if the connection has already been created.

SQLSETPROP() and SQLGETPROP() allow you to set or get the properties for a particular SPT handle. They work the same way as the connection properties except that you cannot assign Comment, ConnectString, DataSource, IdleTimeout, or UserID properties. Additionally, you can also get (but not set) ODBChdbc and ODBChstmt which are internal ODBC connection and statement handles that can be used by external library files (FLLs) to call ODBC directly.

The bulk of our SPT work is done with the SQLEXEC() function which allows us to pass an executable SQL command to the back end and, optionally, to pass the name of the (read/write) cursor that will hold our result set.

SQLMORERESULTS() allows us to retrieve more information when we are working in asynchronous mode.

The SQLTABLES() function retrieves the names of the tables of a remote data source into a local cursor. The SQLCOLS() function retrieves the names of the columns and the information about those columns for a specified remote database table and stores that information in a local cursor.

If an SPT function returns an error code, the value of it indicates whether the error is a connection or environment error. SQLERROR() is used in order to return more information about the error. SQLERROR() will give us information at any of the component levels.

As you can see, the SQL Pass Through functions give us a very low-level approach to accessing our back-end data. It is very useful when we need to control things very closely (for instance batching commands for transaction processing or manually calling a stored procedure), but should not typically be required.

View Support

Visual FoxPro supports both local and remote views, and uses this approach in order to provide seamless upsizing capabilities. In essence, you treat local data as if it were remote data and, when you need to upsize, you simply run an "upsizing wizard" (that ships with the Professional Version of Visual FoxPro) which copies your local views to remote views and renames your local views for you. The bottom line is that your application continues to run the same way, but you are accessing remote data! Let's take a quick tour of a Remote View.

A remote view is created using the view designer. Essentially, it is made up of a SQL SELECT statement that is typically *parameterized,* that is, you provide a memory variable that will be used at query time in order to give you a subset of the data. You specify which fields should be accessed and which ones can be modified in your view. Once the view is fetched from the back end, it is treated as a local Visual FoxPro table, and you can use VFP commands on it as usual, typically in a buffered editing mode. When you tell Visual FoxPro to update the table with the modified data, it actually wraps up your changes in either a SQL UPDATE or a matched set of SQL DELETE and SQL INSERT commands (the choice is up to you).

To give a simple example, you can create two views, one on customer (SELECT * FROM Customer WHERE Customer.CustID = ?mCustID), and one on orders (SELECT * FROM Orders WHERE Orders.CustID = ?mCustID). You bind your views to the form's data environment and set up a textbox that asks the user to type in a customer ID. Once the customer ID is entered, you issue the following commands:

```
=REQUERY("CustView")
=REQUERY("OrderView")
thisform.Refresh
```

When you bind views to a form, you can set a property that causes Visual FoxPro to USE the views with a NODATA clause. This causes the connection to be established, with no data coming down the pipeline. Each REQUERY causes the data to be returned down the preestablished connection, allowing you fast throughput. Note that this same code will work with local or remote views.

FoxPro also handles transaction processing in an easy-to-use, yet thorough, manner. You can set transaction processing to automatic (the default) or manual. In automatic mode, Visual FoxPro works in a mode similar to Microsoft Access. It wraps every back-end update in a transaction. In manual mode, you can begin a transaction and send multiple updates until you end or roll back the transaction. The choice is yours and, again, it works seamlessly for both local and remote data.

Combining Views and SQL Pass Through

Very often you may want to combine Visual FoxPro's remote view support with SQL Pass Through. For instance, you may want to begin a remote transaction, issue your TABLEUPDATE() functions to pass information through to the remote server, and then end the transaction or roll it back. The manual transaction support is handled through three functions: SQLSETPROP(), SQLCOMMIT(), and SQLROLLBACK().

SQLSETPROP() allows you to set various properties for a back-end connection. The Transactions property defaults to 1 (automatic transactions), but can be set to 2 (manual transactions). Setting the Transactions property to manual starts a transaction the minute anything changes data on the back end.

SQLCOMMIT() commits any pending transactions.

SQLROLLBACK() rolls back any pending transactions.

In addition to these functions, CURSORGETPROP() can be used in order to get the handle to the connection that your remote view is using. A sample code fragment shows all of these functions in use:

```
#INCLUDE FOXPRO.H

USE Remote_View
```

```
=CURSORSETPROP("BUFFERING",DB_BUFOPTTABLE)  && Set buffering
*-- Do edits to the remote view

lnConnHandle = CURSORGETPROP("ConnectHandle")
=SQLSETPROP(lnConnHandle,"Transactions",2)&& Manual transaction
IF TABLEUPDATE(.T.)
   =SQLUPDATE(lnConnHandle)
ELSE
   =SQLROLLBACK(lnConnHandle)
ENDIF
```

This example uses a remote view, gets the connection handle, and ends the transaction based on whether or not the information made it safely to the back end.

A Simple Form

Let's look at creating two remote views and a simple form that displays the information from the views, allowing one view to be updated. For this example, we'll connect to the PUBS sample data that ships with Microsoft SQL Server 4.2 and create a VFP connection called PUBS_SQL_Server in a database called Pub_Info. Place this database in a project called VFP_CS and create two parameterized views:

Author_info

```
SELECT Authors.Au_id, Authors.Au_lname,   ;
   Authors.Au_fname, Authors.Au_phone ;
FROM Authors ;
WHERE Authors.Au_ID = ?cAuthors_ID
```

Author_titles

```
SELECT  titles.title, titles.price, ;
   titles.ytd_sales, titleauthor.royaltyper, ;
   titles.notes ;
FROM Titleauthor, Titles ;
WHERE Titleauthor.title_id = Titles.title_id
AND Titleauthor.au_id = ?cAuthors_ID
```

Note that neither of these views is updatable at the moment — we'll worry about that later.

Creating Our Form

Go into the project and create a new form. Don't bother running the form wizard, let's do it by hand.

Click on the textbox tool, and drag a textbox into the form. Set its .Name property to "txtInput." Now, drag and drop the three fields: au_fname, au_lname, and au_phone from the project manager onto one line in the form. Change the .Name properties to: txtAu_fname, txtAu_lname, and txtAu_phone. Finally, drag the author_titles view onto the form, where it will be placed as a grid by Visual FoxPro. Name the grid grdAuthor_titles. When you are done, the form should look something like this:

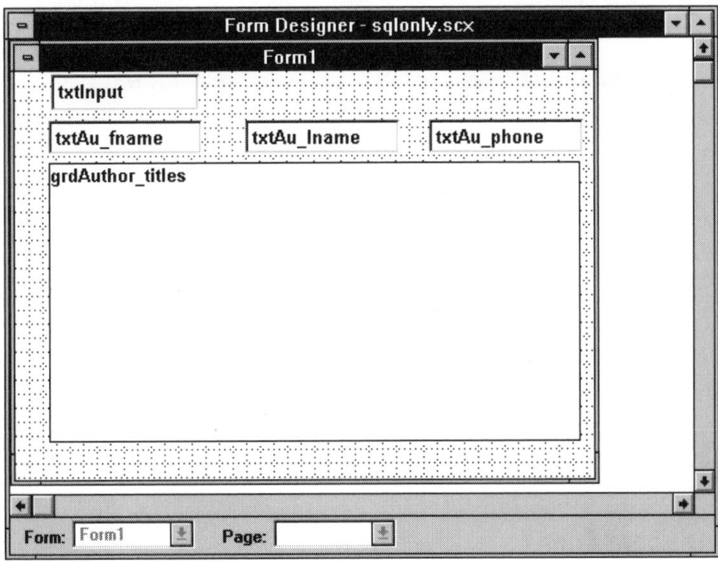

A sample form

Let's look at what we've done so far. When dragging and dropping from a database container to a form, Visual FoxPro automatically does the following things:

1. Creates a textbox or a grid, depending on whether you are dropping a field or a table/view.
2. Adds the table/view that you are using to the forms data environment.
3. If you have a builder lock set on, it calls the appropriate builder.

Setting Up Our Data Environment

Now, let's go into the data environment for the form and make a few changes. To get to the data environment, either right-click on the form and select data environment..., or select that option from the View menu pulldown. When you do so, your data environment will look like this:

The data environment

If the property sheet is not open, right-click on one of the views and open it. Note that each view is known as a Cursor. Cursor stands for CURrent Set Of Records. Visual FoxPro views all data, whether they are coming from a local DBF or from a remote data source, the same way—as a cursor. Change the NoDataOnLoad property for both of these cursors to true. This tells VFP to create the connection to the back end, and prepare the query, but does not actually request that the query be executed until we issue the REQUERY() function. Now, go ahead and close the Data Environment Window.

How About Some Code?

Now that we've done this preparation, let's add a little bit of code to the form. Go to the Valid method of the txtInput textbox and add this code:

```
cAuthors_ID = this.value
=REQUERY("author_info")
=REQUERY("author_titles")
thisform.refresh()
```

The code sets the variable cAuthors_ID to the value of the textbox (whatever you type in at runtime), and then issues a REQUERY() against both views. When the requery runs, it sees that we have a value for cAuthors_ID, so it doesn't pop up the generic window that VFP provides if there is no value for cAuthors_ID. VFP runs the query with the value of the textbox, retrieving the information for both views. Finally, it refreshes the form.

Running the Form

Go ahead and run the form. In the first textbox, type in **172-32-1176** and hit Enter. You should get the following results:

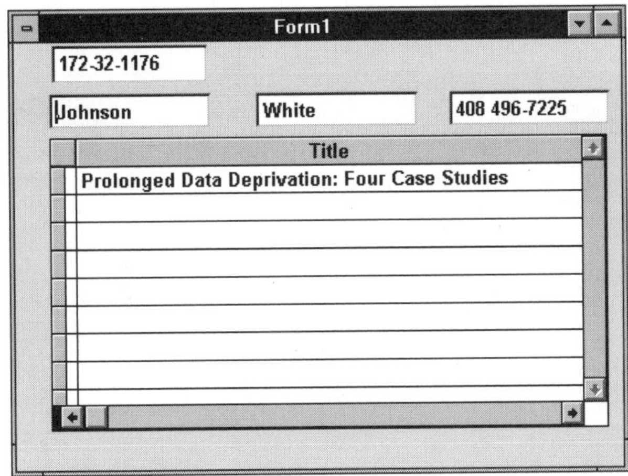

The running form

We now have a simple client-server entry form, that works off three remote tables in two remote views. However, it's not yet updatable. To see that, change the name Johnson to Smith, select the txtInput textbox and hit Enter again. You'll see that the Smith changes back to Johnson. You can make changes to the data on the form, because you're really only changing your local cursor of the data. No updates are being sent to the back end. Let's fix that.

Making Our Remote Views Updatable

Let's go ahead and make our author information updatable. To do so, modify the Author_Info remote view and click on the Update Criteria tab. You'll see something like this:

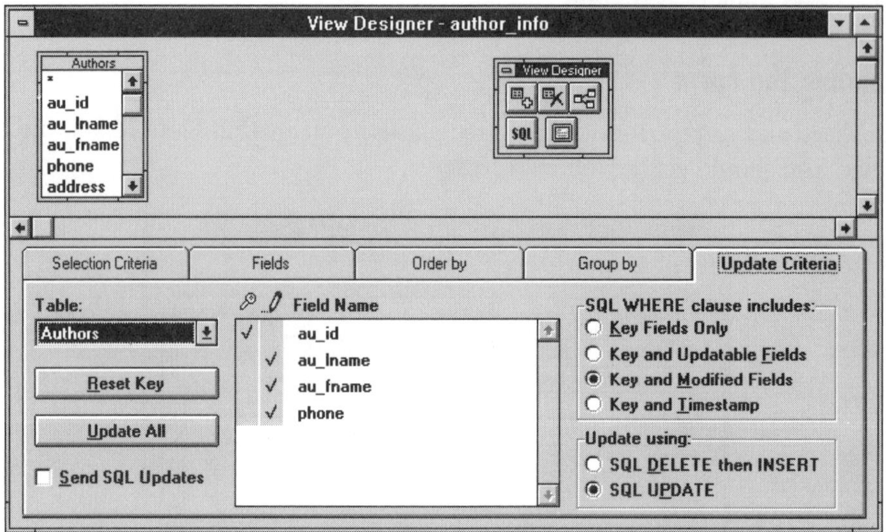

The Update Criteria tab

This dialog allows you to set up many of the updating options for a view. We can see that au_id is marked as the key field—it will be used to tie any local changes to the back end. We also have the three other fields marked as updatable. Clicking on the Send SQL Updates checkbox will make our form an updatable one. That's all there is to it!

Let's take a look at the other two areas on the form and discuss how they work. *Update using* allows you to specify whether an update is handled through the SQL UPDATE command or through a matched SQL DELETE and SQL INSERT. Depending on the server that you are using, what indices it is using and other factors, your DBA may want you to use a matched DELETE/INSERT for performance reasons.

The "SQL WHERE clause includes" tells VFP how to set up the statement that is sent to the back end, and decides when updates are rejected:

Option	Description
Key fields only	As long as the key field hasn't changed on the back end, allow the update to go through.
Key and Updatable fields	As long as the key field hasn't changed and none of the fields marked updatable has changed, allow the update to go through.
Key and Modified fields	As long as the key field hasn't changed and none of the actually modified fields has changed, allow the update to go through.
Key and Timestamp	If the back end allows for a timestamp field (as SQL Server does), make sure that the key field hasn't changed and that the timestamp on the row hasn't changed. In effect, this doesn't allow an update if any field in the row has changed.

Conclusion

Visual FoxPro provides robust client-server capabilities, both through its heterogeneous updatable views, as well as through its SQL Pass Through capabilities. Combining these capabilities with the ability to create a form with multiple data sources allows the developer to create very powerful applications that allow for intelligently distributed data.

Chapter 8

The New Event Model

Introduction

Many of the new features in Visual FoxPro 3 are dramatically changing the way applications are built. For example, the internal event model, and thus the entire concept of event handling within an application, has drastically changed from the approach used in FoxPro 2.x. It is now much easier than ever before to create modeless, multi-window event-driven programs with FoxPro. In this chapter, we'll briefly review how the new event model works in Visual FoxPro 3.

So Long, Foundation READ!

Although still supported for backward compatibility, use of the Foundation READ statement is no longer required to cause the application to enter a *wait state* to prevent the application from returning to the command window. Instead, a new clause has been added to the READ command that begins application-wide event processing. The complete command is:

```
READ EVENTS
```

This single statement is all that is needed! Thanks to the new events (more on events later) that we can respond to, we no longer have to write event handler code for our modeless multi-window applications. Instead, we simply respond to the multitude of events that Visual FoxPro triggers for us in response to user or system actions. When the user wishes to quit the application, we can simply issue the following command:

```
CLEAR EVENTS
```

This command signals the end of event processing, and thus, the end of the application.

Let's take a look at some of the new constructs that can now be supported thanks to this new, simplified event model.

Forms

A form is really not much different than a standard FoxPro 2.x window, but it operates at a much higher level of abstraction. This means that we can perceive forms to be self-contained objects without having to worry about all the messy details that we had to worry about in FoxPro 2.x. *Self-contained* means that a form has properties that can be set to control the appearance or behavior of the form and events that are triggered when certain actions occur in the system.

This differs from the 2.x approach where the concept of a form did not exist. An entry screen or window built using the FoxPro 2.x Screen Builder is not an object, although using the Screen Builder gives us the illusion that it is. When you examine the generated code, you see the DEFINE WINDOW statement, the code for the GET fields, and the READ command which causes FoxPro to enter a wait state that allows the user to input data. Optional clauses can be attached to the READ command that allow the developer to write code that runs at certain times. For example, code in the ACTIVATE clause executes whenever a different window in the READ becomes active. One of the problems with the READ approach to data entry is that clauses like ACTIVATE and DEACTIVATE don't map well with what the user is actually trying to do. Nor do they map well to the Windows event-driven approach for window manipulation.

In the new event model, you no longer have to:

- Use a READ to get user input
- Generate code
- Use the "@ GET" construct for data entry

When you design a form in Visual FoxPro using the brand new Form Designer, you begin much as you do in FoxPro 2.x—with a blank "canvas" on which you draw user-interface objects. Unlike a window generated with FoxPro 2.x's Screen Builder, the form itself is an object. It has properties that manipulate the form's appearance or change the way the form behaves. You normally set these properties at design time using the property sheet, although most of the properties can also be changed at run time.

You can immediately run the form you just created with the DO FORM command, which has the following syntax:

```
DO FORM <FormName>
```

Notice that you can jump from design mode directly into run mode without having to generate code. As you enter code in code-editing windows in the Form Designer, VFP automatically compiles the code and saves it to the appropriate OBJCODE memo field of the SCX file.

The DO FORM command also includes an optional clause that allows you to specify a name for the form. This name can then be used to retrieve or set properties for the form.

```
DO FORM <FormName> NAME frmCustomer
```

Note that if you do not explicitly specify a name, Visual FoxPro will use the name of the SCX file as the name of the form (without the SCX extension, of course). To set the caption of the form (in FoxPro 2.x the caption is equivalent to the window title), you refer to the Caption property using dot notation:

```
frmCustomer.Caption = "Customer Entry"
```

Using this same notation, you could also retrieve the caption at runtime and store it to a memory variable:

```
lcCaption = frmCustomer.Caption.
```

The main advantage of using properties over the various commands available for the same purpose in FoxPro is consistency. Rather than remembering many different commands, each with a different syntax, all you have to remember is the property name.

The following table compares manipulation of the title of a FoxPro 2.x window with manipulation of the caption of a Visual FoxPro form.

Action	FoxPro	Visual FoxPro 3
Set Title	DEFINE WINDOW <<window name>> TITLE "My Title"	form.Caption = "My Title"
Change Title	MODIFY WINDOW <<window name >> ... TITLE "Your Title"	form.Caption = "Your Title"
Get Title	lcTitle = WTITLE(<<window>>)	lcTitle = form.Caption

Events

An event is an action recognized by an object, such as clicking the mouse or pressing a key. An event can be triggered as a result of a user action or directly from the system. An example of a user-generated event is clicking the mouse on a form. When the mouse is clicked, Visual FoxPro triggers the Click event. Any code defined in the Click() event method is executed whenever the Click event occurs. An example of a system generated event would be the Timer event for a timer control. (More on controls later in this chapter.) Each time the specified interval is reached for the timer control, Visual FoxPro triggers the Timer event for that control. Any code defined in the Timer() event method is executed whenever the Timer event occurs. Note that the name of the event method is exactly the same as the event itself.

This table lists some of the more common events for the form object:

Event	Triggered when...
Load	form is first loaded
Unload	form is being unloaded
Init	form is initialized (after the Load event, and after all controls on the form have been initialized)
Destroy	form is being destroyed
GotFocus	form receives focus, i.e., when clicking from another form
LostFocus	form loses focus, i.e., when clicking off of the form
MouseMove	mouse moves over the form
Resize	form is resized

Why do we take care to distinguish between an event and an event method? Because you cannot programmatically initiate an event, at least not directly, but you can call an event method directly. To be precise, when the following command is issued:

```
RELEASE frmCustomer
```

the form with the name "frmCustomer" is released, causing the form object to be destroyed (and eventually unloaded). As a result of the form object being destroyed, Visual FoxPro triggers the Destroy event, causing code in the Destroy() event method to execute. In code, if you were to explicitly call the Destroy() event method:

```
frmCustomer.Destroy()
```

code defined in the Destroy() event method would execute, but the Destroy event *would never occur!* Thus, after executing the above code, the form "frmCustomer" will still exist!

Controls

The objects you place on a form to allow the user to interact with your program are called controls. These controls, like a form, are "self-contained." This means that controls can be manipulated through properties and methods, and can also respond to events.

All controls are assigned names. Once a name is assigned to a control, you can set or retrieve the control's properties using dot notation. For example, to set the text displayed in a text box named txtName on a form called frmCustomer, you reference the Value property:

```
frmCustomer.txtName.Value = "Joe Smith"
```

Retrieving the text from a text box is just as easy:

```
lcName = frmCustomer.txtName.Value
```

This table lists some typical properties and their meanings:

Property	Meaning
Enabled	True if the control is enabled
FontName	The font the control is using
Left	The position of the left border of the control relative to its container
Top	The position of the top border of the control relative to its container
Visible	True if the control is visible

Controls can also respond to events triggered either by user action or directly from the system. For example, if the user clicks on a command button, Visual FoxPro triggers the Click event. Code placed in the Click() event method executes whenever the Click event occurs.

This table lists some typical (common) events that you can respond to by putting code in the corresponding event method:

Event	Triggered when...
Init	control is being initialized
Destroy	control is being destroyed
Click	user clicks on control
GotFocus	control receives focus, i.e., when clicking from another control

Event	Triggered when...
LostFocus	control loses focus, i.e., when clicking to another control
MouseMove	mouse moves over the control

Custom Controls

There is no denying that one of the main contributing factors to the success of Visual Basic is the explosion of third-party custom controls. These controls appear on your control palette alongside all the built-in controls and are manipulated in the same fashion: by setting properties and responding to events. The functionality that these controls provide covers an incredibly broad spectrum, ranging from an enhanced edit box to a full-blown scheduling system! The controls themselves are written in C and packaged as a special kind of dynamic link library (DLL) called a VBX.

Microsoft has announced that VBXs will no longer be supported in favor of the new OLE-based custom control solution: OCXs. While VBX controls were designed exclusively for Visual Basic, OCX controls are designed to be used in any product capable of supporting them. This means that, for example, your OCX control which downloads stock information in real time can be used in Excel, Visual FoxPro, and Access.

The abundance of third-party custom controls has led to the evolution of what is known as component-based software development. Software is constructed by using OLE container applications (i.e., Visual FoxPro, Visual Basic, etc.) as the "glue" that seamlessly binds these powerful custom controls together with minimal effort, resulting in a very robust application.

Visual FoxPro takes the concept of custom controls a step further by allowing you to:

- Subclass built-in controls
- Create new controls based on the VFP Custom class
- Subclass OCX controls

This means that you can create customized or unique versions of any type of control and add them directly to your control palette to be used in any Visual FoxPro application.

Chapter 9

The Visual FoxPro Object Model

Introduction

The Visual FoxPro object model is based on a strong foundation of object-oriented principles. User-defined classes, protected class members, inheritance—it has everything you would expect to find in a robust object model. The model includes a set of built-in classes that you use as a basis for creating your own classes. These built-in classes are called *base classes.*

Base classes are grouped into controls and containers. The difference is that a container can include other controls or even other containers within itself, while a control cannot. (The "control" control is something of an exception to this rule, since it allows us to refer to multiple controls as if they were one.) A good example of a container is a form that contains a group of text boxes. The form is referred to as the *parent,* while the text boxes are referred to as *children* (or child controls).

Here is the current list of base classes:

Controls	Non-Visual	Containers	Non-Visual
CheckBox		Container	
ComboBox		FormSet	X
CommandButton		Form	
Control		Grid	
Custom	X	Column	
EditBox		PageFrame	X
Header		Page	
Image		ToolBar	
Label		OptionButtonGroup	
Line		CommandButtonGroup	
ListBox			
Shape			
Spinner			
TextBox			
Timer	X		

Base Class Properties

An object has properties used to describe the object or to hold values that represent the object's state. All Visual FoxPro base classes share a common minimum set of properties:

Property	Description
Class	The name of the class of the object
BaseClass	The name of the base class of the object
ClassLibrary	The full path of the class library where this class is defined
ParentClass	The name of the class of the parent class of the object

You are free to add custom properties to any new class you create. I'll show you how in just a moment.

Base Class Events and Event Methods

Most objects also exhibit some kind of behavior in the form of methods. In Visual FoxPro, an object can also respond to events that occur in the system. For example, when the user clicks on a command button, Visual FoxPro invokes the Click event. You can place code in a command button's Click() event method that will automatically run whenever the button is clicked.

All Visual FoxPro base classes can respond to a common minimum set of events:

Event	Description
Init	Invoked when the object is created
Destroy	Invoked when the object is released
Error	Invoked when an error occurs inside one of the object's methods

Class Definition Syntax

While it's possible and probably more desirable to create all your classes, including non-visual ones, using the Class Designer, it's easier and more straightforward in a chapter of this nature to demonstrate the features of the language in code. The code that follows can be typed directly into a PRG. Just be sure to place the CREATEOBJECT() function calls *before* any class definitions!

When creating new classes, we use the new DEFINE CLASS command:

```
DEFINE CLASS MaintenanceForm AS Form
ENDDEFINE

DEFINE CLASS Transaction AS Custom
ENDDEFINE
```

These statements create new classes based on Visual FoxPro's built-in classes. More precisely, we are subclassing a Visual FoxPro base class. Through the power of inheritance, we automatically inherit any properties and methods defined in the class that we are subclassing, and thus can treat them as if they were actual members of our new classes:

```
*-- Create an instance of the Transaction class and print the
*-- value of the Class property.
oCreditCardTransaction = CREATEOBJECT("Transaction")
? oCreditCardTransaction.Class  && Prints "Transaction" on screen
```

Let's modify our transaction class definition to show how the Init() and Destroy() event methods work:

```
DEFINE CLASS Transaction AS Custom
  FUNCTION Init()
    WAIT WINDOW "Creating object"
  ENDFUNC

  FUNCTION Destroy()
    WAIT WINDOW "Destroying object"
  ENDFUNC
ENDDEFINE
```

The Init event is invoked by Visual FoxPro whenever an object is created. The Init event causes code defined in the Init() event method to be executed. The generic object-oriented term for this type of event method is a *constructor*. It is commonly used to initialize properties of the object or to ensure that the environment is correctly set up before the object is used.

The Destroy event is invoked by Visual FoxPro whenever an object is destroyed. The Destroy event causes code defined in the Destroy() event method to be executed. The generic object-oriented term for this type of event method is a *destructor*. It is commonly used to clean up the environment when an object is being released.

(Note: If you looked carefully, you may have noticed the empty parentheses after the method name. This is not an error. In fact, instead of using the PARAMETERS statement, or more accurately LPARAMETERS, you can now define parameters within parentheses immediately after the method name. The empty parentheses are a matter of coding style and are strictly optional.)

Creating Instances

As you may have already guessed, the syntax for creating an instance of a class is:

```
oObjectReference = CREATEOBJECT(cClassName)
```

The CREATEOBJECT() function accepts a class name as a parameter and returns a reference to an object. This object reference is really just a memory variable with a data type of O, which stands for object. Variables that represent objects are very similar to other types of variables. For example, it is perfectly legal, although not good programming practice, to assign a value of a different data type to a variable that represents an object:

```
oTransaction = CREATEOBJECT("Transaction")
oTransaction = "A line of text"  && an object is just a var.
```

Note that when passing objects as parameters to a function or method, the object is always passed by reference, never by value. Also, when assigning an object to another memory variable, the new variable is a reference to *the same object!*

```
*-- Both oTransaction2 and oTransaction refer to the same
*-- object in memory
oTransaction2 = oTransaction
```

Releasing Instances

You can release an object the same way you release a memory variable:

```
RELEASE oTransaction
```

When you release an object, its Destroy event is fired, and any code defined in the Destroy() event method is executed. It's important to note that the object remains in memory until *all* references to it have been released.

Subclassing User-Defined Classes

Not only does Visual FoxPro allow you to create new classes based on the built-in base classes, but you can also create new classes based on your own user-defined classes. For example:

```
DEFINE CLASS BaseForm AS Form
ENDDEFINE

DEFINE CLASS MaintenanceForm AS BaseForm
ENDDEFINE
```

Here we first define a new form class called BaseForm and then use that form class as the basis for yet another new form class, MaintenanceForm. If we wish, we could then create a new class based on the MaintenanceForm class and then create a new class on that, and so on, and so on. I would recommend keeping the depth of the class hierarchy as "shallow" as possible, but without placing a specific number on just how deep to go. Use your best judgment.

We Pause for a Look at Our Dictionary...

Before we get too submerged in a sea of terminology, it is desirable to pause for a moment to examine some terms.

The term *superclass* refers to any class that is being used as the basis for creating other classes. You may have seen other object-oriented texts refer to a superclass as a *base class*. In fact, this is acceptable terminology. However, it is important to understand that Visual FoxPro uses the term base class to refer to its own built-in class hierarchy, *not* an arbitrary superclass that you create.

Visual FoxPro uses the term *parentclass* to mean exactly the same thing as superclass. This is unfortunate because it seems that most other object-oriented products and literature have standardized the use of the term superclass. Additionally, Visual FoxPro uses the term *parent* to refer to an object that contains other objects. It can get confusing when trying to talk about the class of an object's parent versus an object's parentclass—they are not the same thing.

I bring up this issue of terminology to help you avoid confusion when discussing object-oriented topics with your associates, or when reading a non-language-specific object-oriented book or article. Just remember that in generic object-oriented terms, base class, superclass, and parent class all mean the same thing. But remember that a base class is just a parent class that has special meaning in Visual FoxPro, and that superclass and parentclass mean exactly the same thing, but parentclass is preferred.

Back to Your Regularly Scheduled Object Model...

So how do we add custom properties to our classes? Here's the syntax:

```
DEFINE CLASS Customer AS Custom
  *-- Custom property definitions
  cName = "Ivar Jacobsen"
  nAge = 40
  lHasMethodolgy = .T.

  *-- Method definitions follow
ENDDEFINE
```

Basically, custom properties are defined before any method code for that class. You could also use this space to initialize built-in properties:

```
DEFINE CLASS MyForm AS Form
  Caption = "My Form"
  AutoCenter = .T.
  BorderStyle = 2
ENDDEFINE
```

Note that if you need to initialize a property to the result of an expression or UDF, you'll have to do this in the Init() event method for the class:

```
DEFINE CLASS Table AS Custom
  cFullName = ""

  FUNCTION Init()
    this.cFullName = DBF()
  ENDFUNC
ENDDEFINE
```

What's THIS All About?

In the Init() event method of the above example, I used the new **this** keyword to refer to the property of the class. Visual FoxPro has added this keyword, along with the **thisform** and **thisformset** keywords to provide access to properties or methods that are scoped to the class, form, or formset, respectively. The following table illustrates this concept further:

Keyword	Meaning
this	Used in method code to refer to a property or method of the current class.
thisform	Used in method code in a form to refer to a property or method of the current form. Can be used from anywhere within that form, including methods of controls on that form.
thisformset	Used in method code in a formset to refer to a property or method of the current formset. Can be used anywhere within that formset, including methods of forms contained within that formset, or controls contained on any form in the formset.

What About Protection?

Encapsulation is the ability to bind both data and functions (or procedures) to a class. What if you have a situation where you have defined properties or methods for a class that you do not want to be accessed directly using the object.Property or object.Method() syntax? Like any robust object model, Visual FoxPro allows you to do this through use of the **PROTECTED** keyword.

```
DEFINE CLASS Customer AS Custom
  PROTECTED cName

  PROTECTED FUNCTION ChangeName(tcNewName)
    this.cName = tcNewName
  ENDFUNC
ENDDEFINE
```

If we instantiate an instance of class Customer:

```
oCustomer = CREATEOBJECT("Customer")
```

and attempt to access either the protected property or method of that class, we will get an error:

```
oCustomer.cName = "Grady Booch"         && Error!
oCustomer.ChangeName("Grady Booch")     && Error!
```

Why would you want to protect class members? Let's assume that certain properties of a class represented an object's state. If you couldn't prevent those properties from being accessed directly from outside the class, how could you ever guarantee the state of that object? If you protect the property, you could then create a custom method that would be used to assign values to that property. The method could contain validation code to ensure that the value is set properly. Since the property value is assigned in just one place, the code becomes much easier to debug and maintain.

Another reason for having the ability to protect members of a class comes up when you have utility methods that serve a particular purpose for a specific class, but are not meant to be called from outside that class. Leaving those methods unprotected could have disastrous results!

Add Those Objects!

A property of a class is not limited to being just a simple variable. It can also be an object of another class. For example, if you want to add a command button to a form in code, you would use the following syntax:

```
DEFINE CLASS MyForm AS Form
  ADD OBJECT oCommandButton AS CommandButton
ENDDEFINE
```

Once you create an instance of this form, you could then refer to the oCommandButton just like you would a normal property:

```
oMyForm = CREATEOBJECT("MyForm")
? oMyForm.oCommandButton.Caption
* Prints the button's caption
```

The form is now considered the parent of the command button. In fact, the form can be accessed by referencing the command button's Parent property. From the Click() event method of the command button:

```
WAIT WINDOW this.Parent.Caption     && Print the form's caption
```

Conclusion

The Visual FoxPro object model is based on a solid foundation of object-oriented concepts that have been in place for years. As a result, developers will be able to create more complex applications that are easier to debug, easier to maintain, and conform more closely to user requirements than ever before.

Chapter 10

Technical Standards and Guidelines

Introduction

This chapter details some of the standards and guidelines that I have found useful in team development efforts. They cover such things as variable and field naming conventions, and standards for commenting of code.

Please note that it is not so important that you follow these rules, as much as it is crucial that you select a set of rules for your development work, document those rules, and use them.

Naming Conventions

With Visual FoxPro 3 presenting a new development approach to the FoxPro developer, we have a chance to agree on a standard set of naming conventions that can be used by everyone in their development efforts, making the development and maintenance of applications an easier job for everyone. Proposals presented here are not earth-shattering or totally new. The guidelines I present follow recommendations by Microsoft and other experienced developers in the Visual Basic arena. Visual FoxPro 3 is moving toward a Visual Basic view of objects that are manipulated, and it follows that naming conventions should be similar in order to ease the way of a developer moving among Microsoft products. These guidelines have been formulated and tuned through the knowledge gained in developing FoxPro, Access, and Visual Basic for Windows applications.

Object Naming Conventions

In keeping with Visual Basic standards, each object will begin with a three-character, lowercase prefix that denotes the type of object. Each distinct word in the name should be capitalized but not underscored.

Object	Prefix	Example
Check box	chk	chkReadOnly
Combo box	cbo	cboEnglish
Command button	cmd	cmdCancel
Container	cnt	cntCustomerInfo

Object	Prefix	Example
Control	ctl	ctlMisc
Edit box	edt	edtComments
Form	frm	frmFileOpen
FormPage	fpg	fpgList
FormSet	frs	frsCustomerInfo
Grid	grd	grdPrices
GridColumn	grc	grcCompanyName
GridHeader	grh	grhLineTotal
Image	img	imgIcon
Label	lbl	lblHelpMessage
Line	lin	linVertical
List box	lst	lstPolicyCodes
OLE	ole	oleObject1
Option button	opt	optFrench
Option group	opg	opgType
Outline control	otl	otlViews
PageFrame	pgf	pgfLeft
Shape (circle, square, oval, rectangle, rounded rectangle, and rounded square)	shp	shpCircle
Spinner	spn	spnDaysShown
Text box	txt	txtGetText
Timer	tmr	tmrAlarm
Toolbar	tbr	tbrEditReport

Variable Naming Conventions

Variables will be used less often in FoxPro 3. The capability of using and manipulating object names directly without the need of assigning a variable to each object will reduce variable use. These standards follow the Hungarian notation used by Microsoft in the object-naming conventions. Every variable will begin with a two-character, lowercase prefix. The first character will denote the variable scope, the second will denote the variable type. Each key word in the variable name should be capitalized but not underscored. Please note that an Object Instance will only use one character, "o," to designate it. Adding a scoping character to an object is optional.

Scope	Prefix	Example
Public/Global	g	gcUserName
Private	p	pcState
Local	l	lnCounter
Parameter	t	tdRun
Class	<none>	Customer
Constant (#DEFINE)	ALLCAPS	TRUE

Type	Prefix	Example
Character	c	cLastName
Numeric	n	nRangeLo
Logical	l	lMarried
Date	d	dPurchased
Memo	m	mComments
General	g	gWordDoc
Currency	y	ySalary

Type	Prefix	Example
Float	f	fResults
Double	b	bValue
Picture	p	pEmployee
DateTime	t	tRecorded
Object Instance	o	oJanitor
Array	a	aMonths

Coding Conventions

In order to differentiate between methods and properties of an object, a method call should be followed by a parenthesis:

```
x = oObject.Value          && Property
x = oObject.Click()        && Method
```

Process Conventions

Parameter Passing and Returned Values

Never rely on the existence of a variable in a sub-procedure. Note the following examples:

The method to avoid:

```
A  =  4
B  =  2
C  =  0
DO abc WITH a,b
WAIT WINDOW STR(C)

PROCEDURE abc
PARAMETERS num1,num2
c  =  num1*num2
RETURN c
```

A better approach:

```
A   =  4
B   =  2
C   =  abc(a,b)
WAIT WINDOW STR(C)

FUNCTION abc
PARAMETERS num1,num2
PRIVATE num3
num3 = num1*num2
RETURN num3
```

Arrays

Arrays should be passed *by reference* as opposed to *by value* to avoid the error of passing only the first element of the array (which is the result of passing by value) instead of the whole array. In functions, use the @ sign to reference the whole array. For example:

```
=sizearry(@laCDList)
```

Source Code Format

Consistent, legible code formatting greatly aids in code readability and can allow for the automated extraction of vital development information.

Header Format

Type of Code	Header Example
Standard Programs	* Program * Author * Project * Created * Copyright *) Description * Major change list

Type of Code	Header Example
Procedure/Function	PROCEDURE Sample * Name of procedure * Author * Date created * Copyright notice *) Description of procedure * Major change list

Note the use of a close parenthesis on the description line to allow extraction and processing of the description comments.

Commands and Functions

Do not use abbreviations for Visual FoxPro commands.

Comments

Keep code blocks together and keep the logical flow of the code intact.

If the comment can be put ahead of or following a code block (in the white space between) do so (use * to indicate comment lines). Otherwise, use an embedded comment (use && to indicate comment lines).

Standard Comment Keys	Description
*--	for pseudo code
*	for commented-out code or for header information
*{	for start of change/modification notes
*}	for end of change/modification notes
*?	for programmer comments (e.g. future ideas, enhancements, questions, or problems)

Line Length

Use a physical line length of around 50 characters. This allows you to see all of your code without panning around a code window.

In-line comments begin at column 55 (use double ampersand—&&) and are limited to 15 characters in width so they are visible on the screen without horizontal scrolling.

Use semicolons for dividing long statements over multiple lines but note that you must have a legal statement without the semicolon.

Upper/Lowercase

Use uppercase for Visual FoxPro language statements such as GET, INDEX ON, STORE etc.

Use mixed case for programmer-defined items such as field names and variable names.

Use lowercase for DOS items such as file names and report names.

White Space

Use white space and individual blank lines to visually signal breaks between logical program sections.

Long Command Statements

Anything that takes an argument gets its own line within a long statement (such as a SQL SELECT or BROWSE). For example:

```
BROWSE NOMODIFY NODELETE NOAPPEND ;
   WINDOW  wbwindow ;
   TITLE "This is my browse" ;
   FIELDS ;
      one   :5    :H = "Hi" ;
      two   :3    :H = "Bye" ;
      three :10   :H = "Howdy" ;
etc.
```

Code Changes/Modifications

Changes in Logical Implementation

You must document changes in code that reflect a change in the system specification or the underlying business rules for processing.

Changes in Technical Implementation

Documenting changes in code that reflect changes based on technical reasons (e.g. performance optimization, bug work-arounds) is left to the discretion and good judgment of the programmer.

Change/Modification Format

```
*{ YAG 5/12/92  reason for change
<<New code goes here>>
*}
```

If removing or modifying code, comment-out but retain the original code.

```
*{ YAG 5/15/92  removed call to
* Employee file, call EMP alias instead
* SELECT Employee
SELECT Emp
*}
```

Chapter 11

Object Linking and Embedding

Introduction

Since the introduction of FoxPro for Windows, developers have enjoyed the ability to embed or link documents from other applications directly into FoxPro tables thanks to OLE technology. While you still have this capability with OLE 2.0, the new specification goes much, much further than that. In fact, Microsoft has publicly stated that the future of all Windows-based products, as well as future versions of Windows itself, will be based on this technology. This chapter focuses on OLE Automation, showing you how to use it to incorporate the power built into other Microsoft Office products like Word and Excel into your own application.

What and Why?

OLE Automation was designed to allow application developers and end-users to control applications through a common interface. An application that is OLE Automation-enabled allows other external applications to control it by exposing certain parts of its internal structure in the form of objects. These objects have properties and methods. Properties allow you to retrieve values that might represent the state of the object, a count of some number items, another object, etc. Methods allow you to perform an action on a specific object, like opening a new document, printing a file, recalculating a range of cells, etc.

Why would you want to use this functionality? How many of us have had to write sophisticated financial routines when we knew that the same routine was already available in our favorite spreadsheet? How many of us have written scheduling routines when we wished we could somehow hook into our favorite project management software? Through the power of OLE Automation, we now have the capability to hook into other applications and use them as if they were a part of our own application. Imagine having all of Excel's built-in functions available at your fingertips. Even better, imagine having Excel's powerful charting capabilities built into your own application! Imagine no more! All this is now possible and readily accessible through OLE Automation!

Quick Review

There are only two Visual FoxPro functions you need to worry about in order to retrieve another application's objects. Once you have obtained the object, you can immediately begin to access properties and methods of the object.

CREATEOBJECT( )

CREATEOBJECT( ) creates an object from a class definition or an OLE object. This command is also used to create objects from built-in Visual FoxPro or user-defined classes. Since this chapter is about creating OLE objects, I will intentionally leave out the syntax and descriptions of creating other types of classes to avoid confusion. For consistency with Microsoft documentation, much of the information in this section is derived directly from Visual FoxPro's help file.

Syntax:

```
<memvar> = CREATEOBJECT(cClassName)
```

cClassName: This specifies the OLE object from which the new object is created. FoxPro will search for the class name you specify in the following order:

1. Visual FoxPro base classes
2. User-defined class definitions in memory in the order they were loaded
3. Classes in the current program
4. Classes in .VCX class libraries opened with SET CLASSLIB
5. Classes in procedure files opened with SET PROCEDURE
6. Classes in the Visual FoxPro program execution chain
7. The Windows Registry (for OLE objects)

OLE objects are created using the following syntax for cClassName:

```
ApplicationName.Class
```

For example, to create a Microsoft Excel object using OLE Automation, you can use the following syntax:

```
xl = CREATEOBJECT("Excel.Application")
```

When this code is run, Microsoft Excel is started but is not visible. You will not see Excel if you ALT+TAB through all your running applications, nor will you see it if you bring up the Task Manager with CTRL+ESC. Note that if Excel is already running, another separate instance will be created when you execute this command. Also note that Microsoft Word functions a little differently, as will be explained in the section titled "The WinWord Class" later in this chapter.

GETOBJECT( )

This function activates an OLE Automation object and creates a reference to the object.

Syntax:

```
GETOBJECT([cFileName [, cClassName]])
```

cFileName: This parameter specifies the full path and name of the file to activate. The application does not need to be specified, because the OLE dynamic link libraries determine the application to start based on the file name you provide.

For example, the following code launches Microsoft Excel, opens a file named BUDGET.XLS, and creates a reference through an object memory variable named xlBudget:

```
xlBudget = GETOBJECT("C:\EXCEL\WORK\BUDGET.XLS")
```

cClassName: The cClassName parameter specifies the class name of the object to retrieve. Some applications can store more than one object type in the same file, allowing you to use the class name to specify the object to activate. For example, if a word processing application stores its documents, macro definitions, and toolbar objects in the same file, you can create a reference to the document file with the following command:

```
mDocFile = GETOBJECT("C:\WRDPROC\MYDOC.DOC", "WrdProc.Document")
```

If you do not specify a string for cFileName, GETOBJECT( ) creates a reference to the currently active object of the class you include. For example, if Microsoft Excel is running, you can create a reference to it with the following command:

```
xl = GETOBJECT(, "Excel.Application")
```

If Excel is not running, a trappable error will be generated. Trapping the error and resorting to the CREATEOBJECT( ) function is a common technique to test if an application is already running. An alternative technique is to use DDE to establish a link with the server application on the System topic, which all DDE applications support. If the link is successfully established, the application is running.

Note that Visual FoxPro now allows you to skip a parameter by not including it in a function call. When using this in native Visual FoxPro functions, Visual FoxPro will substitute a .F. for you. In OLE calls, it will pass the lack of a parameter to the called object.

Dealing with Complex Object Models

At first glimpse, Microsoft Excel's object model is very intimidating. There are over 100 objects available to the OLE Automation developer. Each of these objects puts a myriad of properties and methods at the programmer's disposal. You don't have to memorize each and every one of these properties and methods to be productive with Excel; however, it helps at least to become familiar with what's there.

A great way to learn how to use these properties and methods is through Visual Basic for Applications (VBA), Excel's built-in macro language. You may be wondering how learning another programming language will help you understand how to use Excel's object model from Visual FoxPro. The answer is in knowing how VBA communicates with its host environment, Excel.

VBA uses the same objects, properties, and methods that are available to FoxPro through OLE Automation. In fact, VBA itself uses OLE Automation to communicate with Excel. Knowing this, we can use Excel's built-in macro recorder to record the functionality that we are trying to model. The macro recorder generates VBA code, which you can examine to see how various objects are being utilized. Not every construct in VBA is directly portable to FoxPro, but VBA interacts with Excel in much the same way that Visual FoxPro does. The syntax when dealing with Excel objects is almost identical. In many cases, you will discover new objects or techniques that you didn't previously know existed.

Another great way to become familiar with an application's objects is through the command window, from which you can interactively create objects, set object properties, call object methods, and just plain have fun with OLE Automation.

Hardware Requirements

All this power does not come for free, of course. Memory is the most important requirement when setting out to write OLE Automation applications. The more memory you have, the better. Determining exactly how much memory you need depends on the memory requirements of the operating system you're using, as well as the memory requirements of the application you wish to control. For bare minimums, I would recommend the following:

Operating System	Minimum Memory for OLE Automation
DOS/Windows 3.11 or WFW 3.11 with WIN32s	16MB
Windows NT Workstation 3.5	24MB
Windows 95	16MB

The Registration Database

The registration database is where FoxPro looks for the class name you specify with both the CREATEOBJECT( ) and GETOBJECT( ) functions. Under Windows 3.11 and Windows for WorkGroups 3.11, entries into the registration database are stored as a key and a corresponding value for each key in a tree-like structure. You can view the registration database with a program called REGEDIT.EXE, which is located in the directory where you installed Windows. Running REGEDIT with the /V option, which stands for verbose, will produce the following screen.

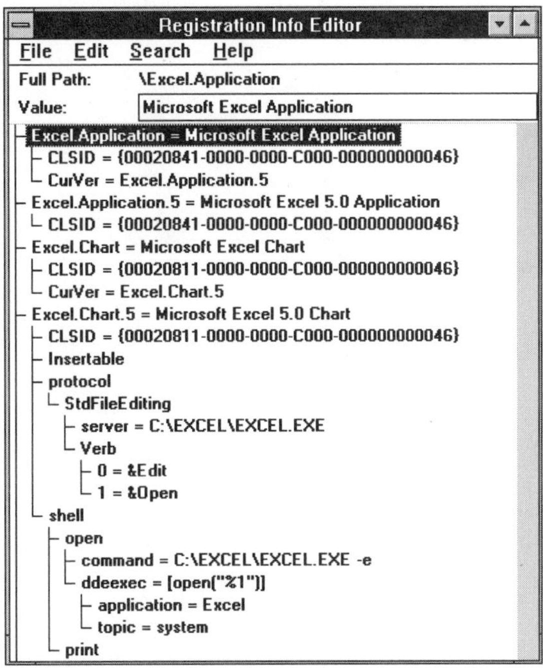

16-bit registration database

Under Windows NT and Windows 95, the tree-like structure remains but the entries are grouped in different categories. Look under the HKEY_CLASSES_ROOT category or window to find entries for OLE Automation objects. The Windows NT 3.5 registration database editor was invoked by running the REGEDT32.EXE program with no options. REGEDT32.EXE can be found in the SYSTEM32 subdirectory under the directory where Windows NT was installed. Note that other windows of the registration database are not shown. Below is a view of the editor with the HKEY_CLASSES_ROOT windows maximized.

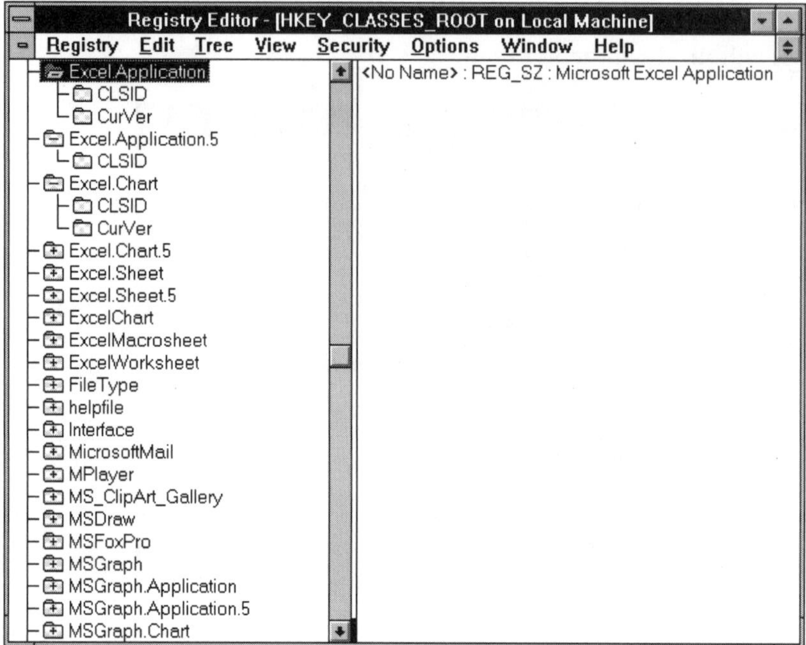

Windows NT registration database

Creating a Generic OLEApplication Class

One of the greatest advantages of using OLE Automation from within Visual FoxPro is due to the new object-oriented extensions. You now have the ability to create custom classes, and because classes serve to encapsulate both data and behavior, you can build classes that shield you from having to worry about the peculiarities of a specific type of OLE server application.

To illustrate this, let's look at the differences between controlling Word and Excel by beginning to develop a class that defines how we'll want to control all of our OLE applications. We will not design this class to be instantiated directly (classes that are designed in this fashion are called *abstract classes*). Rather, we will create a subclass of this class for each specific OLE application that we want to control.

```
#INCLUDE "\VFP\FOXPRO.H"

DEFINE CLASS OLEApplication AS Custom
  *-- oOLEApp - Holds reference to the OLE Application Server
```

```
*-- cOLERegName - The name of the server object as found in
*--     the registration database.
*-- lCloseAppWhenDone - .T. if we started the server for the
*--      first time within this class
PROTECTED oOLEApp, ;
    cOLERegName, ;
    lCloseAppWhenDone

oOLEApp = ""
cOLERegName = ""
lCloseAppWhenDone = .T.

*-- Methods
FUNCTION Init()
  *-- First make sure that the user is not trying to create
  *-- an instance of this class.
  IF EMPTY(this.cOLERegName)
    =MessageBox("Cannot create object directly from class" +;
          " OLEApplication.", ;
          MB_ICONSTOP, ;
          "")
    RETURN .F.
  ENDIF

  *-- Attempt to start the application
  *-- First, check to see if app is already running
  IF this.AppRunning()
    *-- Grab the current instance
    this.oOLEApp = this.GetCurrentInstance()
  ELSE
    *-- Create a new instance.
    this.oOLEApp = this.CreateNewInstance()
  ENDIF
ENDFUNC

*-- Protected functions
PROTECTED FUNCTION AppRunning()
  *-- Returns .T. if app is already running
  LOCAL lcOldError, ;
    llRunning

  llRunning = .T.
  lcOldError = ON("ERROR")
```

```
    ON ERROR llRunning = .F.
    *-- Attempt to get a reference to a running application
    =GETOBJECT(, this.cOLERegName)
    ON ERROR &lcOldError

    this.lCloseAppWhenDone = !llRunning
    RETURN llRunning
  ENDFUNC

  PROTECTED FUNCTION CreateNewInstance()
    RETURN CREATEOBJECT(this.cOLERegName)
  ENDFUNC

  PROTECTED FUNCTION GetCurrentInstance()
    RETURN GETOBJECT(, this.cOLERegName)
  ENDFUNC

ENDDEFINE
```

This defines the core functionality of our abstract OLEApplication class. We first check to make sure that the user of the class is not trying to instantiate it directly. If they are, we just cancel the INIT method, which prevents the object from being created. Secondly, we check to see if the application is running. If it is, we create a reference to it. If not, we create a new instance.

You may be wondering why you need to determine if the application you're trying to control is currently running. The reason is that certain applications let you create multiple instances, while others do not. If you were to execute the following three commands from the command window, you would wind up with three separate running instances of Excel:

```
xl1 = CREATEOBJECT("Excel.Application")
xl2 = CREATEOBJECT("Excel.Application")
xl3 = CREATEOBJECT("Excel.Application")
```

If you try this with Word, you'll wind up with just one instance and three references to the same instance. So how do we determine if an application is already running? Here are two suggestions.

The first way involves the use of the GETOBJECT( ) function to attempt to retrieve a reference to an OLE Automation server. At the time of this writing, this option works fine with Excel, but not with Word. We'll override this function when we define our WinWord class, but for now, let's define this option as a protected function within our OLEApplication class. We define the function as protected because we will only be calling this function from within the OLEApplication class or any class that we derive from it. There is no need to expose it to the "outside world."

```
PROTECTED FUNCTION AppRunning()
   *-- Returns .T. if app is already running
   LOCAL lcOldError, ;
         llRunning

   llRunning = .T.
   lcOldError = ON("ERROR")
   ON ERROR llRunning = .F.
   *-- Attempt to get a reference to a running application
   =GETOBJECT("", this.cOLERegName)
   ON ERROR &lcOldError

   this.lCloseAppWhenDone = !llRunning
   RETURN llRunning
ENDFUNC
```

The second way of determining if an application is already running involves the use of DDE. So as not to disrupt the definition we are building of the OLEApplication class, I will defer discussing this alternative method until we create our WinWord class, a subclass of the OLEApplication class.

To complete the definition of the OLEApplication class, we create two methods, also defined as protected functions, that we will use to create references to new instances or retrieve references to current instances. You'll notice that each method contains only one statement. We could have eliminated the overhead of the function call and placed the CREATEOBJECT() and GETOBJECT() calls directly in the Init method, but, if we needed to, we would not be able to customize the behavior of these methods in our subclasses. An example of customizing the behavior of these methods can be found in the GetCurrentInstance() method of the WinWord class discussed later in this chapter.

```
PROTECTED FUNCTION CreateNewInstance()
   RETURN CREATEOBJECT(this.cOLERegName)
ENDFUNC

PROTECTED FUNCTION GetCurrentInstance()
   RETURN GETOBJECT(, this.cOLERegName)
ENDFUNC
```

The Excel Class

Let's define our first subclass to handle OLE Automation with Excel. Most of the inherited functionality from the OLEApplication class works just fine with Excel. The first thing we need to do is initialize the cOLERegName property with the appropriate name of the Excel Application object as it appears in the registration database (Excel.Application). Secondly, we need to set up a Destroy event method that sends the Quit command to Excel whenever the object is being destroyed. The Destroy event method will fire whenever we explicitly release an Excel object, or whenever the Excel object goes out of scope.

Note that we do not tell Excel to quit if the internal flag, lCloseAppWhenDone, is set. This flag will be .F. if Excel was already running when we created an instance of this class. By providing this functionality, we are making Excel more closely resemble Word, where the application is closed when the reference to it is released from memory.

```
DEFINE CLASS Excel AS OLEApplication
  *-- Inherited properties
  cOLERegName = "Excel.Application"

  *-- Inherited Methods
  FUNCTION Destroy()
    IF TYPE("this.oOLEApp") == "O" AND ;
      this.lCloseAppWhenDone
        this.oOLEApp.Quit()
    ENDIF
  ENDFUNC

  PROTECTED FUNCTION CreateNewInstance()
    LOCAL loExcel
    loExcel = CREATEOBJECT(this.cOLERegName)
    loExcel.Workbooks.Add
    RETURN loExcel
  ENDFUNC

ENDDEFINE
```

The WinWord Class

Our second subclass deals with the intricacies of dealing with Word. Word is not any more difficult to deal with than Excel, it just responds differently in various situations. I mentioned earlier that the GETOBJECT( ) function does not work properly with Word to check if an instance is running. We therefore turn to DDE to attempt to establish a link with Word. If we are successful, we know that Word is running, and we immediately terminate the link.

```
DEFINE CLASS Word AS OLEApplication
  *-- Inherited properties
  cOLERegName = "Word.Basic"

  PROTECTED FUNCTION AppRunning()
    *-- Word does not accept GETOBJECT(, "WORD.BASIC"). Passing
    *-- an empty string as the first parameter will start an
    *-- instance of Word if it is not running. We therefore
    *-- use DDE to determine if Word is running.
    LOCAL lnChannel, ;
          lRunning, ;
          llDDEOldSafety

    llDDEOldSafety = DDESETOPTION("Safety")

    *-- Prevent the prompt to start the application
    =DDESETOPTION("Safety", .F.)
    lnChannel = DDEINITIATE("WinWord", "System")
    IF lnChannel <> -1
      *-- It's running
      this.lCloseAppWhenDone = .F.
      =DDETERMINATE(lnChannel)
      lRunning = .T.
    ENDIF

    =DDESETOPTION("Safety", llDDEOldSafety)

    RETURN lRunning
  ENDFUNC

  PROTECTED FUNCTION GetCurrentInstance()
    RETURN GETOBJECT("", this.cOLERegName)
  ENDFUNC
```

```
    PROTECTED FUNCTION CreateNewInstance()
      LOCAL loWord
      loWord = CREATEOBJECT(this.cOLERegName)
      loWord.AppMinimize
      loWord.FileNew
      RETURN loWord
    ENDFUNC

    *-- New Methods
    FUNCTION Insert(tcText)
      this.oOLEApp.Insert(tcText)
    ENDFUNC

ENDDEFINE
```

Notice that we have also defined a new implementation for the GetCurrent-Instance() method. This is because of Word's inability to respond to the missing parameter in the GETOBJECT() function. To get the current instance of Word, we can safely use the GETOBJECT() method with an empty string.

It is interesting to note that Word does not support creating multiple instances of itself through OLE Automation, while Excel does. The use of the classes presented here will prevent you from having to worry about inadvertently creating another instance of Excel.

Another interesting difference between these two applications is that when releasing a reference to Word that was started via OLE Automation, the Word instance is automatically terminated. However, a reference to Excel will not terminate in this fashion. Instead, we must send the Quit method to the Excel object, explicitly instructing it to terminate. Furthermore, Excel will terminate even if the reference to it was created from a previously running instance.

In either case, however, as application developers the differences don't affect us! We've written a class that handles the functionality that we need (GetCurrent-Instance, CreateNewInstance), and it handles the differences in OLE implementation for us. We can subclass our OLEAutomation class to add capabilities for as many OLE automation servers as we have to work with, and our application can call them in a consistent manner.

More Ideas

Although you could if you wanted to, you probably won't want to create custom methods for every single method of every single object in an OLE server application. Instead, you may want to provide a quick way to indirectly access the properties and methods of the application object itself, without removing its protected status. If we were to simply provide direct access to the application instance, we would lose control over it. The user would then have the ability to disrupt the environment by incorrectly setting properties or calling methods that we may not want them to call. Instead, we can keep the application instance as a protected member of our class and create three methods that provide indirect access to the internal application instance.

The first two methods are implemented the same way. They are intentionally left as two separate methods because they serve two different purposes, and also to make it easier to subclass in the future.

```
*-- The following 3 methods, Do(), Get(), and Set(), can be
*-- used to execute a method, get the value of a property,
*-- or set a property on the protected reference to the
*-- OLE Automation server (this.oOLEApp).

*-- This method takes a method name as a parameter
*-- and executes it.
FUNCTION Do(tcMethod)
  RETURN EVAL("this.oOLEApp." + tcMethod)
ENDFUNC

*-- This method takes a property name as a parameter
*-- and returns its value. (It can even return references
*-- to container objects).
*-- For example, to get a ref to the active sheet from the
*-- command window:
*-- oActiveSheet = oExcel.Get("ActiveSheet")
*-- You could then use the oActiveSheet object directly!
*-- oActiveSheet.Cells(1,1).Value = 10
FUNCTION Get(tcProperty)
  RETURN EVAL("this.oOLEApp." + tcProperty)
ENDFUNC

*-- This method takes a property name and a value as
*-- parameters, and sets the value of the property
*-- to the value parameter.
```

```
FUNCTION Set(tcProperty, tuValue)
  LOCAL lcCommand
  lcCommand = "this.oOLEApp." + tcProperty + "="
  lcCommand = lcCommand + this.ConvertToChar(tuValue)
  &lcCommand
ENDFUNC
```

We'll add just one more method here to convert a generic parameter of any type to a character value. This method could just as easily have been implemented as a stand-alone function in its own PRG, or as a function of a procedure file. For now, it remains a protected method of this class.

```
*-- Takes a parameter of any type and converts it
*-- a character string for use in the Set method.
PROTECTED FUNCTION ConvertToChar(tuParam)
  LOCAL lcRetVal, ;
      lcType
  lcRetVal = ""
  lcType = TYPE("tuParam")

  DO CASE
    CASE lcType = "C"
      LOCAL llSQuote, llDQuote, llBracket
      llSQuote  = ['] $ tuParam
      llDQuote  = ["] $ tuParam
      llBracket = "[" $ tuParam
      DO CASE
        CASE !llSQuote
          lcRetVal = ['] + tuParam + [']
        CASE !llDQuote
          lcRetVal = ["] + tuParam + ["]
        CASE !llBracket
          lcRetVal = "[" + tuParam + "]"
        OTHERWISE
          =MESSAGEBOX("Cannot create string")
          lcRetVal = ""
      ENDCASE
    CASE INLIST(lcType, "N", "B", "Y")
      lcRetVal  = STR(tuParam)
    CASE lcType = "L"
      lcRetVal  = IIF(tuParam, ".T.", ".F.")
    CASE lcType = "D"
       lcRetVal = DTOS(tuParam)
```

```
        CASE lcType = "T"
            lcRetVal = TTOC(tuParam)
    ENDCASE
    RETURN lcRetVal
ENDFUNC
```

And that's all there is to it. Through these methods, we provide access to the internal application instance through a custom interface to the class. We could implement a set of rules governing which methods we want the user to be able to call, thereby protecting users of the class from doing anything they aren't supposed to do.

If we desire, we could ultimately remove these three methods (actually four if you include the ConvertToChar utility method) and add custom methods that perform specific tasks we want to accomplish. You don't have to restrict yourself by mapping each and every method of each and every object. Rather, you could create higher level methods which perform higher level tasks, which shield the user of the class from having to know the details of the OLE Automation commands that are required to perform the desired functionality. We could do this gradually as application requirements change, while still retaining the core functionality we have here.

Conclusion

I hope that this chapter has given you some idea of the power of OLE 2.0, especially when combined with Visual FoxPro's object model. Using the power of objects with OLE allows us to provide a higher level of access to OLE, streamlining our development efforts.

Chapter 12

A Set of MOVER Classes

Introduction

Codebook 2.6 included a reusable screen that allowed the user to move items from one list into another. The screen, called MOVER.SCX, accepted parameters for two arrays (one to hold the entire list and the other to hold the list of selected items) and showed the arrays in scrolling lists side by side with CommandButtons to move from one list to another. Double-clicking on an item in a list would move that item to the other list as well.

This chapter presents a series of classes for implementing this type of functionality in Visual FoxPro applications.

Design Philosophy

In redesigning the screen for Visual FoxPro, a few thoughts came to mind:

- MOVER type functionality is useful not only as a dialog on its own but also as part of other forms and dialogs.
- Different types of MOVER may be required. For example, we had an internal version of MOVER called BIGMOVE which had the lists horizontally oriented to allow for longer list item descriptions.

The new version of MOVER, then, was not designed as a single form but rather as a series of classes that can be combined and subclassed to provide MOVER functionality in a myriad of ways.

MOVER.VCX Class Hierarchy

The class hierarchy used in the MOVER class library is shown in the next figure:

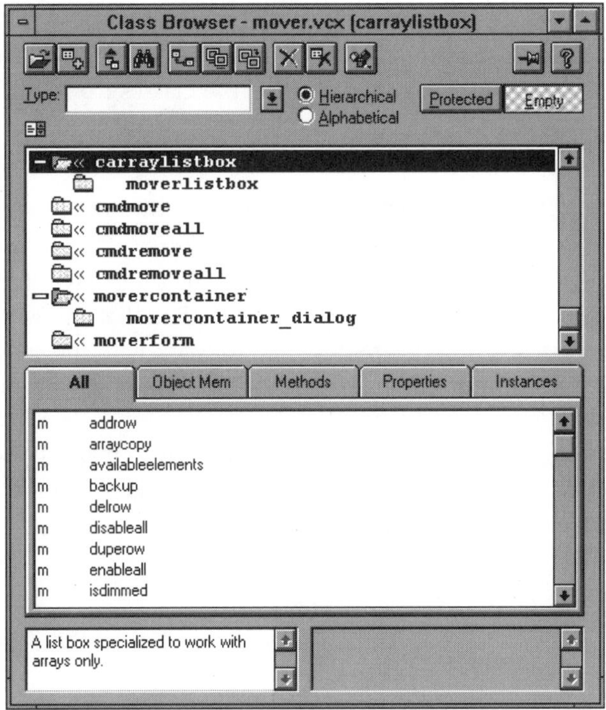

MOVER class hierarchy

There are three major branches to this tree. They are:

1. ArrayListBox Classes
2. Container Classes
3. Form Classes

The CommandButton classes are the CommandButtons that handle the MOVE and REMOVE type functionality and are not really major branches in the class hierarchy.

The ArrayListBox classes define the ListBox classes used for MOVER type lists. The Container classes combine different sets of functionality for MOVER functionality. The Form classes combine a form and the Container classes for final effect.

Let's discuss each branch individually.

Showing the Classes

Visual FoxPro presents somewhat of a challenge in presenting classes in written form. The classes are created visually but a book is a written medium. They don't go together very well.

For the purposes of showing the classes here, we will show the code exported from the Class Browser. On the disc, the classes from this chapter can be found as part of the Codebook Framework classes.

Class: CArrayListBox (CListBox)

This class, the first in our trip down MOVER lane, is a subclass of the framework CListBox class and is designed to create a generic ListBox that will work with arrays.

As we know, ListBox objects are designed to work with internal arrays. Array RowSourceTypes are supported but you cannot use methods like AddItem() and RemoveItem() with array-based lists.

When designing the MOVER hierarchy, it seemed to make sense to abstract out the array-based ListBox functionality into its own class. After all, array-based ListBoxes are something we use quite a lot.

Here's the code:

```
*  Class.............: Carraylistbox
*  Author............: Menachem Bazian, CPA
*  Project...........: Visual FoxPro Codebook
*  Copyright.........: (c) Flash Creative Management, Inc. 1995
*  Notes.............: Exported code from Class Browser.
************************************************
*-- Class:        carraylistbox
*-- ParentClass:  clistbox
*-- BaseClass:    listbox
*-- A list box specialized to work with arrays only.
*
#INCLUDE
"d:\clients\cdbk30\app\cdbk30\common30\include\framewrk.h"
*
DEFINE CLASS carraylistbox AS clistbox


   RowSourceType = 5
   RowSource = ""
```

```
Height = 250
Width = 185
*-- Defines what happens when an item is REMOVED from the list.
*-- May be DELETEd or DIMmed.
cdeltype = "DIM"
*-- Should additions be checked against rowsource or not?
caddtype = "CHECK"
*-- # elements available in the list
nelementsavailable = 0
*-- Should the array be sorted?
lsorted = .T.
Name = "carraylistbox"

*-- Should incoming array be backed up prior to loading.
lbackup = .F.

*-- Backup of the row source to allow for reverting the
*-- list to original form.
DIMENSION arowsourcebackup[1]
PROTECTED rowsourcetype


*-- Adds a row to the rowsource.
PROCEDURE addrow
   *-- Adds a row to the rowsource array.

   LOCAL lcArray, lnRows
   lcArray = this.rowsource
   lnRows = this.numrows()

   IF this.multidimensional()
      DECLARE &lcArray[lnRows+1, this.numcols()]
   ELSE
      DECLARE &lcArray[lnRows+1]
   ENDIF  this.multidimensional()

   RETURN (lnRows+1)
ENDPROC


*-- Is the array multidimensional (i.e., more than one dimension).
*-- Returns a logical.
PROCEDURE multidimensional
```

```
    *-- Is this a multidimensional or unidimensional array?
    *--
    *-- .T. means that it is a multidimensional array

    LOCAL lcRowSource
    lcRowSource = this.rowsource

    RETURN (ALEN(&lcRowSource,2) > 0)
ENDPROC


*-- Number of rows in the list. (The old SizeArry.PRG)
PROCEDURE numrows
    *-- Returns the number of ROWS in the rowsource array.
    *-- This is adaptation of the old
    *-- SizeArry function written by Yair Alan Griver in
    *-- "The FoxPro Codebook"

    LOCAL lnCount, lcRowSource
    llMultCol = this.multidimensional()
    lcRowSource = this.rowsource

    FOR m.lnCount = ALEN(&lcRowSource,1) TO 1 STEP -1
       IF (llMultCol AND !EMPTY(EVAL(this.rowsource - ;
         "[m.lnCount,1]")) OR ;
         !llMultCol AND !EMPTY(EVAL(this.rowsource - ;
         "[m.lnCount]")))
          EXIT && Filled item
       ENDIF
    ENDFOR

    RETURN lnCount
ENDPROC


*-- Return # of Columns in the rowsource array.
PROCEDURE numcols
    *-- Returns the number of Columns in the rowsource array

    LOCAL lcRowSource
    lcRowSource = this.rowsource
```

```
   RETURN ALEN(&lcRowSource,2)
ENDPROC


*-- Delete a row from the rowsource array
PROCEDURE delrow
   *  Parameter List....: tnIndex - Element number to delete

   *-- Deletes a row from the rowsource. Note how it uses
   *-- an ADEL() and then uses
   *-- a RESIZE to ditch the flotsam.

   LPARAMETERS tnIndex
   LOCAL lcRowSource
   lcRowSource = this.rowsource

   =ADEL(&lcRowSource, tnIndex)
   this.nElementsavailable = this.nElementsavailable - 1
   this.resize()

   RETURN
ENDPROC


*-- # of Available Elements in the Array
PROCEDURE availableelements
   *-- Counts how many elements are available to be worked
   *-- with (i.e., non-dimmed elements)

   LOCAL lnRetVal

   lnRetVal = 0
   lnNumRows = this.NumRows()
   IF this.MultiDimensional()
      lcCkVal = this.RowSource - "[lnCounter,1]"
   ELSE
      lcCkVal = this.RowSource - "[lnCounter]"
   ENDIF

   FOR lnCounter = 1 TO lnNumRows
      IF LEFT(EVAL(lcCkVal),1) # '\'
         lnRetVal = lnRetVal + 1
      ENDIF
```

```
   ENDFOR

   RETURN (lnRetVal)
ENDPROC


*-- Enables all items in a list.
PROCEDURE enableall
   *-- Enables all the elements in the rowsource by
   *-- removing backslashes that might exist.

   LOCAL lnCounter, lnRows, lcCkVal, lcRowSource

   lcRowSource = this.rowsource
   lcCkVal = IIF(this.MultiDimensional(), ;
            lcRowSource-"[lnCounter,1]", ;
            lcRowSource-"[lnCounter]")

   lnRows = this.NumRows()
   FOR lnCounter = 1 TO lnRows
      IF EVAL(lcCkVal) = "\"
         &lcCkVal = SUBS(EVAL(lcCkVal),2)
      ENDIF
   ENDFOR

   this.nElementsAvailable = lnRows
   this.requery()
ENDPROC


*-- Disables all individual items in the list
PROCEDURE disableall
   *-- Adds a backslash to all the elements in the rowsource
   *-- array thus disabling them.

   LOCAL lnCounter, lnRows, lcCkVal, lcRowSource

   lcRowSource = this.rowsource
   lcCkVal = IIF(this.MultiDimensional(), ;
            lcRowSource-"[lnCounter,1]", ;
            lcRowSource-"[lnCounter]")
```

```
   lnRows = this.NumRows()
   FOR lnCounter = 1 TO lnRows
      IF EVAL(lcCkVal) # "\"
         &lcCkVal = '\'-EVAL(lcCkVal)
      ENDIF
   ENDFOR

   this.nElementsAvailable = 0
   this.requery()
ENDPROC


*-- Returns whether a list item is disabled or not.
PROCEDURE isdimmed
   *  Parameter List....: tnIndex - Element number to delete
   *-- Returns .T. if a backslash is the first character of a
   *-- list item.
   *-- tnIndex is the element number to test.

   LPARAMETERS tnIndex

   LOCAL llRetVal

   IF this.multidimensional()
      llRetVal = LEFT(EVAL(this.rowsource-"[tnIndex,1]"),1) == '\'
   ELSE
      llRetVal = LEFT(EVAL(this.rowsource-"[tnIndex]"),1) == '\'
   ENDIF

   RETURN llRetVal
ENDPROC


*-- Copy the contents of a row from the rowsource into the
*-- passed through array.
PROCEDURE duperow
   *-- Duplicates a row from one array into a special array.
   *-- For example, suppose you
   *-- have an array[5,20]. Calling duperow for the 5th row
   *-- would create a second array[20]
   *-- with all the values from the 20 columns in the fifth
   *-- row of the rowsource array.
   *--
```

```
   *-- This is useful to read a row into a table. You could
   *-- use DUPEROW() and then GATHER FROM
   *-- ARRAY (assuming array and table structures are in synch).

   *  Parameter List....: taDestArray - Array to put the copied
   *                                    elements into
   *                    : tnIndex - Element number to delete

   LPARAMETERS taDestArray, tnIndex
   LOCAL lnCounter, lnCols

   lnCols = this.numCols()

   DECLARE taDestArray[MAX(1, lnCols)]

   FOR lnCounter = 1 TO MAX(1, lnCols)
      IF lnCols > 0
         taDestArray[lnCounter] = ;
            EVAL(this.rowsource-"[tnIndex, lnCounter]")
      ELSE
         taDestArray[lnCounter] = ;
            EVAL(this.rowsource-"[tnIndex]")
      ENDIF
   ENDFOR
ENDPROC


*-- Marks a row with a backslash thus, in effect, disabling it.
PROCEDURE markrow
   *  Parameter List....: tnIndex - Element number to delete
   *-- Dims a single row.

   LPARAMETERS tnIndex

   lcRowSource = this.rowsource
   IF this.multidimensional()
      IF EVAL(lcRowSource-"[tnIndex,1]") # '\'
         &lcRowSource.[tnIndex,1] = ;
            "\"-EVAL(lcRowSource-"[tnIndex,1]")
         this.nElementsAvailable = this.nElementsAvailable - 1
      ENDIF
   ELSE
```

```
      IF EVAL(lcRowSource-"[tnIndex]") # '\'
         &lcRowSource.[tnIndex] = ;
            "\"-EVAL(lcRowSource-"[tnIndex]")
         this.nElementsAvailable = this.nElementsAvailable - 1
      ENDIF
   ENDIF
ENDPROC


*-- Packs the list removing all disabled items.
PROCEDURE packlist
   *-- This is a stronger pack than Resize()
   *-- Resize just removes the trailing logical
   *-- values. Packlist converts dimmed rows to deleted ones
   *-- and then calls resize.

   LOCAL lnNumRows, lnCounter, lcRowSource
   lcRowSource = this.rowsource
   lnNumRows = this.numrows()
   llMultiDimensional = this.MultiDimensional()
   IF llMultiDimensional
      lcCkVal = this.rowsource-"[lnCounter,1]"
   ELSE
      lcCkVal = this.rowsource-"[lnCounter]"
   ENDIF

   FOR lnCounter = 1 TO lnNumRows
      IF TYPE(lcCkVal) = "L"
         EXIT
      ENDIF

      IF LEFT(EVAL(lcCkVal),1) = '\'
         =ADEL(&lcRowsource,lnCounter)
         lnCounter = lnCounter - 1
      ENDIF
   ENDFOR

   this.resize()
ENDPROC


*-- Resize the array removing all the deleted rows.
PROCEDURE resize
```

```
   *-- Resizes the array to its true size. Rows deleted
   *-- with ADEL() are sitting at the end of the array
   *-- with logicals in them. This "packs"
   *-- the array by redeclaring the array to the right size.

   LOCAL lcRowSource, lnRows
   lcRowSource = this.rowsource
   lnRows = this.numrows()
   lnCols = this.numcols()

   IF lnRows > 0
      IF lnCols > 0
         DECLARE &lcRowSource.[lnRows, lnCols]
      ELSE
         DECLARE &lcRowSource.[lnRows]
      ENDIF
   ENDIF
ENDPROC


*-- Batch loads the rowsource from an array passed through as
*-- a parameter.
PROCEDURE arraycopy
   *-- This procedure takes a source array and copies it
   *-- into the rowsource. This is a way of "batch loading"
   *-- the rowsource from another array.
   *--
   *-- An example where this would be used would be in a MOVER
   *-- when you are doing a "MOVEALL" type of deal.

   *  Parameter List....: taSourceArray - Array for the copy

   LPARAMETERS taSourceArray

   IF ALEN(taSourceArray,2) # this.numcols()
      =MessageBox(MVR_DIFFERENTSTRUCT_LOC, ;
               16, MVR_ARRAYLISTBOXHDR_LOC)
      RETURN
   ENDIF

   *-- If we got this far, we can get to work.
```

```
   LOCAL lnRows, lnCols, lcRowSource
   lnRows = ALEN(taSourceArray,1)
   lnCols = ALEN(taSourceArray,2)
   lcRowSource = this.RowSource

   IF lnCols > 0
      DECLARE &lcRowSource.[lnRows, lnCols]
   ELSE
      DECLARE &lcRowSource.[lnRows]
   ENDIF

   =ACOPY(taSourceArray, &lcRowSource)
   this.nElementsAvailable = this.AvailableElements()
ENDPROC


*-- Copies the rowsource array into the backup array
*--(aRowSourceBackup)
PROCEDURE backup
   LPARAMETERS tlShowMessage

   IF pCount() = 0 OR TYPE("tlShowMessage") # 'L'
      tlShowmessage = .T.
   ENDIF

   *-- Backup the rowsource array to an internal array
   *-- called ArowSourceBackup.
   *--
   *-- We'll need it if the user hits Cancel and we have
   *-- to revert.

   IF ("AROWSOURCEBACKUP" $ UPPER(ALLTRIM(this.rowsource)))

      IF tlShowMessage
         =Messagebox(MVR_CANNOTBACKUP_LOC, ;
                 16, MVR_ARRAYLISTBOXHDR_LOC)
      ENDIF
      RETURN
   ENDIF

   LOCAL lnNumRows, lnNumCols, lcRowSource
```

```
   lnNumRows = MAX(this.numrows(), 1)
   lnNumCols = this.numcols()
   lcRowSource = this.rowsource

   IF lnNumCols > 0
      DECLARE this.aRowSourceBackup[lnNumRows, lnNumCols]
   ELSE
      DECLARE this.aRowSourceBackup[lnNumRows]
   ENDIF

   =ACOPY(&lcRowSource, this.aRowSourceBackup)
   RETURN
ENDPROC


*-- Copies the backup into the rowsource array.
PROCEDURE revert
   LPARAMETERS tlShowMessage

   IF pCount() = 0 OR TYPE("tlShowMessage") # 'L'
      tlShowMessage = .T.
   ENDIF

   *-- Copies the ArowSourceBackup array into the rowsource.
   *-- Usually called from a cancel button.

   IF ("AROWSOURCEBACKUP" $ UPPER(ALLTRIM(this.rowsource)))
      IF tlShowMessage
         =Messagebox(MVR_CANNOTREVERT_LOC, ;
                  16, MVR_ARRAYLISTBOXHDR_LOC)
      ENDIF
      RETURN
   ENDIF

   LOCAL lnNumRows, lnNumCols, lcRowSource

   lnNumRows = ALEN(this.aRowSourceBackup,1)
   lnNumCols = ALEN(this.aRowSourceBackup,2)
   lcRowSource = this.rowsource

   lcRowSource = this.rowsource
```

```
   IF lnNumCols > 0
      DECLARE &lcRowSource[lnNumRows, lnNumCols]
   ELSE
      DECLARE &lcRowSource[lnNumRows]
   ENDIF

   =ACOPY(this.aRowSourceBackup, (this.rowsource))
   RETURN
ENDPROC


*-- Sets the rowsource property for this list.
PROCEDURE setrowsource
   *-- Set the rowsource. This accepts the name of the array
   *-- and then runs the Init() to
   *-- set everything up properly.

   *  Parameter List....: tcRowSourceName - Name of the array
   *                    :   to use as the new rowsource

   LPARAMETERS tcRowSourceName

   *-- Check to make sure we got a character

   IF TYPE("tcRowSourceName") # 'C'
      =Messagebox(MVR_INVALID_ROWSOURCE_PARMTYPE_LOC, ;
              16, MVR_ARRAYLISTBOXHDR_LOC)
      RETURN
   ENDIF

   *-- First check to make sure that this is an array

   IF TYPE(tcRowSourceName-"[1]") = 'U'
      =Messagebox(MVR_INVALID_ROWSOURCE_LOC, 16, ;
              MVR_ARRAYLISTBOXHDR_LOC)
      RETURN
   ENDIF

   *-- IF we get this far, we can go ahead and set the rowsource

   this.rowsource=tcRowSourceName
   this.init()
   this.requery()
```

```
ENDPROC


PROCEDURE Clear
   *-- Clears out the list and the rowsource array (a ZAP,
   *-- in effect).

   LOCAL lnColumns, lcRowSource

   lnColumns = this.numcols()
   lcRowSource = this.rowSource

   IF lnColumns > 0
      DECLARE &lcRowSource[1, lnColumns]
   ELSE
      DECLARE &lcRowSource[1]
   ENDIF

   &lcRowSource[1] = ""
   this.nElementsAvailable = 0
   this.requery()
ENDPROC


PROCEDURE Requery
   LOCAL lcRowSource

   ListBox::Requery()

   DO CASE
      CASE this.numrows() = 0
         this.enabled = .F.
         lcRowSource = this.rowsource
         &lcRowSource[1] = " "

      CASE this.nElementsAvailable = 0
         this.enabled = .F.

      OTHERWISE
         this.enabled = .T.
   ENDCASE
ENDPROC
```

```
PROCEDURE AddItem
   *  Parameter List....: tuItem - Item to add. Can be
   *                    :   character or an array
   *                    : tlNoRquery  -  Don't requery the
   *                    :   list (defaults to .F.)

   LPARAMETERS tuItem, tlNoRequery

   *-- Adds ONE item to the rowsource array.
   *--
   *-- Here's the deal. The item to be added may be an ARRAY
   *-- row or it may be a character.
   *--
   *-- If the element is an ARRAY, then the next step is
   *-- to determine if it is a multidimensional array or
   *-- a unidimensional one. If it is unidimensional and
   *-- the rowsource is multidimensional, then each element
   *-- in the passed array will be mapped to the
   *-- corresponding column in the rowsource.
   *-- (i.e., element 1 will be mapped to column 1, 2 to column 2)
   *--
   *-- If the passed through element is just a plain old
   *-- character string, it will be added to the rowsource
   *-- in column 1.
   *--
   *-- The item added can be treated in one of two ways. First
   *-- of all, if the cAddType is set to "CHECK", the item that
   *-- we are attempting to add will be checked against
   *-- the rowsource behind this list and, if found, will not
   *-- be added. The additem routine
   *-- will check to see if the item is disabled (with a \ in
   *-- the first character slot) and,
   *-- if it is, will reenable it. If cAddType is set to
   *-- "NOCHECK", the item is explicitly
   *-- added without a check.
   *--
   *-- Using another value for cAddType will generate an error.
   *--
   *-- The check for an array parameter will go against
   *-- the BOUNDCOLUMN of the list.
   *--
```

```
*-- One more point. When an ADDITEM() is done in a "regular"
*-- list box with no special rowsource, the additem
*-- automatically updates the list. By default, this additem()
*-- method will follow that for consistency. However, if we
*-- are adding many items, we may want to suppress that
*-- behavior. Therefore, the second parameter, tlNoRequery,
*-- can be sent through with a logical value. If sent through
*-- as a logical .T.,
*-- the requery will be suppressed.

LOCAL llArray, lcRowSource, lcCkVal, llOkToAdd

*-- Step 1 - Get the type of parameter and check the
*-- parameter for validity.

llArray = TYPE("tuItem[1]") # 'U'
IF !llArray AND TYPE("tuItem") # 'C'
   =Messagebox(MVR_INVALID_ADDITEM_PARMTYPE_LOC, ;
         16, MVR_ARRAYLISTBOXHDR_LOC)
   RETURN
ENDIF

IF TYPE("tlNoRequery") # 'L'
   tlNorequery = .F.
ENDIF

llMultiDimensional = this.MultiDimensional()

IF llArray
   *-- This check will deal with an array.
   *--
   *-- Before I go into the code here, let me discuss the
   *-- issue of handling arrays with a number of elements
   *-- different from what I am expecting. To put it
   *-- simply, I am expecting an array with the same number
   *-- of elements as there are
   *-- columns in the rowsource array.
   *--
   *-- The choices here would call for one of the following
   *-- if the array that I am getting here is not the
   *-- length I am expecting. I can either:
   *--
```

```
   *-- 1. Reject the incoming array
   *-- 2. Fill the rowsource array as far as I can
   *--
   *-- I will opt for the second approach in this case.

   IF (llMultiDimensional AND ;
      (ALEN(tuItem) # this.NumCols())) OR ;
      (!llMultiDimensional AND (ALEN(tuItem) # 1))

      =Messagebox(MVR_INVALID_ADDITEM_PARMARRAY_LOC, ;
            16, MVR_ARRAYLISTBOXHDR_LOC)
      RETURN
   ENDIF
ENDIF  llArray AND (ALEN(tuItem) # this.NumRows())

*-- Step 2 - We know what type of parameter we got.
*-- Let's handle them.
*-- We'll deal with a character type first -- It's easiest.

lcRowSource = this.rowsource

IF !llArray
   lcCkVal = tuItem
ELSE
   lcCkVal = tuItem[1, this.boundcolumn]
ENDIF

llOkToAdd = .F.

DO CASE
   CASE UPPER(ALLTRIM(THIS.cAddType)) = "CHECK"
      lnElmNum = ASCAN(&lcRowSource, lcCkVal)

      DO CASE
         CASE lnElmNum = 0  && Not found
            *-- At this point, we haven't found the item
            *-- yet. However, it may be in the list and
            *-- dimmed. So, we need to check for it.

            *-- This case takes care of a dimmed item. It
            *-- is applicable for
            *-- character params or an array with
            *-- this.boundcolumn = 1. In all
```

```
                *-- other cases, a 0 from the ASCAN means that
                *-- it is not in the array.

                lnElmNum = ASCAN(&lcRowSource, "\"-lcCkVal)
                IF lnElmNum > 0
                   &lcRowSource[lnElmNum] = ;
                      SUBST(EVAL(lcRowSource +"[lnElmNum]"),2)
                   this.nElementsAvailable = ;
                      this.nElementsAvailable + 1
                ELSE
                   llOkToAdd = .T.
                ENDIF

             CASE lnElmNum > 0 AND llArray
                *-- This case takes care of a match when the
                *-- parameter is an array and
                *-- this.boundcolumn is set to > 1. This
                *-- means that we may get a match
                *-- even though the item is dimmed.

                lnElmNum = ASUB(&lcRowSource, lnElmNum, 1)

                IF llMultidimensional AND ;
                   LEFT(EVAL(lcRowSource-"[lnElmNum,1]"),1) ;
                      = "\"
                   &lcRowSource[lnElmNum,1] = ;
                      SUBS(EVAL(lcRowSource-"[lnElmNum,1]"),2)

                   this.nElementsAvailable = ;
                      this.nElementsAvailable + 1
                ENDIF
             OTHERWISE
                llOkToAdd = .F.
          ENDCASE
       CASE UPPER(ALLTRIM(THIS.cAddType)) = "NOCHECK"
          llOkToAdd = .T.

       OTHERWISE
          =MessageBox(MVR_INVALID_CADDTYPE_LOC, ;
                16, MVR_ARRAYLISTBOXHDR_LOC)
          RETURN
    ENDCASE
```

```
   IF llOkToAdd
      lnRow = THIS.addrow()

      IF !llArray
         IF llMultiDimensional
            &lcRowSource[lnRow, 1] = tuItem
         ELSE
            &lcRowSource[lnRow] = tuItem
         ENDIF
      ELSE
         IF llMultiDimensional
            FOR lnCounter = 1 TO ALEN(tuItem)
               &lcRowSource[lnRow, lnCounter] = ;
                  tuItem[lnCounter]
            ENDFOR
         ELSE
            *-- By definition, this is only valid when there ;
            *-- is one column in the
            *-- Rowsource and tuItem.
            &lcRowSource[lnRow] = tuItem[1]
         ENDIF
      ENDIF
      this.nElementsAvailable = this.nElementsAvailable + 1

      IF this.lSorted
         =ASORT(&lcRowSource)
      ENDIF
   ENDIF

   IF !tlNoRequery
      this.requery()
   ENDIF
ENDPROC


PROCEDURE Init
   *  CLASS.............: ARRAYLISTBOX
   *  Author............: Menachem Bazian, CPA
   *  Project...........: Common
   *  Created...........: June 01, 1995 - 12:05:19
   *  Copyright.........: (c) Flash Creative Mgt, Inc., 1995
   *) Description.......: A special list box to work with arrays.
```

```
    *-- The basic idea here is to backup the array in the list
    *-- if neccesary and make
    *-- sure that everything is nice and clean.

    LOCAL lnCounter, lnNumRows, llMultiDimensional, lcRowSource

    *-- Check to make sure that our rowsource is an array and,
    *-- if not, make sure that it is by setting the rowsource
    *-- property to the backup array.

    IF EMPTY(this.rowsource) OR TYPE(this.rowsource-"[1]") = "U"
      this.rowsource = "THIS.AROWSOURCEBACKUP"
    ENDIF

    *-- Back it up if requested to do so (but only if I am
    *-- not working against the rowsource backup array).

    IF this.lBackup AND ;
      !("AROWSOURCEBACKUP" $ UPPER(ALLT(this.RowSource)))
      this.backup()
    ENDIF

    *-- Resize the array that comes in just in case it has some
    *-- flotsam at the end.

    this.resize()
    this.nElementsAvailable = this.AvailableElements()

    IF this.nElementsAvailable = 0
      this.enabled = .F.
    ENDIF

    lcRowSource = this.rowsource

    IF this.lSorted
      =ASORT(&lcRowSource)
    ENDIF
ENDPROC
```

```
PROCEDURE RemoveItem
   *  Parameter List....: tnIndex - Element number to delete
   *                    : tlNoRquery - Don't requery the list
   *                    :   (defaults to .F.)

   *-- Removeitem() made to work with arrays.

   LPARAMETERS tnIndex, tlNoRequery

   *-- This method removes an item from the list by modifying
   *-- the underlying ROWSOURCE. Note the effect of
   *-- this.cDelType on the code here.
   *--
   *-- For information on tlNoRequery, see AddItem()

   DO CASE
      CASE this.cDelType = "DELETE"
         this.delrow(tnIndex)
      CASE this.cDelType = "DIM"
         this.markrow(tnIndex)
      OTHERWISE
         =MessageBox(MVR_INVALID_CDELTYPE_LOC, ;
                  16, MVR_ARRAYLISTBOXHDR_LOC)
         RETURN
   ENDCASE

   IF !tlNoRequery
      this.requery()
   ENDIF
ENDPROC


ENDDEFINE
*
*-- EndDefine: carraylistbox
**************************************************
```

There is a common theme to all the methods in this class. When something is done to the list, it is automatically performed on the RowSource array instead. Thus, when doing an AddItem(), for example, the added item is appended to the RowSource array and the ListBox's Requery() method is called.

Let's go through the custom and overridden properties first. All the properties are set in the declaration section of code in the listing.

Custom/Overridden Properties

Property: **cAddType**
Default Value: **"CHECK"**

This property defines whether a new item is checked against the current list before being added. When set to "CHECK," the ListBox will check to make sure that the item is not a duplicate before adding it to the RowSource array.

A duplicate, by the way, is determined by comparing the first column of the RowSource array against the potential new item.

Property: **cDelType**
Default Value: **"DIM"**

This property determines what happens when an item is removed from the list with RemoveItem(). If set to DIM, the item is not physically deleted, rather it is disabled by appending a backslash to the text in the first column. If set to DELETE, the item is physically deleted from the array.

Property: **lBackup**
Default Value: **.F.**

If set to .T., the RowSource is backed up to the aRowSourceBackup[] property array when the RowSource is set.

Property: **lSorted**
Default Value: **.T.**

Should the list be sorted? This property replaces, for all intents and purposes, the Sorted property that is native to the ListBox class because the Sorted property does not work with array-based ListBoxes.

Property: **nElementsAvailable**
Default Value: **0**

Number of available elements in the list. An item is considered available if it is not deleted and not dimmed. This counter is maintained internally.

Property: **RowSource**
Default Value: **""**

The name of the RowSource array. Usually set with the SetRowSource() method.

PROTECTED Property: **RowSourceType**
Value: **5**

5 means an array. This property is protected because, by definition, this list works off arrays.

Property: **aRowSourceBackup[1]**

This is the backup array for the list.

Custom/Overridden Methods

Here are the methods defined in the CArrayListBox class.

Overridden Method: Init()

The Init() method sets up everything for the array ListBox. It checks to make sure that a RowSource has been set. If none has been set, aRowSourceBackup[] is set as the RowSource so that the object can properly initialize without error. If lBackup has been set to .T. (and RowSource does not point to aRowSourceBackup[]), the RowSource array is backed up. Finally, if lSorted is .T., the RowSource array is sorted.

Overridden Method: AddItem(tcItem | taRow [, tlNoRequery])

This method has been modified to work off the RowSource array.

Note the parameters. Two different types of parameters are supported: a character string or an array.

Allowing a character string supports the original ListBox syntax of olstBox.AddItem("Item"). If a character string is passed through, it is placed in the first column of the row added to the RowSource array.

You can also pass an array. The array would be a unidimensional array with one element for every column in the RowSource array. This allows you to populate the entire array (not just the display portion) when adding an element to the list. This is key functionality for MOVER lists.

The method will check to make sure that a duplicate item is not being added if the cAddType property is set to "CHECK."

By default, the AddItem() method issues a Requery() to refresh the list from the RowSource array. If you are adding a batch of items, you will not want to do this until the last item has been added. In that case, pass a .T. for tlNoRequery.

Overridden Method: RemoveItem(tnIndex [, tlNoRequery])

RemoveItem() basically works like AddItem() but in reverse. Give it the item number in the list to remove and it will. "Remove" means one of two things: It either disables the list item (if cDelType is set to "DIM") or it physically deletes the row.

By default, the RemoveItem() method issues a Requery() to refresh the list from the RowSource array. If you are adding a batch of items, you will not want to do this until the last item has been added. In that case, pass a .T. for tlNoRequery.

Overridden Method: Clear()

"Zaps" the RowSource array and issues a Requery(). This, in effect, clears the list.

Overridden Method: Requery()

Issues the default Requery() from the CListBox class and then checks to make sure that there are still items left in the list. If the list is empty (either the array is empty or nElementsAvailable = 0), the method disables it.

Custom Method: AddRow()

Adds a row to the RowSource array.

Custom Method: ArrayCopy(taArray)

Populates the RowSource array from the array parameter. In effect, the parameter array is copied into the RowSource array.

Custom Method: AvailableElements()

Counts the number of elements available. The method considers a list element available if the first column is not a logical value type and it is not disabled (the first character is not "\".)

Custom Method: Backup()

Copies the RowSource array into aRowSourceBackup[].

Custom Method: DelRow([tnIndex])

Deletes the row in the array indicated by tnIndex (the row number to delete). The row is deleted from the RowSource array with ADEL() and then the array is resized with Resize().

Custom Method: DisableAll()

Dims all elements in the list by adding a backslash to the first column of each row. nElementsAvailable is automatically reset to the number of non-deleted rows in the RowSource array and Requery() is automatically called.

Custom Method: DupeRow(taArray, tnIndex)

Duplicates a row from the RowSource array into taArray. The array is a uni-dimensional representation of the row you are copying. For example, suppose the RowSource array has five rows and 20 columns. Issuing:

```
DECLARE laMyArray[1]
lstArrayList.DupeRow(@laMyArray, 4)
```

would dimension laMyArray to 20 elements and then copy all the values from the fourth row of the RowSource array into laMyArray.

This is useful to read a row into a table. You could use DupeRow() and then GATHER FROM ARRAY (assuming array and table structures are in synch).

For the MOVER, this will be used when moving elements from one list to the other.

Custom Method: EnableAll()

The reverse of DisableAll(). Removes any backslashes at the beginning of the strings in the first column of the RowSource array. nElementsAvailable is automatically reset to the number of non-deleted rows in the RowSource array and Requery() is automatically called.

Custom Method: IsDimmed([tnIndex])

Checks row number tnIndex to see if it is disabled with a backslash.

Custom Method: MarkRow([tnIndex])

Marks a row as disabled with a backslash.

Custom Method: MultiDimensional()

Tests an array to see if it is multi- or unidimensional. Unidimensional arrays return 0 for ALEN(array, 2).

Custom Method: NumCols()

Returns the number of columns in the RowSource array.

Custom Method: NumRows()

Equivalent to the old SizeArry() function. Counts the number of non-deleted rows in the RowSource array.

Custom Method: PackList()

Deletes all disabled items (those marked with a backslash).

Custom Method: Resize()

Redimensions the RowSource array by removing all array elements physically deleted with ADEL().

Custom Method: Revert()

Copies aRowSourceBackup[] into the RowSource array.

Custom Method: SetRowSource([tcRowSourceName)

Accepts the name of an array, sets the list's RowSource property and then runs the Init() to make sure everything is properly set up and in synch.

Class: MoverListBox (CArrayListBox)

This is an ArrayListBox specifically designed for use in a MOVER Container class. The principle difference between this class and the CArrayListBox class is the addition of DragDrop() functionality and a small but important change to the Requery() method.

Here's the exported code:

```
*  Class.............: Moverlistbox
*  Author............: Menachem Bazian, CPA
*  Project...........: Visual FoxPro Codebook
```

```
*  Copyright.........: (c) Flash Creative Management, Inc. 1995
*  Notes.............: Exported code from Class Browser.

**************************************************
*-- Class:        moverlistbox
*-- ParentClass:  carraylistbox
*-- BaseClass:    listbox
*-- Mover version of an array list box.
*
DEFINE CLASS moverlistbox AS carraylistbox


   DragIcon = (HOME() + "samples\graphics\cursors\dragmove.cur")
   Name = "moverlistbox"


   PROCEDURE Requery
      *-- Although the parent class disables the listbox when we
      *-- run out of elements, this
      *-- is not behavior we want in a mover list box (without
      *-- enablement we do not have the drag-drop functionality).

      cArrayListBox::Requery()
      IF this.enabled = .F.
         this.enabled = .T.
      ENDIF
   ENDPROC


   PROCEDURE DragDrop
      *  Program...........: MOVERLISTBOX.DRAGDROP
      *  Author............: Menachem Bazian, CPA
      *  Project...........: Visual FoxPro Codebook 3
      *  Created...........: June 01, 1995 - 15:35:47
      *  Copyright.........: (c) Flash Creative Mgt, Inc., 1995
      *) Description.......: Drag drop event for a mover list box.

      LPARAMETERS oSource, nXCoord, nYCoord

      LOCAL lnCounter, laSource[1]

      IF this.Name = oSource.Name
         RETURN
      ENDIF
```

```
*-- A quick note here. I am relying on certain methods
*-- and properties. I can only
*-- be sure of this if we are dealing with objects of the
*-- same class. true, a subclass
*-- can mess me up but I will trust the subclass developer
*-- to keep things in synch.

IF this.class # osource.class
   =Messagebox(MVR_MUSTBESAMECLASS_LOC, ;
          16, MVR_MOVERLISTBOXHDR_LOC)
   RETURN
ENDIF

*-- Some variables we will need. Specifically, whether
*-- the source array is a
*-- multidimensional array and, if so, how many columns it
*-- has. Then we will
*-- dimension a dummy array which we can use for ADDITEM()
*-- purposes.

lnSourceCols = oSource.NumCols()

DECLARE laSource[MAX(1,lnSourceCols)]

FOR lnCounter = 1 TO oSource.ListCount
   IF oSource.selected(lnCounter) AND ;
      !oSource.Isdimmed(lnCounter)
      oSource.DupeRow(@laSource, lnCounter)
      this.additem(@laSource, .T.)
      oSource.MarkRow(lnCounter)
   ENDIF
ENDFOR

IF oSource.cDelType = "DELETE"
   oSource.PackList()
ENDIF

oSource.Requery()
this.requery()
ENDPROC
```

```
   PROCEDURE MouseMove
      *-- This one is simple. I only want to go into drag mode if
      *-- the user regular clicks, holds
      *-- and then drags. This is what I am checking for...

      LPARAMETERS tnButton, tnShift, tnXCoord, tnYCoord

      IF tnButton = 1 AND tnShift = 0
         this.drag(1)
      ELSE
         this.drag(0)
      ENDIF
   ENDPROC


   PROCEDURE When
      RETURN (this.nElementsAvailable > 0)
   ENDPROC


ENDDEFINE
*
*-- EndDefine: moverlistbox
**************************************************
```

Design

A MoverListBox is different in that the list will accept items dropped on it and it can be dragged on other lists. This requires some code to enable and accept the drags and drops. It also means that the list, even when empty, cannot be disabled because if it's disabled it cannot accept items dropped on it.

Custom/Overridden Methods

Overridden Method: Requery()

Sets the form's LockScreen property to .T. before Calling CArrayListBox's Requery() method and then resetting enabled to .T. This prevents the list from flashing.

Overridden Method: When()

Since the list cannot be disabled, we need to disable the ability to get focus. That's the When()'s job.

Overridden Method: MouseMove(tnButton, tnShift, tnXCoord, tnYCoord)

The MouseMove event checks to see if a drag is being initiated. By definition, a drag is considered initiated when the left button is held down (tnButton = 1), and neither control, shift, nor alt is held down (tnShift = 0). The call to the Drag() method either initiates or terminates a DragDrop session depending on whether a 1 or 0 is passed through to it respectively.

Overridden Method: DragDrop(toSource, tnXCoord, tnYCoord)

toSource is an object reference to the object that was dropped on the list. The list checks to make sure that another MoverListBox has been dropped on it; otherwise it rejects it. Since there are a host of methods in the source list that are assumed to exist, this check is necessary.

DragDrop() loops through the items in the oSource list to see which are selected. Those that are selected are automatically added to this list and removed from the other.

That takes care of the CArrayListBox tree. Now that we have our ListBoxes set up, we can move on to combining these lists into a container. That's our next step.

Class: MoverContainer (CContainer)

The MoverContainer class combines two MoverListBox objects, adds some CommandButtons to handle moving and removing, and provides a common interface to the outside world.

Here's what the class looks like in the designer:

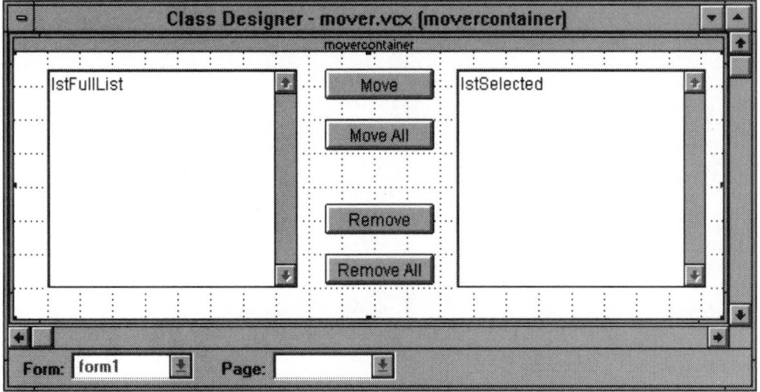

MoverContainer

And here's the class definition:

```
*  Class.............: Movercontainer
*  Author............: Menachem Bazian, CPA
*  Project...........: Visual FoxPro Codebook
*  Copyright.........: (c) Flash Creative Management, Inc. 1995
*  Notes.............: Exported code from Class Browser.
**************************************************
*-- Class:        movercontainer
*-- ParentClass:  ccontainer
*-- BaseClass:    container
*-- A container that combines mover list boxes and command buttons
*-- for use in a form.
*
DEFINE CLASS movercontainer AS ccontainer


   Width = 521
   Height = 190
   *-- Rowsource for the full list.
   cfulllistrowsource = ""
   *-- Rowsource for the list of selected items.
   cselectedlistrowsource = ""
   Name = "movercontainer"
```

```
ADD OBJECT lstfulllist AS moverlistbox WITH ;
   RowSource = "this.arowsourcebackup", ;
   Height = 157, ;
   Left = 24, ;
   Top = 12, ;
   Width = 185, ;
   lbackup = .T., ;
   Name = "lstFullList"


ADD OBJECT lstselected AS moverlistbox WITH ;
   RowSource = "this.arowsourcebackup", ;
   Height = 157, ;
   Left = 324, ;
   Sorted = .F., ;
   Top = 12, ;
   Width = 185, ;
   lbackup = .T., ;
   cdeltype = "DELETE", ;
   Name = "lstSelected"


ADD OBJECT cmdmove AS cmdmove WITH ;
   Top = 12, ;
   Left = 228, ;
   Name = "cmdMove"


ADD OBJECT cmdmoveall AS cmdmoveall WITH ;
   Top = 48, ;
   Left = 228, ;
   Name = "cmdMoveall"


ADD OBJECT cmdremove AS cmdremove WITH ;
   Top = 108, ;
   Left = 228, ;
   Name = "cmdRemove"


ADD OBJECT cmdremoveall AS cmdremoveall WITH ;
```

```
        Top = 144, ;
        Left = 228, ;
        Name = "cmdRemoveall"


*-- Moves only the selected objects from the "All" list to
*-- the "Selected" list.
PROCEDURE moveone
    *-- The functionality to do this already exists in the
    *-- drag drop event. Let's use it.

    this.lstSelected.DragDrop(this.lstFullList)
ENDPROC


*-- Moves the entire "ALL" list to the "Selected" List
PROCEDURE moveall
    *-- Just batchfill the selected list from the full list,
    *-- enable everything in the selected
    *-- list and disable everything in the full list.

    LOCAL lcFullSource
    lcFullSource = this.lstFullList.RowSource
    this.lstSelected.ArrayCopy(@&lcFullSource)
    this.lstSelected.EnableAll()
    this.lstFullList.DisableAll()
ENDPROC


*-- Remove only selected items from the selected list.
PROCEDURE removeone
    *-- The functionality to do this already exists in the
    *-- drag drop event. Let's use it.

    this.lstFullList.DragDrop(this.lstSelected)
ENDPROC


*-- Clear the selected list and enables the entire "All" list.
PROCEDURE removeall
    *-- Clear the selected list and enable everything in the
    *-- Full List.
```

```
   this.lstFullList.EnableAll()
   this.lstSelected.Clear()
ENDPROC


PROCEDURE Init
   *  Program...........: MOVERCONTAINER.INIT
   *  Author............: Menachem Bazian, CPA
   *  Project...........: Visual Codebook 3
   *  Created...........: June 01, 1995 - 15:44:22
   *  Copyright.........: (c) Flash Creative Mgt, Inc, 1995
   *) Description.......: A container that combines elements
   *)                   : needed for mover functionality.
   *  Calling Samples...:
   *  Parameter List....:
   *  Major change list.:

   this.lstFullList.SetRowSource(this.cFullListRowSource)

this.lstSelected.SetRowSource(this.cSelectedListRowSource)
ENDPROC


*-- Reverts both lists.
PROCEDURE revert
   LPARAMETERS tlShowMessage

   *-- This method serves as an interface to the lists
   *-- in the container.

   this.lstFullList.Revert(tlShowMessage)
   this.lstSelected.Revert(tlShowMessage)
ENDPROC


PROCEDURE lstfulllist.DblClick
   *-- Why not use Moveone? For speed reasons. I know I am
   *-- only using the element they are double clicking on here.

   IF this.nElementsAvailable > 0
      lnSourceCols = this.numcols()
```

```
      DECLARE laSource[MAX(1,lnSourceCols)]

      this.DupeRow(@laSource, this.ListIndex)
      this.parent.lstSelected.Additem(@laSource)
      this.removeitem(this.ListIndex)
   ENDIF
ENDPROC


PROCEDURE lstfulllist.Requery
   MoverListBox::Requery()
   this.parent.cmdMove.enabled = ;
      (this.nElementsAvailable > 0)
   this.parent.cmdMoveAll.enabled = ;
      (this.nElementsAvailable > 0)

   IF this.nElementsAvailable = 0
      this.selected(1) = .F.
      this.parent.lstSelected.SetFocus()
   ENDIF
ENDPROC


PROCEDURE lstselected.DblClick
   *-- Why not use Moveone? For speed reasons. I know I am
   *-- only using the element they are double clicking on here.

   IF this.nElementsAvailable > 0
      lnSourceCols = this.numcols()

      DECLARE laSource[MAX(1,lnSourceCols)]

      this.DupeRow(@laSource, this.ListIndex)
      this.parent.lstFullList.Additem(@laSource)
      this.removeitem(this.ListIndex)
   ENDIF
ENDPROC


PROCEDURE lstselected.Requery
   MoverListBox::Requery()
   this.parent.cmdReMove.enabled= ;
      (this.nElementsAvailable > 0)
```

```
        this.parent.cmdReMoveAll.enabled = ;
           (this.nElementsAvailable > 0)

        IF this.nElementsAvailable = 0
           this.selected(1) = .F.
           this.parent.lstFullList.SetFocus()
        ENDIF
     ENDPROC


ENDDEFINE
*
*-- EndDefine: movercontainer
**************************************************
```

Custom/Overridden Properties

Property: **cFullListRowSource**
Default Value: **""**

The name of the array making up the "full list" or the list of items that *may* be selected.

Property: **cSelectedListRowSource**
Default Value: **""**

The name of the array that holds the list of selected items.

Object Members

lstFullList (MoverListBox)

MoverListBox for the list of items that may be selected. Note that it is set to backup the array on Init(). By default (as inherited from the class hierarchy), it is set to sort, and dim items when removing them.

lstSelected (MoverListBox)

MoverListBox for the list of selected items. Also set to backup, this ListBox deletes items when they are removed and does not sort the array.

cmdMove (cmdMove)

CommandButton that calls the container's MoveOne() method.

cmdMoveAll (cmdMoveAll)

CommandButton that calls the container's MoveAll() method.

cmdRemove (cmdRemove)

CommandButton that calls the container's ReMoveOne() method.

cmdRemoveAll (cmdRemoveAll)

CommandButton that calls the container's ReMoveAll() method.

Custom/Overidden Methods

Custom Method: moveone()

Moves only the selected items in the FullList to the SelectedList. Note that it accomplishes this by calling the DragDrop() method of lstSelectedList and sends through lstFullList as a parameter. The reason for this is simple enough: the function of the DragDrop() method and moving only selected items are the same.

Custom Method: moveall()

Copies the FullList into the SelectedList and disables everything in the FullList.

Custom Method: removeone()

Same as MoveOne() but in reverse.

Custom Method: removeall()

Clears out lstSelected and enables everything in lstFullList.

Overridden Method: Init()

Sets the list RowSource properties based on the container's cFullListRowSource and cSelectedListRowSource properties.

Custom Method: Revert()

Calls the Revert() methods of the two lists.

Overridden Method: lstFullList.DblClick()

Moves one item over to lstSelected. Note that DragDrop() is not called. This is because a double-click, by definition, means that you are moving one item. If MultiSelect is set to .T. on the lists, you could have to move more than one in a DragDrop() or MoveOne() call.

Overridden Method: lstFullList.Requery()

Does the parent class' Requery() and then enables or disables the Move and Move All buttons accordingly.

Overridden Method: lstSelected.DblClick()

Does the same as the DblClick() method for lstFullList but in reverse.

Overridden Method: lstSelected.Requery()

Does the parent class' Requery() and then enables or disables the Remove and Remove All buttons accordingly.

Class: MoverContainer_Dialog (MoverContainer)

This class, a subclass of MoverContainer, adds OK and Cancel buttons to the MoverContainer. Why not put this in the MoverContainer class? Again, the key to abstraction is to plan for reusability. In this case, MoverContainer can be well used on a dialog that does things other than just MOVER stuff. Hence, the abstraction.

Here's what this class looks like in the designer followed by the class definition:

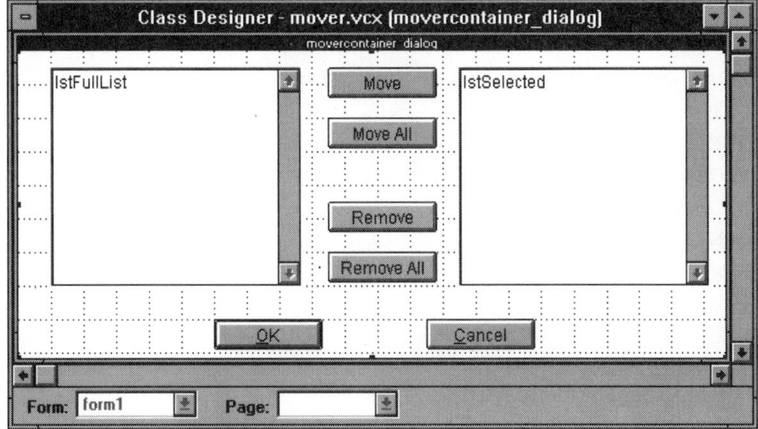

MoverContainer_dialog

```
*  Class.............: Movercontainer_dialog
*  Author............: Menachem Bazian, CPA
*  Project...........: Visual FoxPro Codebook
*  Copyright.........: (c) Flash Creative Management, Inc. 1995
*  Notes.............: Exported code from Class Browser.

**************************************************
*-- Class:        movercontainer_dialog
*-- ParentClass:  movercontainer
*-- BaseClass:    container
*-- A subclass of the MoverContainer class that adds
*-- OK and Cancel buttons.
*
DEFINE CLASS movercontainer_dialog AS movercontainer


   Width = 521
   Height = 221
   Name = "movercontainer_dialog"
   lstFullList.Name = "lstFullList"
   lstSelected.Name = "lstSelected"
   cmdmove.Name = "cmdmove"
```

```
    cmdmoveall.Name = "cmdmoveall"
    cmdRemove.Name = "cmdRemove"
    cmdremoveall.Name = "cmdremoveall"


    ADD OBJECT cmdok AS ccommandbutton WITH ;
      Top = 192, ;
      Left = 144, ;
      Caption = "\<OK", ;
      Default = .T., ;
      Name = "cmdOK"


    ADD OBJECT cmdcancel AS ccommandbutton WITH ;
      Top = 192, ;
      Left = 300, ;
      Cancel = .T., ;
      Caption = "\<Cancel", ;
      Name = "cmdCancel"

    PROCEDURE cmdok.Click
      thisform.release()
    ENDPROC


    PROCEDURE cmdcancel.Click
      this.parent.revert(.F.)
      RELEASE thisform
    ENDPROC


ENDDEFINE
*
*-- EndDefine: movercontainer_dialog
**************************************************
```

Object Members

cmdOk (CCommandButton)

Releases the form.

cmdCancel (CCommandButton)

Calls the container's REVERT method and then releases the form.

At this point, we have everything we need to create a mover dialog. So it's simple. Just create a form and drop the MoverContainer_Dialog class on it. That's class MoverForm.

Class: MoverForm (CBaseModalForm)

```
*  Class.............: Moverform
*  Author............: Menachem Bazian, CPA
*  Project...........: Visual FoxPro Codebook
*  Copyright.........: (c) Flash Creative Management, Inc. 1995
*  Notes.............: Exported code from Class Browser.
**************************************************
*-- Class:        moverform
*-- ParentClass:  cbasemodalform
*-- BaseClass:    form
*-- Modal form with a MoverContainerDialog object on it.
*
#INCLUDE "include\framewrk.h"
*
DEFINE CLASS moverform AS cbasemodalform

   Height = 223
   Width = 529
   DoCreate = .T.
   ShowTips = .T.
   Caption = "Mover"
   Closable = .F.
   MinButton = .F.
   cfulllistrowsource = ""
   cselectedlistrowsource = ""
   Name = "moverform"


   ADD OBJECT movercontainer_dialog1 AS movercontainer_dialog WITH ;
      Top = 0, ;
      Left = 0, ;
      Width = 521, ;
```

```
      Height = 221, ;
      Name = "Movercontainer_dialog1", ;
      lstFullList.Name = "lstFullList", ;
      lstSelected.Name = "lstSelected", ;
      cmdmove.Name = "cmdmove", ;
      cmdmoveall.Name = "cmdmoveall", ;
      cmdRemove.Name = "cmdRemove", ;
      cmdremoveall.Name = "cmdremoveall", ;
      cmdOK.Name = "cmdOK", ;
      cmdCancel.Name = "cmdCancel"


   PROCEDURE Refresh
      LOCAL llReinit
      llReinit = .F.

      IF TYPE("this.MoverContainer_Dialog1.cFullListRowSource") = "C"
         this.MoverContainer_Dialog1.cFullListRowSource = ;
            this.cFullListRowSource
         llReInit = .T.
      ENDIF

      IF TYPE("this.MoverContainer_Dialog1.cFullListRowSource") = "C"
         this.MoverContainer_Dialog1.cSelectedListRowSource = ;
            this.cSelectedListRowSource
         llReinit = .T.
      ENDIF

      IF llReinit
         this.MoverContainer_Dialog1.Init()
      ENDIF
   ENDPROC


ENDDEFINE
*
*-- EndDefine: moverform
**************************************************
```

There really isn't much to this form. It has an instance of MoverContainer_Dialog on it and one overridden method.

Custom/Overridden Methods

Overridden Method: Refresh()

Checks to see if the RowSources have changed. If they have, it calls the MoverContainer_Dialog's Init() to make sure everything is in synch.

Using the MOVER Form

In order to make the interface to the mover form as easy as possible, and to show the similarity to the version of Mover in *The FoxPro 2.6 Codebook*, here's a wrapper program you can use with MoverForm.

```
*  Program...........: MOVER.PRG
*  Author............: Menachem Bazian, CPA
*  Project...........: Visual Codebook 3
*  Created...........: June 01, 1995 - 17:05:04
*  Copyright.........: (c) Flash Creative Management, Inc., 1995
*) Description.......: A wrapper for the standard mover dialog
*  Calling Samples...:
*  Parameter List....: taFullList - Array with the full list in it
*                    : taSelectedList - Array to hold the
*                    :   selected items
*                    : tlNoSort - Whether the FullList should not
*                    :   be sorted
*  Major change list.:

PARAMETERS taFullList, taSelectedList, tlNoSort
LOCAL loMoverForm

loMoverForm                     = CREATEOBJECT("moverform")
loMoverForm.cSelectedListRowSource = "taSelectedList"
loMoverForm.cFullListRowSource     = "taFullList"
loMoverForm.MoverContainer_DIalog1.lstFullList.lSorted = !tlNoSort
loMoverForm.Refresh()

loMoverForm.Show(1)
```

All the program does is accept three parameters and then pass them through to the Mover Form class.

Here's a sample program that shows how all this comes together, followed by the resulting view.

```
*  Program...........: SAMPMVR.PRG
*  Author............: Menachem Bazian, CPA
*  Project...........: Visual Codebook 3
*  Created...........: June 15, 1995 - 14:16:41
*  Copyright.........: (c) Flash Creative Management, Inc., 1995
*) Description.......: Sample program for Mover
*  Calling Samples...:
*  Parameter List....:
*  Major change list.:


*-- Make sure everything is clear and set.

CLOSE ALL
SET CLASS TO mover

*-- Open the sample data so we can build an array

OPEN DATA home()+"samples\data\testdata"
use customer

*-- Declare the arrays PUBLIC so we can see them afterwards

PUBLIC laAllCust[1,1], laSelCust[1,1]

*-- Build the Full array

SELECT customer.company FROM customer into array laAllCust

*-- Call mover

DO mover WITH laAllCust, laSelCust, .T.
```

When you run this program, you'll see the following screen:

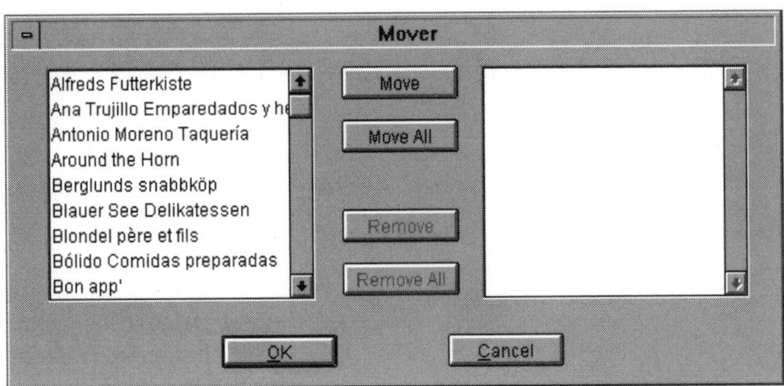

MoverForm called from SampMvr.Prg

Move some items over and you will notice the Remove and Remove All buttons are enabled and the moved items are dimmed on the FullList side.

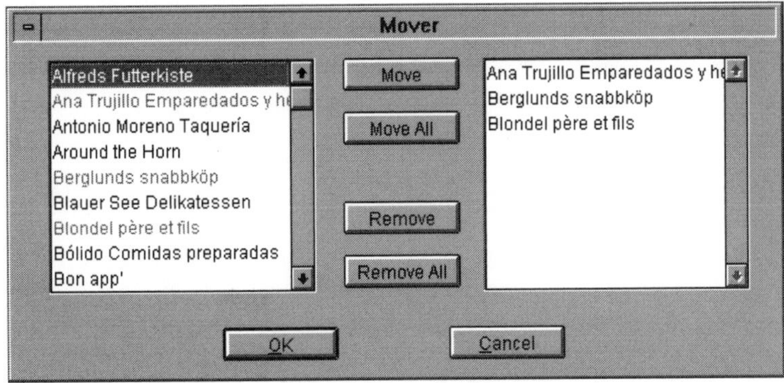

MoverForm after some selections

Finally, selecting OK will leave the items you selected in the laSelCust array.

Conclusion

This chapter not only showed the new version of Mover in Visual FoxPro but also showed a good example of designing functionality for reuse. The classes developed for the MoverForm present a basis for a great deal of functionality both within and outside the realm of MOVER-type functionality.

PART 3

The Codebook Foundation Classes

Chapter 13

The Codebook Foundation Classes

Introduction

This book includes a sample application that is based on a set of *Foundation Classes* which automate the development of robust applications. It is through the use of these classes in your own development efforts, whether through direct usage or subclassing, that you can achieve the full power of Visual FoxPro 3 against local or remote data.

This chapter gives an overview of the Codebook Foundation Classes, and describes the basic hierarchy of the framework for which they are the basis.

What Are Foundation Classes?

There are three basic types of classes that you can create or purchase. They are:

Class Type	Description
Interface	These classes typically handle presentation issues and occasionally are used in system behavior control.
Control	These classes organize internal system behavior.
Entity	These classes manage business information.

A set of Foundation Classes typically provides interface and control classes, allowing the developer who is familiar with the problem set that causes the development effort to focus on the entity classes that make up the solution. So it is with the Codebook Foundation Classes. These classes handle the basics of window, menu, toolbar, and application management so that you can focus on the development of business related classes that make up your solution set.

The Codebook Foundation Classes also include an abstract class of business objects that can be subclassed in order to quickly model your specific business classes.

The Codebook Class Hierarchy

The Codebook Foundation Classes are made up of 16 class libraries which contain over 100 separate classes that can be used in your application development efforts. Separated by type of class, they are:

Interface Classes

VCX Name	Description
CContrls	Common control classes that are subclasses from the Visual FoxPro 3 standard controls.
CCtlLib	Classes that are used to build custom controls.
CCustCtl	Custom controls that can be dropped on a form to provide functionality.
CCustFrm	Custom forms that provide functionality.
CForms	Standard forms that can be used in order to build a system.
CMenus	Base menu classes that are used to provide Visual FoxPro 3 with an object-oriented menu system.
CMover	A set of classes that provide "mover" functionality.
CToolbar	A set of classes that are used to create toolbars for an application.
CUsrPref	Classes that are used to provide user preference functionality, writing the results to .INI files or the Windows '95 and Windows NT Registries.
CBizness	Abstract classes that form the base for business-specific classes.

Control Classes

VCX Name	Description
CApp	The abstract "application" level class.
CBhavior	Data behavior classes.
CCollect	Abstract "collection" classes which are subclassed for various things like form, menu, and toolbar collections.
CEnviron	Environment handling classes.
CUtils	Various utility classes.

Entity Classes

VCX Name	Description
CBizness	Abstract classes that form the base for business-specific classes.
CDataEnv	Data Environment classes.

Foundation Class Naming Conventions

The Codebook Foundation Classes were named in keeping with the standards used by Microsoft in its Microsoft Foundation Classes for C++ development. As a result, all foundation classes begin with the letter 'C,' and the hierarchy within a library is reflected in the name of the classes.

If we look at the hierarchy in CForms, for instance, we can see that it looks like this:

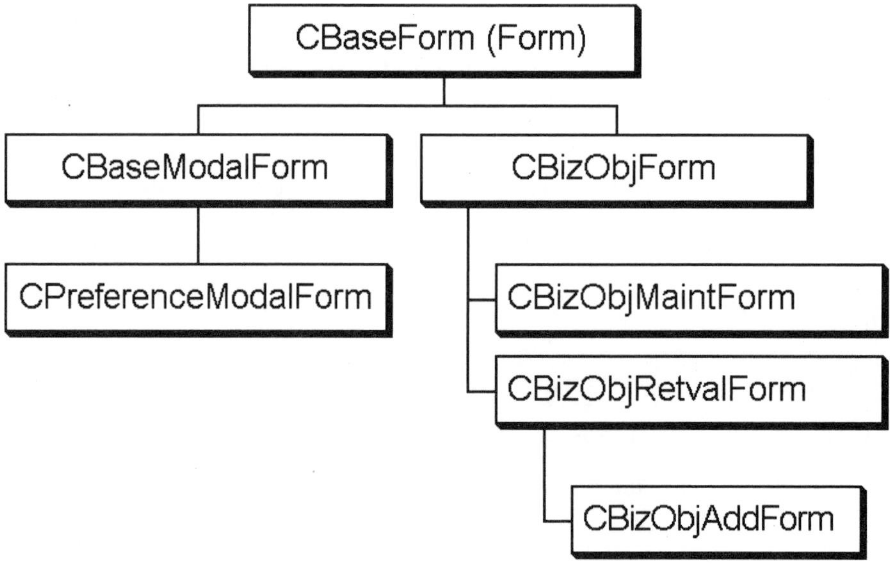

CForms.vcx class library hierarchy

A Detailed Look

The following chapters provide detailed looks at the Codebook Foundation Classes. Each of them is named after the class library that it discusses; and each begins with an overall description of the library, followed by a listing of the classes in that library. Each class lists its superclass and base class, followed by a description of the class itself, any particularly interesting code associated with the class, and finally tables of unique properties and methods of the class. Any PROTECTED properties or methods are *italicized*.

After the description of the classes, there is an example of a consulting effort at an imaginary compact disc mail order supplier. It begins with the Enterprise Model, selects a particular process to automate, continues with the use-case diagrams, and ends with a description of the application-specific classes, data and code and how they fit into the framework.

Chapter 14

CLASSLIB: CCONTRLS.VCX

Introduction

CCONTROLS is a class library that contains subclasses of each of the Visual FoxPro 3 base controls and adds any necessary functionality to those controls. In this manner, the developer can have complete control over the default values of any control. For instance, many of the controls have been modified to provide more of a Windows '95 look and feel. Additionally, any control that does not have a native Release() method has been modified to include one that simply does a "RELEASE this." In this way, we can work with all controls in a standardized manner.

Finally, certain controls that are typically bound to data have an added property called cViewParameter. This property allows the developer to store the name of a View Parameter and allows the framework to automatically handle Requery() functions to local or remote data sources. For example, let's assume that we have a remote view containing the following SQL SELECT:

```
SELECT * ;
 FROM Customer ;
 WHERE Customer.cLastName = ?vp_cLastName
```

The developer can place a CTextBox object on the criteria page of a form and place "vp_cLastName" in the cViewParameter property of the textbox, and the Codebook framework will make sure that the parameter is properly passed to the remote data source.

Class Name: CImage

Superclass: image

Description: Base image for use in Codebook applications.

Base Class: image

Method	Description
release	To bring all classes in line with VFP's native Release method.

Class Name: CLine

Superclass: line

Description: Base line for use in Codebook applications.

Base Class: line

Method	Description
release	To bring all classes in line with VFP's native Release method.

Class Name: COleBoundControl

Superclass: oleboundcontrol

Description: Base oleboundcontrol for use in Codebook applications.

Base Class: oleboundcontrol

Method	Description
release	To bring all classes in line with VFP's native Release method.

Class Name: CShape

Superclass: shape

Description: Base shape for use in Codebook applications.

Base Class: shape

Method	Description
release	To bring all classes in line with VFP's native Release method.

Class Name: CTimer

Superclass: timer

Description: Base timer for use in Codebook applications.

Base Class: timer

Method	Description
release	To bring all classes in line with VFP's native Release method.

Class Name: CToolbar

Superclass: toolbar

Description: Base toolbar for use in Codebook applications.

Base Class: toolbar

Method	Description
release	To bring all classes in line with VFP's native Release method.

Class Name: CLabel

Superclass: label

Description: Base label for use in Codebook applications.

Base Class: label

Method	Description
release	To bring all classes in line with VFP's native Release method.

Class Name: CCustom

Superclass: custom

Description: Base custom class for use in Codebook applications.

Base Class: custom

Method	Description
release	To bring all classes in line with VFP's native Release method.

Class Name: CCommandGroup

Superclass: commandgroup

Description: Base commandgroup for use in Codebook applications.

Base Class: commandgroup

Method	Description
release	To bring all classes in line with VFP's native Release method.

Class Name: CCommandButton

Superclass: commandbutton

Description: Base commandbutton for use in Codebook applications.

Base Class: commandbutton

Method	Description
release	To bring all classes in line with VFP's native Release method.

Class Name: COptionGroup

Superclass: optiongroup

Description: Base optiongroup for use in Codebook applications.

Base Class: optiongroup

Method	Description
release	To bring all classes in line with VFP's native Release method.

Class Name: CCheckBox

Superclass: checkbox

Description: Base checkbox for use in Codebook applications.

Base Class: checkbox

Property	Description
cviewparameter	The name of a view parameter linked to this control. Used in criteria selection forms.

Method	Description
release	To bring all classes in line with VFP's native Release method.

Class Name: CComboBox

Superclass: combobox

Description: Base combobox for use in Codebook applications.

Base Class: combobox

CComboBox is subclassed from the standard combobox base class with the addition of the cViewParameter property and the Release() method. In addition, a new method, GetColumnValue(), has been added. This allows the developer to query the combobox for the value of any column that is bound to the combobox.

Property	Description
cviewparameter	The name of a view parameter linked to this control. Used in criteria selection forms.

Method	Description
release	To bring all classes in line with VFP's native Release method.
getcolumnvalue	Returns the value of the specified column passed as a parameter.

Class Name: CEditBox

Superclass: editbox

Description: Base editbox for use in Codebook applications.

Base Class: editbox

Property	Description
cviewparameter	The name of a view parameter linked to this control. Used in criteria selection forms.

Method	Description
release	To bring all classes in line with VFP's native Release method.

Class Name: CListBox

Superclass: listbox

Description: Base listbox for use in Codebook applications.

Base Class: listbox

Property	Description
cviewparameter	The name of a view parameter linked to this control. Used in criteria selection forms.

Method	Description
release	To bring all classes in line with VFP's native Release method.
getcolumnvalue	Returns the value of the specified column passed as a parameter.

Class Name: CSpinner

Superclass: spinner

Description: Base spinner for use in Codebook applications.

Base Class: spinner

Property	Description
cviewparameter	The name of a view parameter linked to this control. Used in criteria selection forms.

Method	Description
release	To bring all classes in line with VFP's native Release method.

Class Name: CTextBox

Superclass: textbox

Description: Base textbox for use in Codebook applications.

Base Class: textbox

Property	Description
cviewparameter	The name of a view parameter linked to this control. Used in criteria selection forms.

Method	Description
release	To bring all classes in line with VFP's native Release method.

Class Name: CContainer

Superclass: container

Description: Base container for use in Codebook applications.

Base Class: container

Method	Description
release	To bring all classes in line with VFP's native Release method.

Class Name: CGrid

Superclass: grid

Description: Base grid for use in Codebook applications.

Base Class: grid

CGrid is subclassed from the standard grid base class with the addition of the Release() method. In addition, a new method, GetColumnNumber(), has been added. This allows the developer to query the grid for the position of any column given the caption of the header. In this manner, a developer can manipulate grid information without worrying that the user may have moved the columns to other positions.

Method	Description
release	To bring all classes in line with VFP's native Release method.
getcolumnnumber	Returns the column number whose caption is equal to the column's header caption passed as a parameter (case insensitive). Returns 0 if not found.

Class Name: CPageFrame

Superclass: pageframe

Description: Base pageframe for use in Codebook applications.

Base Class: pageframe

CPageFrame is subclassed from the standard pageframe base class with the addition of the Release() method. In addition, a new property, lFirstActivate, and a new method, GetPageNumber(), have been added.

lFirstActivate is set to .T. when the page is created, and allows the developer to do any specific set-up work that has to happen when the page is first accessed. It should be set to .F. after performing that action. For example, this property can be used to avoid having to requery data multiple times when a form is being created, thereby decreasing form load time.

GetPageNumber() allows the developer to query the pageframe for the number of any page given the caption of the header. This is useful for those cases where the developer has added, moved, or removed pageframes and wants to keep the code generic.

Property	Description
cviewparameter	The name of a view parameter linked to this control. Used in criteria selection forms.

Method	Description
release	To bring all classes in line with VFP's native Release method.
getpagenumber	Returns the page number whose caption is equal to the page caption passed as a parameter (case insensitive). Returns 0 if not found.

Chapter 15

CLASSLIB: CCOLLECT.VCT

Introduction

CCOLLECT is a class library that contains much of the basic functionality of the Codebook Framework. Essentially, Codebook manages much of its functionality by looking at things as "collections" of objects. For instance, when a form is created, it adds itself to the forms collection, which can handle things like properly naming multiple instances of forms. We have three basic types of collections that are used in Codebook. The first simply adds the object to the collection, (CReferenceCollection) the second adds the object as a child of the collection (CChildCollection), and the third only allows one instance of any object to be added to the collection (CToolbarCollection).

The collection class hierarchy looks like this:

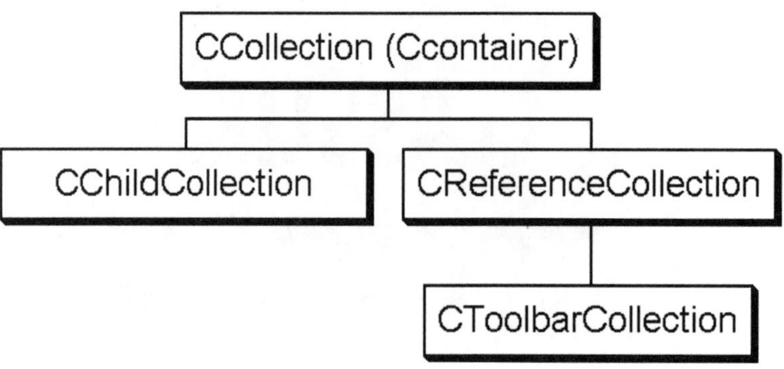

CCollect.vcx class hierarchy

Class Name: CCollection

Superclass: ccontainer (ccontrls.vcx)

Description: The superclass of all collection classes.

Base Class: container

CCollection is an abstract superclass of all collection classes. It is based on our CContainer class, and contains the basic functionality for all of our containers with very little code. The public interface for these classes includes an array of classes that are to be created and stored in the collection when the collection is instantiated, and a set of methods that allow you to add items to and remove items from the collection, as well as methods that allow you to perform actions when certain events occur.

Property	Description
achildren[1,4]	An array of class names and optional object names to add to the collection when the collection is instantiated. Used internally by CReference-Collection to store instances.

Method	Description
add	Adds an item to the collection.
remove	Removes an item from the collection.
isempty	Returns .T. if the collection contains no items.
ispartof	Scans the collection for an object or object name passed as a parameter. Returns .T. if found.
get	Retrieves an object from the collection and returns a reference to it. If not found, returns .NULL.
getfromback	Retrieves an object from the end of the collection and returns a reference to it. Returns .NULL. if not found.
scan	Scans the collection for an object or object name passed as a parameter. Returns index of instance if found, 0 if not.
getobjectcount	Returns the number of objects in the collection.

Method	Description
setenabled	Enables or disables all objects in the collection.
loadchildren	*Creates a predefined list of class names to load to this collection and stores the list to the aChildren[] array.*
createchildren	*Iterates the aChildren[] array calling the Add method for each class name in the array.*

Class Name: CChildCollection

Superclass: ccollection (ccollect.vcx)

Description: A collection class whose objects are children of the collection (i.e., each object's Parent property refers to the collection object).

Base Class: container

CChildCollection is subclassed from CCollection. Objects are loaded in a CChildCollection internally with the .AddObject() method, and can therefore use the .Parent property to call back to that collection.

Class Name: CReferenceCollection

Superclass: ccollection (ccollect.vcx)

Description: A collection class whose objects are stored as references to the actual object itself.

Base Class: container

CReferenceCollection is similar to CChildCollection except that objects are created with CREATEOBJECT() and therefore are stand-alone objects and cannot use the .Parent property to refer back to their collection.

Class Name: CToolbarCollection

Superclass: creferencecollection (ccollect.vcx)

Description: A special class used exclusively to store toolbars.

Base Class: container

CToolbarCollection is subclassed from CReferenceCollection. The main difference in functionality is that CReferenceCollection allows you to add the same class to it multiple times. In CToolbarCollection, we check if the object being added (typically a toolbar) already exists, and if so, we simply increment an instance count for that object. The object does not get destroyed when passed to the Remove() method unless the instance count hits zero.

Chapter 16

CLASSLIB: CUTILS.VCX

Introduction

CUTILS contains utility classes that are used throughout the Codebook framework, as well as wrapper classes around some of Visual FoxPro 3's external libraries.

Class Name: CMessage(cMessage)

Superclass: ccustom (ccontrls.vcx)

Base Class: custom

Parameters: cMessage—The message you want to display.

CMessage allows the developer to add messages to the application by simply instantiating this object and passing it the message to be displayed. Messages default to the status bar, but this class can be easily subclassed to add any form of messaging that is required. The class saves the current message and displays the new one, resetting the message when the class is destroyed.

Property	Description
coldmessage	*Holds the setting of SET('MESSAGE', 1).*

Method	Description
show	Shows the message.

Class Name: CSystemSetting

Superclass: ccontainer (ccontrls.vcx)

Base Class: container

CSystemSetting is an abstract class that is used to define the functionality for reading and writing information to some type of system storage. The Codebook Framework provides two subclasses, one of which reads and writes to .INI files for 16-bit Windows operating systems, and one of which reads and writes to the Windows '95 and Window NT registries. The developer doesn't care how this is done. All that is necessary is that he or she issues the GET() or SET() method, and the classes take care of the rest!

The CSystemSetting class hierarchy looks like this:

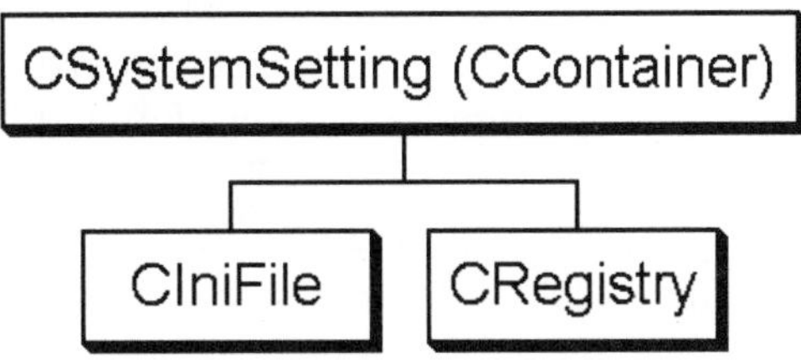

The CSystemSetting class hierarchy

Method	Description
set(cSection, cEntryName, uValue, [cINIFile])	Sets the system setting. This method is passed a section, an entry, a value to save to the entry, and an .INI file to use.
get(cSection, cEntryName, [uDefault,cINIFile])	Retrieves the system setting. This method is passed a section, an entry, a default value to return (in case the entry doesn't exist), and an .INI file to use.

Class Name: CIniFile([cIniFile])

Superclass: csystemsetting (cutils.vcx)

Base Class: container

Parameters: cIniFile—An optional .INI file name if you don't want to write to the default file.

CIniFile is subclassed from CSystemSetting and is used to read and write to .INI files. It does this by declaring and calling the following Windows DLL functions:

Function	Description
GetProfileString	Reads information from WIN.INI.
GetPrivateProfileString	Reads information from a private (application specific) .INI file.
WriteProfileString	Writes information to WIN.INI.
WritePrivateProfileString	Writes information to a private (application-specific) .INI file.

Let's take a look at some of the code behind this class. The INIT() method for the class uses the new DECLARE - DLL functionality of Visual FoxPro 3 to prototype the DLL functions, so that VFP 3 can treat them as native functions:

```
LPARAMETERS tcINIFile

*-- DECLARE DLL statements for reading/writing to private INI files
DECLARE INTEGER GetPrivateProfileString IN Win32API ;
   String cSection, String cKey, String cDefault, String @cBuffer, ;
   Integer nBufferSize, String cINIFile

DECLARE INTEGER WritePrivateProfileString IN Win32API ;
   String cSection, String cKey, String cValue, String cINIFile
```

```
*-- DECLARE DLL statements for reading/writing to WIN.INI file
DECLARE INTEGER GetProfileString IN Win32API ;
   String cSection, String cKey, String cDefault, ;
   String @cBuffer, Integer nBufferSize

DECLARE INTEGER WriteProfileString IN Win32API ;
   String cSection, String cKey, String cValue

IF PCOUNT() >= 1
   this.cINIFile = tcINIFile
ELSE
   this.cINIFile = "WIN.INI"
ENDIF
```

Let's look at one of the DECLARE statements and see how it works:

```
DECLARE INTEGER GetProfileString IN Win32API ;
   String cSection, String cKey, String cDefault, ;
   String @cBuffer, Integer nBufferSize
```

The keyword DECLARE is followed by the type of value that the DLL function returns (in our case, INTEGER). We then let Visual FoxPro 3 know which function we are prototyping (GetProfileString), and tell it where to find the function. In this case, we are using the keyword Win32API, which tells Visual FoxPro 3 that it can find the function in one of the standard DLLs that ships with Windows. The command continues with a list of types of values that will be passed to the function, and keywords that can be used to describe those values. For instance, "String cSection" lets us know that we have to pass a string containing the "Section" of the .INI file in which to look.

The "String @cBuffer" lets Visual FoxPro 3 know that we'll be passing this variable by reference, not value.

The Get() and Set() methods simply make sure that the proper parameters are passed and call the proper DLL functions.

Property	Description
cinifile	*The name of the .INI file to read/write to. Initialized in Init(), but can be overridden in Set() or Get().*

Class Name: CRegistry([nMainKey])

Superclass: csystemsetting (cutils.vcx)

Base Class: container

Parameters: nMainKey—An optional main key to write to (defaults to HKEY_CURRENT_USER).

CRegistry is also subclassed from CSystemSetting and is used to read and write to the Windows '95 and Window NT Registries. It does this by declaring and calling the following Windows DLL functions:

Function	Description
RegCloseKey	Closes the specified key.
RegCreateKeyEx	Creates the specified key.
RegFlushKey	Writes the attributes of the specified key to the registry.
RegOpenKeyEx	Opens the specified key.
RegQueryValueEx	Retrieves the type and data for a specified value in the registry.
RegSetValueEx	Stores data to a specified key.

Again, the developer simply uses Get() and Set() to actually write and read to and from the registry. For those who may be unfamiliar with the Windows Registry, you can look at it by running REGEDT32.EXE. The current user is always in the window HKEY_CURRENT_USER, and Microsoft recommends putting application-specific information in HKEY_CURRENT_USER under the path of:

Software\Company_Name\Application_Name\Version_Number\Key

Here's an example of the Windows NT Registry, showing the CDTrak sample application's Windows Positions values (which store the last position of the window):

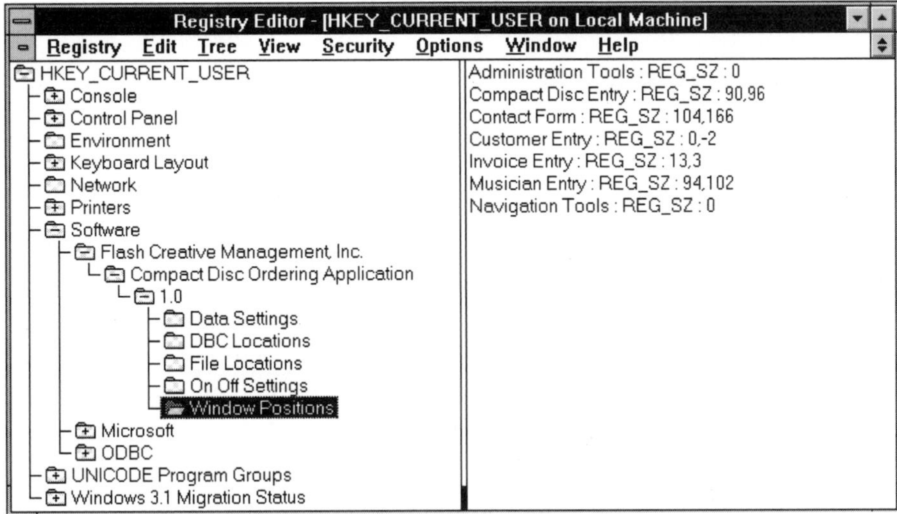

The registration database

Property	**Description**
nmainkey	*The handle to the main registry key (HKEY_xxx).*
ncurrentkeyhandle	*The handle to the currently open subkey.*

Method	**Description**
openkey	*Opens the specified key. Creates the key if it does not exist.*
createkey	*Creates the specified key in the registry.*
deletekey	*Deletes the specified key from the registry. Returns .T. if successful.*
closekey	*Closes the specified key.*

Class Name: CSet(uArg1 [, uArg2, lNoRestore])

Superclass: ccustom (ccontrls.vcx)

Description: Used to save, set, and restore SET commands.

Base Class: custom

Parameters: uArg1
uArg2
lNoRestore

CSet is used to save and restore environmental settings. One of the interesting points of the VFP object model is that since an object is a variable, it automatically gets destroyed if it goes out of scope. We can use this to our advantage by creating a class that, when instantiated, saves the current setting of a SET command and sets it as we would like. The DESTROY() method of the class can reset the SET command to what it was. The upshot of this is that you can instantiate an object from the CSet class in a program or method, and when the object variable goes out of scope, it will automatically call the DESTROY() of the CSet-based object, resetting the SET for you. Here's an example:

```
lcOldExact = CREATEOBJECT("cSet","EXACT","OFF")
*-- do function here
RETURN
```

At the RETURN, lcOldExact will lose focus, causing the DESTROY() to run, resetting EXACT for us. We no longer have to remember to reset SET commands when using this class.

This class allows you to return the current setting of any SET command and the original setting, allows you to find out what SET command an object instance is handling for you, and allows you to force the setting to remain in place, even when the object is destroyed. For instance if you have SET CLOCK STATUS, you can issue the following commands:

Typed in Command Window	Results
oClock =CREATEOBJECT('cset','clock','on')	Clock is in top-right corner.
? oClock.getsetcommand()	Returns "CLOCK."

Typed in Command Window	Results
? oClock.get()	Returns "ON."
? oClock.get(1)	Returns 0.000, 122.333 (clock's position).
? oClock.get(0)	Returns "STATUS."
oClock.release()	Clock is on status bar.

Property	Description
csetcommand	*The SET command name.*
uoldvalue	*The original setting of the SET command as SET(<command>).*
uoldvalue1	*The original setting of the SET command as SET(<command>,1).*
uoldvalue2	*The original setting of the SET command as SET(<command>,2).*
lerror	*Indicates an error occurred during the execution of the SET command.*
lnorestore	*Specifies if the original SET values are restored when the object is released.*

Method	Description
get	No parameter returns the current SET() value. 1 returns the current SET(,1) value. 2 returns the current SET(,2) value. 0 returns the original SET() value. -1 returns the original SET(,1) value. -2 returns the original SET(,2) value.
getsetcommand	Returns the SET command name.

Method	Description
disablerestore	Disables automatic settings restore when in object release mode.
checkvalue	*Returns the proper SET(<command>) value based on the SET command name.*
restore	*Restores the original SET settings.*
set	*uArgument1 [, uArgument2] [, lNoRestore]*

Class Name: CDELoader

Superclass: ccontainer (ccontrls.vcx)

Base Class: container

CDELoader is used to load a CDataEnvironment-derived class. The Codebook Framework does not use DataEnvironments directly, rather it subclasses the Visual FoxPro DataEnvironment classes (DataEnvironment, Cursor, Relation) in order to add functionality such as automatically switching between local and remote data. This class automatically loads a Codebook DataEnvironment for an instance of a business object, whether it is visible (on a form) or not. It allows us to place bound controls directly on a subclass of a business object, since this class exists in the CBizObj superclass, and is created before any of the bound controls are created.

Property	Description
cdataenvironment	Specifies the name of the CDataEnvironment derived class to instantiate.
odataenvironment	Contains a reference to the business object's CDataEnvironment object.

Class Name: CSetAll([oParent, cProperty, cExpr, cBaseClassList, lNoContainerMode, lErrorWait])

Superclass: ccustom (ccontrls.vcx)

Base Class: custom

Parameters: oParent—The object to drill down on.
cProperty—The property to set or method to call.
cExpr—The value to set the property to.
cBaseClassList—Limit the drill down to this base class list.
lNoContainerMode—Don't drill down into containers.
lErrorWait—Set to .T. if the user should be alerted to errors.

This class mimics the SetAll() method of containers, but allows you to drill down through multiple levels, allows you to call methods, and even to evaluate expressions on each object. Here's an example of its use:

```
SET LIBRARY TO CUtils
oSet = CREATEOBJECT('csetall')
xx = CREATEOBJECT('form')
xx.addobject('check','checkbox')
xx.addobject('lbl','label')                            && Note: these are
                                                       && invisible
xx.lbl.top = 40
xx.show()                                              && Form shown, no
                                                       && objects visible
oSet.send(xx,'Visible',.t.)                            && All object
                                                       && visible
oSet.send(xx,'Left',55)                                && All object at
                                                       && position 55
oSet.send(xx,'Left','(this.left+55)')                  && All objects move
                                                       && 55 to right
oSet.send(xx,'Left','(this.left-55)','checkbox')       && Checkbox moves
                                                       && left
```

As you can see, this class can be very useful when you have to drill through a group of objects, performing an action on their relative positions.

Property	Description
cobjectname	*The name of the object to perform the action on.*
cproperty	*The name of the property to set, or the name of the method to call on the object.*
cexpr	*An expression literal or a character expression enclosed in parentheses whose return value will be assigned to the property of the object. Ignored if executing a method on the object.*
cevalexpr	*Holds an expression to evaluate.*
lerrorflag	*Specifies internal error condition.*
lerrorwait	*Specifies if user should be informed of any errors encountered.*

Method	Description
send((oParent, cProperty, [cExpr, cBaseClassList, lNoContainerMode, lErrorWait])	Performs the requested action on the specified object. The parameters are the same ones that can be sent to the object.

Class Name: CSelect(cAlias)

Superclass: ccustom (ccontrls.vcx)

Base Class: custom

Parameter: cAlias—The alias that you would like to SELECT.

This class works just like CSet, except that it is designed to save and restore the current alias.

Property	Description
noldarea	*Holds the return value of SELECT() when the class was instantiated. The work area stored in this parameter is SELECTed in the Destroy() event method.*

Class Name: CWaitMessage

Superclass: ccustom (ccontrls.vcx)

Description: Class that displays a WAIT WINDOW message and then does a WAIT CLEAR when released.

Base Class: custom

This class displays a WAIT WINDOW message that stays up while the class is in scope (as long as the user doesn't remove it). This is useful for putting up a message while other code runs.

Method	Description
show	Show the wait window message.

Class Name: CFoxtools

Superclass: custom

Base Class: custom

This is an example of a wrapper class. It wraps some of the functionality of Foxtools into a class. The main advantage to this over calling Foxtools directly is that the Error() method checks to see if the function failed because Foxtools wasn't loaded, and if so, loads it and runs the function again. You no longer have to make sure that Foxtools is loaded.

Please note that this is a sample. It wraps some, but not all, of the functionality of Foxtools, and adds in a few new functions that are similar.

Property	Description
lloaded	Was Foxtools loaded when the class was instantiated?
lerror	*Flag to track if RETRY fails in the Error event method. Prevents event recursion.*
clibrary	*Specifies the fully qualified file name of FOXTOOLS.FLL.*

Method	Description
loadlib	Checks if Foxtools is loaded, and if not, loads it.
drivetype(cDrive)	Returns the type of drive as follows: 0 - No drive 2 - Floppy disk 3 - Hard disk 4 - Removable drive or network drive 5 - CD ROM 6 - RAM disk
justfname(cPath)	Returns the file name from a complete path.
juststem(cPath)	Returns the stem (first eight characters) of a file name from a complete path.
justpath(cPath)	Returns the path from a complete path.
justdrive(cPath)	Returns just the drive letter from a complete path.
justpathnodrive	Returns the path without a drive letter from a complete path.
addbs(cFileName)	Adds a backslash to a file name, if needed.
isdir(cDirPath)	Does the directory exist?
cleandir(cDirPath)	Returns a clean directory name from a relative path.
cut	Cuts the highlighted text to the clipboard.
copy	Copies the highlighted text to the clipboard.
paste	Pastes the text that is in the clipboard.

Chapter 17

CLASSLIB: CENVIRON.VCX

Introduction

CENVIRON.VCX is a class library that handles the environment settings (SET and ON commands) for your application. It is made up of an abstract class, CEnvironment, that is subclassed into two classes: CGlobalEnvironment and CSessionEnvironment, which set up the environment for your application and private data sessions, respectively. Here is the class hierarchy:

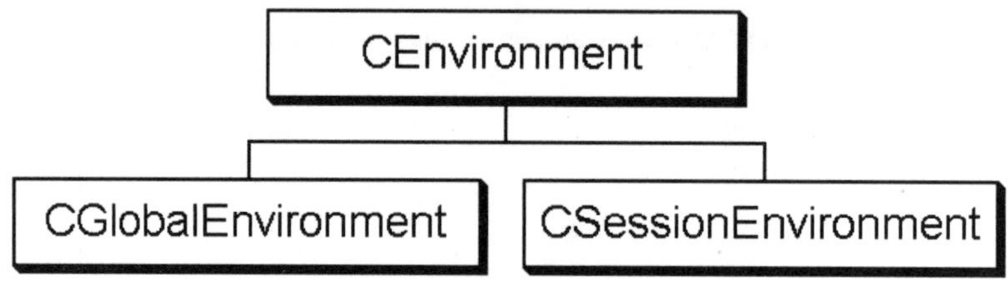

The CEnvironment class hierarchy

Class Name: CEnvironment

Superclass: ccontainer (ccontrls.vcx)

Base Class: container

CEnvironment is an abstract class that defines the functionality for our environment handling classes. It consists of three methods and a property. Using these methods, you can save the original settings of your environment, set them to new settings, and reset them when the object is destroyed.

Property	Description
lsaveoldsettings	Set to .F. to prevent the saving and restoring of the original settings. Useful in private data sessions since all settings are scoped to the session.

Method	Description
set	Sets all the SET commands.
reset	Resets the SET commands to their original value.
saveoldsettings	Saves the original values of the settings to custom properties.

Class Name: CGlobalEnvironment

Superclass: cenvironment (cenviron.vcx)

Base Class: container

CGlobalEnvironment is subclassed from CEnvironment and contains properties that store the original settings of your environment. It contains an instance of CSessionEnvironment which is used to store the settings for the common environment commands that are saved with each session (why write it twice, when we can just "borrow" it from somewhere?).

Note that a number of the saved properties are coming from PUBLIC variables. When a Codebook-based application runs, it sets up a few public variables until the main application class is instantiated. That class instantiates the CGlobal-Environment class which saves the values in the variables which are then released.

Property	Description
calternate	Specifies initial value of SET('ALTERNATE')
calternateto	Specifies initial value of SET('ALTERNATE', 1)
caplabout	Specifies initial value of SET('APLABOUT')
caplaboutprompt	Specifies initial value of SET('APLABOUT', 1)
cbell	Specifies initial value of SET('BELL')
cblink	Specifies initial value of SET('BLINK')
cbrstatus	Specifies initial value of SET('BRSTATUS')
cclear	Specifies initial value of SET('CLEAR')
cclock	Specifies initial value of SET('CLOCK')

Property	Description
ccompatible	Specifies initial value of SET('COMPATIBLE')
cconsole	Specifies initial value of SET('CONSOLE')
ccpdialog	Specifies initial value of SET('CPDIALOG')
ccursor	Specifies initial value of SET('CURSOR')
cdebug	Specifies initial value of SET('DEBUG')
cdevelopment	Specifies initial value of SET('DEVELOPMENT')
cdevice	Specifies initial value of SET('DEVICE')
cdohistory	Specifies initial value of SET('DOHISTORY')
cdohistoryto	Specifies initial value of SET('DOHISTORY', 1)
cecho	Specifies initial value of SET('ECHO')
cescape	Specifies initial value of SET('ESCAPE')
cformat	Specifies initial value of SET('FORMAT')
cfullpath	Specifies initial value of SET('FULLPATH')
cheadings	Specifies initial value of SET('HEADINGS')
chelpfilter	Specifies initial value of SET('HELPFILTER')
chelpto	Specifies initial value of SET('HELP', 1)
cintensity	Specifies initial value of SET('INTENSITY')
ckeycomp	Specifies initial value of SET('KEYCOMP')
clibrary	Specifies initial value of SET('LIBRARY')
clogerrors	Specifies initial value of SET('LOGERRORS')
cmacdesktop	Specifies initial value of SET('MACDESKTOP')
cmachelp	Specifies initial value of SET('MACHELP')
cmachelpprompt	Specifies initial value of SET('MACHELP', 1)
cmackey	Specifies initial value of SET('MACKEY')
cnotify	Specifies initial value of SET('NOTIFY')

Property	Description
coleobject	Specifies initial value of SET('OLEOBJECT')
coptimize	Specifies initial value of SET('OPTIMIZE')
cpalette	Specifies initial value of SET('PALETTE')
cprinter	Specifies initial value of SET('PRINTER')
cprinterto	Specifies initial value of SET('PRINTER', 1)
creadborder	Specifies initial value of SET('READBORDER')
cresource	Specifies initial value of SET('RESOURCE')
cresourceto	Specifies initial value of SET('RESOURCE', 1)
cscoreboard	Specifies initial value of SET('SCOREBOARD')
cseconds	Specifies initial value of SET('SECONDS')
cshadows	Specifies initial value of SET('SHADOWS')
cspace	Specifies initial value of SET('SPACE')
cstatus	Specifies initial value of SET('STATUS')
cstatusbar	Specifies initial value of SET('STATUS BAR')
csticky	Specifies initial value of SET('STICKY')
ctalk	Specifies initial value of SET('TALK')
ctextmerge	Specifies initial value of SET('TEXTMERGE')
ctextmergedelimiters	Specifies initial value of SET('TEXTMERGE', 1)
ctopic	Specifies initial value of SET('TOPIC')
ctopicid	Specifies initial value of SET('TOPIC ID')
cudfparms	Specifies initial value of SET('UDFPARMS')
ncpcompile	Specifies initial value of SET('CPCOMPILE')
nfdow	Specifies initial value of SET('FDOW')
nfweek	Specifies initial value of SET('FWEEK')
nhours	Specifies initial value of SET('HOURS')

Property	Description
nmargin	Specifies initial value of SET('MARGIN')
nodometer	Specifies initial value of SET('ODOMETER')
nrefresh	Specifies initial value of SET('REFRESH')
ntypeahead	Specifies initial value of SET('TYPEAHEAD')
chelp	Specifies initial value of SET('HELP')
coldalternate	*Original value of SET('ALTERNATE')*
coldalternateto	*Original value of SET('ALTERNATE', 1)*
coldaplabout	*Original value of SET('APLABOUT')*
coldaplaboutprompt	*Original value of SET('APLABOUT', 1)*
coldbell	*Original value of SET('BELL')*
coldblink	*Original value of SET('BLINK')*
coldbrstatus	*Original value of SET('BRSTATUS')*
coldclasslib	*Original value of gcClassLib*
coldclear	*Original value of SET('CLEAR')*
coldclock	*Original value of SET('CLOCK')*
coldcompatible	*Original value of SET('COMPATIBLE')*
coldconsole	*Original value of SET('CONSOLE')*
coldcpdialog	*Original value of SET('CPDIALOG')*
coldcursor	*Original value of SET('CURSOR')*
colddebug	*Original value of SET('DEBUG')*
colddevelopment	*Original value of SET('DEVELOPMENT')*
colddevice	*Original value of SET('DEVICE')*
colddir	*Value of gcOldDir*
colddohistory	*Original value of SET('DOHISTORY')*
colddohistoryto	*Original value of SET('DOHISTORY', 1)*

Property	Description
coldecho	*Original value of SET('ECHO')*
coldescape	*Original value of SET('ESCAPE')*
coldformat	*Original value of SET('FORMAT')*
coldfullpath	*Original value of SET('FULLPATH')*
coldheadings	*Original value of SET('HEADINGS')*
coldhelp	*Original value of SET('HELP')*
coldhelpfilter	*Original value of SET('HELPFILTER')*
coldhelpto	*Original value of SET('HELP', 1)*
coldintensity	*Original value of SET('INTENSITY')*
coldkeycomp	*Original value of SET('KEYCOMP')*
coldlibrary	*Original value of SET('LIBRARY')*
coldlogerrors	*Original value of SET('LOGERRORS')*
coldmacdesktop	*Original value of SET('MACDESKTOP')*
coldmachelp	*Original value of SET('MACHELP')*
coldmachelpprompt	*Original value of SET('MACHELP', 1)*
coldmackey	*Original value of SET('MACKEY')*
coldnotify	*Original value of SET('NOTIFY')*
coldoleobject	*Original value of SET('OLEOBJECT')*
coldoptimize	*Original value of SET('OPTIMIZE')*
coldpalette	*Original value of SET('PALETTE')*
coldpath	*Original value of gcOldPath*
coldprinter	*Original value of SET('PRINTER')*
coldprinterto	*Original value of SET('PRINTER', 1)*
coldprocedure	*Original value of gcOldProcedure*
coldreadborder	*Original value of SET('READBORDER')*

Property	Description
coldresource	*Original value of SET('RESOURCE')*
coldresourceto	*Original value of SET('RESOURCE', 1)*
coldscoreboard	*Original value of SET('SCOREBOARD')*
coldseconds	*Original value of SET('SECONDS')*
coldshadows	*Original value of SET('SHADOWS')*
coldspace	*Original value of SET('SPACE')*
coldstatus	*Original value of SET('STATUS')*
coldstatusbar	*Original value of SET('STATUS BAR')*
coldsticky	*Original value of SET('STICKY')*
coldtalk	*Original value of gcOldTalk*
coldtextmerge	*Original value of SET('TEXTMERGE')*
coldtextmergedelimiters	*Original value of SET('TEXTMERGE', 1)*
coldtopic	*Original value of SET('TOPIC')*
coldtopicid	*Original value of SET('TOPIC ID')*
coldudfparms	*Original value of SET('UDFPARMS')*
noldcpcompile	*Original value of SET('CPCOMPILE')*
noldfdow	*Original value of SET('FDOW')*
noldfweek	*Original value of SET('FWEEK')*
noldhours	*Original value of SET('HOURS')*
noldmargin	*Original value of SET('MARGIN')*
noldodometer	*Original value of SET('ODOMETER')*
noldrefresh	*Original value of SET('REFRESH')*
noldtypeahead	*Original value of SET('TYPEAHEAD')*

Class Name: CSessionEnvironment

Superclass: cenvironment (cenviron.vcx)

Base Class: container

This class saves, sets, and restores all of the environment settings that are affected by private data sessions. When you start a private data session, Visual FoxPro 3 resets these SET commands to the global defaults that were set at startup. This class allows you to decide how these SET commands should be set up. Note that since we have created properties for the initial settings, there is no code to write; the developer simply fills in any properties that should be changed. The class takes care of the rest.

Property	Description
cansi	Specifies initial value of SET('ANSI')
ccarry	Specifies initial value of SET('CARRY')
ccentury	Specifies initial value of SET('CENTURY')
ccollate	Specifies initial value of SET('COLLATE')
cconfirm	Specifies initial value of SET('CONFIRM)
ccurrency	Specifies initial value of SET('CURRENCY')
ccurrencyto	Specifies initial value of SET('CURRENCY', 1)
cdatabase	Specifies initial value of SET('DATABASE')
cdate	Specifies initial value of SET('DATE')
cdeleted	Specifies initial value of SET('DELETED')
cdelimiters	Specifies initial value of SET('DELIMITERS')
cdelimitersto	Specifies initial value of SET('DELIMITERS', 1)
cexact	Specifies initial value of SET('EXACT')
cexclusive	Specifies initial value of SET('EXCLUSIVE')
cfields	Specifies initial value of SET('FIELDS')
cfieldsscope	Specifies initial value of SET('FIELDS', 2)

Property	Description
cfieldsto	Specifies initial value of SET('FIELDS', 1)
cfixed	Specifies initial value of SET('FIXED')
clock	Specifies initial value of SET('LOCK')
cmark	Specifies initial value of SET('MARK')
cmultilocks	Specifies initial value of SET('MULTILOCKS')
cnear	Specifies initial value of SET('NEAR')
cnull	Specifies initial value of SET('NULL')
cpoint	Specifies initial value of SET('POINT')
creprocess	Specifies initial value of SET('REPROCESS')
csafety	Specifies initial value of SET('SAFETY')
cseparator	Specifies initial value of SET('SEPARATOR')
csysformats	Specifies initial value of SET('SYSFORMATS')
ctalk	Specifies initial value of SET('TALK')
cunique	Specifies initial value of SET('UNIQUE')
nblocksize	Specifies initial value of SET('BLOCKSIZE')
ndecimals	Specifies initial value of SET('DECIMALS')
nmemowidth	Specifies initial value of SET('MEMOWIDTH')
coldansi	*Original value of SET('ANSI')*
coldcarry	*Original value of SET('CARRY')*
coldcentury	*Original value of SET('CENTURY')*
coldcollate	*Original value of SET('COLLATE')*
coldconfirm	*Original value of SET('CONFIRM')*
coldcurrency	*Original value of SET('CURRENCY')*
coldcurrencyto	*Original value of SET('CURRENCY', 1)*
colddatabase	*Original value of SET('DATABASE')*

Property	Description
colddate	*Original value of SET('DATE')*
colddeleted	*Original value of SET('DELETED')*
colddelimiters	*Original value of SET('DELIMITERS')*
colddelimitersto	*Original value of SET('DELIMITERS', 1)*
coldexact	*Original value of SET('EXACT')*
coldexclusive	*Original value of SET('EXCLUSIVE')*
coldfields	*Original value of SET('FIELDS')*
coldfieldsscope	*Original value of SET('FIELDS', 2)*
coldfieldsto	*Original value of SET('FIELDS', 1)*
coldfixed	*Original value of SET('FIXED')*
coldlock	*Original value of SET('LOCK')*
coldmark	*Original value of SET('MARK')*
coldmultilocks	*Original value of SET('MULTILOCKS')*
coldnear	*Original value of SET('NEAR')*
coldnull	*Original value of SET('NULL')*
coldpoint	*Original value of SET('POINT')*
coldreprocess	*Original value of SET('REPROCESS')*
coldsafety	*Original value of SET('SAFETY')*
coldseparator	*Original value of SET('SEPARATOR')*
coldsysformats	*Original value of SET('SYSFORMATS')*
coldtalk	*Original value of gcOldTalk or SET('TALK')*
coldunique	*Original value of SET('UNIQUE')*
noldblocksize	*Original value of SET('BLOCKSIZE')*
nolddecimals	*Original value of SET('DECIMALS')*
noldmemowidth	*Original value of SET('MEMOWIDTH')*

Chapter 18

CLASSLIB: CDATAENV.PRG

Introduction

CDATAENV is the only class library in the Codebook Framework that is stored in a program file instead of a visual class library. This is because the visual class designer does not allow you to subclass Visual FoxPro's data environment classes. You can subclass them in code, however, and this allows you to add a great deal of functionality to your applications.

Let's start by looking at the base Visual FoxPro data environment classes. They are made up of a container called *dataenvironment* that contains objects called *cursor* and *relation*. A cursor is VFP's view of the data source—whether it is local or remote data. A relation can be used against dbf's to create a relationship, as was the case in earlier versions of FoxPro.

The native data environment structure has some failings, however. The dataenvironment object is created at the start-up of a form, cannot be reused in multiple forms, and cannot be modified at runtime. This means that it is difficult to switch from one data source to another "on the fly."

Creating our own data environment classes that are based on the native ones gives us the following benefits:

- Since the DE is not bound to a form, we can now use a DE just about anywhere we want.
- A DE can be reused and subclassed as necessary.
- It becomes very easy to switch between local or remote data. (Or for that matter, between local views and local tables.)

Class Name: CDataEnvironment

Superclass: dataenvironment

Description: The Codebook Framework data environment.

Base Class: dataenvironment

CDataEnvironment is a subclass of dataenvironment which adds the automatic selection of the proper database container, based on the application needs.

Property	**Description**
nInitialSelectedAlias	The number of the initially selected alias in the aCursors[] array.
cDefaultDatabaseName	The default database name. You should initialize this property when you subclass CDataEnvironment.
cDefaultDatabase	The full path and name of the default database. It is initialized in the GetDefaultDatabase() method.
lUseLocalData	Is the application using the local data path?
aCursors[1]	An array of cursors to be loaded into this dataenvironment.
aRelations[1]	An array of relations to be loaded into this dataenvironment.

Method	**Description**
Release	To standardize on this.Release() to release objects.
LoadCursors	Loads all of the cursors in the aCursors array using the AddObject method.

Method	Description
LoadRelations	Loads all of the relations in the aRelations array using the AddObject method.
GetDefaultDatabase	Returns the default database from the system registry, .INI file or the currently active database. If the application object exists, it tries to look in the registry/INI first. If the application object does not exist and the DEBUGMODEFILE file exists, it looks for an active database container. If there is none, it looks in the DATA\ subdirectory. This latter behavior is useful when you wish to create data environments from the command window for testing or debugging purposes.

Class Name: CCursor

Superclass: cursor

Description: A standard cursor subclass for the data environment.

Base Class: cursor

The CCursor class acts as a regular Visual FoxPro cursor with a few changes in its data handling defaults. CCursor defaults to optimistic row buffering, and uses the database set up in the CDataEnvironment class as its default database.

CCursor is the basis for a hierarchy of various cursor types which provide for on-the-fly switching of data sources and unique reporting capabilities.

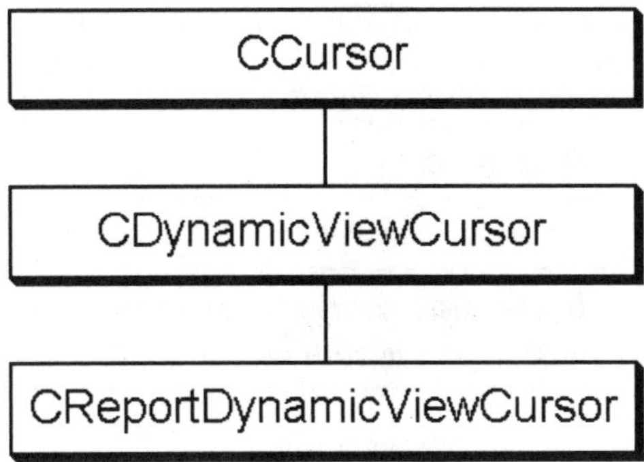

The CCursor class hierarchy

Method	Description
Release	To standardize on this.Release() to release objects.
GetDefaultDatabase	Calls up to its parent (a CDataEnvironment object) and returns the current database.

CDynamicViewCursor

Superclass: ccursor

Description: A cursor that allows "switch-on-the-fly" access to data sources.

Base Class: cursor

The CDynamicViewCursor class is based on CCursor and is meant for views. It allows you to set a property which determines whether or not it looks at a local or remote view for its data.

CDynamicViewCursor's base code assumes that local views will be named lv_<view name> and remote views will be named rv_<view name>. The alias is named v_<view name>. Changing the lLocal property causes the view to be switched, with the alias remaining unchanged.

Additionally, this class sets the NoDataOnLoad property to true as a default, so that our views will not send queries to the data source until we are ready.

Property	Description
cCursorSource	*A variable that contains the alias name for this cursor.*
lUseLocalData	*If set to true, the cursor goes against local data. If set to false, it goes against remote data.*

CReportDynamicViewCursor

Superclass: cdynamicviewcursor

Description: A cursor that contains standard settings for reports.

Base Class: cursor

The CReportDynamicViewCursor class is based on CDynamicViewCursor except that it does run the query and sets the result set to read only.

CRelation

Superclass: relation

Description: A standard relation class for Codebook Foundation applications.

Base Class: relation

The CRelation class is based on the standard Visual FoxPro relation. The only difference is the addition of the Release method to standardize it with other classes.

Method	Description
Release	To standardize on this.Release() to release objects.

CFreeTableCursor

Superclass: cursor

Description: A standard cursor class for free tables in Codebook Foundation applications.

Base Class: cursor

The CFreeTableCursor class is based on the standard Visual FoxPro cursor. The only difference is the addition of the Release method to standardize it with other classes.

Method	Description
Release	To standardize on this.Release() to release objects.

Chapter 19

CLASSLIB: CBHAVIOR.VCX

Introduction

CBHAVIOR.VCX contains the classes that standardize the data manipulation behavior between tables, local views, and remote data. It consists of an abstract class, CDataBehavior, which is subclassed into a CTableBehavior class and another abstract class, CViewBehavior, which is further subclassed into CLocalViewBehavior and CRemoteViewBehavior. Note that CViewBehavior and its subclasses are not currently used. CDataBehavior handles most of the work that we have to do on views, but they are there for later expansion should we find a need.

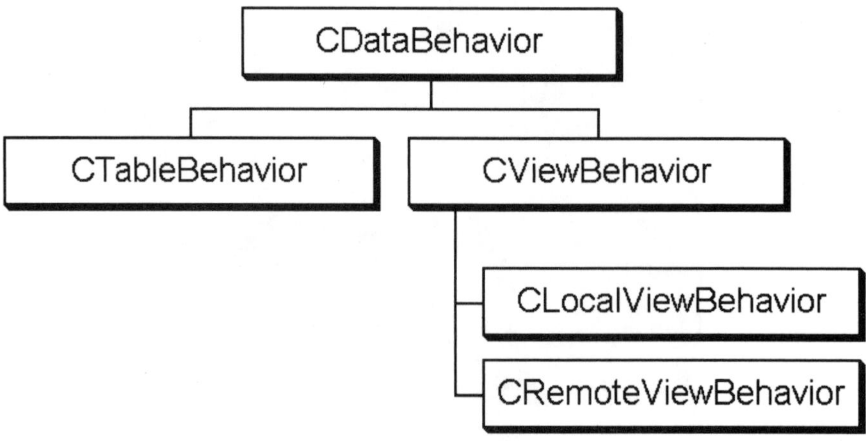

CDataBehavior class hierarchy

Class Name: CDataBehavior

Superclass: ccustom (ccontrls.vcx)

Description: The superclass for all data behavior classes.

Base Class: custom

Method	Description
first	Returns the first record.
prior	Returns the prior record.
next	Returns the next record.
last	Returns the last record.
save	Saves the current record.
cancel	Cancels changes to the current record.
delete	Deletes the current record.
new	Adds a new record.
requery	Requeries the dataset.

Class Name: CTableBehavior

Superclass: cdatabehavior (cbhavior.vcx)

Description: A data behavior class used for tables.

Base Class: custom

Method	Description
reindex	Issues a REINDEX on the currently selected table.
pack	Issues a PACK on the currently selected table.
packmemo	Issues a PACK MEMO on the currently selected table.

Class Name: CViewBehavior

Superclass: cdatabehavior (cbhavior.vcx)

Description: A data behavior superclass used for views.

Base Class: custom

Class Name: CLocalViewBehavior

Superclass: cviewbehavior (cbhavior.vcx)

Description: A data behavior class used for local views.

Base Class: custom

Class Name: CRemoteViewBehavior

Superclass: cviewbehavior (cbhavior.vcx)

Description: A data behavior class used for remote views.

Base Class: custom

Chapter 20

CLASSLIB: CBIZNESS.VCX

Introduction

CBIZNESS.VCX contains the business object classes that are used to create application-specific business objects. Note that the business objects, the behavior classes and the form classes all have some similar methods and properties. This is the way that we implement our three-layer model. When something happens (like clicking on New on the toolbar), that action causes the appropriate method to be called in all three layers (Data, Business Objects, and GUI).

The class hierarchy for CBizObj is very simple, it is made up of CBizObj which is subclassed into COneToManyBizObj.

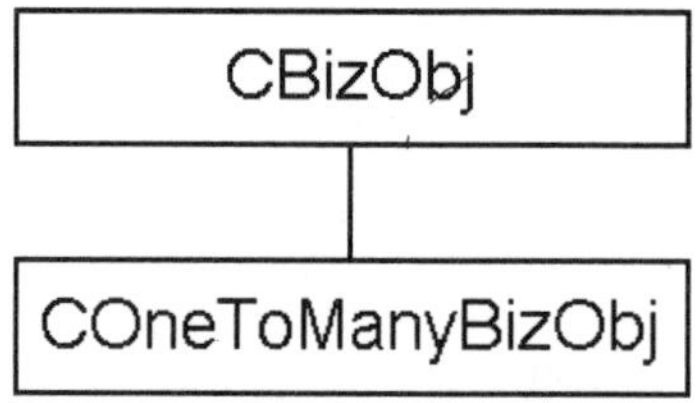

CBizObj class hierarchy

Class Name: CBizObj

Superclass:	ccontainer (ccontrls.vcx)
Description:	The superclass for all business objects.
Base Class:	container

CBizObj is the superclass for all business objects. It is a container with two members that are created from CDataBehavior and CDataEnvironment. These should not be confused with the CSessionEnvironment and CDELoader objects that you see at design time. These objects are used to initialize the SET settings and load the CDataEnvironment class. This allows the business object to manipulate its own data environment and its approach to data access.

Let's take a look at the Init() method of this class, to see how it works.

```
** CBizObj.INIT()
LOCAL llFormIsPresent
llFormIsPresent = (TYPE("thisform") <> "U")

*-- Grab a reference to the DataEnvironment object,
*-- and get rid of the DELoader
IF TYPE("this.oDELoader.oDataEnvironment") == "O"
   this.oDataEnvironment = this.oDELoader.oDataEnvironment
   this.RemoveObject("oDELoader")
ENDIF

this.oBehavior = CREATEOBJECT(this.cBehavior)

IF TYPE("this.Parent") == "O"
   *-- If this business object exists as a child of another
   *-- business object, then set the oChildBizObj property of
   *-- the parent business object to 'this'.
   IF IsA(this.Parent, "CBizObj") AND ;
      TYPE("this.Parent.oChildBizObj") <> "U"
      this.Parent.oChildBizObj = this
   ELSE
      *-- If this object is not a child of another business object
      *-- and appears on a form, then set the value of the form's
      *-- oBizObj property to 'this'.
      IF llFormIsPresent
         thisform.oBizObj = this
      ENDIF
   ENDIF
ENDIF

*-- Put up a custom menu pad if specified
IF !EMPTY(this.cMenuPad) AND ;
      llFormIsPresent AND ;
      TYPE("goApp.oMenu") == "O"
   =EVAL("goApp.oMenu." + this.cMenuPad + ".Show()")
ENDIF
```

When the CBizObj derived class is instantiated, it grabs a reference to its data environment from the contained DELoader class and clears the DELoader. It then loads the proper data behavior class that is set in the cBehavior property of the class (this defaults to CDataBehavior).

It then checks to see if it is a child of another business object or of a form. If so, it sends a reference to itself back to its parent.

Finally, it checks to see if we have specified that a menu should appear whenever this business object is "visible" and, if so, it tells the oMenu collection to show the correct menu.

You can see from the above code that a large part of the functionality of business classes (and object-oriented programming in general) is to parcel out the work that has to be done to the responsible object. The business object doesn't have to know how to put up a menu, it just says "Hey, Menu Collection, old buddy... Do me a favor, put up this menu for me."

Again, for the application developer, none of this implementation code is important. All that is necessary is to fill in a menu in the cMenuPad property and it's all handled for you.

Property	Description
obehavior	An instance of a CDataBehavior derived class that defines generic behavior for the type of recordset (i.e., table, view, etc.) that we are using.
cbehavior	The name of the CDataBehavior derived class to create and store in this.oBehavior.
lignorerecordruleviolations	Specifies whether we wish to ignore record rule violation errors. Useful when record validation rules can generate more than one message.
cinserttriggermsg	Message to be displayed when an insert trigger fails for this business object.
cdeletetriggermsg	Message to be displayed when a delete trigger fails for this business object.
cupdatetriggermsg	Message to be displayed when an update trigger fails for this business object.
lallowforcedupdates	Specifies if user is allowed to force updates on a field-by-field basis when update conflicts occur.

Property	**Description**
lallowselectall	Specifies if user is allowed to see all records at once. (Not recommended for large datasets.)
cmenupad	Specifies the name of a custom menu pad object to create when this business object is created on a form.
lsetfocusonnew	Specifies if focus should be automatically set to the first enabled control when adding a new record.
lconfirmondelete	Specifies if user should be prompted before deleting a record.
lonsavenew	*Allows a subclass to control if OnSaveNew is called. This is useful when using transactions and you don't want to call OnSaveNew until the transaction has been committed.*
odataenvironment	*An instance of a CDataEnvironment derived class.*

Method	**Description**
first	Returns the first business object.
prior	Returns the prior business object.
next	Returns the next business object.
last	Returns the last business object.
cancel	Cancels changes to the current business object.
delete	Deletes the current business object.
getdataenvironment	Returns a reference to the business object's data environment. Returns .NULL. if no data environment exists.

Method	Description
requery	When using a view, called when the view needs to be requeried.
ischanged	Returns .T. if the current business object or one of its child objects has changed.
isnewandempty	Returns .T. if user is adding a new business object but has not yet entered any data for this business object or one of its children.
getalias	Returns the alias stored in the InitialSelectedAlias property of the business object's data environment.
ondeletelastrecord	Called from the Delete() method after the last record is deleted.
new	Adds a new business object.
save	Saves the current business object.
errorfieldrule	*Code to handle field rule errors.*
errorrecordrule	*Code to handle record rule errors.*
errortrigger	*Code to handle failed triggers.*
errorupdateconflict	*Code to handle update conflict errors.*
handleerror	*Custom error handling dispatch for certain types of error messages. Returns .T. if error was handled.*
erroruniqueindexviolated	*Code to handle unique key violation errors.*
setchildfocus	*Sets focus to the control whose ControlSource property is set to the name of the field passed as a parameter.*
setfocustofirst	*Finds the first control whose TabIndex property = 1 and sets focus to it.*
onsavenew	*Called from the Save method after a new record is successfully saved.*

Method	Description
onnew	*Called by the New() method immediately upon the successful addition of a new blank record. Useful for pre-fetching candidate key values.*
allownew	*Called just before calling oDataBehavior.New(). Gives the object a chance to deny the addition of a new record.*

Class Name: COneToManyBizObj

Superclass: cbizobj (cbizness.vcx)

Description: A superclass used for business objects that appear on the "one" side of a one-to-many relation.

Base Class: container

COneToManyBizObj is a subclass of CBizObj which adds a reference to the child business object. It also allows you to specify if a child should be requeried when a parent is saved and if a new row should be added to the child when a new one is added to the parent.

Property	Description
ochildbizobj	A generic reference to a child business object.
lrequerychildonsave	*Specifies if child object should be requeried each time the parent object is saved.*
lnewchildonnew	*Specifies if a new record should be added to the child object every time a new record is added to the parent object.*

Chapter 21

CLASSLIB: CFORMS.VCX

Introduction

CFORMS.VCX is the class library that controls the forms-based interface of our application. It consists of a base class that is subclassed into multiple types of forms including modal forms, forms that interface with the operating system, and forms that are designed to work with business objects.

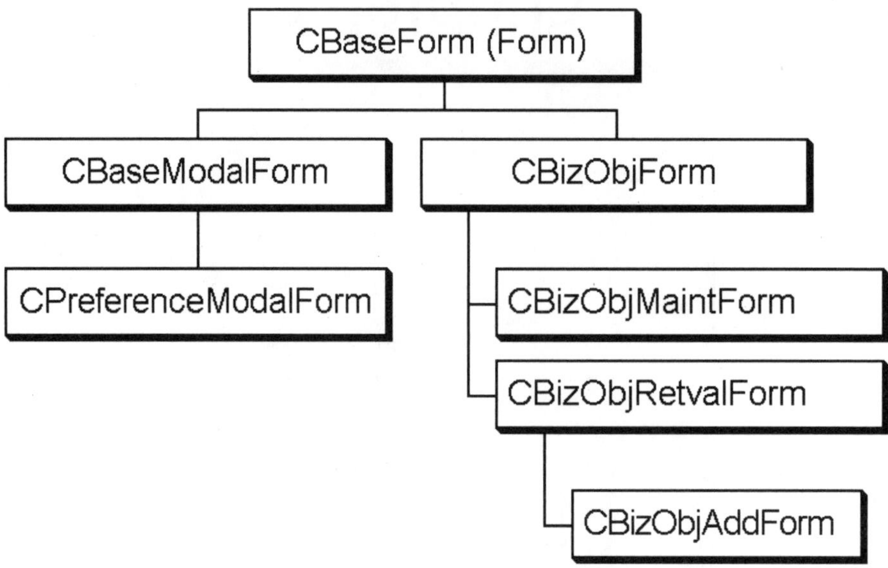

The CForms class hierarchy

Class Name: CBaseForm

Superclass: form

Description: The form superclass for all forms.

Base Class: form

CBaseForm is the base form that is subclassed for all of our forms classes. It contains added capabilities beyond the standard Visual FoxPro form class that include the capability of being bound to a toolbar, whether or not to cascade multiple instances of forms, and if so, how to name them. It also includes a few methods that are used to automate common tasks. Let's look at two of them, WaitMode() and RefreshForm().

```
*-- CBaseForm.WaitMode()
LPARAMETERS tlWaitMode

lnMousePointer = IIF(tlWaitMode, MOUSE_HOURGLASS, MOUSE_DEFAULT)
this.MousePointer = lnMousePointer
_screen.MousePointer = lnMousePointer
this.SetAll('MousePointer', lnMousePointer)
```

Very often during an application, we want an hourglass to appear when the user has the mouse over a form. WaitMode() accepts a logical parameter: if true, it sets the pointer to an hourglass; if false, it resets it. We can't just use the MousePointer property of the form because if the mouse goes over any object on the form, it will be set to that object's MousePointer property. Therefore, this method adds the call to the SetAll() method which sets the MousePointer property for all objects on the form, and issues the same call to _screen, which sets the mouse correctly when the user is over the background of the application.

With this method, a developer simply issues:

```
thisform.WaitMode(.T.)
```

and the mouse pointer is set to an hourglass.

```
*-- CBaseForm.RefreshForm()
LOCAL llResetLockScreen
*-- If LockScreen() is already .T., then allow the calling method
*-- to reset it by not resetting it here.

llResetLockScreen = (this.LockScreen = .F.)
this.LockScreen = .T.
this.Refresh()

*-- If this form is using a toolbar, refresh it
IF TYPE("this.oToolbar") == "O" AND !ISNULL(this.oToolbar)
   this.oToolbar.Refresh()
ENDIF

IF llResetLockScreen
   this.LockScreen = .F.
ENDIF
```

RefreshForm() does a number of functions for us. First of all, it sets the LockScreen property to true, stopping any changes to the screen from occurring. It then refreshes the form and, optionally, an associated toolbar. Finally, it sets LockScreen to false, allowing the changes to display. To the user, this seems much faster than watching each pixel refresh.

Property	Description
ctoolbar	Holds the name of the toolbar to create.
cformnumberseparator	Specifies the character to use to separate form caption from form number if lUseFormNumbers is .T.
otoolbar	Contains a reference to the toolbar that is servicing this form.
lsaveposition	*Specifies whether or not to save the form's position when it is destroyed and restore it when it is initialized.*
luseformnumbers	*True if a number suffix should be added to the form's caption. Useful for forms that can be instantiated multiple times.*
lcascadeforms	*True if multiple instances of the same form should be cascaded.*
nformnumber	*Specifies number of this form even if lUseFormNumbers is .F.*
ncascadefromleft	*Number of pixels to cascade the form from the left.*
ncascadefromtop	*Number of pixels to cascade the form from the top.*

Method	Description
waitmode(lWaitMode)	Pass this method .T. to indicate a wait state for the current form.
getformnumber	Returns the nFormNumber property.

Method	Description
createtoolbar	Creates the toolbar whose class is specified in the form's cToolbar property.
refreshform	Sets this.LockScreen to .T., refreshes the current form, then sets this.LockScreen to .F. Also refreshes this form's toolbar, if applicable.
restoreposition	*Restores the form's last known position.*
saveposition	*Saves the form's position.*
initmultipleinstance	*Called from the form's Init when the form is non-modal and using a private data session. Used to do specific initialization for multiple instances of a form.*

Class Name: CBaseModalForm

Superclass: cbaseform (cforms.vcx)

Description: The form superclass for all modal forms.

Base Class: form

CBaseModalForm is a subclass of CBaseForm that is meant to be used for dialogs. It has a dialog type border automatically set, and it disables any active toolbars automatically as well.

Class Name: CPreferenceModalForm

Superclass: cbasemodalform (cforms.vcx)

Description: The form superclass for all forms that display user preferences.

Base Class: form

This form class is a dialog that is meant to store user preferences. It defaults to having a two-tabbed pageframe for data and general information. The pageframe is subclassed from the CUserPrefPageFrame class (described in the chapter titled CUSERPREF.VCX).

The form (through its pageframe) knows how to read from and write to the 16-bit Windows .INI files or the Windows '95 and Windows NT Registry Databases. In essence, each preference object knows how to save itself, and the pageframe knows how to iterate through all preference objects on each page, enabling all preferences to be retrieved, saved, or written at once. All a developer has to do is add the preferences that he or she wishes to store, and the form takes care of the rest.

Class Name: CBizObjForm

Superclass:	cbaseform (cforms.vcx)
Description:	The superclass form for all forms that support a business object (i.e., an instance of CBizObj or one of its subclasses).
Base Class:	form

CBizObjForm is the superclass for all forms that display business objects. It contains a subclass of the business object, and includes properties and methods that are called as the business object is manipulated. For instance, clicking on the first button on the toolbar will automatically call the forms First() method. The message that first was selected will ripple through the business object and the data handling object. Only code that affects the graphical display of the object should be placed in the appropriate methods of the form.

Additionally, to speed up display issues, a number of properties that let that framework (or a developer) query the state of the business object are surfaced. These include: lEOF, lBOF, lAllowNew, and others.

This form has a number of interesting methods which allow for automatic gathering of view parameters, dialog boxes that ask if the user wishes to save his or her changes, and others. The form works by allowing the user to be in edit mode at all times. Therefore, the method IsChanged() is called from most methods to see if a change was made before the method itself is run. IsChanged() simply asks the business object if any change was made.

An interesting method to look at is WriteBuffer(). This method points out an interesting behavior of Visual FoxPro. When a user enters information into a control (like a textbox), the information is stored in the .Value property. When the control loses focus, Visual FoxPro places the information into the user's buffer. A toolbar never gains focus, however, so clicking on a toolbar will not place any typed information from the current field into the buffer! That means that we can't tell if information has been typed in. Enter WriteBuffer().

```
*--CBizObjForm.WriteBuffer
LOCAL llRetval
llRetVal = .T.

*-- Code to save field value to buffer when
*-- clicking on toolbar without leaving the field
*-- Don't do this for a grid since a grid may change
*-- work areas unexpectedly
*-- GETFLDSTATE(0) % 2 will be 0 if GETFLDSTATE(0) returns
*-- a 2 or a 4, indicating that the deletion status has changed
*-- for the current record. No need to flush the buffer if the current
*-- record has been deleted.
IF GETFLDSTATE(0) % 2 = 1 AND TYPE("this.ActiveControl") == "O" AND ;
      UPPER(this.ActiveControl.BaseClass) <> "GRID"
   IF TYPE("this.ActiveControl.ControlSource") <> "U" AND ;
         !EMPTY(this.ActiveControl.ControlSource)
      IF EVAL(this.ActiveControl.ControlSource) <> ;
         this.ActiveControl.Value
         REPLACE (this.ActiveControl.ControlSource) WITH ;
            this.ActiveControl.Value
         *-- We rely on the fact that we revert the field's value
         *-- before this next line of code.
         llRetVal = (EVAL(this.ActiveControl.ControlSource) = ;
            this.ActiveControl.Value)
      ENDIF
   ENDIF
ENDIF

RETURN llRetVal
```

The key to WriteBuffer() are the two lines that are highlighted above. They check to see if the active control's ControlSource property (the data buffer) is different from the active control's Value property (what the user typed in). If so, we force the write to the buffer with a REPLACE command. This takes care of the control-to-buffer writing issue for us, and becomes a standard behavior of all of our forms that work with business objects—we never have to worry about it again.

Property	Description
obizobj	A generic reference to the business object contained on this form.
leof	Specifies an end-of-file condition.
lbof	Specifies a beginning-of-file condition.
lhavecriteria	Specifies if user has entered criteria. Only meaningful when data is coming from views.
lallownew	Specifies if user is allowed to add new business objects.
lallowsave	Specifies if user is allowed to save business objects.
lallowdelete	Specifies if user is allowed to delete business objects.
cnorecordsmsg	Specifies message to display when no records are returned from a requery.
ldisplaynorecordsmsg	Specifies if the message stored in this.cNoRecordsMsg should be displayed when a user enters selection criteria that returns zero records.

Method	Description
first	Displays the first record on the current form.
prior	Displays the prior record on the current form.
next	Displays the next record on the current form.
last	Displays the last record on the current form.

Method	Description
save([lAllRows, lForce])	Saves the current record on the current form.
cancel([lAllRows])	Cancels changes to the current record on the current form.
delete	Deletes the current record on the current form.
asktosave	Prompts user to save his or her changes.
ischanged	Returns .T. if data on the current form has changed.
isnewandempty	Returns .T. if user has added a new record but not changed anything.
new	Displays a new record on the current form.
requery	Refreshes the current view if applicable.
iscursorempty	Returns .T. if the current cursor (i.e., table or view) contains no records.
ondeletelastrecord	Called from the Delete() method after the user has deleted the last record.
oncancelfirstrecord	Called from the Cancel() method after the user has canceled the addition of the first record, which will leave the cursor empty.
getviewparameters (oContainer, aViewParameters)	Returns a two-dimensional array (via a parameter) containing view parameter names and their values.
selectalias	Selects the appropriate alias for this form.
writebuffer	*Saves contents of current control to table buffer.*

Class Name: CBizObjMaintForm

Superclass: cbizobjform (cforms.vcx)

Description: A generic form superclass used as the basis for all maintenance-style forms.

Base Class: form

CBizObjMaintForm is subclassed from the CBizObjForm. It is a standard form that is used by the sample application for all maintenance forms. It consists of a three-tab pageframe, allowing the entry of criteria for a view, a form-based view of the current business object, and a list view of all accessed business objects. The code in the form's methods automatically sets the pages to fit nicely in the form. It also makes sure that if the user is editing a business object, and that user clicks from one page to another, the standard "Are You Sure?" dialog comes up.

Only one property is added to CBizObjForm. This property, lAutoSizeGrid controls whether or not the grid on the list view is automatically sized to the size of the form.

Property	Description
lautosizegrid	Specifies if the grid on the list page should be automatically sized to fill the page.

Class Name: CBizObjRetvalForm

Superclass: cbizobjform (cforms.vcx)

Description: The form superclass that is used for forms that support business objects and return values.

Base Class: form

CBizObjRetvalForm is used to return a value from a form that contains a business object. One example of this is shown in the next subclass, CBizObjAddForm, which allows you to add a business object and returns the ID of the added object.

Instead of the form being released when the user closes it, it is simply hidden, with the uRetval property being set to the return value. Once the return value has been saved, the form can then be released.

Property	Description
uretval	Property used to hold the return value of the form.

Method	Description
getretval	Called by the cmdOK::Click() method to load the uRetVal property of the form.

Class Name: CBizObjAddForm

Superclass: cbizobjretvalform (cforms.vcx)

Description: A form class used for adding business objects "on the fly."

Base Class: form

CBizObjAddForm is a specialized type of CBizObjRetvalForm which is used to automatically add business objects in the course of working with an application. For instance, if a user types in a customer ID in an invoice form, and that ID isn't found, a form of CBizObjAddForm type can be automatically called, allowing the user to add the customer and then continue with the invoice.

Chapter 22

CLASSLIB: CMENUS.VCX

Introduction

CMENUS.VCX is an object-oriented wrapper around Visual FoxPro 3's menu commands. When we created this wrapper, we wanted to allow developers to access menus in the same way they access other objects, and also to allow developers to easily bind a menu option to a toolbar which performs the same action.

At the same time, it meant that we could no longer use the menu builder. We feel that this can be easily overcome by either building a custom menu builder that is designed to work with menu objects, or by creating a custom GENMENU that generates the classes.

These menu classes make development with Visual FoxPro 3 much simpler, since you can now treat menus using a similar interface as the rest of the product. For instance, you can run the sample application, suspend it, and in the command window type:

```
goApp.oMenu.oUtilitiesPad.Hide
goApp.oMenu.oNavigationPad.Hide
goApp.oMenu.oUtilitiesPad.Show
goApp.oMenu.oNavigationPad.Show
```

and you will see the expected results. You can also easily call the oMenu.Add() method to add a menu pad and popup "on the fly" as necessary. This capability is how we allow business objects to automatically add unique menu options as they are called for.

In design mode, you can bind a toolbar button to a menu bar by specifying the name of the pad and the name of the bar in the proper toolbar properties, and by specifying the action to take in the cToolbarCommand property of the menu bar. Once you have done that, dimming the toolbar button will automatically dim the associated menu bar. This customization can be enhanced in the future at will.

Class Name: CMenu

Superclass: cchildcollection (ccollect.vcx)

Description: A wrapper class for the VFP DEFINE MENU command. CMenu is a CChildCollection of CPads.

Base Class: container

CMenu is subclassed from CChildCollection and contains multiple instances of the CPad class. Two custom methods have been defined, AddBar() and RemoveBar(), which allow the developer to add and remove menu bars "on the fly."

Property	Description
cinstancename	The instance name and object path to the menu.

Method	Description
addbar	Adds a bar to the popup of the specified pad.
removebar	Removes a bar from the popup of the specified pad.

Class Name: CPad

Superclass: ccontainer (ccontrls.vcx)

Description: A wrapper class for the VFP DEFINE PAD command. A CPad is a CContainer that contains a single CPopup.

Base Class: container

CPad encapsulates the functionality of a Visual FoxPro 3 menu pad with the addition of Hide() and Show() methods.

Property	Description
cmessage	Text that is displayed in the status bar when this pad is highlighted.
cmenu	Specifies the name of the menu to which this pad will be "attached." Default value is _msysmenu.
cpopup	Specifies the class name of the popup to activate when this pad is chosen. If not specified, the word Pad in the pad's class name will be replaced with the word Popup and the result used as the class name for the popup.
ckey	Specifies a character expression used for the KEY clause of the DEFINE PAD command.
cskipfor	Specifies a logical expression to be used for the SKIP for clause of the DEFINE PAD command.
ccaption	The caption to display for this menu pad.
opopup	A generic reference to the popup belonging to this pad.
cpadbefore	*The name of the pad that appears before this pad on the menu bar.*
cpadafter	*The name of the pad that appears after this pad on the menu bar.*
lvisible	Specifies if the pad is visible or not.

Method	Description
define	Code to build and execute the DEFINE PAD command.
hide	Hides the menu pad by removing the pad from the menu.
show	Shows the menu pad by redefining it.

Class Name: CPopup

Superclass: cchildcollection (ccollect.vcx)

Description: A wrapper class for the VFP DEFINE POPUP command. CPopup is a CChildCollection of CBars.

Base Class: container

CPopup is a collection class that contains objects that are subclassed from CBar.

Class Name: CBar

Superclass: ccontainer (ccontrls.vcx)

Description: Wrapper class for a VFP menu bar.

Base Class: container

CBar is the superclass for a hierarchy of menu bars. A developer puts the action to perform when this bar is selected in the Click() method of the class. It is subclassed into various types of bars with various functionality.

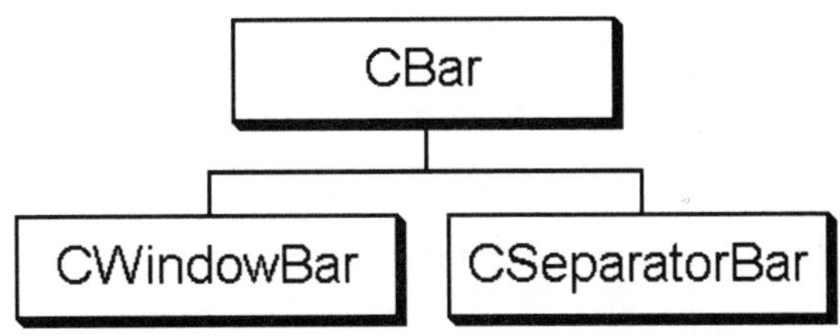

CBar class hierarchy

Property	Description
cskipfor	Specifies a logical expression used in the SKIP FOR clause of the DEFINE BAR command. The bar's Enabled property is always used in the SKIP FOR clause.

Property	Description
cmessage	Text that is displayed in the status bar when this bar is highlighted.
nbarnumber	Specifies the number of the bar. Used internally to store the bar's number or can be used to specify a system bar number, as in _MWI_TRACE.
ckey	Specifies a character expression used for the KEY clause of the DEFINE BAR command.
ccaption	The text to display for this bar.
cpopupname	The name of the popup object that this bar belongs to. This also represents the actual popup name and is needed when removing bars from the popup.
ctoolbarcommand	Specifies a command to execute on a reference to the current toolbar.
lvisible	Specifies if the bar is visible or not.
nbarbefore	*The number of the bar that appears before this bar on the menu popup.*
nbarafter	*The number of the bar that appears after this bar on the menu popup.*

Method	Description
hide	Hides the menu bar by releasing it from its popup.
show	Shows the menu bar by redefining it.
define	Code to define and execute the DEFINE BAR command.

Class Name: CWindowBar

Superclass: cbar (cmenus.vcx)

Description: A special bar class used for bars on the Window menu pad. Subclass of CBar.

Base Class: container

CWindowBar is a specialized version of CBar that is meant to go on the Window pad and is tied to a window. It replaces the Codebook 2.6 functions called AddBar() and KillBar().

Property	Description
cwindowname	The name of the window to activate when this bar is chosen.

Class Name: CSeparatorBar

Superclass: cbar (cmenus.vcx)

Description: A special bar class used for menu separators. Subclassed from CBar.

Base Class: container

CSeparatorBar is a subclass of CBar that adds a separator to a menu.

Chapter 23

CLASSLIB: CTOOLBAR.VCX

Class Name: CToolbarButton

Superclass: ccommandbutton (ccontrls.vcx)

Description: A superclass for all command buttons that will be used in a toolbar.

Base Class: commandbutton

CToolbarButton is the superclass for all command buttons that will be used in a toolbar. The button is defaulted to the Microsoft standard size of 22 by 22 pixels. It also has much of the standard functionality that is required. The button "knows" which menu pad and bar it is associated with, and can be "told" not to execute a click if some process is running.

The .Enabled property is protected and a SetEnabled() method is added which is called in order to enable or disable the button. This is done so that whenever the button is enabled or disabled, the framework can similarly enable or disable the corresponding menu option.

CToolbarButton is subclassed into a number of toolbar buttons that can be used to create custom toolbars quickly. These buttons range from a standard superclass for "administration" toolbar buttons that are always visible and call forms, to buttons like New and Cancel that perform specific actions.

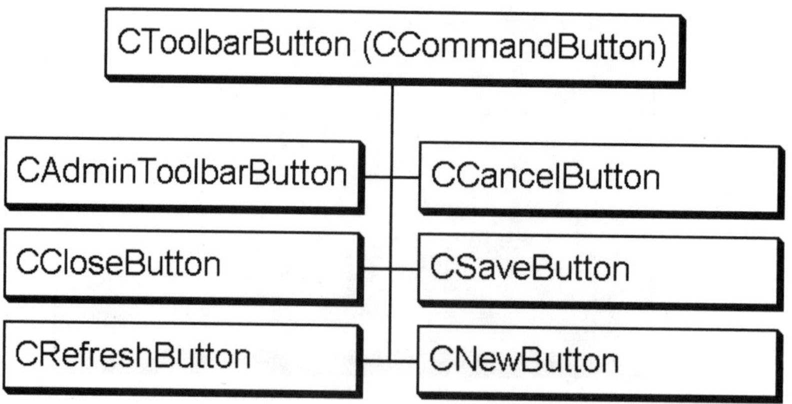

CToolbarButton class hierarchy

Let's take a look at how we achieve the functionality inherent in canceling a click if the current form doesn't know how to work with the clicked toolbar button. This involves the use of two event methods: MouseDown() and MouseUp().

```
*--CToolbarButton.MouseDown()
LPARAMETERS nButton, nShift, nXCoord, nYCoord
this.lCancelClick = .F.
IF !this.OKToSend()
   this.lCancelClick = .T.
   ?? CHR(7)
   NODEFAULT
ENDIF
*--CToolbarButton.MouseUp()
LPARAMETERS nButton, nShift, nXCoord, nYCoord
IF this.lCancelClick
   this.lCancelClick = .F.
   NODEFAULT
ENDIF
```

If the current object cannot work with the toolbar (for instance, we are debugging and have the command window active), we want to "eat" the click. In other words, we'd like to duplicate the functionality of Microsoft Word for Windows and beep with the button not showing that it has been clicked (displaying itself as depressed and then normal). In order to do this, the MouseDown() method checks if it is okay to send the click through (through the OKToSend() method), and if not, it sets a property, lCancelClick to true, beeps, and then issues the **NODEFAULT** keyword.

When you inherit from a Visual FoxPro base class, the behavior of that base class continues unless you issue a NODEFAULT. By placing the NODEFAULT in the MouseDown() and MouseUp() event methods, we are telling Visual FoxPro 3 to forget about displaying the button as it is clicked. That's all there is to it. From now on, any button subclassed from CToolbarbutton will only click when it is able to.

Property	Description
cmenubar	Specifies a menu bar object name to keep in sync with the current button.
cmenupad	Specifies a pad object name on which this.cMenuBar appears.
lcancelclick	.T. if not OK to execute Click() event method.

Method	Description
oktosend	Returns .T. if the active form can accept messages.
setenabled(lEnabled)	Used for setting the value of the Enabled property, which is protected.

Class Name: CAdminToolbarButton

Superclass: ctoolbarbutton (ctoolbar.vcx)

Description: A superclass for buttons that will be used in a CAdminToolbar.

Base Class: commandbutton

A CAdminToolbarButton is a toolbar button that is meant to go on a toolbar that is always available (for instance, one that is used to call the common forms in an application). It works exactly like CToolbarButton, except that the OKToSend() method always returns a true.

Class Name: CCancelButton

Superclass: ctoolbarbutton (ctoolbar.vcx)

Description: A toolbar button to cancel changes to the current form.

Base Class: commandbutton

CCancelButton is a standard button that you may wish to use on a toolbar. It simply passes the Cancel message on to whatever form is currently active (using the _screen.ActiveForm property). The tooltip and bitmap properties of the button have already been set for the developer; it is just a matter of selecting the button and dropping it on a toolbar.

Class Name: CCloseButton

Superclass: ctoolbarbutton (ctoolbar.vcx)

Description: A toolbar button to close the current form.

Base Class: commandbutton

CCloseButton is a standard button that you may wish to use on a toolbar. It simply passes the Close message on to whatever form is currently active (using the _screen.ActiveForm property). The tooltip and bitmap properties of the button have already been set for the developer; it is just a matter of selecting the button and dropping it on a toolbar.

Class Name: CNewButton

Superclass: ctoolbarbutton (ctoolbar.vcx)

Description: A toolbar button to add new records to the current form.

Base Class: commandbutton

CNewButton is a standard button that you may wish to use on a toolbar. It simply passes the New message on to whatever form is currently active (using the _screen.ActiveForm property). The tooltip and bitmap properties of the button have already been set for the developer: it is just a matter of selecting the button and dropping it on a toolbar.

Class Name: CRefreshButton

Superclass: ctoolbarbutton (ctoolbar.vcx)

Description: A toolbar button to refresh the view in the current form.

Base Class: commandbutton

CRefreshButton is a standard button that you may wish to use on a toolbar. It simply passes the Refresh message on to whatever form is currently active (using the _screen.ActiveForm property). The tooltip and bitmap properties of the button have already been set for the developer; it is just a matter of selecting the button and dropping it on a toolbar.

Class Name: CSaveButton

Superclass: ctoolbarbutton (ctoolbar.vcx)

Description: A toolbar button to save changes to the current form.

Base Class: commandbutton

CSaveButton is a standard button that you may wish to use on a toolbar. It simply passes the Save message on to whatever form is currently active (using the _screen.ActiveForm property). The tooltip and bitmap properties of the button have already been set for the developer; it is just a matter of selecting the button and dropping it on a toolbar.

Class Name: CNavButtons

Superclass: ccontainer (ccontrls.vcx)

Description: A container class that contains record navigation buttons.

Base Class: container

CNavButtons is another class that is meant to aid the developer in quickly creating a toolbar. It consists of a container of navigation buttons (first, prior, next, and last). These buttons were not created separately because they are used together as a group, though a developer could definitely subclass CToolbarButton and create each of these buttons separately, adding them to this container for common use.

The buttons, when clicked, call the proper method of the form that they're working with and then call the container's Refresh() method, which enables or disables the buttons appropriately.

Method	Description
first	Calls the Click() method of the cmdFirst button.
last	Calls the Click() method of the cmdLast button.
next	Calls the Click() method of the cmdNext button.
prior	Calls the Click() method of the cmdPrior button.
setenabled	Enables or disables all navigation buttons.

Class Name: CToolbar

Superclass: toolbar

Description: The superclass for all toolbars.

Base Class: toolbar

CToolbar is the base class for all Codebook Foundation toolbars. It acts like a standard toolbar except that it has the capability of saving its position when it is destroyed and restoring it when it is next created.

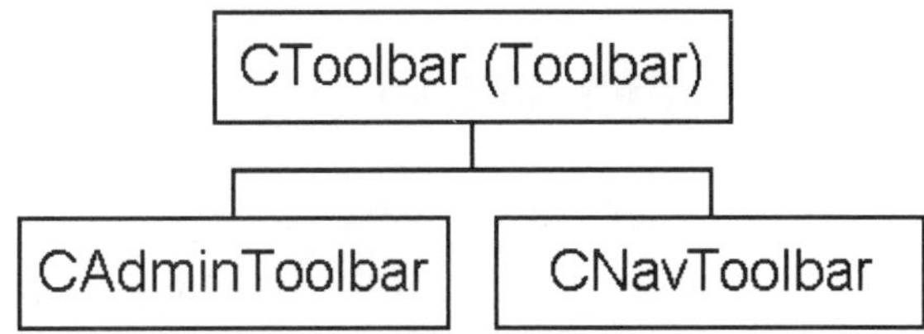

CToolbar class hierarchy

Property	Description
lsaveposition	Specifies whether or not to save the toolbar's position when it is destroyed and restore it when it is initialized.

Method	Description
release	Releases the current instance.
setenabled	Enables or disables the toolbar and all its controls.
restoreposition	*Restores the toolbar's last known position.*
saveposition	*Saves the toolbar's position.*

Class Name: CNavToolbar

Superclass: ctoolbar (ctoolbar.vcx)

Description: The superclass for all navigation toolbars.

Base Class: toolbar

CNavToolbar is a CToolbar that has an instance of CNavButtons as well as the most common editing buttons placed on it. It is there to give the developer a standard "navigation" toolbar that can be used in an application.

Class Name: CAdminToolbar

Superclass: ctoolbar (ctoolbar.vcx)

Description: A superclass used for administration toolbars (i.e., toolbars that are visible for the entire application).

Base Class: toolbar

CAdminToolbar is a CToolbar that is used to create an application-specific administration toolbar, which will typically contain calls to the standard business forms that are used in an application.

Chapter 24

CLASSLIB: CAPP.VCX

Class Name: CApplication

Superclass: cchildcollection (ccollect.vcx)

Description: The main application class.

Base Class: container

CApplication is the superclass for all Codebook-Framework-created applications. Applications simply subclass CApplication, set some properties, and are ready to go. As such, CApplication has a good bit of functionality built into it. Let's take a look at some of the various methods and see how they work.

```
*--CApplication.ReleaseVFPToolbars
LOCAL lnToolbar, ;
  laVFPToolbars[ALEN(this.aVFPToolbars, 1), ALEN(this.aVFPToolbars, 2)]

*-- For now, we hard code the VFP toolbar names
laVFPToolbars[1,1] = "Form Designer"
laVFPToolbars[2,1] = "Standard"
laVFPToolbars[3,1] = "Layout"
laVFPToolbars[4,1] = "Query Designer"
laVFPToolbars[5,1] = "View Designer"
laVFPToolbars[6,1] = "Color Palette"
laVFPToolbars[7,1] = "Form Controls"
laVFPToolbars[8,1] = "Database Designer"
laVFPToolbars[9,1] = "Report Designer"
laVFPToolbars[10,1]  = "Report Controls"
laVFPToolbars[11,1]  = "Print Preview"

*-- German toolbar names
laVFPToolbars[12,1]  = "Abfragedesigner"
laVFPToolbars[13,1]  = "Ansichtsdesigner"
laVFPToolbars[14,1]  = "Berichtsdesigner"
laVFPToolbars[15,1]  = "Bericht-Steuerelemente"
laVFPToolbars[16,1]  = "Datenbankdesigner"
laVFPToolbars[17,1]  = "Farbpalette"
laVFPToolbars[18,1]  = "Formulardesigner"
laVFPToolbars[19,1]  = "Formular-Steuerelemente"
laVFPToolbars[20,1]  = "Seitenansicht"
```

```
FOR lnToolbar = 1 TO ALEN(laVFPToolbars, 1)
   laVFPToolbars[lnToolbar, 2] = WVISIBLE(laVFPToolbars[lnToolbar, 1])
   IF laVFPToolbars[lnToolbar, 2]
      HIDE WINDOW (laVFPToolbars[lnToolbar, 1])
   ENDIF
ENDFOR

=ACOPY(laVFPToolbars, this.aVFPToolbars)
```

Visual FoxPro 3 gives us ways of looking at all forms that are contained within it (_screen.FormCount and the _screen.Forms collection), we can look at the controls within a form (form.ControlCount and the form.Controls collection), we can look at the columns in a grid and pages in a pageframe, but we cannot find out what Visual FoxPro toolbars are currently active. Our only way to turn them off is to check the WVISIBLE() function of the toolbar, and if it's around, use HIDE WINDOW to hide it.

We want to turn off all Visual FoxPro toolbars when beginning our application and reset them afterwards. The methods ReleaseVFPToolbars() and ShowVFPToolbars() accomplish this. The code that appears with the Codebook framework includes the English and German names of the toolbars. If you are working in another language, simply add to the array.

An interesting performance trick is found in these methods. Note that a local array is created using the dimensions of the aVFPToolbars member array. All work is done on laVFPToolbars, and then the results are copied back to the member array. Testing has shown the Visual FoxPro 3 works on local arrays much faster than on member arrays, so whenever there is a decent amount of array work to be done in a method, it is faster to copy the member array to a local array and work from that.

```
*-- CApplication.GetSetting
LPARAMETERS tcSection, tcEntryName, tuDefault

LOCAL lcSection, ;
        luINIFile, ;
        luDefault

*-- Setup default value
IF PCOUNT() >= 3
   luDefault = tuDefault
ELSE
   luDefault = ""
ENDIF
```

```
*-- cRegistry will be empty for 16-bit environments
*-- cINIFile will be empty for 32-bit environments
lcSection = this.cRegistryKey + tcSection
luINIFile = IIF(EMPTY(this.cINIFile), .F., this.cINIFile)

RETURN ;
  this.oSystemSetting.Get(lcSection, tcEntryName, luDefault, luINIFile)
```

GetSetting and SaveSetting are two wrapper methods that provide easy access to reading from and writing to the Windows Registry or .INI files. They handle the call to the CRegistry or CINIFile classes. For example, all an application developer has to do to read the value of the Window Positions entry for the Customer Entry Form is:

goApp.GetSetting("Window Positions," "Customer Entry Form")

When an application class is instantiated it does the following:

- Releases the VFP toolbars
- Shows the splash screen (if one exists)
- Saves the old caption and sets the application caption
- Sets up the use of the registry or .INI file to store information

Once the application is created, a Do() method can be called to begin the application. The Do() method creates a message class to display what is happening as the application begins, adds the application menu, removes the splash screen, and adds the main toolbar (if one exists). From that point on, the user is in charge.

Property	Description
avfptoolbars[20,2]	Holds the name of each toolbar and whether or not it was visible at the start of the program.
cmessageclass	Specifies the name of the class to use for messaging.
omaintoolbar	A reference to the main application toolbar.
cinifile	*Name of the application .INI file. Only valid for 16-bit Windows environments.*

Property	Description
cmainmenuclass	*Specifies the name of the main menu class to create when the application is run.*
cmaintoolbarclass	*Specifies the name of the main toolbar class to create when the application is run.*
coldmainwindcaption	*Holds the original value of the main window caption.*
cregistrykey	*Specifies the key to use to write application settings to the system registry. Only valid for Windows 32-bit environments.*
csplashimage	*The name of the image class to add to _screen to be used for the initial "splash screen."*
lisclean	*True if the environment has been cleaned up by the CleanUp method.*
lshowsplash	*Specifies whether or not to show the splash form at application startup.*
luseinifile	*Set to .T. to override the system-determined file to use to store system settings.*

Method	Description
cleanup	Cleans up the environment when the application is closing.
do	After the application object and its composite objects have been properly initialized, this method begins the application.
getsetting	Retrieves an application setting.
savesetting	Saves an application setting.
releasevfptoolbars	*Releases all VFP toolbars.*
showsplash	*Shows the splash screen.*
showvfptoolbars	*Shows all toolbars that were released in the ReleaseVFPToolbars method.*

Chapter 25

CLASSLIB: CCTLLIB.VCX

Introduction

This visual class library holds a "library" of objects that are used in order to create custom controls that exist in the framework classes. We felt that it would be best to place these in a separate VCX, so that they don't clutter up the toolbar during development time.

Class Name: CCmdGetVal

Superclass: ccontainer (ccontrls.vcx)

Description: An abstract class used as the superclass for the CCmdGetDir and CCmdGetFile classes.

Base Class: container

CCmdGetVal is a container class that holds a command button with an ellipsis as a caption. It is used for a number of custom controls which allow a user to either type a selection or click on the command button and pick the selection from a dialog.

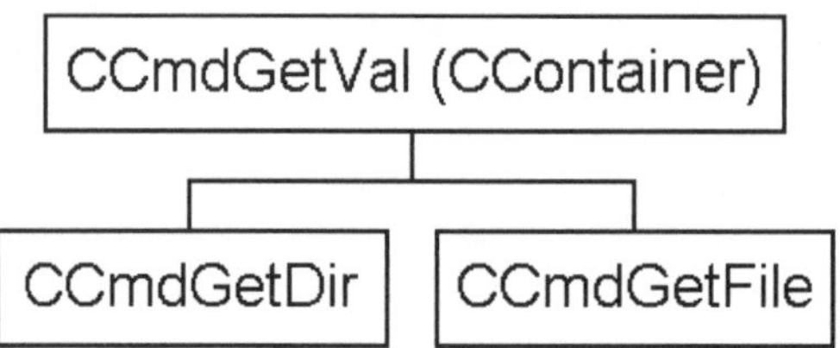

CCmdGetVal class hierarchy

Property	Description
cvalue	This property will accept and hold the return value from the command button.
cdisplaymessage	The message to display with the GETxxx() dialog.

Method	Description
displayvalues	A placeholder for the code that should run when the command button selection's dialog is displayed.

Class Name: CCmdGetDir

Superclass: ccmdgetval (cctllib.vcx)

Description: Adds functionality to the CCmdGetVal class that allows the user to select a directory.

Base Class: container

CCmdGetDir is a subclass of CCmdGetVal with the DisplayValues() method set up to allow the selection of a directory from a GETDIR() dialog.

Class Name: CCmdGetFile

Superclass: ccmdgetval (cctllib.vcx)

Description: Adds functionality to the CCmdGetVal class that allows the user to select a file.

Base Class: container

CCmdGetFile is a subclass of CCmdGetFile with the DisplayValues() method set up to allow the selection of a directory from a GETFile() dialog.

Property	Description
cfileextensions	File extensions to show. See help file on GETFILE() for more information.
copenbuttoncaption	Caption of the OPEN button on the GETFILE() dialog.
lminimumpath	If .T., the path is adjusted to the file and minimized with SYS(2014).
nbuttontype	The type of button scheme to use. See the HELP file on GETFILE() for more information.

Chapter 26

CLASSLIB: CCUSTCTL.VCX

Introduction

This visual class library contains *custom controls* which provide added functionality to the interface of an application. In essence, these are all controls that are commonly used in application development, and which have been created to allow "drag-and-drop" functionality during design time.

Class Name: CDirectoryTextBox

Superclass: ctextbox (ccontrls.vcx)

Description: A custom textbox used for entering directory names.

Base Class: textbox

CDirectoryTextBox is a textbox that has validation built into it that ensures that a proper directory name has been entered by the user. Let's take a look and see how this is done.

```
*--CDirectoryTextBox.Valid()
LOCAL llRetVal

IF TYPE("goApp") = "O"
   this.Value = ALLTRIM(goApp.oFoxTools.AddBs(this.Value))
   llRetVal = goApp.oFoxTools.IsDir(this.Value)
ELSE
   this.Value = ALLTRIM(_screen.oFoxTools.AddBs(this.Value))
   llRetVal = _screen.oFoxTools.IsDir(this.Value)
ENDIF

IF !llRetVal
   =ErrorMsg(DIRNOTFOUND_LOC+": " + ALLTRIM(this.Value))
ENDIF

RETURN llRetVal
```

CDirectoryTextBox uses the functions built into the Foxtools wrapper class (see the chapter on CUTILS.VCX). It adds a backslash to the directory name that was typed in (if one didn't exist), and calls the IsDir() method of the Foxtools class to see if it is an existing directory.

Class Name: CFileNameTextBox

Superclass: ctextbox (ccontrls.vcx)

Description: A custom textbox used for entering file names.

Base Class: textbox

CFileNameTextBox is similar to CDirectoryTextBox except that it checks to see if the entry is an existing file name. If you set the lAllowBlank property to true, the textbox allows the user to leave the file name empty.

Property	Description
lallowblank	Specifies if a blank entry is allowed.

Class Name: CZipCodeTextBox

Superclass: ctextbox (ccontrls.vcx)

Description: A custom textbox used to enter zip codes.

Base Class: textbox

CZipCodeTextBox presets all properties to ensure that a properly formatted United States zip code has been entered.

Class Name: CPhoneTextBox

Superclass: ctextbox (ccontrls.vcx)

Description: A custom textbox used for entering phone numbers.

Base Class: textbox

CPhoneTextBox presets all properties to ensure that a properly formatted United States phone number (with area code) has been entered.

Class Name: CStateComboBox

Superclass: ccombobox (ccontrls.vcx)

Description: A custom combobox used to select states.

Base Class: combobox

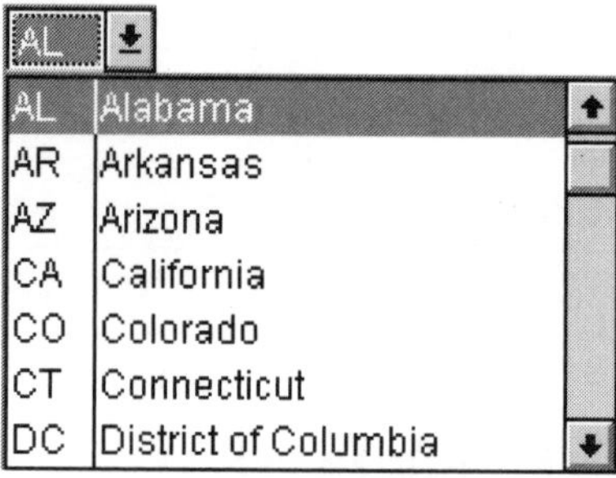

An instance of CStateComboBox

CStateComboBox allows the developer to drop a combobox onto a form, and immediately allow the selection of one of the states in the United States from that box. When closed, it displays the two-character abbreviation of a state, and when open, it displays that abbreviation followed by the full name of the state.

In order to keep this class self-contained, the Init() method uses the AddListItem() method multiple times to add all 50 states to the list. In this manner, the class can be dropped on any form and can take care of initializing itself.

Setting lAllowBlank to true allows a blank entry to appear at the top of the drop-down list. This is useful whenever you may need to allow the selection of no specific state.

Property	Description
lallowblank	Set to .T. to add a blank entry to the drop-down list. Useful in criteria selection forms.

Class Name: CSetOrderGrid

Superclass: cgrid (ccontrls.vcx)

Description: A custom grid that allows for the setting of an order by clicking on a column header.

Base Class: grid

CSetOrderGrid is a specialized grid control that includes a new method, SetOrder(). This method, when called from the Click() method of a grid header automatically sets the order of the grid to that column, if an index tag exists.

```
*--CSetOrderGrid.SetOrder()
LPARAMETERS tcControlSource
LOCAL lnCount, lcField

*-- Sets the order to the currently selected
*-- controlsource if possible

*-- Get the fieldname being used
lcField = ;
    SUBSTR(tcControlSource, AT(".", tcControlSource) + 1)

*-- See if the field name is in the leftmost part of the index
*-- expression. If so, SET ORDER TO the index.
FOR lnCount = 1 TO TAGCOUNT()
    IF UPPER(SYS(14, lnCount)) = UPPER(lcField)
      SET ORDER TO lnCount
      IF TYPE("thisform") == "O"
         thisform.Refresh()
      ENDIF
      EXIT
    ENDIF
ENDFOR
```

As you can see, SetOrder() accepts a parameter which contains the ControlSource of the column. It uses that ControlSource to get the field that is being used, and looks for a matching index. If it is found, it sets the order and refreshes the form.

Method	Description
setorder(cControlSource)	This method checks if there is a tag for the current column's rowsource, and if so, sets the order to it.

Class Name: CGetDirectory

Superclass: ccmdgetdir (cctllib.vcx)

Description: A custom control used for entering directory names.

Base Class: container

CGetDirectory combines a CCmdGetDir button (see the chapter on CCTLLIB.VCX) with a CDirectoryTextBox to provide the standard interface made up of a textbox and commandbutton with which the user can either type a directory or select one by clicking on the button.

Class Name: CGetFileName

Superclass: ccmdgetfile (cctllib.vcx)

Description: A custom control used for entering file names.

Base Class: container

CGetFileName combines a CCmdGetFile button (see the chapter on CCTLLIB.VCX) with a CFileNameTextBox to provide the standard interface made up of a textbox and command button with which the user can either type a file name or select one by clicking on the button.

Class Name: CDateTextBox

Superclass: ctextbox (ccontrls.vcx)

Description: A custom textbox used for entering dates.

Base Class: textbox

CDateTextBox allows the developer to drop a control onto a form that "knows" how to ease data entry. It allows the user to manipulate the date being entered in the following ways:

Keys Pressed	Results
Numeric Key	Standard date entry
+,=	Forward one day
-,_	Backward one day
T,t	Today's date
M,m	First day of month
H,h	Last day of month
Y,y	First day of year
R,r	Last day of year

Let's take a look at the two methods of this control and see what they do.

```
CDateTextBox.Init()
*-- Make sure that we're using a DATE type of controlsource.
IF CTextBox::Init()
   IF TYPE(this.Controlsource) # "D"
      =MESSAGEBOX(NON_DATE_SOURCE_LOC)
      RETURN .F.
   ENDIF
ENDIF
```

The Init() method calls up to the superclass Init() and then makes sure that the developer has bound a date to the CDateTextBox control. If not, it RETURNs false, preventing the control from being created.

```
CDateTextBox.KeyPress()
*-- This method checks the key pressed, allowing the following
*-- unique behaviors:
*--       +,=   next day
*--       -,_   previous day
*--       T,t   Today's date
*--       M,m   First day of month
*--       H,h   Last day of month
```

```
*--      Y,y  First day of year
*--      R,r  Last day of year

*-- The NODEFAULT in this case stops the  bell from sounding as
*-- the date is filled.
LPARAMETERS nKeyCode, nShiftAltCtrl
LOCAL lcValue, lcMonth, lcYear, ldValue

DO CASE
   CASE nKeyCode = ASC("+") OR nKeyCode = ASC("=")
      this.Value = this.Value + 1
      NODEFAULT
   CASE nKeyCode = ASC("-") OR nKeyCode = ASC("_")
      this.Value = this.Value - 1
      NODEFAULT
   CASE nKeyCode = ASC("T") or nKeyCode = ASC("t")
      this.Value = DATE()
      NODEFAULT
   CASE nKeyCode = ASC("M") or nKeyCode = ASC("m")
      lcMonth = STR(MONTH(this.Value))
      lcYear  = STR(YEAR(this.Value))
      lcValue = lcMonth + "/" + "01" + "/" + lcYear
      this.Value = CTOD(lcValue)
      NODEFAULT
   CASE nKeyCode = ASC("H") or nKeyCode = ASC("h")
      ldValue = GOMONTH(this.Value,1)
      lcMonth = STR(MONTH(ldValue))
      lcYear  = STR(YEAR(ldValue))
      lcValue = lcMonth + "/" + "01" + "/" + lcYear
      this.Value = CTOD(lcValue) - 1
      NODEFAULT
   CASE nKeyCode = ASC("Y") or nKeyCode = ASC("y")
      lcValue = "01/01/" + STR(YEAR(this.Value))
      this.Value = CTOD(lcValue)
      NODEFAULT
   CASE nKeyCode = ASC("R") or nKeyCode = ASC("r")
      lcValue = "12/31/" + STR(YEAR(this.Value))
      this.Value = CTOD(lcValue)
      NODEFAULT
ENDCASE
```

The KeyPress() event method checks to see which key was pressed and acts accordingly. If one of the keys that we're checking for was pressed, it modifies the .Value property, which changes the value of the control, and then issues a NODEFAULT. This stops Visual FoxPro 3 from doing its default behavior, which would be to beep because we entered an invalid key in a date field.

Class Name: ClfComboBox

Superclass: ccombobox (ccontrls.vcx)

Description: A custom combobox that performs an incremental seek for each key press.

Base Class: combobox

This is our "intellifind" combobox. It consists of a combobox that automatically performs an incremental seek as the user types in a value. The developer can customize this control in a number of ways. If lCaseSensitive is set to True, it does a case sensitive search. The property lLimitToList forces the user to type in only values that exist in the list.

If cFormName is set to a form class, then that form is displayed whenever the user types in a non-existent name. This allows the developer to place an intellifind combobox on an invoice form, allowing users to enter a customer name. If the customer name isn't found, it can automatically call up a subclass of CBizObjAddForm to enter a new customer, at which point the invoice form will continue to run with the newly entered customer. All this functionality is accomplished with no code on the developer's part, simply good design and setting of properties!

Property	Description
caddmessage	Specifies text to prompt user when an entry is typed that is not in the list. Only valid if a form name is specified in this.cFormName.
cformname	Specifies name of form class to run if user entry is not in list.

Property	Description
ctag	Since you can only specify 10 characters for tag names, this property is used to specify a tag name for the field that is being searched. If not specified, the first 10 characters of the field name are used.
lcasesensitive	Specifies whether character typed should be auto-converted to uppercase.
llimittolist	True if user is limited to adding items that are already in the list.
calias	*Specifies the alias to do the search on.*
cfield	*Specifies name of field to evaluate in the textbox portion of the control.*
csearchstring	*Holds the text the user is typing.*
linitialized	*.T. if control has been properly initialized.*

Chapter 27

CLASSLIB: CCUSTFRM.VCX

Introduction

CCUSTFRM.VCX is very similar in intent to CCUSTCTL.VCX in that it consists of some reusable custom forms. All of the forms in this class library are common forms that will probably be used in all applications.

Class Name: CReportForm

Superclass: cbasemodalform (cforms.vcx)

Description: A custom form used for report selection.

Base Class: form

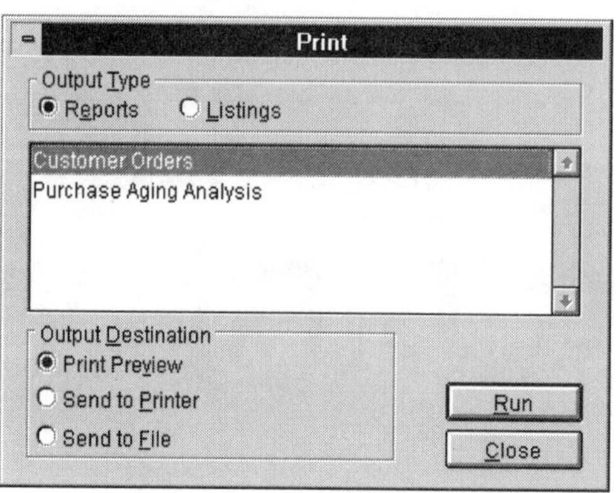

An instance of CReportForm

This form is a standard report selection form. It allows the user to select a report from a list, and then either display it, print it, or save it as a file. Those of you who have read the earlier versions of Codebook will be familiar with this form, and will be amazed at how much simpler it has become thanks to Visual FoxPro's 3 use of data environments in the report as well as the new REPORT FORM ... ASCII clause.

CReportForm works off a free table called REPOLIST.DBF. The structure of Repolist is:

Field Name	Type	Width
cDOSName	C	8
cFullName	C	30
cType	C	4

cDOSName contains the file name of the FRX report file, cFullName is the name of the report that is shown in the listbox, and cType is either LIST or REPO, depending on whether it should appear when Listings or Reports is selected in the Output Type option group.

There is very little code in this form class. The Load() method makes sure that Repolist.dbf is USEd.

Most methods are done to make things "interface friendly." The Init() of the listbox returns a false if Repolist is empty, ensuring that the form doesn't display in that case. The DoubleClick() method of the listbox calls the Click() of the Run button, so that the user can double-click on a report to run it. Likewise, the KeyPress() method of the listbox calls the Click() of the Run button if Enter has been pressed, allowing the user to select a report and hit Enter.

Most of the code is in the Click() method of the Run button.

```
*-- cmdRun.Click()
LOCAL lcSeleReport

lcSeleReport = "REPORTS\" + ALLTRIM(repoList.cdosname) + ".FRX"

IF NOT FILE(lcSeleReport)
   =MESSAGEBOX(REPORTNOTFOUND_LOC, MB_ICONEXCLAMATION)
   RETURN
ENDIF

DO CASE
   CASE thisform.opgOutput.optPreview.Value = 1   && To screen
      REPORT FORM (lcSeleReport) PREVIEW
   CASE thisform.opgOutput.optPrinter.Value = 1   && To printer
      IF PRINTSTATUS()
         REPORT FORM (lcSeleReport) ;
            TO PRINTER NOCONSOLE
      ELSE
```

```
         =MESSAGEBOX(PRINTERNOTREADY_LOC, MB_ICONEXCLAMATION)
      ENDIF
   CASE thisform.opgOutput.optFile.Value = 1      && To file
      lcTextFile  = ALLTRIM(Repolist.cDosName)+".TXT"
      REPORT FORM (lcSeleReport) TO FILE (lcTextFile) ASCII
      =MESSAGEBOX(FILESAVEDAS_LOC + FULLPATH(lcTextFile), ;
                      MB_ICONINFORMATION)
ENDCASE
```

This code checks to see if the report exists, and then, depending on the Output option that is selected, runs the REPORT FORM command with the PREVIEW, PRINTER, or ASCII clause. That's all there is to it!

Class Name: CDbManageForm

Superclass:	cbasemodalform (cforms.vcx)
Description:	DataBase Management Form. Allows for Reindex, Pack, and PackMemo.
Base Class:	form

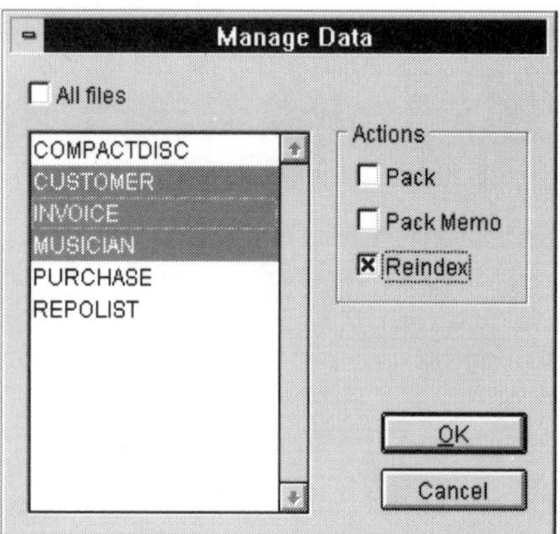

An instance of CDbManageForm

CDbManageForm is a form class that allows the selection of various database management functions. It contains a CSessionEnvironment instance that saves our SET commands, a CDELoader instance that loads a data environment

(LocalTablesEnvironment) which contains all local tables that can be manipulated, and an instance of the CTableBehavior class which has the logic for handling behavior that is unique to tables (see the chapter on CBEHAVIOR.VCX).

One interesting point to note is that the DoActions() method simply calls the appropriate oTableBehavior method (for instance: this.oTableBehavior.Pack()). These methods have already enhanced the base Visual FoxPro 3 command to include a WAIT WINDOW that states what is happening. Therefore, simply by saying, "Hey table, pack yourself," the user gets a message that the table is being packed.

Method	Description
doactions	Performs the requested actions on the database.

Class Name: CAboutForm

Superclass: cbasemodalform (cforms.vcx)

Description: A standard About form with a call to MSInfo (if it exists).

Base Class: form

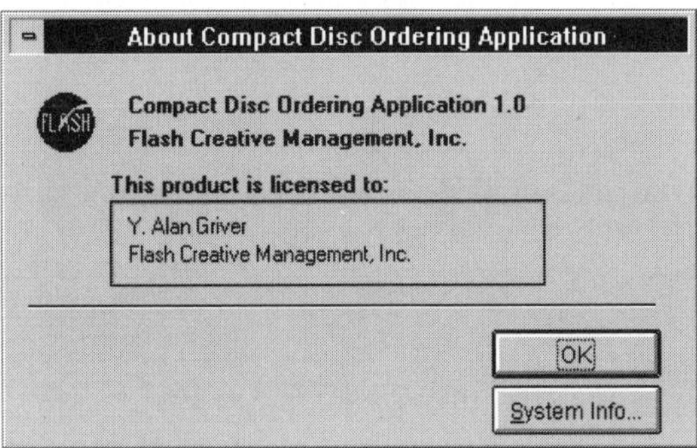

An instance of CAboutForm

CAboutForm calls up a standard "about" window with the registered user's name inside a box on the form. The System Info... button appears if MSINFO has been installed on the user's machine. Most of the code happens in the Init() method of the form.

```
CAboutForm.Init()
LOCAL loSystemSetting, ;
        lcKey

*-- Initialize the form caption and various label captions
this.Caption = ABOUT_LOC + " " + APPNAME_LOC
this.lblName.Caption = APPNAME_LOC + " " + VERSION_LOC
this.lblCopyright.Caption = COMPANYNAME_LOC

DO CASE
  CASE UPPER(OS()) = "WINDOWS NT" OR UPPER(OS()) = "WINDOWS 4"
    *-- Gets default user name, organization,
    *--  and location of MSINFO.EXE from
    *--  system registry
    loSystemSetting = CREATEOBJECT("CRegistry")
    this.cMSInfo = ;
      loSystemSetting.Get(KEY_SHARED_TOOLS_LOCATION, ;
        "MSINFO", "", HKEY_LOCAL_MACHINE)
    lcKey = IIF("NT" $ UPPER(OS()), KEY_NTCURRENTVERSION, ;
      KEY_WIN4CURRENTVERSION)
    this.lblUserName.Caption = ;
      loSystemSetting.Get(lcKey, "RegisteredOwner", "", ;
        HKEY_LOCAL_MACHINE)
    this.lblOrganization.Caption = ;
      loSystemSetting.Get(lcKey, "RegisteredOrganization", "", ;
        HKEY_LOCAL_MACHINE)

  OTHERWISE
    *-- Gets default user name, organization, and location of
    *-- MSINFO.EXE from WIN.INI (for Windows 3.x machines)
    loSystemSetting = CREATEOBJECT("CINIFile")
    this.cMSInfo = ;
      loSystemSetting.Get("MICROSOFT SYSTEM INFO", "MSINFO", "", ;
        "WIN.INI")
    this.lblUserName.Caption = ;
      loSystemSetting.Get("MS USER INFO", "DEFNAME", "", "WIN.INI")
    this.lblOrganization.Caption = ;
      loSystemSetting.Get("MS USER INFO", "DEFCOMPANY", "", ;
        "WIN.INI")
ENDCASE
```

```
*-- Check if MSINFO.EXE exists, otherwise remove the System Info
*-- command button and shorten the form
IF !EMPTY(thisform.cMSInfo)
   thisform.cMSInfo = thisform.cMSInfo + "\MSINFO.EXE"
ENDIF

IF !FILE(thisform.cMSInfo)
   thisform.cmdSystemInfo.Enabled = .F.
   thisform.Height = 175
ENDIF

RETURN CBaseModalForm::Init()
```

This code checks to see if we're running in a 16- or 32-bit version of Microsoft Windows and loads the information on the user and MSInfo accordingly. If MSInfo doesn't exist, it disables the System Info... button and resizes the form.

Property	Description
cmsinfo	Specifies the fully qualified file name of the MSINFO.EXE program, if present.

Chapter 28

CLASSLIB: CUSRPREF.VCX

Introduction

CUSRPREF.VCX contains a set of classes that automate the creation of an interface that includes reading from and writing to the Windows Registry or an .INI file. These classes are most commonly used in a File/Preferences or Tools/Options type of dialog box.

The class library is made up of an abstract CPreference class with a number of visual subclasses and a pageframe class that has the capability of iterating through all preference objects that it contains, reading and writing the appropriate preferences.

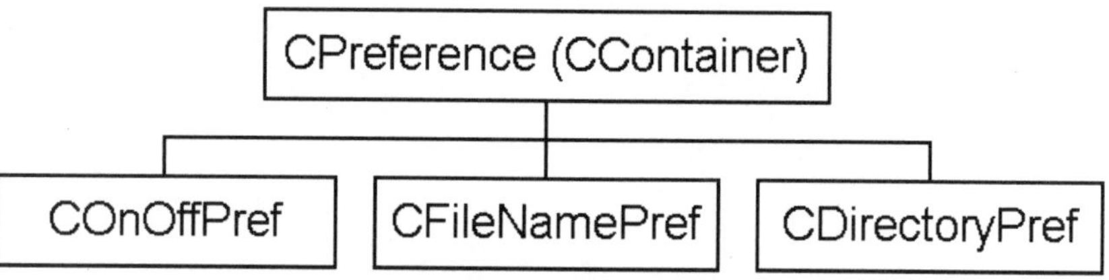

The CPreference class hierarchy

Class Name: CPreference

Superclass:	ccontainer (ccontrls.vcx)
Description:	An abstract class used as the superclass of other user preference classes.
Base Class:	container

This abstract class contains the base behavior that preference-aware containers must have. It includes properties which the developer can fill in to specify which preference should be tied to the objects contained within the CPreference container, as well as methods that read from and write to the preference file (however it is handled by the application) as well as a method to issue the proper Visual FoxPro 3 command to set the preference.

Property	Description
cpreferencename	Specifies the name of the preference to store in the system setting file.
cpreferencesection	Specifies the name of the section used to store the preference in the system setting file.
cpreferencevalue	The value of the preference. You can use this property to provide a default value for the preference when setting it for the first time.
csetcommand	The command to issue in order to set the command. Used by SETPREFERENCE() by default. Combined with cPreferenceValue to get the executed command.

Method	Description
getpreferencevalue	Retrieves the value of the preference from the system setting file.
setpreferencevalue	Issues the command to set up the preference based on the value of cPreferenceValue.
writepreferencevalue	Writes the value of the preference from the system setting file.

Class Name: COnOffPref

Superclass: cpreference (cusrpref.vcx)

Description: A user preference class used for On/Off settings.

Base Class: container

COnOffPref is a subclass of CPreference which provides the visual behavior of a checkbox, allowing the developer to use it for any preference that stores a Yes/No or On/Off value. The methods of this class have been enhanced to specifically handle those types of values.

Class Name: CFileNamePref

Superclass: cpreference (cusrpref.vcx)

Description: A user preference class used for file names.

Base Class: container

CFileNamePref is a subclass of CPreference which contains a CGetFileName instance (see the chapter on CCUSTCTL.VCX) that allows the user to enter or select an existing file name.

Class Name: CDirectoryPref

Superclass: cpreference (cusrpref.vcx)

Description: A user preference class used for directory names.

Base Class: container

CDirectoryPref is a subclass of CPreference which contains a CGetDirectory instance (see the chapter on CCUSTCTL.VCX) that allows the user to enter or select an existing directory.

Class Name: CUserPrefPageframe

Superclass: cpageframe (ccontrls.vcx)

Description: A pageframe that contains custom methods used to iterate through all embedded user preference classes that allow retrieving, setting, and writing all preferences at once.

Base Class: pageframe

CUserPrefPageframe is the standard User Interface container that will be subclassed by a developer to provide a Tools/Options or File/Preferences interface. All the developer has to do is to drop an instance of this class on a form (typically a CBaseModalForm) and then drop instances of the other classes in this visual class library for each preference that must be provided. In fact, CPreference-ModalForm (see the chapter on CFORMS.VCX) does just this for you.

The CUserPrefPageframe class includes methods for iterating through all the pages and reading from or writing to the appropriate preference storage. It also includes a method that calls the proper Visual FoxPro 3 code to set the preference.

This is done by iterating through all pages and all controls on the pages, calling the appropriate method of each control in turn. Let's look at the code in the WriteAllPreferences() method and see how this works.

```
*--CPageFrame.WriteAllPreferences()
LOCAL lnCounter, lnCount2

FOR lnCounter = 1 TO this.PageCount
  FOR lnCount2 = 1 TO this.Pages(lnCounter).ControlCount
    IF TYPE("this.Pages(lnCounter). ;
        Controls(lnCount2).cPreferencename") = 'C'
      this.Pages(lnCounter).Controls(lnCount2). ;
        WritePreferenceValue()
    ENDIF
  ENDFOR
ENDFOR
```

The code uses the .PageCount and .ControlCount properties to get the total number of pages in the pageframe and controls in the page. It also uses the Pages() and Controls() control arrays to iterate through the pages and controls one at a time. For each control, it calls the WritePreferenceValue() method, allowing the control to handle how it writes itself to the preference storage. Again, all the developer cares about is calling the WriteAllPreferences() method. The classes take care of themselves.

Method	Description
getallpreferences	Calls the custom GetPreferenceValue() for each user preference object on each page in the pageframe.
setallpreferences	Calls the custom SetPreferenceValue() for each user preference object on each page in the pageframe.
writeallpreferences	Calls the custom WritePreferenceValue() for each user preference object on each page in the pageframe.

Chapter 29

CLASSLIB: CMOVER.VCX

Introduction

This class library is fully described in the chapter titled "A Set of Mover Classes." It provides for a set of classes that together allow you to create mover type functionality with various interfaces.

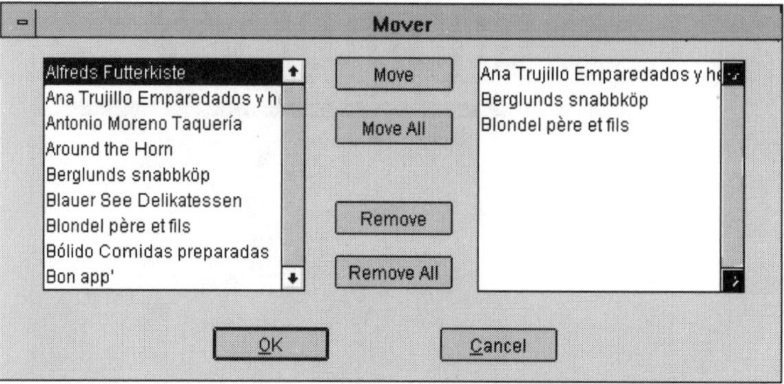

An instance of MoverForm

Class Name: CArrayListBox

Superclass: clistbox (ccontrls.vcx)

Description: A listbox specialized to work with arrays only.

Base Class: listbox

This subclass of CListBox has been created to work with arrays, allowing a developer to use methods like AddItem() and RemoveItem() against array-based lists as well as standard lists. It also adds some functionality, including whether a row is removed from a list or just dimmed in the listbox.

Property	Description
cdeltype	Defines what happens when an item is REMOVED from the list. May be DELETEd or DIMmed.
caddtype	Should additions be checked against rowsource or not?

Property	Description
nelementsavailable	# elements available in the list.
lsorted	Should the array be sorted?
lbackup	Should incoming array be backed up prior to loading?
arowsourcebackup[1,0]	Backup of the row source to allow for reverting the list to original form.

Method	Description
addrow	Adds a row to the rowsource.
multidimensional	Is the array multidimensional (i.e., more than one dimension)? Returns a logical.
numrows	Number of rows in the list. (The old SizeArry.PRG.)
numcols	Returns # of columns in the rowsource array.
delrow	Deletes a row from the rowsource array.
availableelements	# of available elements in the array.
enableall	Enables all items in a list.
disableall	Disables all individual items in the list.
isdimmed	Returns whether a list item is disabled or not.
duperow	Copies the contents of a row from the rowsource into the passed-through array.
markrow	Marks a row with a backslash, in effect disabling it.
packlist	Packs the list, removing all disabled items.
resize	Resizes the array, removing all the deleted rows.

Method	Description
arraycopy	Batch loads the rowsource from an array passed through as a parameter.
backup	Copies the rowsource array into the backup array (aRowSourceBackup).
revert	Copies the backup into the rowsource array.
setrowsource	Sets the rowsource property for this list.

Class Name: MoverListBox

Superclass: carraylistbox (cmover.vcx)

Description: Mover version of an array listbox.

Base Class: listbox

MoverListBox is a subclass of CArrayListBox to which drag-and-drop functionality has been added. Since Mover dialogs involve moving items from one listbox to another, drag-and-drop seemed to make sense as a basic function.

Class Name: CmdMove

Superclass: ccommandbutton (ccontrls.vcx)

Description: A command button to move a single item from the full list to the selected list.

Base Class: commandbutton

This button calls its parent's MoveOne() method.

Class Name: CmdRemove

Superclass: ccommandbutton (ccontrls.vcx)

Description: A command button to remove a single item from the full list to the selected list.

Base Class: commandbutton

This button calls its parent's RemoveOne() method.

Class Name: CmdMoveAll

Superclass: ccommandbutton (ccontrls.vcx)

Description: A command button to move all items from the full list to the selected list.

Base Class: commandbutton

This button calls its parent's MoveAll() method.

Class Name: CmdRemoveAll

Superclass: ccommandbutton (ccontrls.vcx)

Description: A command button to remove all items from the full list to the selected list.

Base Class: commandbutton

This button calls its parent's RemoveAll() method.

Class Name: MoverContainer

Superclass: ccontainer (ccontrls.vcx)

Description: A container that combines mover listboxes and command buttons for use in a form.

Base Class: container

This class is a container that provides all of the functionality of a Mover dialog box. It allows the developer to drop it on a form where this functionality is required.

Property	Description
cfulllistrowsource	Rowsource for the full list.
cselectedlistrowsource	Rowsource for the list of selected items.

Method	Description
moveone	Moves only the selected objects from the “All” list to the “Selected” list.
moveall	Moves the entire All list to the Selected list.
removeone	Removes only selected items from the Selected list.
removeall	Clears the Selected list and enables the entire All list.
revert	Reverts both lists.

Class Name: MoverContainer_Dialog

Superclass: movercontainer (cmover.vcx)

Description: A subclass of the MoverContainer class that adds OK and Cancel buttons.

Base Class: container

This container includes OK and Cancel buttons with a Mover dialog box.

Class Name: MoverForm

Superclass: cbasemodalform (cforms.vcx)

Description: Modal form with a MoverContainerDialog object on it.

Base Class: form

This is a form that includes a mover with OK and Cancel buttons.

Property	Description
cfulllistrowsource	This property contains the name of the full list source.
cselectedlistrowsource	This property contains the name of the selected list source.

Chapter 30

THE CODEBOOK FRAMEWORK — PUTTING IT ALL TOGETHER

Introduction

We have covered all of the class libraries that make up the Codebook Foundation Classes. There are a number of additional files that provide the remaining functionality of the foundation.

File Name	Description
MAIN.PRG	This is a stub program that allows the framework to "learn" where the various files are found, allowing development to take place without generating an APP. This is set as the "Main" program.
SETUP.PRG	This is the program that sets up an application, creating the application object.
UTILITY.PRG	This program file contains a set of utility functions that are called throughout the application.
APPINCL.H	This INCLUDE file contains application-specific constants.
ERRORS.H	This INCLUDE file contains standard error constants.
FRAMEWRK.H	This INCLUDE file contains constants that are required by the framework.
STRINGS.H	This INCLUDE file contains any strings that are used by the framework.
DEBUG.TXT	Placing a file with this name in an application's root directory will cause your application to go into Debug mode, adding a Utilities menu for your use, among other things (see SETUP.PRG, later in this chapter).

This chapter describes these files, the recommended directory structure, and the Visual FoxPro 3 Tools/Options settings that allow the full benefits of using the Codebook Framework.

Directory Structure

As in past Codebooks, we highly recommend creating a set of directories which store your reusable code, as well as an application-specific set of directories in which to store application-specific code.

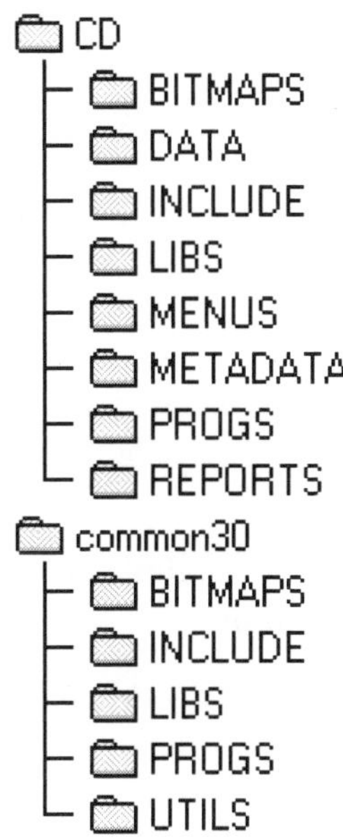

The Codebook directory structure

All of the foundation class code goes into the various COMMON30 subdirectories with the exception of MAIN.PRG, which is included in every application's PROGS subdirectory. As will be described, this program is simply a stub, allowing the framework to "understand" where the application components reside.

Visual FoxPro 3's Tools/Options Settings

There are a number of recommended options that you can use in Visual FoxPro 3's Tools/Options settings in order to speed development.

Controls Tab

Add the following two Visual Class Libraries: CCONTROLS, CCUSTCTL. This will give you immediate access to the most commonly used Codebook controls and custom controls.

Forms Tab

We like setting the horizontal and vertical spacing to five pixels each. It allows us to move controls finely with the mouse, but not so finely that it's a pain to move them.

File Locations

You can have a Codebook Framework-based application automatically find all the files that it needs, without you having to build an APP in one of two ways:

- Set the PATH to all of the subdirectories of the application-specific path and the COMMON30\PROGS subdirectory. This works fine if you are working on only one application.
- Modify APPINCL.H so that the COMMONPATH constant points to a relative path to your COMMON30 subdirectory. Set your default directory (using CD or SET DEFAULT TO) to the root application directory. Compile PROGS\MAIN. That should do it. From that point on, the framework will SET PATH for you, and reset it at the end. This will work for all applications that you work on, based on which application's root directory you are in when you begin.

In either case, to begin the application, simply type **DO PROGS\MAIN**.

MAIN.PRG

This stub program is used to allow you to easily start an application, even though the application's real code is based in the COMMON30\PROGS subdirectory (SETUP.PRG). It consists of two lines of code (and lots of comments):

```
*--MAIN.PRG
*-- This program is necessary in order for code in SETUP.PRG,
*-- which is located in COMMON30\PROGS, to be able to find where
*-- the project directory structure is without having to know
```

```
*-- the name or main directory of the project. Note that this
*-- is really only necessary when running the PRG directly,
*-- since the APP will reside in the same directory as the project.
#INCLUDE "INCLUDE\APPINCL.H"
DO COMMONPATH\PROGS\Setup
```

The first line #INCLUDEs APPINCL.H so that COMMONPATH will be found. The next line simply runs Setup for you.

SETUP.PRG

SETUP.PRG does all of the application initialization and setup for you. It is somewhat similar to TRAFICOP.PRG in *The FoxPro 2.6 Codebook*. It sets a number of public variables whose values will be saved by the CGlobal-Environment object, sets the path properly and instantiates the application object. (An instance of the CGlobalEnvironment class is added to the application object as the application object is being created.) Two functions, SetPath() and BuildMeta(), exist in this program.

SetPath() checks to see if we are running an .APP or a .PRG. If the latter, it sets the path to all of the local subdirectories and the COMMONPATH's PROGS subdirectory. This allows the application to run as usual. SetPath() then looks for a table called METADATA.DBF. This table contains a list of all class libraries and programs used in the application and is used to build SET CLASSLIB TO and SET PROC TO strings which ensure that everything is loaded into memory.

BuildMeta() is called if we are in DEBUG mode (a file called DEBUG.TXT exists in the application's root directory). It USEs the project file, and builds the METADATA.DBF file for us. In this manner, METADATA.DBF is maintained for us, ensuring that whenever we add a class library or program, the application "knows" that it is there without us having to change any code!

UTILITY.PRG

This program file contains a number of procedures that are reused throughout the application.

IsTag (cTagName, cAlias)

IsTag() accepts a tag name and an alias, and returns a true if the tag name exists for that alias.

NotYet()

NotYet() puts up a message box that states that the function is not yet implemented.

FileSize(cFileName)

This function returns the size of a file.

FormIsObject()

This function returns a true if the active form is an object.

IsAbstract(cClass, cClassName)

This function returns a true if the class is an abstract class. This allows the developer to put the following code in the Init() method of an abstract class:

```
*-- Sample Init() method
IF IsAbstract(this.Class, "<Class Name>")
   RETURN .F.
ENDIF
```

ErrorMsg(cMessage[, nOptions, cTitle])

This function creates a message box that defaults to an error bitmap, an OK button, and the title of the application.

DoForm(cClassName[, uParam1])

DoForm() allows a developer to quickly call a form that is in a class library and show it.

ARColHead(nNumDays)

This is a simple function that calculates headers for a 30/60/90 type of aging report.

ConvertToChar(uParam)

This function takes a parameter of any type and converts it to a character string.

IsA(oObject, cClass)

This function returns a true if the object that is passed is instantiated from the class that is passed or one of its subclasses.

IsAdding(cAlias)

Returns .T. if the user is in the midst of adding a record to the alias specified in the tcAlias parameter.

LockScreen(lValue)

This speeds up refreshes by locking the active form or the _screen object while the refresh is done, then unlocking them.

CSZ(cCity, cState, cZip)

This function formats a U. S. City, State, and Zip Code address line. It correctly handles both five- and nine-digit zip codes.

YesNo(cMessage, [nDialogType, cTitleText, nDefaultButton, lBeep])

This is a specialized version of the native MessageBox() function that forces a Yes/No button choice, and defaults the rest of the options intelligently. The default text for the message is "Are You Sure?" with a question mark icon.

GetMessageClass()

This function returns what type of message should be displayed. If the application is running, it returns whatever message type has been set for the application (it defaults to status bar types of messages), otherwise it returns CMESSAGE as the class to use.

APPINCL.H

This is the application-specific INCLUDE file. It contains settings that will be specific to each application, yet are accessible by the common framework classes. It allows you to specify your company name, the application name, a path to the common directories, and more. All of these constants must be defined for an application.

ERRORS.H

This INCLUDE file contains all of the error handling constants required by the framework.

FRAMEWRK.H

This is the INCLUDE file that is #INCLUDEd in every program, class library, and form in the application. It #INCLUDEs all of the other necessary INCLUDE files for you. The constants in this file are used throughout the entire framework.

STRINGS.H

This file contains all strings that are used in the application.

DEBUG.TXT

This file does not have to contain anything. APPINCL.H includes the line:

```
#DEFINE DEBUGMODEFILE "DEBUG.TXT"
```

When DEBUGMODEFILE is found in the application root directory, a Codebook Framework-based application goes into DEBUG mode, forcing the creation of METADATA.DBF and adding a Utilities menu option so that the developer can use the trace, debug, command, or class browser windows.

PART 4

A Sample Application

Chapter 31

CDs R Us Enterprise Model

Introduction

In order to properly undertake any development effort, we must have an understanding of the *business* that we are working with. The Enterprise Model allows us to look at the business by asking all of the necessary questions: Who, What, Where, When, and Why.

Once we have an understanding of the general business (the Enterprise Model), the company can select a process for automation, if that is needed.

The following pages include a sample Enterprise Model.

CDs R Us
101 Old Long View Road
Suite 307
East Nutley, NJ 07023

CD Order Entry System

Enterprise Model

Yair Alan Griver
Flash Creative Management
Continental Plaza
433 Hackensack Ave.
12th Floor
Hackensack, NJ 07602
201-489-2500

Introduction

This document contains an Enterprise Model that describes CDs R Us from a number of perspectives. This model will be used to help management to focus on the changes required as the business grows, as well as to specify the order in which any required automation will take place. It, in essence, serves as a map for the future growth of the business. In order to build this road map, we use a modified version of Zachman's Information System Architecture which is explained below.

Through a number of meetings with management and other personnel, we have discussed each of the questions that has arisen through the use of the framework. The results are listed in this document.

The Information System Architecture

The ISA framework walks through a list of questions that allows us to picture the business and its information systems in all of its facets. We use the first two rows of the framework in order to capture business issues. This abbreviated version is listed below.

	What	**How**	**Where**	**Who**	**When**	**Why**
	Data	Function	Network	People	Time	Motivation
Objectives/ Scope	List of Important Business Things	List of Business Processes	List of Business Locations	List of Org. Units	List of Business Events/ Cycles	List of Business Goals/ Strategies
Business Model (Example)	Entity Relationship Diagram	Function Flow Diagram of Process Map	Logistics Network	Org. Chart	Master Schedule, PERT Chart	Business Plan

CDs R Us – Objectives/Scope

We began with *what* things are important to the business and continued from left to right across the row. The responses from the CD company owners follow.

Important Business Things List

Employees

Customers

Supplies

Catalogs

CDs

Sales Orders

Vendors

Business Processes

Making the catalog

Mailing the catalog

Monitoring the market

Shipping

Paying our bills

Inventory & ordering CDs

Ordering supplies

Managing relationships

Advertising

Accounting

Marketing

Business Locations

One location with one building/office

Organizational Units

Administration/Accounting

Marketing

Sales

Shipping

Business Events (Cycles)

1st Quarter - Recovery, restock, catalog by 4/1

2nd & 3rd Quarter - Sales pick up, prepare

4th Quarter - Holiday rush, catalog by 10/15, hire temp help

Business Goals

Best price/benefit for customers

Profitable & enjoyable business for employees

Reasonable growth without more locations

Increase revenues with automation efficiency

As we discussed in our meetings, it is appropriate to review the obvious because what is obvious may be different to two different people. For instance, by discussing the number of locations (*where*), even for a small business with only one location, we may discover plans to expand or the use of a vendor for packaging and shipping that effects the business and therefore the scope of any possible application. The *who*, *when,* and *why* lists help set boundaries on the business and any applications by capturing the number of employees, maximum load, and expected growth.

The above lists taken together give us a very complete sketch of the business. The next row of the framework focuses on turning that sketch into a clearer picture. We worked backwards (from right to left) across the second row turning our lists into more organized documents that we can discuss.

CDs R Us – Business Plan and Event Cycles

The meetings with management resulted in the creation of a business plan for the company, as well as an outline of four company-wide goals and supporting sub-goals for the year.

The business plan for CDs R Us company follows, along with a calendar for recording business events (cycles).

CD Company Business Plan, 1995	
Increase sales by 50 percent over last year	Implement marketing program Implement inventory strategy Automate order & inventory tracking
Increase profits to 20 percent of revenue	
Achieve 99 percent customer satisfaction	Implement quality program Liberalize return policy Automate customer service tracking
Achieve recognition as industry leader	

CD Company Monthly Planner	Events
January	Recover from holiday rush Restock inventory
February	Prepare catalog

CD Company Monthly Planner	Events
March	Mail catalog Financial information to bank
April	Catalog orders pick up
May	ASCAP Convention
June	Financial information to bank
July	Restock inventory
August	ASCAP Convention
September	Prepare holiday catalog Financial information to bank
October	Mail catalog Hire temporary help
November	Train temporary help
December	Holiday rush Financial information to bank

The Organizational Units and Logistics Network

Proceeding across row two to the left, the next two cells represent the organizational units in the company and the business locations. An "org chart" is a good way to represent the business units and is commonly recognized by business people.

A sample organizational chart

A logistics network is a way to show required workflow by location. This logistics network shows an idealized example of CDs coming from one supplier. Traditionally, a logistics network only deals with company locations, but it was felt that it made sense to include suppliers.

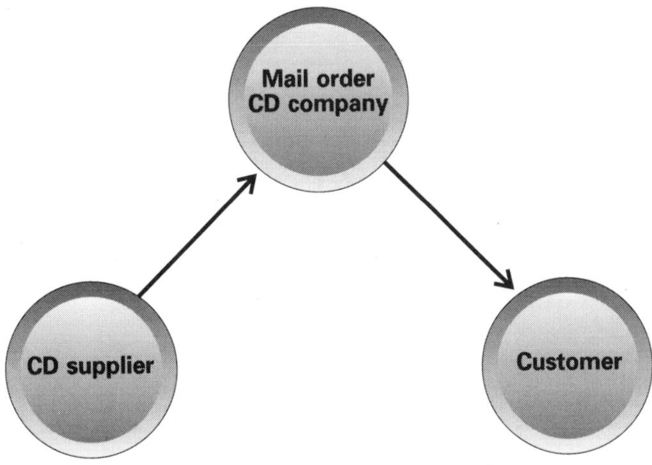

A logistics network

Entity Relationships and Process Maps

The last two cells (remember we are going right to left) show the major process maps for the company as well as an entity-relationship diagram, which shows the important business things, and how they connect.

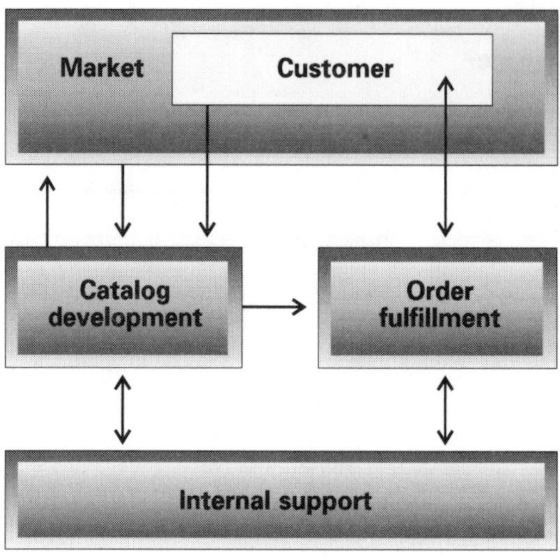

A process map

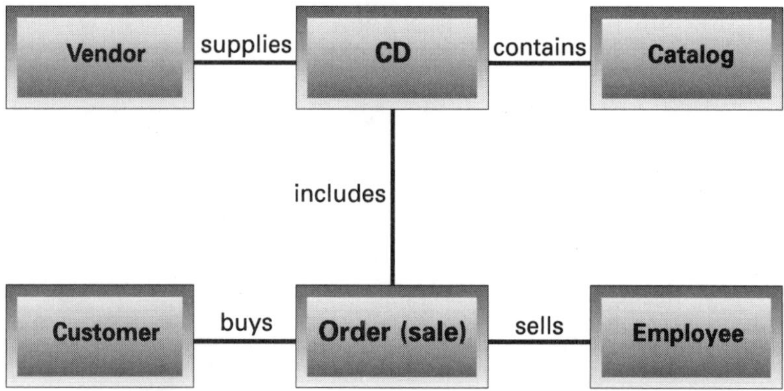

A high level Entity-Relationship diagram

The Conclusions

Upon reviewing the Enterprise Model, management has decided to make some workflow changes in the company, and has decided to begin automation with the *Order Fulfillment* process. Management feels that only through automation can the goals of a 50 percent sales increase as well as an ease of the holiday rush be achieved. Other automation projects may follow.

Chapter 32

Functional Analysis Document

Introduction

Once we have an understanding of the general business (the Enterprise Model), the company can select a process for automation, if that is needed.

Upon selection, a functional analysis is created, which includes process maps and use-case diagrams that show the business needs that have to be met. After the functional analysis is agreed upon, an iterative cycle of technical analysis, prototyping, and documentation is begun.

The following pages include a sample functional analysis document.

CDs R Us
101 Old Long View Road
Suite 307
East Nutley, NJ 07023

CD Order Entry System

Functional Analysis
Draft - September 12, 1995

Yair Alan Griver
Flash Creative Management
Continental Plaza
433 Hackensack Ave.
12th Floor
Hackensack, NJ 07602
201-489-2500

Overview

CDs R Us is in need of a new solution for processing orders and tracking their customers and products, and has engaged Flash Creative Management, Inc. to design, develop, and implement the system.

The purpose of this document is to outline and detail the needs of a CD Order Tracking System (CDTrak). System structure, architecture, and other such technical details are beyond the scope of this document and will be addressed in the next step in the process, the *technical specification.*

This document represents our understanding of the needs of CDs R Us and will be the basis for determining a proper design of the CDTrak System.

Flash Creative Management has been invited to develop a FoxPro-based software solution to replace the existing system. The new system will be used to track orders placed by telephone, and will enable printing of various reports. The new system will be a Microsoft Windows application, allowing a link between FoxPro and a word processor for printing mail-merge letters, and the capability to directly mail reports to various employees in the company.

Document Scope

A *functional analysis* is a review of the business requirements which will have to be addressed by the application to be developed. Although your group has begun this process, the functional analysis must be complete and exhaustive. The purpose of the functional analysis is to provide you and the development team with a proper basis for determining the business requirements and the functionality needed in a system to automate procedures.

Only once all agree about the requirements of the organization can the next phase, designing the system and developing a technical specification, be undertaken.

In accordance with these goals, Flash Creative Management met with management of CDs R Us. During the course of this meeting, we discussed the basis for current operations. We identified the information which the new system would have to store and how that data relates to the required functionality of the system.

Overview of Current Operations/Procedures

How an Order Is Processed

Currently, all orders are taken by phone and are processed. All orders are paid for by credit card at the time the order is placed. No other form of payment is accepted. If a credit card is refused, the order is not taken. The order is entered, the total price is calculated from the order, and the employee calls in for credit card verification. No shipping charge is added. After the order is taken, and verification is received, it is shipped out to the customer.

Product Management

A list of CDs currently carried by CDs R Us is kept for reference purposes. The data in this list contains the CD title, artist, and price. Availability is currently not tracked, if an item is not available at ship time, it is cross-shipped by a different vendor.

As CDs R Us is just a mail-order company, catalogs are sent to customers with product information. This is the only means of advertising and communication with the consumer. CDs R Us tracks customer ordering habits. A list is kept of all the CDs ordered by each customer. With this information, CDs R Us can target customers with catalogs aimed at their specific interests. CDs are not yet divided into individual categories, but this is something CDs R Us may want to implement in the future.

Current Hardware and Software Overview

CDs R Us is currently not computerized.

Statement of Goals

A new, multiuser automated system will be constructed to handle the ordering and tracking processes. Automated CD, customer, and ordering maintenance will be implemented, with corresponding specialized reports.

When an order is taken by phone, it will immediately be entered into the new system. To facilitate this process, customer and CD information will be readily available. The order total will be calculated automatically and stored with the rest of the order information. Customer information will be updated whenever an order is placed. As a result, all data will be current and available in specialized reports. Reports such as customer quarterly purchases, and product and customer listings will be available for analytical and forecasting purposes, as well as customer labels for mailing lists.

Problems and Needs in Current Operation

Currently there is no automated system and all orders and lists are maintained manually. As a result, the ordering process is extremely time consuming and leaves a wide margin for human error. Data is not readily available and extensive time is required to reference any information.

The mailing of catalogs is very difficult due to the hand-mailing that must currently take place. Having the system mail merge the current customer list with a catalog mailing will halve the time it takes to distribute a catalog, allowing CDs R Us to move to quarterly mailings.

Use Cases

Use cases detail each process that is done within the system. They provide an overview of the work performed by various people or groups of people. Each process is detailed further in the document.

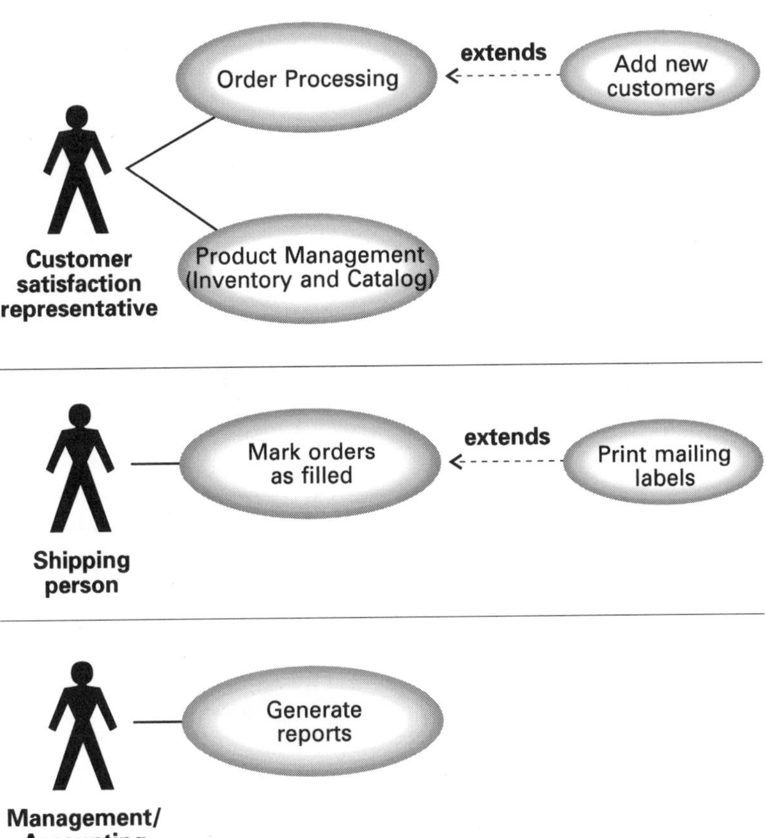

Process Models

The process models provide a graphical description of each of the processes described above.

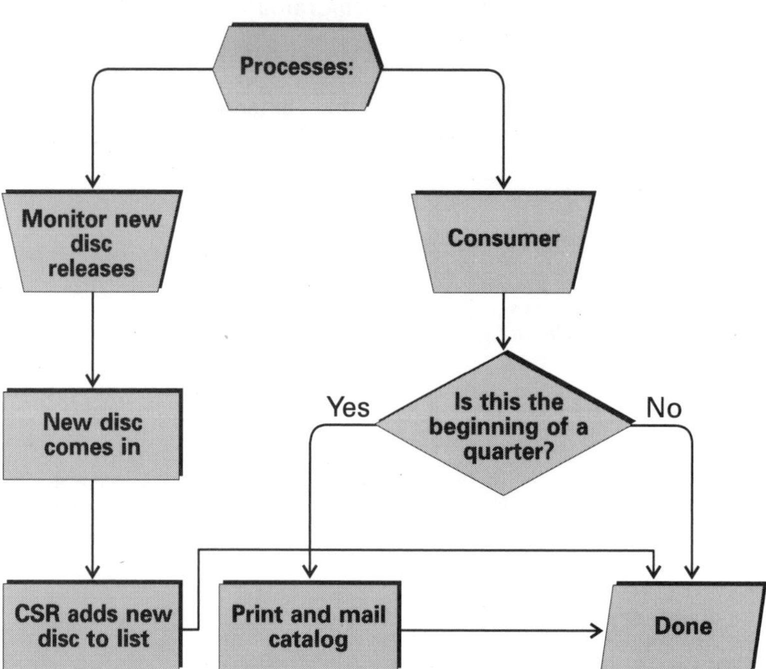

Order Processing

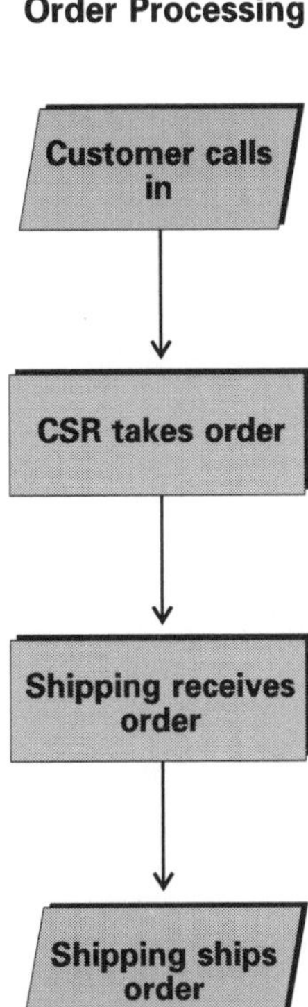

Functional Detail

The functional detail deals with the work flow and processes that will take place under the new CDTrak system.

Entry of Orders

When an order is phoned in by a new customer, the system will allow the customer satisfaction representative (CSR) to easily add that customer and a new order. If an existing customer has called in, the system will allow the CSR to quickly find that customer and enter the order or look at previous orders for that customer.

Mail Enabling

Any report that is created may be mailed to an employee via Microsoft Mail. When a report is directed to Mail, a list of employees will appear, allowing the user to select the recipients of the report. The report will then be sent out to those recipients automatically.

Please note that those employees with access to a fax/modem will be able to fax the reports directly from the Mail system as well.

Assumptions

Our understanding is that CDTrak does not have to track employee or supplier information. There is no current desire to track inventory, although that may be required in the future.

Work Responsibilities

Customer Satisfaction Representative

Take Customer Orders:

The customer satisfaction representative's responsibility is to receive customer phone orders and enter them into the system. Upon receiving a phone call, the following information will be entered:

Customer name

Invoice date

Invoice number (automatically generated)

Each compact disc's name

Each compact disc's quantity

Each compact disc's cost

The total price of the order will be calculated automatically by the system and displayed on the invoice entry screen.

The use case will be completed when the customer order has been entered into the system.

Add New Customers:

When a customer calls for the first time, the CSR will have the ability to enter all relevant customer information without first having to exit the invoice-entry process. Customer information will include:

Name

Address

City

State

Zip

Phone number

Once the customer information has been entered, the CSR will continue entering the remaining information on the invoice. The customer's name will not have to be reentered.

Send Out Catalog:

At the beginning of every quarter (January, April, July, October), the CSR group will create a new catalog from the current list of available CDs, and send a text file listing every customer to the mailing house so that the company can mail out the new catalog.

Shipping Person

Mark Orders As Filled:

The shipping person needs to mark orders that have been filled. This implies that the order has already been entered into the system, the shipping box has been filled with the appropriate materials, the mailing label has been printed and attached, and the box placed in a bin to be shipped.

Print Mailing Labels:

The shipping person should be able to print mailing labels for the current order being filled.

Management/Accounting

Generate Reports:

Management/accounting personnel need to be able to generate reports.

Outline of Plan

After the functional analysis is approved by CDs R Us, Flash Creative Management will proceed with the technical specification. The technical specification is a document which explicitly describes the functionality the new system will contain and includes iterative prototypes of the system. Once that is completed and approved, work on the actual system will begin.

Chapter 33

CDTRAK — OUR SAMPLE APPLICATION

Introduction

The upcoming chapters in the book go through the application-specific database, classes, programs, and reports that make up the CDTrak sample application. Once the Enterprise Model and Functional Analysis have been done, we move into a cycle of concurrent analysis, development, and prototyping while developing our system. As you'll see from the upcoming chapters, most of the code that is created is focused on the business processes with which we are working.

The CD Project

As always, work begins with the creation of an application-specific set of directories as discussed in Chapter 30, "The Codebook Framework—Putting It All Together." Once we have our directory structure in place, we create a project in the root directory, add a copy of MAIN.PRG (remember, this is the stub program to make our lives easier during testing) to the PROGS directory, and create a DEBUG.TXT file in the application root directory.

The CDBK30 Database

The CDTrak sample application works from local views, though the classes could just as easily work against a different type of data. As such, the DATAENV classes contain CURSOR subclassed definitions that use the local views in this database.

This database contains the application data. It is made up of tables, local views, and stored procedures which are described below.

Table	Description
CompactDisc	Contains compact disc inventory information.
Customer	Contains customer information.
Musician	Contains musician information.
Invoice	Contains invoice header information.
Purchase	Contains invoice detail information.

Table	Description
ID	Holds IDs used by the system—both primary keys and invoice numbers.

Local View	Description
lv_compactdisc	A view of the compact disc information.
lv_compact_disc_listing	A read-only view of the compact disc information used in a compact disc listing.
lv_customer	A view of the customer information.
lv_customerinvoice	A read-only view of the customer information used in invoice business objects.
lv_customer_listing	A read-only view of the customer information used for a customer listing.
lv_customer_orders	A read-only view of customer order information used for an invoice report.
lv_invoice	A view of the invoice information.
lv_markinvoice	A view of invoice shipping information.
lv_musician	A view of the musician information.
lv_purchase	A view of the purchase (invoice detail) information.
lv_purchase_history	A view of purchase history information used to generate 30/60/90 aging reports.

Stored Procedure	Description
NewID	Gets the next ID from the ID table and increments the ID table using IncrementBase62().
IncrementBase10	Increments a base 10 number.

Stored Procedure	Description
IncrementBase62	Increments a base 62 number. Unique IDs are stored as a base 62 number. In a 6-byte character string, this gives us 62^6 possible values. Since 62^6 is greater than the maximum number of records allowed in a FoxPro table (2 billion), we will never reach this limit. (Base 62 numbers include the following range of values: 0-9, A-Z, a-z.)
InvoiceDelete	Called from the Delete trigger for the Invoice table. Ensures that invoices that have shipped are not deleted.
InvoiceUpdate	Called from the Update trigger for the Invoice table. Ensures that invoices that have shipped are not updated.
PurchaseUpdate	Called from the Update trigger for the Purchase table. Ensures that invoice line items for invoices that have shipped are not updated.
RIDelete	This stored procedure is generated for us by the Visual FoxPro Referential Integrity Builder. This procedure deletes the current row.
RIUpdate	This stored procedure is generated for us by the Visual FoxPro Referential Integrity Builder. This procedure updates a field with a new value.
RIError	This stored procedure is generated for us by the Visual FoxPro Referential Integrity Builder. This procedure is the error handler for the RI code.

Stored Procedure	Description
RIOpen	This stored procedure is generated for us by the Visual FoxPro Referential Integrity Builder. This procedure opens a table for RI work.
RIEnd	This stored procedure is generated for us by the Visual FoxPro Referential Integrity Builder. This procedure ends our RI work with an END TRANSACTION or ROLLBACK and resets the state of the system.
RIReUse	This stored procedure is generated for us by the Visual FoxPro Referential Integrity Builder. This procedure sets up work areas for reuse.
__ri_delete_compactdisc	This stored procedure is generated for us by the Visual FoxPro Referential Integrity Builder. This is the RI code for the delete trigger of the compactdisc table.
__ri_delete_customer	This stored procedure is generated for us by the Visual FoxPro Referential Integrity Builder. This is the RI code for the delete trigger of the customer table.
__ri_delete_invoice	This stored procedure is generated for us by the Visual FoxPro Referential Integrity Builder. This is the RI code for the delete trigger of the invoice table.
__ri_delete_musician	This stored procedure is generated for us by the Visual FoxPro Referential Integrity Builder. This is the RI code for the delete trigger of the musician table.

Stored Procedure	Description
__ri_insert_compactdisc	This stored procedure is generated for us by the Visual FoxPro Referential Integrity Builder. This is the RI code for the insert trigger of the compactdisc table.
__ri_insert_invoice	This stored procedure is generated for us by the Visual FoxPro Referential Integrity Builder. This is the RI code for the insert trigger of the invoice table.
__ri_insert_purchase	This stored procedure is generated for us by the Visual FoxPro Referential Integrity Builder. This is the RI code for the insert trigger of the purchase table.
__ri_update_compactdisc	This stored procedure is generated for us by the Visual FoxPro Referential Integrity Builder. This is the RI code for the update trigger of the compactdisc table.
__ri_update_customer	This stored procedure is generated for us by the Visual FoxPro Referential Integrity Builder. This is the RI code for the update trigger of the customer table.
__ri_update_invoice	This stored procedure is generated for us by the Visual FoxPro Referential Integrity Builder. This is the RI code for the update trigger of the invoice table.
__ri_update_musician	This stored procedure is generated for us by the Visual FoxPro Referential Integrity Builder. This is the RI code for the update trigger of the musician table.

Stored Procedure	Description
__ri_update_purchase	This stored procedure is generated for us by the Visual FoxPro Referential Integrity Builder. This is the RI code for the update trigger of the purchase table.

```
Table    compactdisc
                  Path            cd.dbf
                  DeleteTrigger   __ri_delete_compactdisc()
                  UpdateTrigger   __ri_update_compactdisc()
                  InsertTrigger   __ri_insert_compactdisc()
                  PrimaryKey      cid
                  Comment         Compact Discs
  Index    delrec
  Index    ctitle
  Index    cid
  Index    cmusiciani
  Relation Relation 1
                  RelatedChild    cmusiciani
                  RelatedTable    musician
                  RelatedTag      cid
  Field    cid                    CID         C        6        0
                  Caption         Primary Key
                  DefaultValue    newid()
  Field    cmusicianid            CMUSICIANID C        6        0
                  Caption         Musician ID
  Field    ctitle                 CTITLE      C       45        0
                  Caption         Title
                  RuleExpression  .NOT.EMPTY(ctitle)
                  RuleText        "Must specify a title."
  Field    ycost                  YCOST       Y        8        4
                  Caption         Cost
                  DefaultValue    0
                  RuleExpression  ycost=>0
                  RuleText        "Cost cannot be less than zero."
  Field    yprice                 YPRICE      Y        8        4
                  Caption         Price
                  DefaultValue    0
                  RuleExpression  yprice=>ycost
                  RuleText        "Price must be greater than or
                                    equal to cost."
  Field    mdescription           MDESCRIPTIO M        4        0
                  Caption         Description
```

```
Table    customer
                    Path             customer.dbf
                    DeleteTrigger    __ri_delete_customer()
                    UpdateTrigger    __ri_update_customer()
                    PrimaryKey       cid
                    Comment          Customers
  Index    cfirstname
  Index    ccity
  Index    cstate
  Index    czip
  Index    cphone
  Index    clastname
  Index    cname
  Index    delrec
  Index    cid
  Field    cid                       CID         C       6        0
                    Caption          Primary Key
                    DefaultValue     newid()
  Field    cfirstname                CFIRSTNAME  C      15        0
                    Caption          First Name
  Field    clastname                 CLASTNAME   C      25        0
                    Caption          Last Name
                    RuleExpression   .NOT.EMPTY(clastname)
                    RuleText         "Last name cannot be empty."
  Field    caddress1                 CADDRESS1   C      40        0
                    Caption          Address 1
                    RuleExpression   .NOT.EMPTY(caddress1)
                    RuleText         "First address line cannot be
                                        empty."
  Field    caddress2                 CADDRESS2   C      40        0
                    Caption          Address 2
  Field    ccity                     CCITY       C      20        0
                    Caption          City
                    RuleExpression   .NOT.EMPTY(ccity)
                    RuleText         "City cannot be empty."
  Field    cstate                    CSTATE      C       2        0
                    Caption          State
                    RuleExpression   .NOT.EMPTY(cstate)
                    RuleText         "State cannot be empty."
  Field    czip                      CZIP        C       9        0
                    Caption          Zip
                    RuleExpression   .NOT.EMPTY(czip)
                    RuleText         "Zip code cannot be empty."
  Field    cphone                    CPHONE      C      10        0
                    Caption          Phone
```

```
Table    invoice
                    Path              invoice.dbf
                    DeleteTrigger     invoicedelete()
                                        .AND.__ri_delete_invoice()
                    UpdateTrigger     invoiceupdate()
                                        .AND.__ri_update_invoice()
                    InsertTrigger     __ri_insert_invoice()
                    PrimaryKey        cid
                    Comment           Invoices
  Index    delrec
  Index    cid
  Index    ccustomeri
  Relation Relation 1
                    RelatedChild      ccustomeri
                    RelatedTable      customer
                    RelatedTag        cid
  Index    lshipped
  Index    cinvoicenu
  Field    cid                        CID         C          6          0
                    Caption           Primary Key
                    DefaultValue      newid()
  Field    ccustomerid                CCUSTOMERID C          6          0
                    Caption           Customer ID
  Field    cinvoicenumber             CINVOICENUM C          6          0
                    Caption           Invoice Number
                    DefaultValue      newid("cinvoicenumber")
  Field    ddateordered               DDATEORDERE D          8          0
                    Caption           Date Ordered
                    RuleExpression    .NOT.EMPTY(ddateordered)
                    RuleText          "Date ordered cannot be empty."
  Field    lshipped                   LSHIPPED    L          1          0
```

```
Table    purchase
                    Path              purchase.dbf
                    UpdateTrigger
                       purchaseupdate().AND.__ri_update_purchase()
                    InsertTrigger     __ri_insert_purchase()
                    PrimaryKey        cid
                    Comment           Purchases
  Index    delrec
  Index    ccdid
  Index    cinvoiceid
  Index    cid
  Relation Relation 2
                    RelatedChild      ccdid
                    RelatedTable      compactdisc
                    RelatedTag        cid
  Relation Relation 1
                    RelatedChild      cinvoiceid
                    RelatedTable      invoice
                    RelatedTag        cid
  Field    cid                        CID         C          6          0
                    Caption           Primary Key
                    DefaultValue      newid()
```

```
  Field    cinvoiceid                          CINVOICEID  C        6          0
                    Caption                    Invoice ID
  Field    ccdid                               CCDID       C        6          0
                    Caption                    Compact Disc ID
  Field    ycdamount                           YCDAMOUNT   Y        8          4
                    Caption                    Amount
  Field    icdquantity                         ICDQUANTITY I        4          0
                    Caption                    Quantity
                    RuleExpression             icdquantity>0
                    RuleText                   "Quantity ordered cannot be
                                                 zero."
```

```
Table    id
                    Path                       id.dbf
                    Comment                    Holds ids for primary keys
                                                     and invoice numbers
  Index    keyname
  Field    keyname                             KEYNAME     C       20          0
  Field    value                               VALUE       C        6          0
  Field    incrementprocedure                  INCREMENTPR C       64          0
                    DefaultValue               "IncrementBase62(
                                                 RIGHT(id.value, id.maxlength))"
                    Comment                    Specifies stored procedure used
                                                 to increment the value.
  Field    maxlength                           MAXLENGTH   I        4          0
                    DefaultValue               LEN(value)
                    RuleExpression             maxlength<=LEN(value)
                    RuleText                   "Max length must be less than
                                                 or equal to the size of the
                                                 'value' field."
                    Comment                    The maximimun length of the
                                                 value.
```

```
Table    musician
                    Path                       musician.dbf
                    DeleteTrigger              __ri_delete_musician()
                    UpdateTrigger              __ri_update_musician()
                    PrimaryKey                 cid
                    Comment                    Musicians
  Index    cid
  Index    cname
  Field    cid                                 CID         C        6          0
                    Caption                    Primary Key
                    DefaultValue               newid()
  Field    cname                               CNAME       C       30          0
                    Caption                    Name
                    RuleExpression             .NOT.EMPTY(cname)
                    RuleText                   "Name cannot be empty."
```

```
View     lv_compact_disc_listing
                   UpdateType       1
                   WhereType        3
                   FetchMemo        1
                   CrsShareConnect  0
                   SendUpdates      0
                   UseMemoSize      255
                   FetchSize        100
                   CrsMaxRows       -1
                   Tables
                   SQL
                    SELECT Musician.cname, Compactdisc.ctitle,
                      Compactdisc.ycost,  Compactdisc.yprice,
                      Compactdisc.mdescription
                      FROM cdbk30!compactdisc, cdbk30!musician
                      WHERE Musician.cid = Compactdisc.cmusicianid
                      ORDER BY Musician.cname
                   SourceType       1
                   BatchUpdateCoun  1
  Field    cname
                   KeyField
                   Updatable        0
                   UpdateNameList   cdbk30!musician.cname
                   DataType         C(30)
  Field    ctitle
                   KeyField
                   Updatable        0
                   UpdateNameList   cdbk30!compactdisc.ctitle
                   DataType         C(45)
  Field    ycost
                   KeyField
                   Updatable        0
                   UpdateNameList   cdbk30!compactdisc.ycost
                   DataType         Y NOCPTRANS
  Field    yprice
                   KeyField
                   Updatable        0
                   UpdateNameList   cdbk30!compactdisc.yprice
                   DataType         Y NOCPTRANS
  Field    mdescription
                   KeyField
                   Updatable        0
                   UpdateNameList   cdbk30!compactdisc.mdescription
                   DataType         M
```

```
View     lv_customer_listing
                   UpdateType       1
                   WhereType        3
                   FetchMemo        1
                   CrsShareConnect 0
                   SendUpdates      1
                   UseMemoSize      255
                   FetchSize        100
                   CrsMaxRows       -1
                   Tables           cdbk30!customer
                   SQL
                     SELECT * FROM cdbk30!customer
                     ORDER BY Customer.clastname,
                     Customer.cfirstname
                   SourceType       1
                   BatchUpdateCoun 1
  Field    cid
                   KeyField
                   Updatable        0
                   UpdateNameList   cdbk30!customer.cid
                   DataType         C(6)
  Field    cfirstname
                   KeyField
                   Updatable        1
                   UpdateNameList   cdbk30!customer.cfirstname
                   DataType         C(15)
  Field    clastname
                   KeyField
                   Updatable        1
                   UpdateNameList   cdbk30!customer.clastname
                   DataType         C(25)
  Field    caddress1
                   KeyField
                   Updatable        1
                   UpdateNameList   cdbk30!customer.caddress1
                   DataType         C(40)
  Field    caddress2
                   KeyField
                   Updatable        1
                   UpdateNameList   cdbk30!customer.caddress2
                   DataType         C(40)
  Field    ccity
                   KeyField
                   Updatable        1
                   UpdateNameList   cdbk30!customer.ccity
                   DataType         C(20)
  Field    cstate
                   KeyField
                   Updatable        1
                   UpdateNameList   cdbk30!customer.cstate
                   DataType         C(2)
```

```
  Field    czip
                    KeyField
                    Updatable        1
                    UpdateNameList   cdbk30!customer.czip
                    DataType         C(9)
  Field    cphone
                    KeyField
                    Updatable        1
                    UpdateNameList   cdbk30!customer.cphone
                    DataType         C(10)
```

```
View     lv_customer_orders
                    UpdateType       1
                    WhereType        3
                    FetchMemo        1
                    CrsShareConnect  0
                    SendUpdates      0
                    UseMemoSize      255
                    FetchSize        100
                    CrsMaxRows       -1
                    Tables
                    SQL
                      SELECT Customer.clastname, Customer.cfirstname,
                      Musician.cname,  Purchase.ycdamount,
                      Invoice.ddateordered, Invoice.cinvoicenumber,
                      Compactdisc.ctitle, Purchase.icdquantity
                      FROM cdbk30!customer, cdbk30!invoice,
                      cdbk30!purchase, cdbk30!compactdisc,
                      cdbk30!musician
                      WHERE Customer.cid = Invoice.ccustomerid
                      AND Invoice.cid = Purchase.cinvoiceid
                      AND Compactdisc.cid = Purchase.ccdid
                      AND Musician.cid = Compactdisc.cmusicianid
                      ORDER BY Customer.clastname,
                      Customer.cfirstname, Invoice.cinvoicenumber,
                      Musician.cname, Compactdisc.ctitle
                    SourceType       1
                    BatchUpdateCoun  1
  Field    clastname
                    KeyField
                    Updatable        0
                    UpdateNameList   cdbk30!customer.clastname
                    DataType         C(25)
  Field    cfirstname
                    KeyField
                    Updatable        0
                    UpdateNameList   cdbk30!customer.cfirstname
                    DataType         C(15)
  Field    cname
                    KeyField
                    Updatable        0
                    UpdateNameList   cdbk30!musician.cname
                    DataType         C(30)
  Field    ycdamount
                    KeyField
                    Updatable        0
                    UpdateNameList   cdbk30!purchase.ycdamount
                    DataType         Y NOCPTRANS
```

```
Field     ddateordered
                   KeyField
                   Updatable          0
                   UpdateNameList     cdbk30!invoice.ddateordered
                   DataType           D
Field     cinvoicenumber
                   KeyField
                   Updatable          0
                   UpdateNameList     cdbk30!invoice.cinvoicenumber
                   DataType           C(6)
Field     ctitle
                   KeyField
                   Updatable          0
                   UpdateNameList     cdbk30!compactdisc.ctitle
                   DataType           C(45)
Field     icdquantity
                   KeyField
                   Updatable          0
                   UpdateNameList     cdbk30!purchase.icdquantity
                   DataType           I NOCPTRANS
```

```
View      lv_customerinvoice
                   UpdateType         1
                   WhereType          3
                   FetchMemo          1
                   CrsShareConnect    0
                   SendUpdates        0
                   UseMemoSize        255
                   FetchSize          100
                   CrsMaxRows         -1
                   Tables
                   SQL
                     SELECT * FROM cdbk30!customer
                     WHERE Customer.cid = ?vp_ccustomerid
                   SourceType         1
                   ParameterList      vp_ccustomerid,'C'
                   BatchUpdateCoun    1
  Field     cid
                   KeyField
                   Updatable          0
                   UpdateNameList     cdbk30!customer.cid
                   DataType           C(6)
  Field     cfirstname
                   KeyField
                   Updatable          0
                   UpdateNameList     cdbk30!customer.cfirstname
                   DataType           C(15)
  Field     clastname
                   KeyField
                   Updatable          0
                   UpdateNameList     cdbk30!customer.clastname
                   DataType           C(25)
  Field     caddress1
                   KeyField
                   Updatable          0
                   UpdateNameList     cdbk30!customer.caddress1
                   DataType           C(40)
```

```
  Field    caddress2
                    KeyField
                    Updatable        0
                    UpdateNameList   cdbk30!customer.caddress2
                    DataType         C(40)
  Field    ccity
                    KeyField
                    Updatable        0
                    UpdateNameList   cdbk30!customer.ccity
                    DataType         C(20)
  Field    cstate
                    KeyField
                    Updatable        0
                    UpdateNameList   cdbk30!customer.cstate
                    DataType         C(2)
  Field    czip
                    KeyField
                    Updatable        0
                    UpdateNameList   cdbk30!customer.czip
                    DataType         C(9)
  Field    cphone
                    KeyField
                    Updatable        0
                    UpdateNameList   cdbk30!customer.cphone
                    DataType         C(10)
```

```
View     lv_invoice
                    UpdateType       1
                    WhereType        3
                    FetchMemo        1
                    CrsShareConnect  0
                    SendUpdates      1
                    UseMemoSize      255
                    FetchSize        100
                    CrsMaxRows       -1
                    Tables           cdbk30!invoice
                    SQL
                      SELECT Invoice.*,
                      SUM(Purchase.ycdamount * Purchase.icdquantity)
                      as ninvoicetotal,  .T. as lsaved
                      FROM cdbk30!invoice, cdbk30!purchase
                      WHERE Invoice.cid = Purchase.cinvoiceid
                      AND Invoice.ccustomerid = ?vp_ccustomerid
                      GROUP BY Invoice.cid
                    SourceType       1
                    ParameterList    vp_ccustomerid,'C'
                    BatchUpdateCoun 1
  Field    cid
                    KeyField
                    Updatable        1
                    UpdateNameList   cdbk30!invoice.cid
                    DataType         C(6)
  Field    ccustomerid
                    KeyField
                    Updatable        1
                    UpdateNameList   cdbk30!invoice.ccustomerid
                    DataType         C(6)
```

```
  Field    cinvoicenumber
                  KeyField
                  Updatable        1
                  UpdateNameList   cdbk30!invoice.cinvoicenumber
                  DataType         C(6)
  Field    ddateordered
                  KeyField
                  Updatable        1
                  UpdateNameList   cdbk30!invoice.ddateordered
                  DataType         D
  Field    lshipped
                  KeyField
                  Updatable        1
                  UpdateNameList   cdbk30!invoice.lshipped
                  DataType         L
  Field    ninvoicetotal
                  KeyField
                  Updatable        0
                  UpdateNameList   ninvoicetotal
                  DataType         Y NOCPTRANS
  Field    lsaved
                  KeyField
                  Updatable        0
                  UpdateNameList   lsaved
                  DataType         L
```

```
View     lv_markinvoice
                  UpdateType       1
                  WhereType        3
                  FetchMemo        1
                  CrsShareConnect 0
                  SendUpdates      1
                  UseMemoSize      255
                  FetchSize        100
                  CrsMaxRows       -1
                  Tables           cdbk30!invoice
                  SQL
                    SELECT Invoice.cid, Invoice.cinvoicenumber,
                    Customer.clastname,  Customer.cfirstname,
                    Invoice.ddateordered, Invoice.lshipped,
                    SUM(Purchase.ycdamount*Purchase.icdquantity)
                    as ninvoicetotal
                    FROM cdbk30!invoice, cdbk30!customer,
                    cdbk30!purchase
                    WHERE Customer.cid = Invoice.ccustomerid
                    AND Invoice.cid = Purchase.cinvoiceid
                    AND (Customer.clastname = ?vp_clastname
                    AND Invoice.lshipped = .F.)
                    GROUP BY Invoice.cid
                  SourceType       1
                  ParameterList    vp_clastname,'C'
                  BatchUpdateCoun 1
  Field    cid
                  KeyField
                  Updatable        0
                  UpdateNameList   cdbk30!invoice.cid
                  DataType         C(6)
```

```
  Field    cinvoicenumber
                     KeyField
                     Updatable        0
                     UpdateNameList   cdbk30!invoice.cinvoicenumber
                     DataType         C(6)
  Field    clastname
                     KeyField
                     Updatable        0
                     UpdateNameList   cdbk30!customer.clastname
                     DataType         C(25)
  Field    cfirstname
                     KeyField
                     Updatable        0
                     UpdateNameList   cdbk30!customer.cfirstname
                     DataType         C(15)
  Field    ddateordered
                     KeyField
                     Updatable        0
                     UpdateNameList   cdbk30!invoice.ddateordered
                     DataType         D
  Field    lshipped
                     KeyField
                     Updatable        1
                     UpdateNameList   cdbk30!invoice.lshipped
                     DataType         L
  Field    ninvoicetotal
                     KeyField
                     Updatable        0
                     UpdateNameList   ninvoicetotal
                     DataType         Y NOCPTRANS
```

```
View     lv_musician
                     UpdateType       1
                     WhereType        3
                     FetchMemo        1
                     CrsShareConnect 0
                     SendUpdates      1
                     UseMemoSize      255
                     FetchSize        100
                     CrsMaxRows       -1
                     Tables           cdbk30!musician
                     SQL
                       SELECT * FROM cdbk30!musician
                       WHERE Musician.cname = ?vp_cname
                       ORDER BY Musician.cname
                     SourceType       1
                     ParameterList    vp_cname,'C'
                     BatchUpdateCoun 1
  Field    cid
                     KeyField
                     Updatable        1
                     UpdateNameList   cdbk30!musician.cid
                     DataType         C(6)
  Field    cname
                     KeyField
                     Updatable        1
                     UpdateNameList   cdbk30!musician.cname
                     DataType         C(30)
```

```
View     lv_purchase
                    UpdateType      1
                    WhereType       3
                    FetchMemo       1
                    CrsShareConnect 0
                    SendUpdates     1
                    UseMemoSize     255
                    FetchSize       100
                    CrsMaxRows      -1
                    Tables          cdbk30!purchase
                    SQL
                      SELECT Purchase.*, Compactdisc.ctitle,
                      Musician.cname
                      FROM cdbk30!purchase, cdbk30!compactdisc,
                      cdbk30!musician
                      WHERE Purchase.ccdid = Compactdisc.cid
                      AND Compactdisc.cmusicianid = Musician.cid
                      AND Purchase.cinvoiceid = ?v_invoice.cid
                    SourceType      1
                    ParameterList   v_invoice,'C'
                    BatchUpdateCoun 1
  Field    cid
                    KeyField
                    Updatable       1
                    UpdateNameList  cdbk30!purchase.cid
                    DataType        C(6)
  Field    cinvoiceid
                    KeyField
                    Updatable       1
                    UpdateNameList  cdbk30!purchase.cinvoiceid
                    DataType        C(6)
  Field    ccdid
                    KeyField
                    Updatable       1
                    UpdateNameList  cdbk30!purchase.ccdid
                    DataType        C(6)
  Field    ycdamount
                    KeyField
                    Updatable       1
                    UpdateNameList  cdbk30!purchase.ycdamount
                    DataType        Y NOCPTRANS
  Field    icdquantity
                    KeyField
                    Updatable       1
                    UpdateNameList  cdbk30!purchase.icdquantity
                    DataType        I NOCPTRANS
  Field    ctitle
                    KeyField
                    Updatable       0
                    UpdateNameList  cdbk30!compactdisc.ctitle
                    DataType        C(45)
  Field    cname
                    KeyField
                    Updatable       0
                    UpdateNameList  cdbk30!musician.cname
                    DataType        C(30)
```

```
View     lv_customer
                    UpdateType       1
                    WhereType        3
                    FetchMemo        1
                    CrsShareConnect 0
                    SendUpdates      1
                    UseMemoSize      255
                    FetchSize        100
                    CrsMaxRows       -1
                    Tables           cdbk30!customer
                    SQL
                      SELECT * FROM cdbk30!customer
                      WHERE Customer.clastname = ?vp_clastname
                      AND Customer.cstate = ?vp_cstate
                      AND Customer.czip = ?vp_czip
                      AND Customer.cphone = ?vp_cphone
                      ORDER BY Customer.clastname
                    SourceType       1
                    ParameterList    vp_clastname,'C';
                                     vp_cstate,'C';
                                     vp_czip,'C';
                                     vp_cphone,'C'
                    BatchUpdateCoun 1
  Field    cid
                    KeyField
                    Updatable        1
                    UpdateNameList   cdbk30!customer.cid
                    DataType         C(6)
  Field    cfirstname
                    KeyField
                    Updatable        1
                    UpdateNameList   cdbk30!customer.cfirstname
                    DataType         C(15)
  Field    clastname
                    KeyField
                    Updatable        1
                    UpdateNameList   cdbk30!customer.clastname
                    DataType         C(25)
  Field    caddress1
                    KeyField
                    Updatable        1
                    UpdateNameList   cdbk30!customer.caddress1
                    DataType         C(40)
  Field    caddress2
                    KeyField
                    Updatable        1
                    UpdateNameList   cdbk30!customer.caddress2
                    DataType         C(40)
  Field    ccity
                    KeyField
                    Updatable        1
                    UpdateNameList   cdbk30!customer.ccity
                    DataType         C(20)
```

```
  Field    cstate
                    KeyField
                    Updatable       1
                    UpdateNameList  cdbk30!customer.cstate
                    DataType        C(2)
  Field    czip
                    KeyField
                    Updatable       1
                    UpdateNameList  cdbk30!customer.czip
                    DataType        C(9)
  Field    cphone
                    KeyField
                    Updatable       1
                    UpdateNameList  cdbk30!customer.cphone
                    DataType        C(10)
```

```
View     lv_compactdisc
                    UpdateType      1
                    WhereType       3
                    FetchMemo       1
                    CrsShareConnect 0
                    SendUpdates     1
                    UseMemoSize     255
                    FetchSize       100
                    CrsMaxRows      -1
                    Tables          cdbk30!compactdisc
                    SQL
                      SELECT Compactdisc.*, Musician.cname
                      FROM cdbk30!compactdisc, cdbk30!musician
                      WHERE Musician.cid = Compactdisc.cmusicianid
                      AND (Musician.cname = ?vp_cname
                      AND Compactdisc.ctitle = ?vp_ctitle
                      AND Compactdisc.ycost > ?vp_ycost)
                      ORDER BY Compactdisc.ctitle
                    SourceType      1
                    ParameterList   vp_cname,'C';
                                    vp_ctitle,'C';
                                    vp_ycost,'Y'
                    BatchUpdateCoun 1
  Field    cid
                    KeyField
                    Updatable       1
                    UpdateNameList  cdbk30!compactdisc.cid
                    DataType        C(6)
  Field    cmusicianid
                    KeyField
                    Updatable       1
                    UpdateNameList  cdbk30!compactdisc.cmusicianid
                    DataType        C(6)
  Field    ctitle
                    KeyField
                    Updatable       1
                    UpdateNameList  cdbk30!compactdisc.ctitle
                    DataType        C(45)
```

```
  Field     ycost
                 KeyField
                 Updatable        1
                 UpdateNameList   cdbk30!compactdisc.ycost
                 DataType         Y NOCPTRANS
  Field     yprice
                 KeyField
                 Updatable        1
                 UpdateNameList   cdbk30!compactdisc.yprice
                 DataType         Y NOCPTRANS
  Field     mdescription
                 KeyField
                 Updatable        1
                 UpdateNameList   cdbk30!compactdisc.mdescription
                 DataType         M
  Field     cname
                 KeyField
                 Updatable        0
                 UpdateNameList   cdbk30!musician.cname
                 DataType         C(30)
```

```
View      lv_purchase_history
                 UpdateType       1
                 WhereType        3
                 FetchMemo        1
                 CrsShareConnect  0
                 SendUpdates      0
                 UseMemoSize      255
                 FetchSize        100
                 CrsMaxRows       -1
                 Tables
                 SQL
                   SELECT ALLTRIM(Customer.clastname)+","
                   +ALLTRIM(Customer.cfirstname),
                   DATE()-Invoice.ddateordered,
                   SUM(Purchase.ycdamount*Purchase.icdquantity)
                   FROM cdbk30!customer, cdbk30!invoice,
                   cdbk30!purchase
                   WHERE Customer.cid = Invoice.ccustomerid
                   AND Invoice.cid = Purchase.cinvoiceid
                   GROUP BY Invoice.cid
                 SourceType       1
                 BatchUpdateCoun  1
  Field     exp_1
                 KeyField
                 Updatable        0
                 UpdateNameList   exp_1
                 DataType         C(42)
  Field     exp_2
                 KeyField
                 Updatable        0
                 UpdateNameList   exp_2
                 DataType         N(10)
  Field     sum_exp_3
                 KeyField
                 Updatable        0
                 UpdateNameList   sum_exp_3
                 DataType         Y NOCPTRANS
```

```
** Stored Procedures
#INCLUDE "..\COMMON30\INCLUDE\FRAMEWRK.H"

FUNCTION NewID(tcAlias)
  LOCAL lcAlias, ;
        lcID, ;
        lnOldReprocess, ;
        lnOldArea

  lnOldArea = SELECT()

  IF PARAMETERS() < 1
    lcAlias = ALIAS()
    IF CURSORGETPROP("SOURCETYPE") = DB_SRCLOCALVIEW
      *-- Attempt to get base table
      lcAlias = UPPER(CURSORGETPROP("TABLES"))
      lcAlias = SUBSTR(lcAlias, AT("!", lcAlias) + 1)
    ENDIF
  ELSE
    lcAlias = UPPER(tcAlias)
  ENDIF

  lcID = ""
  lnOldReprocess = SET('REPROCESS')

  *-- Lock until user presses Esc
  SET REPROCESS TO AUTOMATIC

  IF !USED("id")
    USE id IN 0
  ENDIF
  SELECT id

  IF SEEK(lcAlias, "id", "keyname")
    IF RLOCK()
      lcID = id.value
      REPLACE id.value WITH EVAL(id.IncrementProcedure)
      UNLOCK
    ENDIF
  ENDIF

  SELECT (lnOldArea)
  SET REPROCESS TO lnOldReprocess

  RETURN lcID
ENDFUNC

FUNCTION IncrementBase62(tcValue)
  *-- Unique ID's are stored as a base 62 number. In a 6-byte
  *-- character string, this gives us 62^6 possible values. Since
  *-- 62^6 is greater than the maximum number of records allowed
  *-- in a Foxpro table (2 billion), we will never reach this limit.
  *-- Base 62 numbers include the following range of values:
  *-- '0' - '9'
  *-- 'A' - 'Z'
  *-- 'a' - 'z'
```

```
  *-- Top value of each range
  #DEFINE NINE      57       && ASC('9')
  #DEFINE CAP_Z     90       && ASC('Z')
  #DEFINE LOW_Z     122      && ASC('z')

  LOCAL lnDigit, ;
        lnStringLength, ;
        lnChar, ;
        lcChar, ;
        lcID, ;
        lcValue

  lcValue = tcValue
  lcID = ""

  *-- Loop backwards through the string only as
  *-- many times as necessary to increment the value.
  lnStringLength = LEN(lcValue)
  FOR lnDigit = lnStringLength TO 1 STEP -1
    lnChar = ASC(SUBSTR(lcValue, lnDigit, 1))
    IF lnChar = LOW_Z
      *-- Make the char "0". We'll need to loop again.
      lcValue = LEFT(lcValue, lnDigit - 1) + ;
              "0" + ;
              RIGHT(lcValue, lnStringLength - lnDigit)
    ELSE
      *-- Figure out new value of lcChar. We'll automatically
      *-- exit the loop since no other chars have to be
      *-- incremented.
      DO CASE
        CASE lnChar = NINE
          lcChar = 'A'
        CASE lnChar = CAP_Z
          lcChar = 'a'
        CASE lnChar = KEY_SPACE
          lcChar = '1'
        OTHERWISE
          lcChar = CHR(lnChar + 1)
      ENDCASE
      lcID = LEFT(lcValue, lnDigit - 1) + ;
              lcChar + ;
              RIGHT(lcValue, lnStringLength - lnDigit)
      EXIT
    ENDIF
  ENDFOR

  *-- If lcID is empty, then we have reached the maximum allowable
  *-- value, so replace everything with zeros.
  IF EMPTY(lcID)
    lcID = REPLICATE("0", lnStringLength - 1) + "1"
  ENDIF

  RETURN lcID
ENDFUNC

FUNCTION IncrementBase10(tcValue)
  *-- Increments a base 10 number. This function assumes that
  *-- the length of tcValue represents the maximum number of
```

```
  *-- possible digits for this base 10 number.
  LOCAL lnStringLength
  lnStringLength = LEN(tcValue)
  RETURN PADL(RIGHT(ALLT(STR(VAL(tcValue) + 1)),
lnStringLength), lnStringLength)
ENDFUNC

FUNCTION InvoiceDelete()
  *-- Called from the Delete trigger for the Invoice table. Ensures
  *-- that invoices that have shipped are not deleted.
  RETURN !invoice.lShipped
ENDFUNC

FUNCTION InvoiceUpdate()
  *-- Called from the Update trigger for the Invoice table. Ensures
  *-- that invoices that have shipped are not updated.
  RETURN !OLDVAL("lShipped")
ENDFUNC

FUNCTION PurchaseUpdate()
  *-- Called from the Update trigger for the Purchase table. Ensures
  *-- that invoice line items for invoices that have shipped are not
  *-- updated.
  LOCAL llCloseInvoice, ;
        llRetVal

  llCloseInvoice = !USED("invoice")

  IF llCloseInvoice
    USE invoice IN 0
  ENDIF

  IF invoice.cid <> purchase.cinvoiceid
    =SEEK(purchase.cinvoiceid, "invoice", "cid")
  ENDIF

  llRetVal = !OLDVAL("lShipped", "invoice")

  IF llCloseInvoice
    USE IN invoice
  ENDIF

  RETURN llRetVal
ENDFUNC

**__RI_HEADER!@ Do NOT REMOVE or MODIFY this line!!!! @!__RI_HEADER**
procedure RIDELETE
* ridelete.prg
local llRetVal
llRetVal=.t.
  IF (UPPER(SYS(2011))="RECORD LOCKED" and !deleted()) OR !RLOCK()
    llRetVal=.F.
  ELSE
    IF !deleted()
      DELETE
      UNLOCK RECORD (RECNO())
      llRetVal=pnerror=0
    ENDIF not already deleted
```

```
  ENDIF
return llRetVal

procedure RIUPDATE
* riupdate
parameters tcFieldName,tcNewValue
local llRetVal
llRetVal=.t.
  IF UPPER(SYS(2011))="RECORD LOCKED" OR !RLOCK()
    llRetVal=.F.
  ELSE
    IF EVAL(tcFieldName)<>tcNewValue
      REPLACE (tcFieldName) WITH tcNewValue
      UNLOCK RECORD (RECNO())
      llRetVal=pnerror=0
    ENDIF not already deleted
  ENDIF
return llRetVal

procedure rierror
parameters tnErrNo,tcMessage,tcCode,tcProgram
local lnErrorRows,lnXX
lnErrorRows=alen(gaErrors,1)
if type('gaErrors[lnErrorRows,1]')<>"L"
  dimension gaErrors[lnErrorRows+1,alen(gaErrors,2)]
  lnErrorRows=lnErrorRows+1
endif
gaErrors[lnErrorRows,1]=tnErrNo
gaErrors[lnErrorRows,2]=tcMessage
gaErrors[lnErrorRows,3]=tcCode
gaErrors[lnErrorRows,4]=""
lnXX=1
do while !empty(program(lnXX))
  gaErrors[lnErrorRows,4]=gaErrors[lnErrorRows,4]+","+;
  program(lnXX)
  lnXX=lnXX+1
enddo
gaErrors[lnErrorRows,5]=pcParentDBF
gaErrors[lnErrorRows,6]=pnParentRec
gaErrors[lnErrorRows,7]=pcParentID
gaErrors[lnErrorRows,8]=pcParentExpr
gaErrors[lnErrorRows,9]=pcChildDBF
gaErrors[lnErrorRows,10]=pnChildRec
gaErrors[lnErrorRows,11]=pcChildID
gaErrors[lnErrorRows,12]=pcChildExpr
*=messagebox(str(tnErrNo)+""+ ;
*tcMessage+chr(13)+tcCode+chr(13)+tcProgram)
return tnErrNo


PROCEDURE riopen
PARAMETERS tcTable,tcOrder
local lcCurWkArea,lcNewWkArea,lnInUseSpot
lnInUseSpot=atc(tcTable+"*",pcRIcursors)
IF lnInUseSpot=0
  lcCurWkArea=select()
  SELECT 0
  lcNewWkArea=select()
  IF NOT EMPTY(tcOrder)
```

```
    USE (tcTable) AGAIN ORDER (tcOrder) ;
      ALIAS ("__ri"+LTRIM(STR(SELECT()))) share
  ELSE
    USE (tcTable) AGAIN ALIAS ("__ri"+LTRIM(STR(SELECT()))) share
  ENDIF
  if pnerror=0
    pcRIcursors=pcRIcursors+upper(tcTable)+"?"+STR(SELECT(),5)
  else
    lcNewWkArea=0
  endif something bad happened while attempting to open the file
ELSE
  lcNewWkArea=val(substr(pcRIcursors,lnInUseSpot+len(tcTable)+1,5))
  pcRIcursors = ;
    strtran(pcRIcursors,upper(tcTable)+"*"+str(lcNewWkArea,5),;
    upper(tcTable)+"?"+str(lcNewWkArea,5))
  IF NOT EMPTY(tcOrder)
    SET ORDER TO (tcOrder) IN (lcNewWkArea)
  ENDIF sent an order
  if pnerror<>0
    lcNewWkArea=0
  endif something bad happened while setting order
ENDIF
RETURN (lcNewWkArea)


PROCEDURE riend
PARAMETERS tlSuccess
local lnXX,lnSpot,lcWorkArea
IF tlSuccess
  END TRANSACTION
ELSE
  SET DELETED OFF
  ROLLBACK
  SET DELETED ON
ENDIF
IF EMPTY(pcRIolderror)
  ON ERROR
ELSE
  ON ERROR &pcRIolderror.
ENDIF
FOR lnXX=1 TO occurs("*",pcRIcursors)
  lnSpot=atc("*",pcRIcursors,lnXX)+1
  USE IN (VAL(substr(pcRIcursors,lnSpot,5)))
ENDFOR
IF pcOldDele="OFF"
  SET DELETED OFF
ENDIF
IF pcOldExact="ON"
  SET EXACT ON
ENDIF
IF pcOldTalk="ON"
  SET TALK ON
ENDIF
RETURN .T.


PROCEDURE rireuse
* rireuse.prg
```

```
PARAMETERS tcTableName,tcWkArea
pcRIcursors = ;
  strtran(pcRIcursors,upper(tcTableName)+"?"+str(tcWkArea,5),;
  upper(tcTableName)+"*"+str(tcWkArea,5))
RETURN .t.

************************************************************************
** Referential integrity delete trigger for compactdisc
PROCEDURE __RI_DELETE_compactdisc
LOCAL llRetVal
llRetVal = .t.
IF _triggerlevel=1
  BEGIN TRANSACTION
  PRIVATE pcRIcursors,pcRIwkareas,pcRIolderror,pnerror,;
  pcOldDele,pcOldExact,pcOldTalk
  pcOldTalk=SET("TALK")
  SET TALK OFF
  pcOldDele=SET("DELETED")
  pcOldExact=SET("EXACT")
  SET DELETED ON
  SET EXACT OFF
  pcRIcursors=""
  pcRIwkareas=""
  pcRIolderror=ON("error")
  pnerror=0
  ON ERROR pnerror=rierror(ERROR(),message(),message(1),program())
  IF TYPE('gaErrors(1)')<>"U"
    release gaErrors
  ENDIF
  PUBLIC gaErrors(1,12)
ENDIF first trigger
PRIVATE pcParentDBF,pnParentRec,pcChildDBF,pnChildRec,
PRIVATE pcParentID,pcChildID
PRIVATE pcParentExpr,pcChildExpr
STORE "" TO ;
  pcParentDBF,pcChildDBF,pcParentID,pcChildID,pcParentExpr,pcChildExpr
STORE 0 TO pnParentRec,pnChildRec
LOCAL lcParentID && parent's value to be sought in child
LOCAL lcChildWkArea && child work area handle returned by riopen
LOCAL lcParentWkArea
LOCAL llDelHeaderarea
lcStartArea=select()
llRetVal=.t.
lcParentWkArea=select()
SELECT (lcParentWkArea)
pcParentDBF=dbf()
pnParentRec=recno()
STORE CID TO lcParentID,pcParentID
pcParentExpr="CID"
lcChildWkArea=riopen("purchase","ccdid")
IF lcChildWkArea<=0
  IF _triggerlevel=1
    DO riend WITH .F.
  ENDIF at the end of the highest trigger level
  RETURN .F.
ENDIF not able to open the child work area
pcChildDBF=dbf(lcChildWkArea)
llRetVal=!SEEK(lcParentID,lcChildWkArea)
SELECT (lcChildWkArea)
```

```
pnChildRec=recno()
pcChildID=CCDID
pcChildExpr="CCDID"
IF !llRetVal
  DO rierror with -1,"Delete restrict rule violated.","",""
ENDIF
=rireuse("purchase",lcChildWkArea)
IF NOT llRetVal
  IF _triggerlevel=1
    DO riend WITH llRetVal
  ENDIF at the end of the highest trigger level
  SELECT (lcStartArea)
  RETURN llRetVal
ENDIF
IF _triggerlevel=1
  do riend with llRetVal
ENDIF at the end of the highest trigger level
SELECT (lcStartArea)
RETURN llRetVal
** End of Referential integrity Delete trigger for compactdisc
**********************************************************************

**********************************************************************
procedure __RI_UPDATE_compactdisc
** Referential integrity update trigger for compactdisc
LOCAL llRetVal
llRetVal = .t.
IF _triggerlevel=1
  BEGIN TRANSACTION
  PRIVATE pcRIcursors,pcRIwkareas,pcRIolderror,pnerror,;
  pcOldDele,pcOldExact,pcOldTalk
  pcOldTalk=SET("TALK")
  SET TALK OFF
  pcOldDele=SET("DELETED")
  pcOldExact=SET("EXACT")
  SET DELETED ON
  SET EXACT OFF
  pcRIcursors=""
  pcRIwkareas=""
  pcRIolderror=ON("error")
  pnerror=0
  ON ERROR pnerror=rierror(ERROR(),message(),message(1),program())
  IF TYPE('gaErrors(1)')<>"U"
    release gaErrors
  ENDIF
  PUBLIC gaErrors(1,12)
ENDIF first trigger
PRIVATE pcParentDBF,pnParentRec,pcChildDBF,pnChildRec
PRIVATE pcParentID,pcChildID
PRIVATE pcParentExpr,pcChildExpr
STORE "" TO ;
  pcParentDBF,pcChildDBF,pcParentID,pcChildID,pcParentExpr,pcChildExpr
STORE 0 TO pnParentRec,pnChildRec
LOCAL lcParentID && parent's value to be sought in child
LOCAL lcOldParentID && previous parent id value
LOCAL lcChildWkArea && child work area handle returned by riopen
LOCAL lcChildID && child's value to be sought in parent
LOCAL lcOldChildID && old child id value
```

```
LOCAL lcParentWkArea && parentwork area handle returned by riopen
LOCAL lcStartArea
lcStartArea=select()
llRetVal=.t.
lcChildWkArea=select()
IF _triggerlevel=1
  SELECT (lcChildWkArea)
  lcChildID=CMUSICIANID
  lcOldChildID=oldval("CMUSICIANID")
  pcChildDBF=dbf(lcChildWkArea)
  pnChildRec=recno(lcChildWkArea)
  pcChildID=lcOldChildID
  pcChildExpr="CMUSICIANID"
  IF lcChildID<>lcOldChildID
    lcParentWkArea=riopen("musician","cid")
    IF lcParentWkArea<=0
      IF _triggerlevel=1
        DO riend WITH .F.
      ENDIF at the end of the highest trigger level
      SELECT (lcStartArea)
      RETURN .F.
    ENDIF not able to open the child work area
    pcParentDBF=dbf(lcParentWkArea)
    llRetVal=SEEK(lcChildID,lcParentWkArea)
    pnParentRec=recno(lcParentWkArea)
    =rireuse("musician",lcParentWkArea)
    IF NOT llRetVal
      DO rierror with -1,"Insert restrict rule violated.","",""
      IF _triggerlevel=1
        DO riend WITH llRetVal
      ENDIF at the end of the highest trigger level
      SELECT (lcStartArea)
      RETURN llRetVal
    ENDIF no parent
  ENDIF this value was changed
ENDIF not part of a cascade
lcParentWkArea=lcChildWkArea
SELECT (lcParentWkArea)
pcParentDBF=dbf()
pnParentRec=recno()
lcOldParentID=OLDVAL("CID")
pcParentID=lcOldParentID
pcParentExpr="CID"
lcParentID=CID
IF lcParentID<>lcOldParentID
  lcChildWkArea=riopen("purchase")
  IF lcChildWkArea<=0
    IF _triggerlevel=1
      DO riend WITH .F.
    ENDIF at the end of the highest trigger level
    SELECT (lcStartArea)
    RETURN .F.
  ENDIF not able to open the child work area
  pcChildDBF=dbf(lcChildWkArea)
  SELECT (lcChildWkArea)
  SCAN FOR CCDID=lcOldParentID
    pnChildRec=recno()
    pcChildID=CCDID
    pcChildExpr="CCDID"
```

```
    llRetVal=riupdate("CCDID",lcParentID)
  ENDSCAN get all of the purchase records
  =rireuse("purchase",lcChildWkArea)
  IF NOT llRetVal
    IF _triggerlevel=1
      DO riend WITH llRetVal
    ENDIF at the end of the highest trigger level
    SELECT (lcStartArea)
    RETURN llRetVal
  ENDIF
ENDIF this parent id changed
IF _triggerlevel=1
  do riend with llRetVal
ENDIF at the end of the highest trigger level
SELECT (lcStartArea)
RETURN llRetVal
** End of Referential integrity Update trigger for compactdisc
**************************************************************************

**************************************************************************
** Referential integrity insert trigger for compactdisc
PROCEDURE __RI_INSERT_compactdisc
LOCAL llRetVal
llRetVal = .t.
IF _triggerlevel=1
  BEGIN TRANSACTION
  PRIVATE pcRIcursors,pcRIwkareas,pcRIolderror,pnerror,;
    pcOldDele,pcOldExact,pcOldTalk
  pcOldTalk=SET("TALK")
  SET TALK OFF
  pcOldDele=SET("DELETED")
  pcOldExact=SET("EXACT")
  SET DELETED ON
  SET EXACT OFF
  pcRIcursors=""
  pcRIwkareas=""
  pcRIolderror=ON("error")
  pnerror=0
  ON ERROR pnerror=rierror(ERROR(),message(),message(1),program())
  IF TYPE('gaErrors(1)')<>"U"
    release gaErrors
  ENDIF
  PUBLIC gaErrors(1,12)
ENDIF first trigger
PRIVATE pcParentDBF,pnParentRec,pcChildDBF,pnChildRec
PRIVATE pcParentID,pcChildID
PRIVATE pcParentExpr,pcChildExpr
STORE "" TO ;
  pcParentDBF,pcChildDBF,pcParentID,pcChildID,pcParentExpr,pcChildExpr
STORE 0 TO pnParentRec,pnChildRec
LOCAL lcChildID && child's value to be sought in parent
LOCAL lcParentWkArea && parentwork area handle returned by riopen
LOCAL lcChildWkArea && child's work area
LOCAL lcStartArea
lcStartArea=select()
llRetVal=.t.
lcChildWkArea=SELECT()
SELECT (lcChildWkArea)
```

```
lcChildID=CMUSICIANID
pcChildDBF=dbf(lcChildWkArea)
pnChildRec=recno(lcChildWkArea)
pcChildID=lcChildID
pcChildExpr="CMUSICIANID"
lcParentWkArea=riopen("musician","cid")
IF lcParentWkArea<=0
  IF _triggerlevel=1
    DO riend WITH .F.
  ENDIF at the end of the highest trigger level
  SELECT (lcStartArea)
  RETURN .F.
ENDIF not able to open the child work area
pcParentDBF=dbf(lcParentWkArea)
llRetVal=SEEK(lcChildID,lcParentWkArea)
pnParentRec=recno(lcParentWkArea)
=rireuse("musician",lcParentWkArea)
IF NOT llRetVal
  DO rierror with -1,"Insert restrict rule violated.","",""
  IF _triggerlevel=1
    DO riend WITH llRetVal
  ENDIF at the end of the highest trigger level
  SELECT (lcStartArea)
  RETURN llRetVal
ENDIF
IF _triggerlevel=1
  do riend with llRetVal
ENDIF at the end of the highest trigger level
SELECT (lcStartArea)
RETURN llRetVal
** End of Referential integrity insert trigger for compactdisc
**************************************************************************

**************************************************************************
** Referential integrity delete trigger for customer
PROCEDURE __RI_DELETE_customer
LOCAL llRetVal
llRetVal = .t.
IF _triggerlevel=1
  BEGIN TRANSACTION
  PRIVATE pcRIcursors,pcRIwkareas,pcRIolderror,pnerror,;
    pcOldDele,pcOldExact,pcOldTalk
  pcOldTalk=SET("TALK")
  SET TALK OFF
  pcOldDele=SET("DELETED")
  pcOldExact=SET("EXACT")
  SET DELETED ON
  SET EXACT OFF
  pcRIcursors=""
  pcRIwkareas=""
  pcRIolderror=ON("error")
  pnerror=0
  ON ERROR pnerror=rierror(ERROR(),message(),message(1),program())
  IF TYPE('gaErrors(1)')<>"U"
    release gaErrors
  ENDIF
  PUBLIC gaErrors(1,12)
ENDIF first trigger
PRIVATE pcParentDBF,pnParentRec,pcChildDBF,pnChildRec
```

```
PRIVATE pcParentID,pcChildID
PRIVATE pcParentExpr,pcChildExpr
STORE "" TO ;
  pcParentDBF,pcChildDBF,pcParentID,pcChildID,pcParentExpr,pcChildExpr
STORE 0 TO pnParentRec,pnChildRec
LOCAL lcParentID && parent's value to be sought in child
LOCAL lcChildWkArea && child work area handle returned by riopen
LOCAL lcParentWkArea
LOCAL llDelHeaderarea
lcStartArea=select()
llRetVal=.t.
lcParentWkArea=select()
SELECT (lcParentWkArea)
pcParentDBF=dbf()
pnParentRec=recno()
STORE CID TO lcParentID,pcParentID
pcParentExpr="CID"
lcChildWkArea=riopen("invoice","ccustomeri")
IF lcChildWkArea<=0
  IF _triggerlevel=1
    DO riend WITH .F.
  ENDIF at the end of the highest trigger level
  RETURN .F.
ENDIF not able to open the child work area
pcChildDBF=dbf(lcChildWkArea)
llRetVal=!SEEK(lcParentID,lcChildWkArea)
SELECT (lcChildWkArea)
pnChildRec=recno()
pcChildID=CCUSTOMERID
pcChildExpr="CCUSTOMERID"
IF !llRetVal
  DO rierror with -1,"Delete restrict rule violated.","",""
ENDIF
=rireuse("invoice",lcChildWkArea)
IF NOT llRetVal
  IF _triggerlevel=1
    DO riend WITH llRetVal
  ENDIF at the end of the highest trigger level
  SELECT (lcStartArea)
  RETURN llRetVal
ENDIF
IF _triggerlevel=1
  do riend with llRetVal
ENDIF at the end of the highest trigger level
SELECT (lcStartArea)
RETURN llRetVal
** End of Referential integrity Delete trigger for customer
*************************************************************************

*************************************************************************
procedure __RI_UPDATE_customer
** Referential integrity update trigger for customer
LOCAL llRetVal
llRetVal = .t.
IF _triggerlevel=1
  BEGIN TRANSACTION
  PRIVATE pcRIcursors,pcRIwkareas,pcRIolderror,pnerror,;
    pcOldDele,pcOldExact,pcOldTalk
```

```
  pcOldTalk=SET("TALK")
  SET TALK OFF
  pcOldDele=SET("DELETED")
  pcOldExact=SET("EXACT")
  SET DELETED ON
  SET EXACT OFF
  pcRIcursors=""
  pcRIwkareas=""
  pcRIolderror=ON("error")
  pnerror=0
  ON ERROR pnerror=rierror(ERROR(),message(),message(1),program())
  IF TYPE('gaErrors(1)')<>"U"
    release gaErrors
  ENDIF
  PUBLIC gaErrors(1,12)
ENDIF first trigger
PRIVATE pcParentDBF,pnParentRec,pcChildDBF,pnChildRec
PRIVATE pcParentID,pcChildID
PRIVATE pcParentExpr,pcChildExpr
STORE "" TO ;
  pcParentDBF,pcChildDBF,pcParentID,pcChildID,pcParentExpr,pcChildExpr
STORE 0 TO pnParentRec,pnChildRec
LOCAL lcParentID && parent's value to be sought in child
LOCAL lcOldParentID && previous parent id value
LOCAL lcChildWkArea && child work area handle returned by riopen
LOCAL lcChildID && child's value to be sought in parent
LOCAL lcOldChildID && old child id value
LOCAL lcParentWkArea && parentwork area handle returned by riopen
LOCAL lcStartArea
lcStartArea=select()
llRetVal=.t.
lcParentWkArea=select()
SELECT (lcParentWkArea)
pcParentDBF=dbf()
pnParentRec=recno()
lcOldParentID=OLDVAL("CID")
pcParentID=lcOldParentID
pcParentExpr="CID"
lcParentID=CID
IF lcParentID<>lcOldParentID
  lcChildWkArea=riopen("invoice")
  IF lcChildWkArea<=0
    IF _triggerlevel=1
      DO riend WITH .F.
    ENDIF at the end of the highest trigger level
    SELECT (lcStartArea)
    RETURN .F.
  ENDIF not able to open the child work area
  pcChildDBF=dbf(lcChildWkArea)
  SELECT (lcChildWkArea)
  SCAN FOR CCUSTOMERID=lcOldParentID
    pnChildRec=recno()
    pcChildID=CCUSTOMERID
    pcChildExpr="CCUSTOMERID"
    llRetVal=riupdate("CCUSTOMERID",lcParentID)
  ENDSCAN get all of the invoice records
  =rireuse("invoice",lcChildWkArea)
  IF NOT llRetVal
    IF _triggerlevel=1
```

```
      DO riend WITH llRetVal
    ENDIF at the end of the highest trigger level
    SELECT (lcStartArea)
    RETURN llRetVal
  ENDIF
ENDIF this parent id changed
IF _triggerlevel=1
  do riend with llRetVal
ENDIF at the end of the highest trigger level
SELECT (lcStartArea)
RETURN llRetVal
** End of Referential integrity Update trigger for customer
************************************************************************

************************************************************************
** Referential integrity delete trigger for invoice
PROCEDURE __RI_DELETE_invoice
LOCAL llRetVal
llRetVal = .t.
IF _triggerlevel=1
  BEGIN TRANSACTION
  PRIVATE pcRIcursors,pcRIwkareas,pcRIolderror,pnerror,;
    pcOldDele,pcOldExact,pcOldTalk
  pcOldTalk=SET("TALK")
  SET TALK OFF
  pcOldDele=SET("DELETED")
  pcOldExact=SET("EXACT")
  SET DELETED ON
  SET EXACT OFF
  pcRIcursors=""
  pcRIwkareas=""
  pcRIolderror=ON("error")
  pnerror=0
  ON ERROR pnerror=rierror(ERROR(),message(),message(1),program())
  IF TYPE('gaErrors(1)')<>"U"
    release gaErrors
  ENDIF
  PUBLIC gaErrors(1,12)
ENDIF first trigger
PRIVATE pcParentDBF,pnParentRec,pcChildDBF,pnChildRec
PRIVATE pcParentID,pcChildID
PRIVATE pcParentExpr,pcChildExpr
STORE "" TO ;
pcParentDBF,pcChildDBF,pcParentID,pcChildID,pcParentExpr,pcChildExpr
STORE 0 TO pnParentRec,pnChildRec
LOCAL lcParentID && parent's value to be sought in child
LOCAL lcChildWkArea && child work area handle returned by riopen
LOCAL lcParentWkArea
LOCAL llDelHeaderarea
lcStartArea=select()
llRetVal=.t.
lcParentWkArea=select()
SELECT (lcParentWkArea)
pcParentDBF=dbf()
pnParentRec=recno()
STORE CID TO lcParentID,pcParentID
pcParentExpr="CID"
lcChildWkArea=riopen("purchase","cinvoiceid")
```

```
IF lcChildWkArea<=0
  IF _triggerlevel=1
    DO riend WITH .F.
  ENDIF at the end of the highest trigger level
  RETURN .F.
ENDIF not able to open the child work area
pcChildDBF=dbf(lcChildWkArea)
SELECT (lcChildWkArea)
SEEK lcParentID
SCAN WHILE CINVOICEID=lcParentID AND llRetVal
  pnChildRec=recno()
  pcChildID=CINVOICEID
  pcChildExpr="CINVOICEID"
  llRetVal=ridelete()
ENDSCAN get all of the purchase records
=rireuse("purchase",lcChildWkArea)
IF NOT llRetVal
  IF _triggerlevel=1
    DO riend WITH llRetVal
  ENDIF at the end of the highest trigger level
  SELECT (lcStartArea)
  RETURN llRetVal
ENDIF
IF _triggerlevel=1
  do riend with llRetVal
ENDIF at the end of the highest trigger level
SELECT (lcStartArea)
RETURN llRetVal
** End of Referential integrity Delete trigger for invoice
*************************************************************************

*************************************************************************
procedure __RI_UPDATE_invoice
** Referential integrity update trigger for invoice
LOCAL llRetVal
llRetVal = .t.
IF _triggerlevel=1
  BEGIN TRANSACTION
  PRIVATE pcRIcursors,pcRIwkareas,pcRIolderror,pnerror,;
    pcOldDele,pcOldExact,pcOldTalk
  pcOldTalk=SET("TALK")
  SET TALK OFF
  pcOldDele=SET("DELETED")
  pcOldExact=SET("EXACT")
  SET DELETED ON
  SET EXACT OFF
  pcRIcursors=""
  pcRIwkareas=""
  pcRIolderror=ON("error")
  pnerror=0
  ON ERROR pnerror=rierror(ERROR(),message(),message(1),program())
  IF TYPE('gaErrors(1)')<>"U"
    release gaErrors
  ENDIF
  PUBLIC gaErrors(1,12)
ENDIF first trigger
PRIVATE pcParentDBF,pnParentRec,pcChildDBF,pnChildRec
PRIVATE pcParentID,pcChildID
PRIVATE pcParentExpr,pcChildExpr
```

```
STORE "" TO ;
  pcParentDBF,pcChildDBF,pcParentID,pcChildID,pcParentExpr,pcChildExpr
STORE 0 TO pnParentRec,pnChildRec
LOCAL lcParentID && parent's value to be sought in child
LOCAL lcOldParentID && previous parent id value
LOCAL lcChildWkArea && child work area handle returned by riopen
LOCAL lcChildID && child's value to be sought in parent
LOCAL lcOldChildID && old child id value
LOCAL lcParentWkArea && parentwork area handle returned by riopen
LOCAL lcStartArea
lcStartArea=select()
llRetVal=.t.
lcChildWkArea=select()
IF _triggerlevel=1
  SELECT (lcChildWkArea)
  lcChildID=CCUSTOMERID
  lcOldChildID=oldval("CCUSTOMERID")
  pcChildDBF=dbf(lcChildWkArea)
  pnChildRec=recno(lcChildWkArea)
  pcChildID=lcOldChildID
  pcChildExpr="CCUSTOMERID"
  IF lcChildID<>lcOldChildID
    lcParentWkArea=riopen("customer","cid")
    IF lcParentWkArea<=0
      IF _triggerlevel=1
        DO riend WITH .F.
      ENDIF at the end of the highest trigger level
      SELECT (lcStartArea)
      RETURN .F.
    ENDIF not able to open the child work area
    pcParentDBF=dbf(lcParentWkArea)
    llRetVal=SEEK(lcChildID,lcParentWkArea)
    pnParentRec=recno(lcParentWkArea)
    =rireuse("customer",lcParentWkArea)
    IF NOT llRetVal
      DO rierror with -1,"Insert restrict rule violated.","",""
      IF _triggerlevel=1
        DO riend WITH llRetVal
      ENDIF at the end of the highest trigger level
      SELECT (lcStartArea)
      RETURN llRetVal
    ENDIF no parent
  ENDIF this value was changed
ENDIF not part of a cascade
lcParentWkArea=lcChildWkArea
SELECT (lcParentWkArea)
pcParentDBF=dbf()
pnParentRec=recno()
lcOldParentID=OLDVAL("CID")
pcParentID=lcOldParentID
pcParentExpr="CID"
lcParentID=CID
IF lcParentID<>lcOldParentID
  lcChildWkArea=riopen("purchase")
  IF lcChildWkArea<=0
    IF _triggerlevel=1
      DO riend WITH .F.
    ENDIF at the end of the highest trigger level
```

```
    SELECT (lcStartArea)
    RETURN .F.
  ENDIF not able to open the child work area
  pcChildDBF=dbf(lcChildWkArea)
  SELECT (lcChildWkArea)
  SCAN FOR CINVOICEID=lcOldParentID
    pnChildRec=recno()
    pcChildID=CINVOICEID
    pcChildExpr="CINVOICEID"
    llRetVal=riupdate("CINVOICEID",lcParentID)
  ENDSCAN get all of the purchase records
  =rireuse("purchase",lcChildWkArea)
  IF NOT llRetVal
    IF _triggerlevel=1
      DO riend WITH llRetVal
    ENDIF at the end of the highest trigger level
    SELECT (lcStartArea)
    RETURN llRetVal
  ENDIF
ENDIF this parent id changed
IF _triggerlevel=1
  do riend with llRetVal
ENDIF at the end of the highest trigger level
SELECT (lcStartArea)
RETURN llRetVal
** End of Referential integrity Update trigger for invoice
************************************************************************

************************************************************************
** Referential integrity insert trigger for invoice
PROCEDURE __RI_INSERT_invoice
LOCAL llRetVal
llRetVal = .t.
IF _triggerlevel=1
  BEGIN TRANSACTION
  PRIVATE pcRIcursors,pcRIwkareas,pcRIolderror,pnerror,;
    pcOldDele,pcOldExact,pcOldTalk
  pcOldTalk=SET("TALK")
  SET TALK OFF
  pcOldDele=SET("DELETED")
  pcOldExact=SET("EXACT")
  SET DELETED ON
  SET EXACT OFF
  pcRIcursors=""
  pcRIwkareas=""
  pcRIolderror=ON("error")
  pnerror=0
  ON ERROR pnerror=rierror(ERROR(),message(),message(1),program())
  IF TYPE('gaErrors(1)')<>"U"
    release gaErrors
  ENDIF
  PUBLIC gaErrors(1,12)
ENDIF first trigger
PRIVATE pcParentDBF,pnParentRec,pcChildDBF,pnChildRec
PRIVATE pcParentID,pcChildID
PRIVATE pcParentExpr,pcChildExpr
STORE "" TO ;
  pcParentDBF,pcChildDBF,pcParentID,pcChildID,pcParentExpr,pcChildExpr
STORE 0 TO pnParentRec,pnChildRec
```

```
LOCAL lcChildID && child's value to be sought in parent
LOCAL lcParentWkArea && parentwork area handle returned by riopen
LOCAL lcChildWkArea && child's work area
LOCAL lcStartArea
lcStartArea=select()
llRetVal=.t.
lcChildWkArea=SELECT()
SELECT (lcChildWkArea)
lcChildID=CCUSTOMERID
pcChildDBF=dbf(lcChildWkArea)
pnChildRec=recno(lcChildWkArea)
pcChildID=lcChildID
pcChildExpr="CCUSTOMERID"
lcParentWkArea=riopen("customer","cid")
IF lcParentWkArea<=0
  IF _triggerlevel=1
    DO riend WITH .F.
  ENDIF at the end of the highest trigger level
  SELECT (lcStartArea)
  RETURN .F.
ENDIF not able to open the child work area
pcParentDBF=dbf(lcParentWkArea)
llRetVal=SEEK(lcChildID,lcParentWkArea)
pnParentRec=recno(lcParentWkArea)
=rireuse("customer",lcParentWkArea)
IF NOT llRetVal
  DO rierror with -1,"Insert restrict rule violated.","",""
  IF _triggerlevel=1
    DO riend WITH llRetVal
  ENDIF at the end of the highest trigger level
  SELECT (lcStartArea)
  RETURN llRetVal
ENDIF
IF _triggerlevel=1
  do riend with llRetVal
ENDIF at the end of the highest trigger level
SELECT (lcStartArea)
RETURN llRetVal
** End of Referential integrity insert trigger for invoice
**********************************************************************

**********************************************************************
** Referential integrity delete trigger for musician
PROCEDURE __RI_DELETE_musician
LOCAL llRetVal
llRetVal = .t.
IF _triggerlevel=1
  BEGIN TRANSACTION
  PRIVATE pcRIcursors,pcRIwkareas,pcRIolderror,pnerror,;
    pcOldDele,pcOldExact,pcOldTalk
  pcOldTalk=SET("TALK")
  SET TALK OFF
  pcOldDele=SET("DELETED")
  pcOldExact=SET("EXACT")
  SET DELETED ON
  SET EXACT OFF
  pcRIcursors=""
  pcRIwkareas=""
```

```
  pcRIolderror=ON("error")
  pnerror=0
  ON ERROR pnerror=rierror(ERROR(),message(),message(1),program())
  IF TYPE('gaErrors(1)')<>"U"
    release gaErrors
  ENDIF
  PUBLIC gaErrors(1,12)
ENDIF first trigger
PRIVATE pcParentDBF,pnParentRec,pcChildDBF,pnChildRec
PRIVATE pcParentID,pcChildID
PRIVATE pcParentExpr,pcChildExpr
STORE "" TO ;
  pcParentDBF,pcChildDBF,pcParentID,pcChildID,pcParentExpr,pcChildExpr
STORE 0 TO pnParentRec,pnChildRec
LOCAL lcParentID && parent's value to be sought in child
LOCAL lcChildWkArea && child work area handle returned by riopen
LOCAL lcParentWkArea
LOCAL llDelHeaderarea
lcStartArea=select()
llRetVal=.t.
lcParentWkArea=select()
SELECT (lcParentWkArea)
pcParentDBF=dbf()
pnParentRec=recno()
STORE CID TO lcParentID,pcParentID
pcParentExpr="CID"
lcChildWkArea=riopen("compactdisc","cmusiciani")
IF lcChildWkArea<=0
  IF _triggerlevel=1
    DO riend WITH .F.
  ENDIF at the end of the highest trigger level
  RETURN .F.
ENDIF not able to open the child work area
pcChildDBF=dbf(lcChildWkArea)
llRetVal=!SEEK(lcParentID,lcChildWkArea)
SELECT (lcChildWkArea)
pnChildRec=recno()
pcChildID=CMUSICIANID
pcChildExpr="CMUSICIANID"
IF !llRetVal
  DO rierror with -1,"Delete restrict rule violated.","",""
ENDIF
=rireuse("compactdisc",lcChildWkArea)
IF NOT llRetVal
  IF _triggerlevel=1
    DO riend WITH llRetVal
  ENDIF at the end of the highest trigger level
  SELECT (lcStartArea)
  RETURN llRetVal
ENDIF
IF _triggerlevel=1
  do riend with llRetVal
ENDIF at the end of the highest trigger level
SELECT (lcStartArea)
RETURN llRetVal
** End of Referential integrity Delete trigger for musician
***************************************************************************
```

```
*************************************************************************
procedure __RI_UPDATE_musician
** Referential integrity update trigger for musician
LOCAL llRetVal
llRetVal = .t.
IF _triggerlevel=1
  BEGIN TRANSACTION
  PRIVATE pcRIcursors,pcRIwkareas,pcRIolderror,pnerror,;
    pcOldDele,pcOldExact,pcOldTalk
  pcOldTalk=SET("TALK")
  SET TALK OFF
  pcOldDele=SET("DELETED")
  pcOldExact=SET("EXACT")
  SET DELETED ON
  SET EXACT OFF
  pcRIcursors=""
  pcRIwkareas=""
  pcRIolderror=ON("error")
  pnerror=0
  ON ERROR pnerror=rierror(ERROR(),message(),message(1),program())
  IF TYPE('gaErrors(1)')<>"U"
    release gaErrors
  ENDIF
  PUBLIC gaErrors(1,12)
ENDIF first trigger
PRIVATE pcParentDBF,pnParentRec,pcChildDBF,pnChildRec
PRIVATE pcParentID,pcChildID
PRIVATE pcParentExpr,pcChildExpr
STORE "" TO ;
  pcParentDBF,pcChildDBF,pcParentID,pcChildID,pcParentExpr,pcChildExpr
STORE 0 TO pnParentRec,pnChildRec
LOCAL lcParentID && parent's value to be sought in child
LOCAL lcOldParentID && previous parent id value
LOCAL lcChildWkArea && child work area handle returned by riopen
LOCAL lcChildID && child's value to be sought in parent
LOCAL lcOldChildID && old child id value
LOCAL lcParentWkArea && parentwork area handle returned by riopen
LOCAL lcStartArea
lcStartArea=select()
llRetVal=.t.
lcParentWkArea=select()
SELECT (lcParentWkArea)
pcParentDBF=dbf()
pnParentRec=recno()
lcOldParentID=OLDVAL("CID")
pcParentID=lcOldParentID
pcParentExpr="CID"
lcParentID=CID
IF lcParentID<>lcOldParentID
  lcChildWkArea=riopen("compactdisc")
  IF lcChildWkArea<=0
    IF _triggerlevel=1
      DO riend WITH .F.
    ENDIF at the end of the highest trigger level
    SELECT (lcStartArea)
    RETURN .F.
  ENDIF not able to open the child work area
  pcChildDBF=dbf(lcChildWkArea)
```

```
  SELECT (lcChildWkArea)
  SCAN FOR CMUSICIANID=lcOldParentID
    pnChildRec=recno()
    pcChildID=CMUSICIANID
    pcChildExpr="CMUSICIANID"
    llRetVal=riupdate("CMUSICIANID",lcParentID)
  ENDSCAN get all of the compactdisc records
  =rireuse("compactdisc",lcChildWkArea)
  IF NOT llRetVal
    IF _triggerlevel=1
      DO riend WITH llRetVal
    ENDIF at the end of the highest trigger level
    SELECT (lcStartArea)
    RETURN llRetVal
  ENDIF
ENDIF this parent id changed
IF _triggerlevel=1
  do riend with llRetVal
ENDIF at the end of the highest trigger level
SELECT (lcStartArea)
RETURN llRetVal
** End of Referential integrity Update trigger for musician
**********************************************************************

**********************************************************************
procedure __RI_UPDATE_purchase
** Referential integrity update trigger for purchase
LOCAL llRetVal
llRetVal = .t.
IF _triggerlevel=1
  BEGIN TRANSACTION
  PRIVATE pcRIcursors,pcRIwkareas,pcRIolderror,pnerror,;
    pcOldDele,pcOldExact,pcOldTalk
  pcOldTalk=SET("TALK")
  SET TALK OFF
  pcOldDele=SET("DELETED")
  pcOldExact=SET("EXACT")
  SET DELETED ON
  SET EXACT OFF
  pcRIcursors=""
  pcRIwkareas=""
  pcRIolderror=ON("error")
  pnerror=0
  ON ERROR pnerror=rierror(ERROR(),message(),message(1),program())
  IF TYPE('gaErrors(1)')<>"U"
    release gaErrors
  ENDIF
  PUBLIC gaErrors(1,12)
ENDIF first trigger
PRIVATE pcParentDBF,pnParentRec,pcChildDBF,pnChildRec
PRIVATE pcParentID,pcChildID
PRIVATE pcParentExpr,pcChildExpr
STORE "" TO ;
  pcParentDBF,pcChildDBF,pcParentID,pcChildID,pcParentExpr,pcChildExpr
STORE 0 TO pnParentRec,pnChildRec
LOCAL lcParentID && parent's value to be sought in child
LOCAL lcOldParentID && previous parent id value
LOCAL lcChildWkArea && child work area handle returned by riopen
LOCAL lcChildID && child's value to be sought in parent
```

```
LOCAL lcOldChildID && old child id value
LOCAL lcParentWkArea && parentwork area handle returned by riopen
LOCAL lcStartArea
lcStartArea=select()
llRetVal=.t.
lcChildWkArea=select()
IF _triggerlevel=1
  SELECT (lcChildWkArea)
  lcChildID=CCDID
  lcOldChildID=oldval("CCDID")
  pcChildDBF=dbf(lcChildWkArea)
  pnChildRec=recno(lcChildWkArea)
  pcChildID=lcOldChildID
  pcChildExpr="CCDID"
  IF lcChildID<>lcOldChildID
    lcParentWkArea=riopen("compactdisc","cid")
    IF lcParentWkArea<=0
      IF _triggerlevel=1
        DO riend WITH .F.
      ENDIF at the end of the highest trigger level
      SELECT (lcStartArea)
      RETURN .F.
    ENDIF not able to open the child work area
    pcParentDBF=dbf(lcParentWkArea)
    llRetVal=SEEK(lcChildID,lcParentWkArea)
    pnParentRec=recno(lcParentWkArea)
    =rireuse("compactdisc",lcParentWkArea)
    IF NOT llRetVal
      DO rierror with -1,"Insert restrict rule violated.","",""
      IF _triggerlevel=1
        DO riend WITH llRetVal
      ENDIF at the end of the highest trigger level
      SELECT (lcStartArea)
      RETURN llRetVal
    ENDIF no parent
  ENDIF this value was changed
  SELECT (lcChildWkArea)
  lcChildID=CINVOICEID
  lcOldChildID=oldval("CINVOICEID")
  pcChildDBF=dbf(lcChildWkArea)
  pnChildRec=recno(lcChildWkArea)
  pcChildID=lcOldChildID
  pcChildExpr="CINVOICEID"
  IF lcChildID<>lcOldChildID
    lcParentWkArea=riopen("invoice","cid")
    IF lcParentWkArea<=0
      IF _triggerlevel=1
        DO riend WITH .F.
      ENDIF at the end of the highest trigger level
      SELECT (lcStartArea)
      RETURN .F.
    ENDIF not able to open the child work area
    pcParentDBF=dbf(lcParentWkArea)
    llRetVal=SEEK(lcChildID,lcParentWkArea)
    pnParentRec=recno(lcParentWkArea)
    =rireuse("invoice",lcParentWkArea)
    IF NOT llRetVal
      DO rierror with -1,"Insert restrict rule violated.","",""
```

```
      IF _triggerlevel=1
        DO riend WITH llRetVal
      ENDIF at the end of the highest trigger level
      SELECT (lcStartArea)
      RETURN llRetVal
    ENDIF no parent
  ENDIF this value was changed
ENDIF not part of a cascade
lcParentWkArea=lcChildWkArea
IF _triggerlevel=1
  do riend with llRetVal
ENDIF at the end of the highest trigger level
SELECT (lcStartArea)
RETURN llRetVal
** End of Referential integrity Update trigger for purchase
************************************************************************

************************************************************************
** Referential integrity insert trigger for purchase
PROCEDURE __RI_INSERT_purchase
LOCAL llRetVal
llRetVal = .t.
IF _triggerlevel=1
  BEGIN TRANSACTION
  PRIVATE pcRIcursors,pcRIwkareas,pcRIolderror,pnerror,;
    pcOldDele,pcOldExact,pcOldTalk
  pcOldTalk=SET("TALK")
  SET TALK OFF
  pcOldDele=SET("DELETED")
  pcOldExact=SET("EXACT")
  SET DELETED ON
  SET EXACT OFF
  pcRIcursors=""
  pcRIwkareas=""
  pcRIolderror=ON("error")
  pnerror=0
  ON ERROR pnerror=rierror(ERROR(),message(),message(1),program())
  IF TYPE('gaErrors(1)')<>"U"
    release gaErrors
  ENDIF
  PUBLIC gaErrors(1,12)
ENDIF first trigger
PRIVATE pcParentDBF,pnParentRec,pcChildDBF,pnChildRec
PRIVATE pcParentID,pcChildID
PRIVATE pcParentExpr,pcChildExpr
STORE "" TO ;
  pcParentDBF,pcChildDBF,pcParentID,pcChildID,pcParentExpr,pcChildExpr
STORE 0 TO pnParentRec,pnChildRec
LOCAL lcChildID && child's value to be sought in parent
LOCAL lcParentWkArea && parentwork area handle returned by riopen
LOCAL lcChildWkArea && child's work area
LOCAL lcStartArea
lcStartArea=select()
llRetVal=.t.
lcChildWkArea=SELECT()
SELECT (lcChildWkArea)
lcChildID=CCDID
pcChildDBF=dbf(lcChildWkArea)
pnChildRec=recno(lcChildWkArea)
```

```
pcChildID=lcChildID
pcChildExpr="CCDID"
lcParentWkArea=riopen("compactdisc","cid")
IF lcParentWkArea<=0
  IF _triggerlevel=1
    DO riend WITH .F.
  ENDIF at the end of the highest trigger level
  SELECT (lcStartArea)
  RETURN .F.
ENDIF not able to open the child work area
pcParentDBF=dbf(lcParentWkArea)
llRetVal=SEEK(lcChildID,lcParentWkArea)
pnParentRec=recno(lcParentWkArea)
=rireuse("compactdisc",lcParentWkArea)
IF NOT llRetVal
  DO rierror with -1,"Insert restrict rule violated.","",""
  IF _triggerlevel=1
    DO riend WITH llRetVal
  ENDIF at the end of the highest trigger level
  SELECT (lcStartArea)
  RETURN llRetVal
ENDIF
SELECT (lcChildWkArea)
lcChildID=CINVOICEID
pcChildDBF=dbf(lcChildWkArea)
pnChildRec=recno(lcChildWkArea)
pcChildID=lcChildID
pcChildExpr="CINVOICEID"
lcParentWkArea=riopen("invoice","cid")
IF lcParentWkArea<=0
  IF _triggerlevel=1
    DO riend WITH .F.
  ENDIF at the end of the highest trigger level
  SELECT (lcStartArea)
  RETURN .F.
ENDIF not able to open the child work area
pcParentDBF=dbf(lcParentWkArea)
llRetVal=SEEK(lcChildID,lcParentWkArea)
pnParentRec=recno(lcParentWkArea)
=rireuse("invoice",lcParentWkArea)
IF NOT llRetVal
  DO rierror with -1,"Insert restrict rule violated.","",""
  IF _triggerlevel=1
    DO riend WITH llRetVal
  ENDIF at the end of the highest trigger level
  SELECT (lcStartArea)
  RETURN llRetVal
ENDIF
IF _triggerlevel=1
  do riend with llRetVal
ENDIF at the end of the highest trigger level
SELECT (lcStartArea)
RETURN llRetVal
** End of Referential integrity insert trigger for purchase
************************************************************************
**__RI_FOOTER!@ Do NOT REMOVE or MODIFY this line!!!! @!__RI_FOOTER**
```

Once our database is complete, we move on to building an application class, menu classes, toolbars, business objects, data environments, form classes, and reports. The upcoming chapters detail each of these in turn.

Chapter 34

CLASSLIB: AAPP.VCX

Class Name: SplashImage

Superclass: cimage (..\..\common30\libs\ccontrls.vcx)

Description: The image class used for the initial "splash screen."

Base Class: image

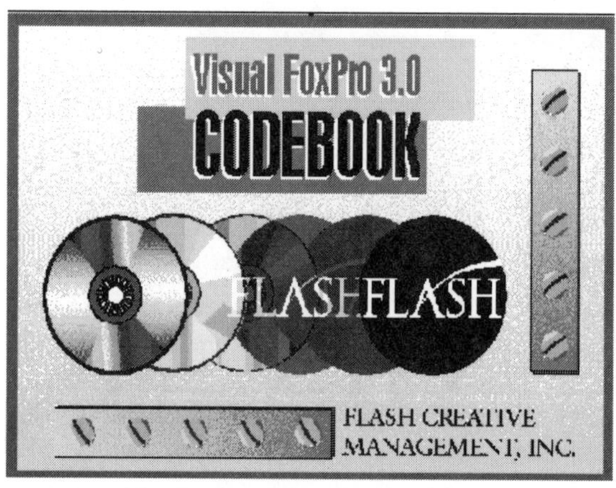

The SplashImage picture

SplashImage is the CImage class that is used for the initial splash screen. It is used because we have filled in the cSplashImage property of the Codebook Application object with the name of this class, and the lShowSplash property is set to true.

Class Name: Codebook

Superclass: capplication (..\..\common30\libs\capp.vcx)

Description: The Codebook application class.

Base Class: container

This is our application class. It is automatically created in SETUP.PRG and given an instance name of goApp. We have simply modified two properties, cSplash-Image and lShowSplash. The rest of the behavior of an application is done for us.

We have, however, extended the Do() method for the application, so that it checks if this is the first time the application is running and, if so, brings up the User Preferences form so that they can point to their data and do other actions.

```
*--Codebook.Do()
*-- Override to ensure that user preference settings have been
*-- entered. We cannot put this code in the Init() since
*-- PreferenceForm needs to access methods of the application
*-- object, which would not yet exist.

*-- For this application, if Use Local Data isn't found in the
*-- settings storage (whether an INI or Registry), we know
*-- we're running this app for the first time.
IF EMPTY(this.GetSetting("Data Settings","Use Local Data", ""))
   *-- Need to specify settings
   ?? CHR(7)
   =MESSAGEBOX(SELECTPREFERENCE_LOC,MB_ICONINFORMATION,APPNAME_LOC)
   IF DOFORM("preferenceform")
      RETURN CApplication::Do()
   ELSE
      this.Release()
   ENDIF
ELSE
   RETURN CApplication::Do()
ENDIF
```

One fun thing to try is change the cMessageClass property from CMessage to CWaitMessage. Now run the application again. Notice how all the messages that take place while a process is running show up in WAIT WINDOWs? The cMessageClass property stores the default message type to use for the application. Almost all places that call a message use the GetMessageClass() function (found in UTILITY.PRG) to find out which message class to use, and then call it. Changing this one behavior changes messaging functions for the whole application!

Chapter 35

CLASSLIB: AMENUS.VCX

Class Name: MainMenu

Superclass: cmenu (..\..\common30\libs\cmenus.vcx)

Description: The main menu class.

Base Class: container

This CMenu-based class is the container for our menu. It, like all the containers in this class, is based on our CContainer hierarchy (see the chapter on CCONTAINER.VCX). We simply fill in the LoadChildren() method with the classes that we want to be "part" of this menu, and the superclasses handle the rest.

```
*-- MainMenu.LoadChildren()
#DEFINE NUMCHILDREN 8
LOCAL laChildren[NUMCHILDREN, ALEN(this.aChildren, 2)]

laChildren[1, CHILD_CLASS] = "FilePad"
laChildren[2, CHILD_CLASS] = "EditPad"
laChildren[3, CHILD_CLASS] = "AdministrationPad"
laChildren[4, CHILD_CLASS] = "NavigationPad"
laChildren[5, CHILD_CLASS] = "UtilitiesPad"
laChildren[6, CHILD_CLASS] = "InvoicePad"
laChildren[7, CHILD_CLASS] = "WindowPad"
laChildren[8, CHILD_CLASS] = "HelpPad"

DIMENSION this.aChildren[NUMCHILDREN, ALEN(laChildren, 2)]
=ACOPY(laChildren, this.aChildren)

RETURN NUMCHILDREN
```

Class Name: FilePad

Superclass: cpad (..\..\common30\libs\cmenus.vcx)

Description: The menu class for the File menu pad.

Base Class: container

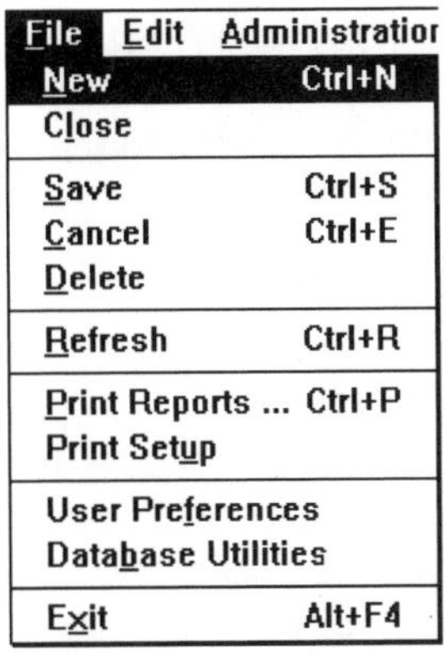

The File Pad and Popup

This is the File Pad for our menu system. All we do here is override a number of properties including:

Property	Setting
cCaption	\<File
cKey	Alt+F, "Alt+F"
cMessage	Create, save, delete, and restore records; close forms, print reports, or quit application.

Class Name: FilePopup

Superclass: cpopup (..\..\common30\libs\cmenus.vcx)

Description: The menu class for the File menu popup.

Base Class: container

FilePopup is the popup that contains our File menu bars. Like Mainmenu, it has an overridden LoadChildren() method.

```
*--FilePopup.LoadChildren()
#DEFINE NUMCHILDREN 16
LOCAL laChildren[NUMCHILDREN, ALEN(this.aChildren, 2)]
```

```
laChildren[1, CHILD_CLASS] = "FileNewBar"
laChildren[2, CHILD_CLASS] = "FileCloseBar"
laChildren[3, CHILD_CLASS] = "CSeparatorBar"
laChildren[4, CHILD_CLASS] = "FileSaveBar"
laChildren[5, CHILD_CLASS] = "FileCancelBar"
laChildren[6, CHILD_CLASS] = "FileDeleteBar"
laChildren[7, CHILD_CLASS] = "CSeparatorBar"
laChildren[8, CHILD_CLASS] = "FileRefreshBar"
laChildren[9, CHILD_CLASS] = "CSeparatorBar"
laChildren[10,CHILD_CLASS] = "FilePrintReportsBar"
laChildren[11, CHILD_CLASS] = "FilePrintSetupBar"
laChildren[12, CHILD_CLASS] = "CSeparatorBar"
laChildren[13, CHILD_CLASS] = "FileUserPrefBar"
laChildren[14, CHILD_CLASS] = "FileDBUtilsBar"
laChildren[15, CHILD_CLASS] = "CSeparatorBar"
laChildren[16, CHILD_CLASS] = "FileExitBar"

DIMENSION this.aChildren[NUMCHILDREN, ALEN(laChildren, 2)]
=ACOPY(laChildren, this.aChildren)

RETURN NUMCHILDREN
```

Class Name: FileNewBar

Superclass: cbar (..\..\common30\libs\cmenus.vcx)

Description: Adds a new record.

Base Class: container

This bar allows the user to add a new business object to the database. Since it is tied to a toolbar button, we don't have to add any Click() code, we simply point to the button that it works with, and that button's Click() method is called when this menu option is selected.

As with any visible menu class, we set certain properties.

Property	Setting
cCaption	\<New
cKey	Alt+N, "Alt+N"

Property	Setting
cMessage	Creates a new record in the active form.
cSkipFor	!FormIsObject()
cToolbarCommand	cmdNew.Click()

Class Name: FileCloseBar

Superclass: cbar (..\..\common30\libs\cmenus.vcx)

Description: Closes the open form.

Base Class: container

This bar allows the user to close the current window. Since it is tied to a toolbar button, we don't have to add any Click() code, we simply point to the button that it works with, and that button's Click() method is called when this menu option is selected.

As with any visible menu class, we set certain properties.

Property	Setting
cCaption	C\<lose
cMessage	Closes the active form.
cSkipFor	!FormIsObject()
cToolbarCommand	cmdClose.Click()

Class Name: FileSaveBar

Superclass: cbar (..\..\common30\libs\cmenus.vcx)

Description: Saves the current record.

Base Class: container

This bar allows the user to save the current business object. Since it is tied to a toolbar button, we don't have to add any Click() code, we simply point to the button that it works with, and that button's Click() method is called when this menu option is selected.

As with any visible menu class, we set certain properties.

Property	Setting
cCaption	\<Save
cKey	Ctrl+S, "Ctrl+S"
cMessage	Saves the current record in the active form.
cSkipFor	!FormIsObject()
cToolbarCommand	cmdSave.Click()

Class Name FileCancelBar

Superclass: cbar (..\..\common30\libs\cmenus.vcx)

Description: Cancels changes.

Base Class: container

This bar allows the user to cancel the current edit. Since it is tied to a toolbar button, we don't have to add any Click() code, we simply point to the button that it works with, and that button's Click() method is called when this menu option is selected.

As with any visible menu class, we set certain properties.

Property	Setting
cCaption	\<Cancel
cKey	Ctrl+E, "Ctrl+E"
cMessage	Cancels any changes made to the current record.
cSkipFor	!FormIsObject()
cToolbarCommand	cmdCancel.Click()

Class Name: FileDeleteBar

Superclass: cbar (..\..\common30\libs\cmenus.vcx)

Description: Deletes the current record.

Base Class: container

This bar allows the user to delete the current business object. We don't tie this option to a toolbar button, because it is destructive. Therefore, we modify the Click() method so that it looks to see if we have assigned it to a toolbar (there may be an application where we are asked to do this). If we have assigned it, it runs the toolbar's Click() method, otherwise, it runs the current form's Delete() method.

As with any visible menu class, we set certain properties.

Property	Setting
cCaption	\<Delete
cMessage	Deletes the current record in the active form.
cSkipFor	!FormIsObject()
cToolbarCommand	cmd.Click()

Method	Description
allowdelete	Code used to control enabling this menu bar.

Class Name: FileRefreshBar

Superclass: cbar (..\..\common30\libs\cmenus.vcx)

Description: Refreshes the current view.

Base Class: container

This bar allows the user to refresh his or her current data. Since it is tied to a toolbar button, we don't have to add any Click() code, we simply point to the button that it works with, and that button's Click() method is called when this menu option is selected.

As with any visible menu class, we set certain properties.

Property	Setting
cCaption	\<Refresh
cKey	Ctrl+R, "Ctrl+R"
cMessage	Refreshes the current view.
cSkipFor	!FormIsObject()
cToolbarCommand	cmdRefresh.Click()

Class Name FilePrintReportsBar

Superclass: cbar (..\..\common30\libs\cmenus.vcx)

Description: Runs the CReportForm form.

Base Class: container

This bar allows the user to select a report to print, display, or save. Since it is not tied to a toolbar button, we add specific Click() code that is called when this menu option is selected.

For this menu bar, the click code is:

```
*-- .Click() Method
=DoForm("CReportForm")
```

As with any visible menu class, we set certain properties.

Property	Setting
cCaption	\<Print Reports...
cKey	Ctrl+P, "Ctrl+P"
cMessage	Runs the report and list selection form.

Class Name: FilePrintSetupBar

Superclass: cbar (..\..\common30\libs\cmenus.vcx)

Description: Runs the printer setup dialog.

Base Class: container

This bar allows the user to select a printer. Since it is not tied to a toolbar button, we add specific Click() code that is called when this menu option is selected. For this menu bar, the click code is:

```
*-- .Click() Method
LOCAL loMsg
loMsg = CREATEOBJECT(GetMessageClass(), "Printer Setup")
=GETPRINTER()
```

We create our own message "Printer Setup" because we are calling a standard Windows dialog, which does not place a message on the status bar. The addition of this message makes this window act like one of our standard windows.

As with any visible menu class, we set certain properties.

Property	Setting
cCaption	Print Set\<up
cMessage	Changes the page layout and printer settings.

Class Name: FileUserPrefBar

Superclass: cbar (..\..\common30\libs\cmenus.vcx)

Description: Runs the user preferences dialog.

Base Class: container

This bar runs the user preferences dialog, allowing the user to set preferences for the application. Since it is not tied to a toolbar button, we add specific Click() code that is called when this menu option is selected.

For this menu bar, the click code is:

```
*-- .Click() Method
=DoForm("PreferenceForm")
```

As with any visible menu class, we set certain properties.

Property	Setting
cCaption	User Pre\<ferences
cMessage	Change user preferences.
cSkipFor	!EMPTY(WONTOP())

Class Name FileDBUtilsBar

Superclass: cbar (..\..\common30\libs\cmenus.vcx)

Description: Runs the CDBManage form.

Base Class: container

This bar runs the database management form, allowing the user to perform database functions like REINDEX and PACK. Since it is not tied to a toolbar button, we add specific Click() code that is called when this menu option is selected.

For this menu bar, the click code is:

```
*-- .Click() Method
=DoForm("CDBManageForm")
```

As with any visible menu class, we set certain properties.

Property	Setting
cCaption	Data\<base Utilities
cMessage	Pack, pack memo, and reindex utilities.
cSkipFor	!EMPTY(WONTOP())

Class Name FileExitBar

Superclass: cbar (..\..\common30\libs\cmenus.vcx)

Description: Exits the application.

Base Class: container

Selecting this bar ends the application. Since it is not tied to a toolbar button, we add specific Click() code that is called when this menu option is selected.

For this menu bar, the click code is:

```
*-- .Click() Method
goApp.CleanUp()
RELEASE goApp
```

This code tells the application to clean up after itself, and then it releases the application object.

As with any visible menu class, we set certain properties.

Property	Setting
cCaption	E\<xit
cKey	Alt+F4, "Alt+F4"
cMessage	Exit the application.

Class Name EditPad

Superclass: cpad (..\..\common30\libs\cmenus.vcx)

Description: The menu class for the Edit menu pad.

Base Class: container

Edit Administratio
Undo Ctrl+Z
Redo Ctrl+R
Cut Ctrl+X
Copy Ctrl+C
Paste Ctrl+V
Select All Ctrl+A

The Edit Pad and Popup

This is the Edit Pad for our menu system. All we do here is override a number of properties including:

Property	Setting
cCaption	\<Edit
cKey	Alt+E, "Alt+E"
cMessage	Edits text or current selection.
cSkipFor	EMPTY(WONTOP())

Class Name EditPopup

Superclass: cpopup (..\..\common30\libs\cmenus.vcx)

Description: The menu class for the Edit menu popup.

Base Class: container

EditPopup is the popup that contains our Edit menu bars. Like Mainmenu, it has an overridden LoadChildren() method.

```
*--EditPopup.LoadChildren
#DEFINE NUMCHILDREN 8
LOCAL laChildren[NUMCHILDREN, ALEN(this.aChildren, 2)]

laChildren[1, CHILD_CLASS] = "EditUndoBar"
laChildren[2, CHILD_CLASS] = "EditRedoBar"
laChildren[3, CHILD_CLASS] = "CSeparatorBar"
laChildren[4, CHILD_CLASS] = "EditCutBar"
```

```
laChildren[5, CHILD_CLASS] = "EditCopyBar"
laChildren[6, CHILD_CLASS] = "EditPasteBar"
laChildren[7, CHILD_CLASS] = "CSeparatorBar"
laChildren[8, CHILD_CLASS] = "EditSelectAllBar"

DIMENSION this.aChildren[NUMCHILDREN, ALEN(laChildren, 2)]
=ACOPY(laChildren, this.aChildren)

RETURN NUMCHILDREN
```

Class Name EditUndoBar

Superclass: cbar (..\..\common30\libs\cmenus.vcx)

Description: Undo text menu bar.

Base Class: container

This bar allows the user to undo his or her most recent change. It is not tied to a toolbar button, but since it is tied to a native Visual FoxPro feature (using nBarNumber), we don't have to add any Click() code.

As with any visible menu class, we set certain properties.

Property	Setting
cCaption	\<Undo
cKey	Ctrl+Z, "Ctrl+Z"
cMessage	Undoes the last change made to the current control of the active form.
nBarNumber	_med_undo

Class Name EditRedoBar

Superclass: cbar (..\..\common30\libs\cmenus.vcx)

Description: Redo changes menu bar.

Base Class: container

This bar allows the user to redo his or her most recently undone change. It is not tied to a toolbar button, but since it is tied to a native Visual FoxPro feature (using nBarNumber), we don't have to add any Click() code.

As with any visible menu class, we set certain properties.

Property	Setting
cCaption	\<Redo
cKey	Ctrl+R, "Ctrl+R"
cMessage	Repeats the last change made to the current control of the active form.
nBarNumber	_med_redo

Class Name EditCutBar

Superclass: cbar (..\..\common30\libs\cmenus.vcx)

Description: Cut text menu bar.

Base Class: container

This bar allows the user to cut the currently selected text to the clipboard. It is not tied to a toolbar button, but since it is tied to a native Visual FoxPro feature (using nBarNumber), we don't have to add any Click() code.

As with any visible menu class, we set certain properties.

Property	Setting
cCaption	Cu\<t
cKey	Ctrl+X, "Ctrl+X"
cMessage	Removes the selection and places it onto the clipboard.
nBarNumber	_med_cut

Class Name EditCopyBar

Superclass: cbar (..\..\common30\libs\cmenus.vcx)

Description: Copy text menu bar.

Base Class: container

This bar allows the user to copy the selected text to the clipboard. It is not tied to a toolbar button, but since it is tied to a native Visual FoxPro feature (using nBarNumber), we don't have to add any Click() code.

As with any visible menu class, we set certain properties.

Property	Setting
cCaption	\<Copy
cKey	Ctrl+C, "Ctrl+C"
cMessage	Copies the selection onto the clipboard.
nBarNumber	_med_copy

Class Name EditPasteBar

Superclass: cbar (..\..\common30\libs\cmenus.vcx)

Description: Paste text menu bar.

Base Class: container

This bar allows the user to paste the data currently in the clipboard. It is not tied to a toolbar button, but since it is tied to a native Visual FoxPro feature (using nBarNumber), we don't have to add any Click() code.

As with any visible menu class, we set certain properties.

Property	Setting
cCaption	\<Paste
cKey	Ctrl+V, "Ctrl+V"
cMessage	Pastes the contents of the clipboard.
nBarNumber	_med_paste

Class Name EditSelectallBar

Superclass: cbar (..\..\common30\libs\cmenus.vcx)

Description: Select all text menu bar.

Base Class: container

This bar allows the user to select all the text in the current control. It is not tied to a toolbar button, but since it is tied to a native Visual FoxPro feature (using nBarNumber), we don't have to add any Click() code.

As with any visible menu class, we set certain properties.

Property	Setting
cCaption	Select \<All
cKey	Ctrl+A, "Ctrl+A"
cMessage	Selects all text in the current control of the active form.
nBarNumber	_med_slcta

Class Name AdministrationPad

Superclass: cpad (..\..\common30\libs\cmenus.vcx)

Description: The menu class for the Administration menu pad.

Base Class: container

The Administration Pad and Popup

This is the Administration pad for our menu system. All we do here is override a number of properties including:

Property	Setting
cCaption	\<Administration
cKey	Alt+A, "Alt+A"
cMessage	Access to all maintenance forms.

Class Name AdministrationPopup

Superclass: cpopup (..\..\common30\libs\cmenus.vcx)

Description: The menu class for the Administration menu popup.

Base Class: container

AdministrationPopup is the popup that contains our Administration menu bars. Like Mainmenu, it has an overridden LoadChildren() method.

```
*--AdministrationPopup.LoadChildren()
#DEFINE NUMCHILDREN 5
LOCAL laChildren[NUMCHILDREN, ALEN(this.aChildren, 2)]

laChildren[1, CHILD_CLASS] = "AdminCustomerBar"
laChildren[2, CHILD_CLASS] = "AdminMusicianBar"
laChildren[3, CHILD_CLASS] = "AdminCompactDiscBar"
laChildren[4, CHILD_CLASS] = "AdminInvoiceBar"
laChildren[5, CHILD_CLASS] = "AdminMarkInvoiceBar"

DIMENSION this.aChildren[NUMCHILDREN, ALEN(laChildren, 2)]
=ACOPY(laChildren, this.aChildren)

RETURN NUMCHILDREN
```

Class Name AdminCustomerBar

Superclass: cbar (..\..\common30\libs\cmenus.vcx)

Description: Runs the customer form.

Base Class: container

This bar allows the user to run an instance of the customer form. We have overridden the Click() method, however, so that it checks for the application toolbar object first, otherwise it just runs the form.

```
*-- Click() Method
IF TYPE("goApp.oMainToolbar") == "O"
   goApp.oMainToolbar.cmdCustomer.Click()
ELSE
   =DoForm("customerform")
ENDIF
```

As with any visible menu class, we set certain properties.

Property	Setting
cCaption	\<Customers
cMessage	Add, edit, or delete customers.

Class Name AdminMusicianBar

Superclass: cbar (..\..\common30\libs\cmenus.vcx)

Description: Runs the musician form.

Base Class: container

This bar allows the user to run an instance of the musician form. We have overridden the click method, however, so that it checks for the application toolbar object first, otherwise it just runs the form.

As with any visible menu class, we set certain properties.

Property	Setting
cCaption	\<Musicians
cMessage	Add, edit, or delete musicians.

Class Name AdminCompactDiscBar

Superclass: cbar (..\..\common30\libs\cmenus.vcx)

Description: Runs the compact disc form.

Base Class: container

This bar allows the user to run an instance of the compact disc form. We have overridden the Click() method, however, so that it checks for the application toolbar object first, otherwise it just runs the form.

As with any visible menu class, we set certain properties.

Property	Setting
cCaption	Compact \<Discs
cMessage	Add, edit, or delete compact discs.

Class Name: AdminInvoiceBar

Superclass: cbar (..\..\common30\libs\cmenus.vcx)

Description: Runs the invoice form.

Base Class: container

This bar allows the user to run an instance of the invoice form. We have overridden the Click() method, however, so that it checks for the application toolbar object first, otherwise it just runs the form.

As with any visible menu class, we set certain properties.

Property	Setting
cCaption	\<Invoices
cMessage	Add, edit, or delete invoices.

Class Name: AdminMarkInvoiceBar

Superclass: cbar (..\..\common30\libs\cmenus.vcx)

Description: Runs the mark invoice form.

Base Class: container

This bar allows the user to run an instance of the mark invoice as shipped form. We have overridden the Click() method, however, so that it checks for the application toolbar object first, otherwise it just runs the form.

As with any visible menu class, we set certain properties.

Property	Setting
cCaption	Mar\<k Invoices
cMessage	Mark invoices as shipped.

Class Name: NavigationPad

Superclass: cpad (..\..\common30\libs\cmenus.vcx)

Description: The menu class for the Navigation menu pad.

Base Class: container

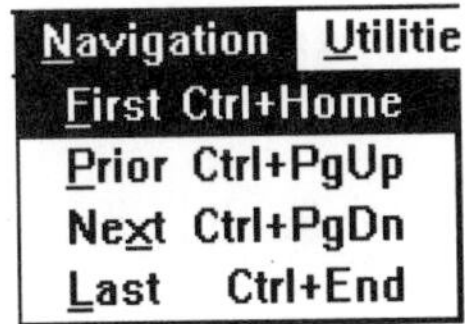

The Navigation Pad and Popup

This is the Navigation pad for our menu system. All we do here is override a number of properties including:

Property	Setting
cCaption	\<Navigation
cKey	Alt+N, "Alt+N"
cMessage	Commands to navigate through records on the active form.
cSkipFor	EMPTY(WONTOP())

Class Name NavigationPopup

Superclass: cpopup (..\..\common30\libs\cmenus.vcx)

Description: The menu class for the Navigation menu popup.

Base Class: container

NavigationPopup is the popup that contains our Navigation menu bars. Like Mainmenu, it has an overridden LoadChildren() method.

```
*--NavigationPopup.LoadChildren()
#DEFINE NUMCHILDREN 4
LOCAL laChildren[NUMCHILDREN, ALEN(this.aChildren, 2)]

laChildren[1, CHILD_CLASS] = "NavFirstBar"
laChildren[2, CHILD_CLASS] = "NavPriorBar"
laChildren[3, CHILD_CLASS] = "NavNextBar"
laChildren[4, CHILD_CLASS] = "NavLastBar"

DIMENSION this.aChildren[NUMCHILDREN, ALEN(laChildren, 2)]
=ACOPY(laChildren, this.aChildren)

RETURN NUMCHILDREN
```

Class Name NavFirstBar

Superclass: cbar (..\..\common30\libs\cmenus.vcx)

Description: Advances the record pointer to the first record.

Base Class: container

This bar allows the user to move the record pointer of the current alias to the first record. Since it is tied to a toolbar button, we don't have to add any Click() code, we simply point to the button that it works with, and that button's Click() method is called when this menu option is selected.

As with any visible menu class, we set certain properties.

Property	Setting
cCaption	\<First
cKey	CTRL+HOME, "Ctrl+Home"
cMessage	Moves the record pointer of the current alias to the first record.
cSkipFor	!FormIsObject()
cToolbarCommand	cntNavButtons.First()

Class Name NavPriorBar

Superclass: cbar (..\..\common30\libs\cmenus.vcx)

Description: Advances the record pointer to the prior record.

Base Class: container

This bar allows the user to move the record pointer of the current alias to the previous record. Since it is tied to a toolbar button, we don't have to add any Click() code, we simply point to the button that it works with, and that button's Click() method is called when this menu option is selected.

As with any visible menu class, we set certain properties.

Property	Setting
cCaption	\<Prior
cKey	CTRL+PGUP, "Ctrl+PgUp"
cMessage	Moves the record pointer of the current alias to the previous record.
cSkipFor	!FormIsObject()
cToolbarCommand	cntNavButtons.Prior()

Class Name NavNextBar

Superclass: cbar (..\..\common30\libs\cmenus.vcx)

Description: Advances the record pointer to the next record.

Base Class: container

This bar allows the user to move the record pointer of the current alias to the next record. Since it is tied to a toolbar button, we don't have to add any Click() code, we simply point to the button that it works with, and that button's Click() method is called when this menu option is selected.

As with any visible menu class, we set certain properties.

Property	Setting
cCaption	Ne\<xt
cKey	CTRL+PGDN, "Ctrl+PgDn"
cMessage	Moves the record pointer of the current alias to the next record.
cSkipFor	!FormIsObject()
cToolbarCommand	cntNavButtons.Next()

Class Name: NavLastBar

Superclass: cbar (..\..\common30\libs\cmenus.vcx)

Description: Advances the record pointer to the last record.

Base Class: container

This bar allows the user to move the record pointer of the current alias to the last record. Since it is tied to a toolbar button, we don't have to add any Click() code, we simply point to the button that it works with, and that button's Click() method is called when this menu option is selected.

As with any visible menu class, we set certain properties.

Property	Setting
cCaption	\<Last
cKey	CTRL+END, "Ctrl+End"
cMessage	Moves the record pointer of the current alias to the last record.
cSkipFor	!FormIsObject()
cToolbarCommand	cntNavButtons.Last()

Class Name: MrGoodBar

Superclass: cchocolate (..\..\common30\libs\chershey.vcx)

Description: Yummy in the tummy.

Base Class: ccandy

This bar allows the user to get a quick burst of energy while reading through this rather lengthy documentation. It is not included in the standard version of the framework (you must purchase the professional version), and exists here because surely you have a sense of humor. (OK, we'll stop calling you Shirley.)

As with any edible menu class, we set certain properties.

Property	Setting
lCrunchy	.T.
lMilky	.T.
nPeanuts	15
cWrapperColor	255, 255, 0
nCalories	=IIF(developer, .NULL., IIF(management, ∞, 300), 300)

Class Name UtilitiesPad

Superclass: cpad (..\..\common30\libs\cmenus.vcx)

Description: The menu class for the Utilities menu pad.

Base Class: container

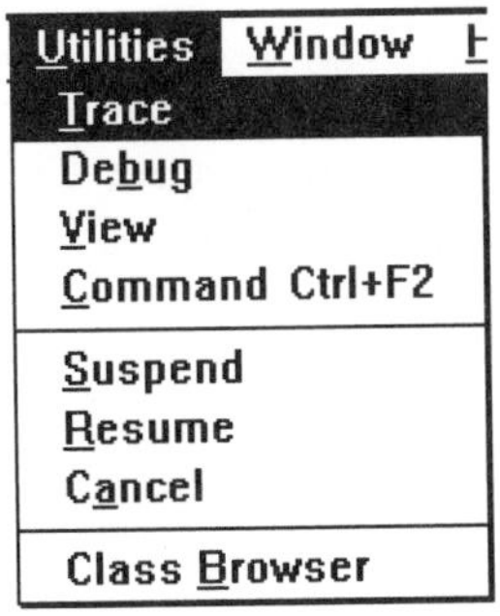

Utilities	Window	H
Trace		
Debug		
View		
Command Ctrl+F2		
Suspend		
Resume		
Cancel		
Class Browser		

The Utilities Pad and Popup

This is the Utilities Pad for our menu system. Since we only want this menu pad to appear when we are in debug mode, we add some code to the Init() method. This code checks if the file (DEBUG.TXT) that we use to see if we're in debug mode exists. If not, it sets the .lVisible property of itself to false. It then calls up to the Init() of its superclass.

```
*--UtilitiesPad.Init()
IF !FILE(DEBUGMODEFILE)
   this.lVisible = .F.
ENDIF
CPad::Init()
```

As with all menu pads, all we have to do for the base behavior is override a number of properties including:

Property	Setting
cCaption	\<Utilities
cKey	Alt+U, "Alt+U"
cMessage	Trace, debug, and view windows; suspend, resume, and cancel programs.

Class Name UtilitiesPopup

Superclass: cpopup (..\..\common30\libs\cmenus.vcx)

Description: The menu class for the Utilities menu popup.

Base Class: container

UtilitiesPopup is the popup that contains our Utilities menu bars. Like Mainmenu, it has an overridden LoadChildren() method.

```
*--UtilitiesPopup.LoadChildren()
#DEFINE NUMCHILDREN 10
LOCAL laChildren[NUMCHILDREN, ALEN(this.aChildren, 2)]

laChildren[1, CHILD_CLASS] = "UtilTraceBar"
laChildren[2, CHILD_CLASS] = "UtilDebugBar"
laChildren[3, CHILD_CLASS] = "UtilViewBar"
laChildren[4, CHILD_CLASS] = "UtilCommandBar"
laChildren[5, CHILD_CLASS] = "CSeparatorBar"
laChildren[6, CHILD_CLASS] = "UtilSuspendBar"
laChildren[7, CHILD_CLASS] = "UtilResumeBar"
laChildren[8, CHILD_CLASS] = "UtilCancelBar"
laChildren[9, CHILD_CLASS] = "CSeparatorBar"
laChildren[10, CHILD_CLASS] = "UtilBrowserBar"
```

```
DIMENSION this.aChildren[NUMCHILDREN, ALEN(laChildren, 2)]
=ACOPY(laChildren, this.aChildren)

RETURN NUMCHILDREN
```

Class Name UtilTraceBar

Superclass: cbar (..\..\common30\libs\cmenus.vcx)

Description: Displays the trace window.

Base Class: container

This bar allows the developer to call up the trace window. It is not tied to a toolbar button, but since it is tied to a native Visual FoxPro feature (using nBarNumber), we don't have to add any Click() code.

As with any visible menu class, we set certain properties.

Property	Setting
cCaption	\<Trace
cMessage	Displays the trace window.
nBarNumber	_MWI_TRACE

Class Name UtilDebugBar

Superclass: cbar (..\..\common30\libs\cmenus.vcx)

Description: Displays the debug window.

Base Class: container

This bar allows the developer to call the debug window. It is not tied to a toolbar button, but since it is tied to a native Visual FoxPro feature (using nBarNumber), we don't have to add any Click() code.

As with any visible menu class, we set certain properties.

Property	Setting
cCaption	De\<bug
cMessage	Displays the debug window.
nBarNumber	_MWI_DEBUG

Class Name UtilViewBar

Superclass: cbar (..\..\common30\libs\cmenus.vcx)

Description: Displays the view window.

Base Class: container

This bar allows the developer to call up the view window. It is not tied to a toolbar button, but since it is tied to a native Visual FoxPro feature (using nBarNumber), we don't have to add any Click() code.

As with any visible menu class, we set certain properties.

Property	Setting
cCaption	\<View
cMessage	Displays the view window.
nBarNumber	_MWI_VIEW

Class Name UtilCommandBar

Superclass: cbar (..\..\common30\libs\cmenus.vcx)

Description: Displays the command window.

Base Class: container

This bar allows the developer to call the command window. It is not tied to a toolbar button, but since it is tied to a native Visual FoxPro feature (using nBarNumber), we don't have to add any Click() code.

As with any visible menu class, we set certain properties.

Property	Setting
cCaption	\<Command
cKey	CTRL+F2, "Ctrl+F2"
cMessage	Displays the command window.
nBarNumber	_MWI_CMD

Class Name UtilSuspendBar

Superclass: cbar (..\..\common30\libs\cmenus.vcx)

Description: Suspends the current running program.

Base Class: container

This bar allows the developer to suspend the application. It is not tied to a toolbar button, nor is it tied to a native Visual FoxPro feature (using nBarNumber). We add code to the Click() method.

```
*--UtilSuspendBar.Click()
SUSPEND
```

As with any visible menu class, we set certain properties.

Property	Setting
cCaption	\<Suspend
cMessage	Suspends the currently running program.

Class Name UtilResumeBar

Superclass: cbar (..\..\common30\libs\cmenus.vcx)

Description: Resumes a previously suspended application.

Base Class: container

This bar allows the developer to resume a suspended application. It is not tied to a toolbar button, but since it is tied to a native Visual FoxPro feature (using nBarNumber), we don't have to add any Click() code.

As with any visible menu class, we set certain properties.

Property	Setting
cCaption	\<Resume
cMessage	Resumes running the current suspended program.
nBarNumber	_MPR_RESUM

Class Name: UtilCancelBar

Superclass: cbar (..\..\common30\libs\cmenus.vcx)

Description: Cancels the program.

Base Class: container

This bar allows the developer to cancel the application. It is not tied to a toolbar button, but since it is tied to a native Visual FoxPro feature (using nBarNumber), we don't have to add any Click() code.

As with any visible menu class, we set certain properties.

Property	Setting
cCaption	C\<ancel
cMessage	Stops running the current program.
nBarNumber	_MPR_CANCL

Class Name UtilBrowserBar

Superclass: cbar (..\..\common30\libs\cmenus.vcx)

Base Class: container

This bar allows the developer to call the class browser, if it exists. Since it is not tied to a toolbar button, we add specific Click() code that is called when this menu option is selected.

For this menu bar, the click code is:

```
*-- UtilBrowserBar.Click() Method
DO (_browser)
```

The system memory variable, _browser, points to where the class browser is located. The Init() method of this class has to change as well, because the class browser may not exist—it may not have been loaded on your hard drive, or you may be working with the standard version of Visual FoxPro 3, which doesn't include the class browser.

```
*-- UtilBrowserBar.Init() Method
LPARAMETERS tnBarNumber, tcPopupName

IF VERSION(2) <> 2 OR !FILE(_browser)
   this.Enabled = .F.
ENDIF
CBar::Init(tnBarNumber, tcPopupName)
```

The VERSION() function now takes a parameter. If it is passed a one, it returns the date and serial number of your version of Visual FoxPro 3. A two returns what type of version it is: runtime (0), standard (1), or professional (2). A three returns the localized language that you are running (English, French, Spanish, etc.).

If we are not running the professional version, or if the class browser cannot be found, we set the Enabled property to false, and call up to the Init() of the superclass.

As with any visible menu class, we set certain properties.

Property	Setting
cCaption	Class \<Browser
cSkipFor	!FormIsObject()

Class Name: WindowPad

Superclass: cpad (..\..\common30\libs\cmenus.vcx)

Description: The menu class for the Window menu pad.

Base Class: container

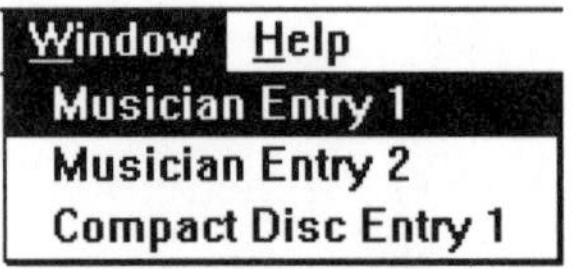

The Window Pad and Popup

This is the Window Pad for our menu system. All we do here is override a number of properties including:

Property	Setting
cCaption	\<Window
cKey	ALT+W, "ALT+W"
cMessage	Window selection
cSkipFor	EMPTY(WONTOP())

Class Name WindowPopup

Superclass: cpopup (..\..\common30\libs\cmenus.vcx)

Description: The menu class for the Window menu popup.

Base Class: container

WindowPopup is the popup that will contain instances of our CWindowBar class. Unlike the other popups, it has no overriding code in the LoadChildren() method, because we don't know what the children of this popup will be at design time. At run time, the children will be filled in as the user calls up new forms.

Class Name HelpPad

Superclass: cpad (..\..\common30\libs\cmenus.vcx)

Description: The menu class for the Help menu pad.

Base Class: container

The Help Pad and Popup

This is the Help Pad for our menu system. All we do here is override a number of properties including:

Property	Setting
cCaption	\<Help
cKey	Alt+H, "Alt+H"
cMessage	Displays help on this application.

Class Name HelpPopup

Superclass: cpopup (..\..\common30\libs\cmenus.vcx)

Description: The menu class for the Help menu popup.

Base Class: container

HelpPopup is the popup that contains our File menu bars. Like Mainmenu, it has an overridden LoadChildren() method.

```
*--HelpPopup.LoadChildren()
#DEFINE NUMCHILDREN 4
LOCAL laChildren[NUMCHILDREN, ALEN(this.aChildren, 2)]
```

```
laChildren[1, CHILD_CLASS] = "HelpContentsBar"
laChildren[2, CHILD_CLASS] = "HelpSearchBar"
laChildren[3, CHILD_CLASS] = "CSeparatorBar"
laChildren[4, CHILD_CLASS] = "HelpAboutBar"

DIMENSION this.aChildren[NUMCHILDREN, ALEN(laChildren, 2)]
=ACOPY(laChildren, this.aChildren)

RETURN NUMCHILDREN
```

Class Name HelpContentsBar

Superclass: cbar (..\..\common30\libs\cmenus.vcx)

Description: Calls up help contents.

Base Class: container

This bar allows the user to access the contents of the help file. It is not tied to a toolbar button, but since it is tied to a native Visual FoxPro 3 feature (using nBarNumber), we don't have to add any Click() code.

As with any visible menu class, we set certain properties.

Property	Setting
cCaption	\<Contents
cKey	F1, "F1"
cMessage	Displays Help table of contents.
nBarNumber	_mst_help

Class Name HelpSearchBar

Superclass: cbar (..\..\common30\libs\cmenus.vcx)

Description: Calls up search engine for help system.

Base Class: container

This bar allows the user to search for a specific topic in the current help file. It is not tied to a toolbar button, but since it is tied to a native Visual FoxPro 3 feature (using nBarNumber), we don't have to add any Click() code.

As with any visible menu class, we set certain properties.

Property	Setting
cCaption	\<Search for Help on...
cMessage	Searches for Help topics by keyword.
nBarNumber	_mst_hpsch

Class Name HelpAboutBar

Superclass: cbar (..\..\common30\libs\cmenus.vcx)

Description: Displays information about the application.

Base Class: container

This bar runs the About dialog, showing the user basic copyright information about the application, and allowing him or her to run MSINFO if it exists. Since it is not tied to a toolbar button, we add specific Click() code that is called when this menu option is selected.

For this menu bar, the Click() code is:

```
*-- HelpAboutBar.Click() Method
=DoForm("CAboutForm")
```

Since we want the caption of this bar to change based on the application (why keep reinventing the wheel?), we modify the Init() method.

```
*-- HelpAboutBar.Init() Method
LPARAMETERS tnBarNumber, tcPopupName

this.cCaption = "\<" + ABOUT_LOC + " " + APPNAME_LOC + "..."
RETURN CBar::Init(tnBarNumber, tcPopupName)
```

The Init() method simply concatenates whatever is stored in the constants ABOUT_LOC and APPNAME_LOC and stores it in the cCaption property. For the sample application, the cCaption property ends up storing:

```
About Compact Disc Ordering Application...
```

As with any visible menu class, we set certain properties.

Property	Setting
cCaption	\<About (this is only used as a default)
cMessage	Displays information about this application and the system configuration.

Class Name InvoicePad

Superclass: cpad (..\..\common30\libs\cmenus.vcx)

Description: The menu class for the Invoice menu pad.

Base Class: container

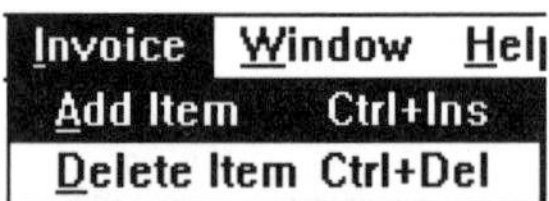

The Invoice Pad and Popup

This is the Invoice Pad for our menu system. It does not appear unless the Invoice Form is instantiated. When the Invoice Form exists, this menu pad remains disabled until the user is in the invoice line items grid.

All we do here is override a number of properties including:

Property	Setting
Enabled	.F.
cCaption	\<Invoice
cKey	Alt+I, "Alt+I"
cMessage	Add and delete line items.
lVisible	.F.

Class Name InvoicePopup

Superclass: cpopup (..\..\common30\libs\cmenus.vcx)

Description: The menu class for the Invoice menu popup.

Base Class: container

InvoicePopup is the popup that contains our Invoice menu bars. Like Mainmenu, it has an overridden LoadChildren() method.

```
*-- InvoicePopup.LoadChildren()
#DEFINE NUMCHILDREN   2
LOCAL laChildren[NUMCHILDREN, ALEN(this.aChildren, 2)]

laChildren[1, CHILD_CLASS] = "InvoiceAddItemBar"
laChildren[2, CHILD_CLASS] = "InvoiceDelItemBar"

DIMENSION this.aChildren[NUMCHILDREN, ALEN(laChildren, 2)]
=ACOPY(laChildren, this.aChildren)

RETURN NUMCHILDREN
```

Class Name InvoiceAddItemBar

Superclass: cbar (..\..\common30\libs\cmenus.vcx)

Description: Adds items to the line item grid in the invoice form.

Base Class: container

This bar adds a blank row to the line item grid in the invoice form, allowing the user to add another item. Since it is not tied to a toolbar button, we add specific Click() code that is called when this menu option is selected.

For this menu bar, the Click() code is:

```
*-- InvoiceAddItemBar.Click() Method
_screen.ActiveForm.oBizObj.oChildBizObj.cmdAdd.Click()
```

This code calls the Click() method of the Add commandbutton of the child business object of the invoice form. As you can see, you can tie menu bars to any existing method or object—not just ones on toolbars.

As with any visible menu class, we set certain properties.

Property	Setting
cCaption	\<Add Item
cKey	CTRL+INS, "Ctrl+Ins"
cMessage	Add line items.

Class Name InvoiceDelItemBar

Superclass: cbar (..\..\common30\libs\cmenus.vcx)

Description: Deletes items to the line item grid in the invoice form.

Base Class: container

This bar removes the current row from the line item grid in the invoice form, removing the item. Since it is not tied to a toolbar button, we add specific Click() code that is called when this menu option is selected.

For this menu bar, the Click() code is:

```
*-- InvoiceDelItemBar.Click() Method
_screen.ActiveForm.oBizObj.oChildBizObj.cmdDelete.Click()
```

As with any visible menu class, we set certain properties.

Property	Setting
cCaption	\<Delete Item
cKey	CTRL+DEL, “Ctrl+Del”
cMessage	Delete line items.

Chapter 36

CLASSLIB: ATOOLBAR.VCX

Introduction

ATOOLBAR.VCX contains any application-specific toolbars used in our application. In this application, the only toolbar that is created is an Admin toolbar that allows quick access to the various forms. All forms use the default CNavToolbar which is described in the chapter on CTOOLBAR.VCX.

Class Name: MainToolbar

Superclass: cadmintoolbar (..\..\common30\libs\ctoolbar.vcx)

Description: The main Codebook admin (application) toolbar

Base Class: toolbar

An instance of MainToolbar

MainToolbar contains our Admin toolbar with a number of buttons, one for each form that can be called from the Administration menu pad. The toolbar is easy to create, we simply subclass CAdminToolbar, and add instances of CAdminToolbarButton to it, setting their Click() methods to call:

```
=DOFORM("<form name>")
```

Button Name: cmdCustomer

This button creates an instance of the CustomerForm class. It is tied to the proper menu pad and menu bar through its cMenuPad and cMenuBar properties. This allows it to automatically disable the correct menu bar when the toolbar button is disabled.

Property	Setting
ToolTipText	Customers
cMenuPad	oAdministrationPad
cMenuBar	oAdminCustomerBar

Button Name: cmdCompactDisc

This button creates an instance of the CompactDiscForm class. It is tied to the proper menu pad and menu bar through its cMenuPad and cMenuBar properties. This allows it to automatically disable the correct menu bar when the toolbar button is disabled.

Property	Setting
ToolTipText	Compact Discs
cMenuPad	oAdministrationPad
cMenuBar	oAdminCompactDiscBar

Button Name: cmdMusician

This button creates an instance of the MusicianForm class. It is tied to the proper menu pad and menu bar through its cMenuPad and cMenuBar properties. This allows it to automatically disable the correct menu bar when the toolbar button is disabled.

Property	Setting
ToolTipText	Musicians
cMenuPad	oAdministrationPad
cMenuBar	oAdminMusicianBar

Button Name: cmdInvoice

This button creates an instance of the InvoiceForm class. It is tied to the proper menu pad and menu bar through its cMenuPad and cMenuBar properties. This allows it to automatically disable the correct menu bar when the toolbar button is disabled.

Property	Setting
ToolTipText	Invoices
cMenuPad	oAdministrationPad
cMenuBar	oAdminInvoiceBar

Button Name: cmdMarkInvoice

This button creates an instance of the MarkInvoiceForm class. It is tied to the proper menu pad and menu bar through its cMenuPad and cMenuBar properties. This allows it to automatically disable the correct menu bar when the toolbar button is disabled.

Property	Setting
ToolTipText	Mark Invoices
cMenuPad	oAdministrationPad
cMenuBar	oAdminMarkInvoiceBar

Chapter 37

CLASSLIB: DATAENV.PRG

Introduction

DATAENV is the only class library in the sample application that is stored in a program file instead of a visual class library. This is because the visual class designer does not allow you to subclass Visual FoxPro 3's data environment classes. You can subclass them in code, however, and this allows you to add a great deal of functionality to your applications.

This program file contains classes subclassed from our CDATAENV set of foundation classes. The program file begins with a #INCLUDE statement that includes our FRAMEWRK.H constants, and continues with the classes that make up the bulk of this .PRG file.

Note that not all of the data environments, cursors, and relations defined here are actually used in the sample application. The sample application makes use of views in order to provide an easy switch from local to remote data. We have defined cursors and relations that go against the table in order to show what it would look like if you wanted to change this application to go directly against DBF files.

Class Name: CodebookEnvironment

Superclass: cdataenvironment

Description: The sample application data environment.

Base Class: dataenvironment

CodebookEnvironment is a subclass of CDataEnvironment with the cDefaultDatabaseName property filled in, allowing all classes that are derived from this to automatically know which database container to use. This saves us from doing this in every data environment, and allows us to easily switch database containers, should we desire to at some later date.

Property	Contents
cDefaultDatabaseName	CDBK30

Class Name: CodebookReportEnvironment

Superclass: codebookenvironment

Description: The environment to use for reports.

Base Class: dataenvironment

CodebookReportEnvironment is a subclass of CodebookEnvironment which is geared towards working with reports. The AutoCloseTables property is set to false because the dataenvironment is instantiated in the Init() method of reports, and would automatically close all the tables when that method ends (since it is a local object and would lose scope) unless you set this property.

Property	Contents
cDefaultDatabaseName	CDBK30
AutoCloseTables	.F.

Class Name: LocalTablesEnvironment

Superclass: codebookenvironment

Description: A data environment that contains all local tables.

Base Class: dataenvironment

LocalTablesEnvironment is a subclass of CodebookEnvironment with the LoadCursors() method filled in so that it loads all of the local tables used in the application. This environment is used by the CDBManageForm, which is called when the user wants to perform table-based functions like PACK or REINDEX.

```
*-- LocalTablesEnvironment.LoadCursors()
DIMENSION this.aCursors[6]
this.aCursors[1] = "Musician"
this.aCursors[2] = "CompactDisc"
this.aCursors[3] = "Customer"
this.aCursors[4] = "Invoice"
this.aCursors[5] = "Purchase"
this.aCursors[6] = "Repolist"
```

Class Name: CompactDiscEnvironment

Superclass: codebookenvironment

Description: A data environment that contains the cursors for the CompactDisc business object.

Base Class: dataenvironment

CompactDiscEnvironment is a subclass of CodebookEnvironment with the LoadCursors() method filled in so that it loads all of the views or tables used in the CompactDisc business object. This environment is used by any processes which require the CompactDisc business object, including the CompactDiscForm.

Notice that this environment includes two cursors, one is based on the CompactDisc view, and the other on the musician table. The CompactDisc business object will have to include a link from the CompactDisc to its Musician.

```
*-- LoadCursors() Method
DIMENSION this.aCursors[2]
this.aCursors[1] = "v_CompactDisc"
this.aCursors[2] = "Musician"
```

Class Name: MusicianEnvironment

Superclass: codebookenvironment

Description: A data environment that contains the cursors for the Musician business object.

Base Class: dataenvironment

MusicianEnvironment is a subclass of CodebookEnvironment with the LoadCursors() method filled in so that it loads all of the views or tables used in the Musician business object. This environment is used by any processes which require this business object, including the MusicianForm and MusicianAddForm.

```
*-- LoadCursors() Method
DIMENSION this.aCursors[1]
this.aCursors[1] = "v_Musician"
```

Class Name: CustomerEnvironment

Superclass: codebookenvironment

Description: A data environment that contains the cursors for the Customer business object.

Base Class: dataenvironment

CustomerEnvironment is a subclass of CodebookEnvironment with the LoadCursors() method filled in so that it loads all of the views or tables used in the Customer business object. This environment is used by any processes which require this business object, including the CustomerForm.

```
*-- LoadCursors() Method
DIMENSION this.aCursors[1]
this.aCursors[1] = "v_Customer"
```

Class Name: InvoiceEnvironment

Superclass: codebookenvironment

Description: A data environment that contains the cursors for the Invoice business object.

Base Class: dataenvironment

InvoiceEnvironment is a subclass of CodebookEnvironment with the LoadCursors() method filled in so that it loads all of the views or tables used in the Invoice business object. This environment is used by any processes which require this business object, including the InvoiceForm.

Notice that this environment includes three cursors, based on the Invoice Header, Invoice Detail (Purchase), and Customer views.

```
*-- LoadCursors() Method
DIMENSION this.aCursors[3]
this.aCursors[1] = "v_Invoice"
this.aCursors[2] = "v_Purchase"
this.aCursors[3] = "v_CustomerInvoice"
```

Class Name: PurchaseEnvironment

Superclass: codebookenvironment

Description: A data environment that contains the cursors for the Purchase business object.

Base Class: dataenvironment

PurchaseEnvironment is a subclass of CodebookEnvironment with the LoadCursors() method filled in so that it loads all of the views or tables used in the Purchase business object. This environment is used by any processes which require this business object, including the InvoiceForm.

Notice that this environment includes two cursors, based on the Invoice Header and Invoice Detail (Purchase). It also sets the initial selected alias to the v_Purchase cursor.

```
*-- LoadCursors() Method
*-- We want the Purchase alias selected
nInitialSelectedAlias = 2

FUNCTION LoadCursors()
   DIMENSION this.aCursors[2]
   this.aCursors[1] = "v_Invoice"
   this.aCursors[2] = "v_Purchase"
ENDFUNC
```

Class Name: MarkInvoiceEnvironment

Superclass: codebookenvironment

Description: A data environment that contains the cursors for the Mark Invoice business object.

Base Class: dataenvironment

MarkInvoiceEnvironment is a subclass of CodebookEnvironment with the LoadCursors() method filled in so that it loads all of the views or tables used in the MarkInvoice business object. This environment is used by any processes which require this business object, including the MarkInvoiceForm.

```
*-- LoadCursors() Method
DIMENSION this.aCursors[1]
this.aCursors[1] = "v_MarkInvoice"
```

Class Name: ListCDEnvironment

Superclass: codebookreportenvironment

Description: A data environment that contains the cursor for the List CD Report.

Base Class: dataenvironment

ListCDEnvironment is a subclass of CodebookReportEnvironment with the LoadCursors() method filled in so that it loads all of the views or tables used in the List CD Report.

```
*-- LoadCursors() Method
DIMENSION this.aCursors[1]
this.aCursors[1] = "v_CompactDiscListing"
```

Class Name: ListCustEnvironment

Superclass: codebookreportenvironment

Description: A data environment that contains the cursor for the List Customer Report.

Base Class: dataenvironment

ListCustEnvironment is a subclass of CodebookReportEnvironment with the LoadCursors() method filled in so that it loads all of the views or tables used in the List Customers Report.

```
*-- LoadCursors() Method
DIMENSION this.aCursors[1]
this.aCursors[1] = "v_CustomerListing"
```

Class Name: OrdersEnvironment

Superclass: codebookreportenvironment

Description: A data environment that contains the cursor for the Customer Orders Report.

Base Class: dataenvironment

OrdersEnvironment is a subclass of CodebookReportEnvironment with the LoadCursors() method filled in so that it loads all of the views or tables used in the Customer Orders Report.

```
*-- LoadCursors() Method
DIMENSION this.aCursors[1]
this.aCursors[1] = "v_CustomerOrders"
```

Class Name: PurchAgeEnvironment

Superclass: codebookreportenvironment

Description: A data environment that contains the cursor for the Aging Report.

Base Class: dataenvironment

PurchAgeEnvironment is a subclass of CodebookReportEnvironment with the LoadCursors() method filled in so that it loads all of the views or tables used in the Aging (30/60/90) Report.

```
*-- LoadCursors() Method
DIMENSION this.aCursors[1]
this.aCursors[1] = "v_PurchaseHistory"
```

Class Name: CompactDisc

Superclass: ccursor

Description: A cursor that points to the compact disc table.

Base Class: cursor

CompactDisc is a subclass of the CCursor class with the CursorSource property set to the correct table.

Property	Setting
CursorSource	CompactDisc

Class Name: v_CompactDisc

Superclass: cdynamicviewcursor

Description: A cursor that points to a view of the compact disc table.

Base Class: cursor

v_CompactDisc is a subclass of the CDynamicViewCursor class with the CursorSource property set to the correct view.

Property	Setting
CursorSource	v_CompactDisc

Class Name: Customer

Superclass: ccursor

Description: A cursor that points to the customer table.

Base Class: cursor

Customer is a subclass of the CCursor class with the CursorSource property set to the correct table.

Property	Setting
CursorSource	Customer

Class Name: v_Customer

Superclass: cdynamicviewcursor

Description: A cursor that points to a view of the compact disc table.

Base Class: cursor

v_Customer is a subclass of the CDynamicViewCursor class with the CursorSource property set to the correct view.

Property	Setting
CursorSource	v_Customer

Class Name: v_CustomerInvoice

Superclass: cdynamicviewcursor

Description: A cursor that points to a view of the customer that is used to query invoices.

Base Class: cursor

v_CustomerInvoice is a subclass of the CDynamicViewCursor class with the CursorSource property set to the correct view.

Property	Setting
CursorSource	v_CustomerInvoice

Class Name: Invoice

Superclass: ccursor

Description: A cursor that points to the invoice.

Base Class: cursor

Invoice is a subclass of the CCursor class with the CursorSource property set to the correct table.

Property	Setting
CursorSource	Invoice

Class Name: v_Invoice

Superclass: cdynamicviewcursor

Description: A cursor that points to a view of the invoice and purchase tables.

Base Class: cursor

v_Invoice is a subclass of the CDynamicViewCursor class with the CursorSource property set to the correct view. It contains a join between the invoice and purchase tables, allowing us to view all of the invoice information (header and detail) in one logical and updatable view.

Property	Setting
CursorSource	v_Invoice

Class Name: v_MarkInvoice

Superclass: cdynamicviewcursor

Description: A cursor that points to a view of the invoice information (based on customer, invoice, and purchase), allowing you to mark a row as shipped.

Base Class: cursor

v_MarkInvoice is a subclass of the CDynamicViewCursor class with the CursorSource property set to the correct view. This view is set to optimistic table buffering, allowing the user to modify multiple rows before saving them all at once.

Property	Setting
CursorSource	v_MarkInvoice
BufferModeOverride	DB_BUFOPTTABLE

Class Name: Purchase

Superclass: ccursor

Description: A cursor that points to the purchase table.

Base Class: cursor

Purchase is a subclass of the CCursor class with the CursorSource property set to the correct table. This cursor is also set to use optimistic table buffering.

Property	Setting
CursorSource	Purchase
BufferModeOverride	DB_BUFOPTTABLE

Class Name: v_Purchase

Superclass: cdynamicviewcursor

Description: A cursor that points to a view of the purchase table.

Base Class: cursor

v_Purchase is a subclass of the CDynamicViewCursor class with the CursorSource property set to the correct view and the buffering default set to optimistic table buffering.

Property	Setting
CursorSource	v_Purchase
BufferModeOverride	DB_BUFOPTTABLE

Class Name: Musician

Superclass: ccursor

Description: A cursor that points to the musician table.

Base Class: cursor

Musician is a subclass of the CCursor class with the CursorSource property set to the correct table.

Property	Setting
CursorSource	Musician

Class Name: v_Musician

Superclass: cdynamicviewcursor

Description: A cursor that points to a view of the musician table.

Base Class: cursor

v_Musician is a subclass of the CDynamicViewCursor class with the CursorSource property set to the correct view.

Property	Setting
CursorSource	v_Musician

Class Name: v_CompactDiscListing

Superclass: creportdynamicviewcursor

Description: A reporting cursor that points to a view of the compact disc table.

Base Class: cursor

v_CompactDiscListing is a subclass of the CReportDynamicViewCursor class with the CursorSource property set to the correct view and an alias set for the view. As this shows, you can set the alias of a view separately from the view name, which can be handy when you have existing reports or forms that are bound to certain aliases.

Property	Setting
CursorSource	v_compact_disc_listing
Alias	compact_disc_listing

Class Name: v_CustomerListing

Superclass: creportdynamicviewcursor

Description: A reporting cursor that points to a view of the customer table.

Base Class: cursor

v_CustomerListing is a subclass of the CReportDynamicViewCursor class with the CursorSource property set to the correct view and an alias set for the view. As this shows, you can set the alias of a view separately from the view name, which can be handy when you have existing reports or forms that are bound to certain aliases.

Property	Setting
CursorSource	v_customer_listing
Alias	customer_listing

Class Name: v_CustomerOrders

Superclass: creportdynamicviewcursor

Description: A reporting cursor that points to a view of customer orders.

Base Class: cursor

v_CustomerOrders is a subclass of the CReportDynamicViewCursor class with the CursorSource property set to the correct view and an alias set for the view.

As this shows, you can set the alias of a view separately from the view name, which can be handy when you have existing reports or forms that are bound to certain aliases.

Property	Setting
CursorSource	v_customer_orders
Alias	customer_orders

Class Name: v_PurchaseHistory

Superclass: creportdynamicviewcursor

Description: A reporting cursor that points to a view of customer purchase history.

Base Class: cursor

v_PurchaseHistory is a subclass of the CReportDynamicViewCursor class with the CursorSource property set to the correct view and an alias set for the view. As this shows, you can set the alias of a view separately from the view name, which can be handy when you have existing reports or forms that are bound to certain aliases.

Property	Setting
CursorSource	v_purchase_history
Alias	purchase_history

Class Name: Repolist

Superclass: cfreetablecursor

Description: A cursor that points to a free table containing report information.

Base Class: cursor

Repolist is a subclass of the CFreeTableCursor class with the CursorSource property set to the correct table. As this shows, you can create a cursor from a free table as well as from tables that are tied to a database container.

Property	Setting
CursorSource	FULLPATH(METAPATH + "repolist.dbf")

Class Name: InvoicePurchaseRelation

Superclass: crelation

Description: A relation that points from invoice to purchase.

Base Class: Relation

InvoicePurchaseRelation is a CRelation that relates the invoice header and detail. This relation class is not used in the application. It is left here as an example of how to set up relations.

Property	Setting
ParentAlias	Invoice
ChildAlias	Purchase
ChildOrder	cInvoiceID
RelationalExpr	cID

Chapter 38

CLASSLIB: ABIZNESS.VCX

Introduction

ABIZNESS.VCX contains our application-specific business objects. They are subclassed from classes that are stored in the CBIZNESS.VCX class library.

Class Name: MusicianObj

Superclass: cbizobj (..\..\common30\libs\cbizness.vcx)

Description: The musician business object.

Base Class: container

The MusicianObj in design view

MusicianObj is an example of a simple business object. It is subclassed from CBizObj and has few specializations.

The container's cDeleteTriggerMsg property has been overridden to say, "There are compact discs belonging to this musician. Cannot delete." This is the message users will get whenever they try to delete a musician who has compact discs. The delete trigger fails, and causes this message to display.

The method, ErrorUniqueIndexViolated() is overridden as follows:

```
*-- MusicianObj.ErrorUniqueIndexViolated()
=ErrorMsg(NAMEALREADYEXISTS_LOC)
*-- Since we have already displayed the error message,
*-- we pass a .T. to the superclass method to prevent the
*-- default error message from being displayed.
CBizObj::ErrorUniqueIndexViolated(.T.)
```

This calls up a specific error message for this business object, and passes a true to its superclass, so that it doesn't display the default error message.

Finally, the lAllowSelectAll property is set to true, allowing all rows to be returned from the view if the user doesn't fill in any of the view parameters on a form.

As with all CBIZOBJ subclasses, this business class includes instances of CSessionEnvironment and CDELoader. CSessionEnvironment is not touched because we don't have to change the default settings of any of our SET commands.

CDELoader has the cDataEnvironment property set to MusicianEnvironment, causing this business object to automatically load the proper data environment whenever it is instantiated (whether it is on a form or is instantiated directly).

We have also provided a default "view" into the business object, which is a simple textbox that has its datasource set to "v_musician.cname."

Class Name: CompactDiscObj

Superclass: cbizobj (..\..\common30\libs\cbizness.vcx)

Description: The compact disc business object.

Base Class: container

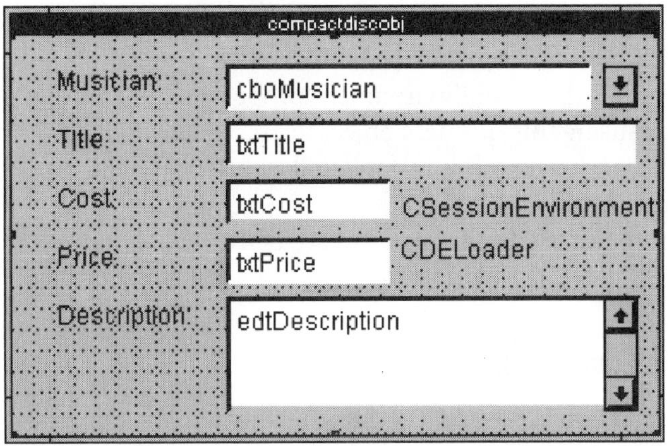

compactdiscobj
Musician: cboMusician
Title: txtTitle
Cost: txtCost CSessionEnvironment
Price: txtPrice CDELoader
Description: edtDescription

The CompactDiscObj in design view

CompactDiscObj is an example of a slightly more complex business object. It is subclassed from CBizObj, and has some interesting specializations, most of which have to do with the musician intellifind combobox.

The container's cDeleteTriggerMsg property has been overridden to say, "This compact disc appears on one or more invoices. Cannot delete." This is the message users will get whenever they try to delete a musician who has compact discs. The delete trigger fails, and causes this message to display. The cInsert-TriggerMsg property has been overridden to say, "Cannot add record. Musician does not exist!" The insert trigger fails if a compact disc is added without there being a corresponding musician.

As with MusicianObj, the lAllowSelectAll property is set to true, allowing all rows to be returned from the view if the user doesn't fill in any of the view parameters on a form.

The lAllowForcedUpdates is set to true, allowing fields to be written even if another user has changed the current business object. If this property is set to false, the user gets a message that his or her changes cannot be saved, and the other user's changes are shown. With this property set to true, the user sees a message box asking if he or she wants to override the other user's changes. The user can answer "yes," and his or her changes will be saved.

The method, Requery() is overridden as follows:

```
*-- CompactDiscObj.Requery()
this.cboMusician.Requery()
RETURN CBizObj::Requery()
```

This allows the business object to keep its musician combobox up to date whenever the business object is brought up to date.

CDELoader has the cDataEnvironment property set to CompactDisc-Environment, causing this business object to automatically load the proper data environment whenever it is instantiated (whether that is on a form or is instantiated directly).

The textboxes on the business object are tied to the v_compactdisc data environment.

The Musician ComboBox

The musician combobox is subclassed from CIFCombobox and has the following specialized properties and methods.

The ControlSource property is set to v_compactdisc.cmusicianid, tying the combobox to the proper column.

Three special properties of the intellifind combobox have been set:

The cFormName property is set to musicianaddform, causing that form to appear if the user types in a musician name that doesn't exist in the musician data. The lCaseSensitive property is set to true, causing the combobox to do a case-sensitive search, and lLimitToList is set to false, allowing the user to type in a name that doesn't already exist.

If you want to test the functionality of the CIFCombobox, run the sample application, bring up the Compact Disc form, and type a new name into the combobox. Three methods of this combobox have been specialized.

```
*--cboMusician.Init()
this.RowSource = "select cname, cid " + ;
                              " from musician " + ;
                              " order by cname " + ;
                              " into cursor cMusician "
CIFCombobox::Init()
```

The Init() method creates a cursor which is used to fill the combobox pulldown.

```
*--cboMusician.InteractiveChange()
CIFCombobox::InteractiveChange()
*-- Update cname field in view. This field should not be updatable.
*-- It is present just for the grid in the list page.
IF CURSORGETPROP("SOURCETYPE") <> DB_SRCTABLE
   REPLACE v_compactdisc.cname WITH this.DisplayValue
ENDIF
```

The InteractiveChange() method calls back to the superclass and then does a REPLACE, putting the current musician name in the compact disc view, so that the "List" page will show the correct name. This is important in case the user changes the musician for an existing compact disc.

```
*--cboMusician.Destroy()
CIFCombobox::Destroy()
IF USED("cMusician")
   USE IN cMusician
ENDIF
```

The Combobox's Destroy() method calls back to its superclass, and then removes the cursor that its Init() method created.

Class Name: CustomerObj

Superclass: cbizobj (..\..\common30\libs\cbizness.vcx)

Description: The customer business object.

Base Class: container

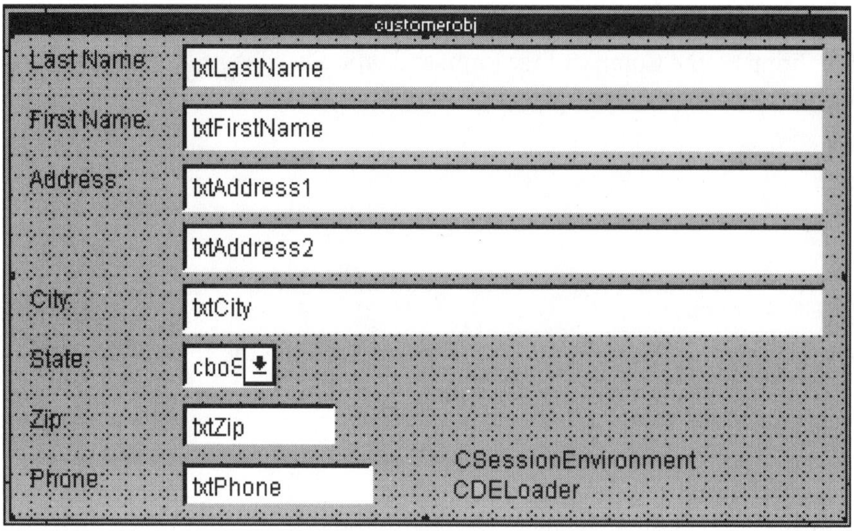

The CustomerObj in design view

CustomerObj is another example of a simple business object. It is subclassed from CBizObj, and has few specializations. It does, however, demonstrate how a custom control (in this case, the state combobox) can ease your development.

The container's cDeleteTriggerMsg property has been overridden to say, "There are invoices belonging to this customer. Cannot delete." This is the message users will get whenever they try to delete a customer who has invoices. The delete trigger fails, and causes this message to display.

There is no specialized code written behind this business object.

As with all CBIZOBJ subclasses, this business class includes instances of CSessionEnvironment and CDELoader. CSessionEnvironment is not touched because we don't have to change the default settings of any of our SET commands.

CDELoader has the cDataEnvironment property set to "CustomerEnvironment," causing this business object to automatically load the proper data environment whenever it is instantiated (whether that is on a form or it is instantiated directly).

The default "view" into the business object is made up mostly of textboxes that are tied to the proper columns of the dataenvironment. One control is based on the CStateComboBox class located in CCUSTCTL.VCX. This control was simply dropped on the form, with the ControlSource property set to v_customer.cstate, just like any other control can have a ControlSource set. The superclass handles all of the state drop-down logic for you.

Class Name: PurchaseObj

Superclass: cbizobj (..\..\common30\libs\cbizness.vcx)

Description: The purchase business object.

Base Class: container

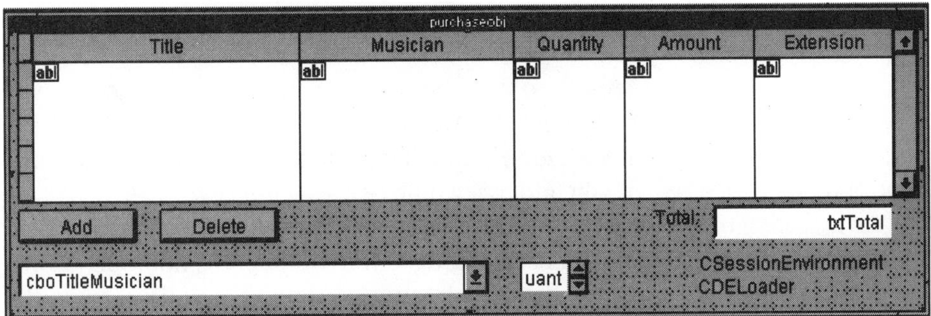

The PurchaseObj in design view

PurchaseObj is an example of a complex business object. It is subclassed from CBizObj, and has many specializations. Purchase is an object which will almost never (I'd say never, but someone will find that one time) be created on its own. This business object is a line item of an invoice. As such, we have set up the default view to look like a portion of an invoice entry form, with a grid containing line items, a control that displays the total, and a "rapid entry" region consisting of Add and Delete buttons, a dropdown of inventory items and a spinner to select the quantity purchased.

Let's look back to the needs of our sample application. It is geared towards a company that takes telephone orders, and as such must allow for easy and fast entry of multiple compact discs. This led us to decide to not use the grid for direct data entry—that would be too slow for the user (don't worry, we have a business object that includes direct grid entry a little later on). In order to speed things up, we allow keyboard entry that loops from the Add button to the dropdown, to the spinner, and back to the Add button. Very fast entry results from this design.

The container's cInsertTriggerMsg property has been overridden to say, "Cannot save invoice. You have either failed to select a compact disc, or the compact disc you have selected has been deleted." This is the message users will get whenever they try to add an invoice with an invalid lineitem. The purchase object's insert trigger fails, and causes this message to display. The cUpdate-TriggerMsg property has been overridden to say, "Cannot save record. Changes are not permitted to invoices that have been shipped."

One interesting property of a business object that is used here is the cMenuPad property. This business object sets the property to oInvoicePad. This ensures that whenever the purchase object has focus, an Invoice menu pad will appear. To see this, run the sample application, bring up an invoice, and click in the lineitems area. Notice that the Invoice Pad appears, with the options to add and delete line items. These options have shortcut keys assigned, allowing a user to hit a key to accomplish the same functions.

Other properties that are key to this object include lConfirmOnDelete which is set to false, so that users don't get an "Are You Sure?" message every time they delete a line item, and lSetFocusOnNew which is set to false, allowing the current control to keep focus when you add a new line item.

As with all CBIZOBJ subclasses, this business class includes instances of CSessionEnvironment and CDELoader. CSessionEnvironment is not touched because we don't have to change the default settings of any of our SET commands.

CDELoader has the cDataEnvironment property set to PurchaseEnvironment, causing this business object to automatically load the proper data environment whenever it is instantiated (whether that is on a form or is instantiated directly).

PurchaseObj has a custom method, GetTotal(), which returns the total of the line items.

```
*-- PurchaseObj.GetTotal()
RETURN this.txtTotal.Value
```

This business object has specialized the behavior of many methods.

```
*-- PurchaseObj.AllowNew()
LOCAL lcAlias, ;
      llAllowNew

lcAlias = this.GetAlias()
llAllowNew = .T.

GO BOTTOM IN (lcAlias)
IF !EOF(lcAlias) AND EMPTY(v_purchase.ccdid)
   llAllowNew = .F.
ENDIF

RETURN llAllowNew
```

The AllowNew() method lets us decide whether a new business object can be created. We test to see if we have the information that is needed in order to add a row (a link to a CD that is being purchased), and if so, allow the add; otherwise, we return a false.

```
*-- PurchaseObj.Delete()
LOCAL loSelect, ;
        lnRetVal, ;
        lyCurrentExtension

loSelect = CREATEOBJECT("CSelect", this.GetAlias())
lyCurrentExtension = icdquantity * ycdamount
IF this.lConfirmOnDelete
   IF (MESSAGEBOX(DELETEREC_LOC, ;
        MB_ICONQUESTION + MB_ICONYESNO, ;
        APPNAME_LOC)) = IDNO
      RETURN
   ENDIF
ENDIF

=LockScreen(.T.)
lnRetVal = CBizObj::Delete()
IF lnRetVal <> FILE_NORECORDS
   this.grdPurchases.SetFocus()
   IF TYPE("goApp.oMenu.oInvoicePad") == "O"
      goApp.oMenu.oInvoicePad.Enabled = .T.
      *-- Force the menu to refresh
      ACTIVATE MENU _MSYSMENU NOWAIT
   ENDIF
ENDIF

*-- Update the total
IF INLIST(lnRetVal, FILE_OK, FILE_NORECORDS)
   this.txtTotal.Value = this.txtTotal.Value - lyCurrentExtension
   this.txtTotal.Refresh()
ENDIF
this.grdPurchases.Refresh()
=LockScreen(.F.)
RETURN lnRetVal
```

Delete() is the method that runs whenever the user deletes a line item. It SELECTs the proper work area, stores the extended amount for the line being deleted, optionally asks the user if he or she wants the deletion to take place (if lConfirmOnDelete gets set to true), and calls up to the superclass to do the delete.

If there are still rows left in the purchase object, it sets focus to the grid, enables the invoice menu, and refreshes it. Finally, it updates the control that displays the total, and refreshes the grid.

```
*-- PurchaseObj.IsChanged()
RETURN (GETNEXTMODIFIED(0, this.GetAlias()) <> 0)
```

The IsChanged() method is overridden so that it checks the proper work area for any changes. It does this by using the GETNEXTMODIFIED() function to check if any other rows in the purchase object have been modified.

```
*-- PurchaseObj.IsNewAndEmpty()
RETURN this.IsChanged()
```

This method simply returns a true if we have any changed rows.

```
*-- PurchaseObj.New()
LOCAL lnRetVal

=LockScreen(.T.)
lnRetVal = CBizObj::New()
this.cboTitleMusician.SetFocus()
=LockScreen(.F.)

RETURN lnRetVal
```

The New() method calls up to its superclass, then sets the focus to the combobox that displays the compact disc title. Therefore, whenever a new purchase object is created, the user is immediately able to select a compact disc.

```
*-- PurchaseObj.OnDeleteLastRecord()
*-- When last record is deleted, automatically add a new
*-- record to the grid.
this.New()
RETURN CBizObj::OnDeleteLastRecord()
```

Purchase should have the behavior of automatically adding a new purchase when the last one is deleted. In this way, a user can delete all of the line items of an invoice, and continue to add new ones.

```
*-- PurchaseObj.OnNew()
CBizObj::OnNew()
```

```
*-- Replace the invoice id so we know what invoice this
*-- record belongs to.
REPLACE cinvoiceid WITH v_invoice.cid
```

When we are adding a new purchase object, we want to default the invoice ID of that purchase object to the currently active invoice.

```
*-- PurchaseObj.Requery()
LOCAL lnRetVal, ;
        loSelect

loSelect = CREATEOBJECT("CSelect", this.GetAlias())
this.cboTitleMusician.Requery()
lnRetVal = CBizObj::Requery()
IF lnRetVal = REQUERY_SUCCESS
   =LockScreen(.T.)
   this.txtTotal.Value = v_invoice.ninvoicetotal
   this.Refresh()
   =LockScreen(.F.)
ENDIF

RETURN lnRetVal
```

When we requery the business object, we select the correct work area, requery the combobox (like we did in the Compact Disc business object), set up the total textbox, and refresh the business object.

The Purchase Grid

The grid that displays the line items has been specialized by setting the following properties:

Property	Value	Description
ColumnCount	5	This is the number of columns that we want in the grid.
DeleteMark	.F.	We don't show the Delete Mark in the grid. This makes it look more like an invoice line item section.
GridLines	2	We only show vertical grid lines.

Property	Value	Description
ReadOnly	.T.	The information in the grid cannot be modified. All modification is done through the "fast entry" section below the grid.
RecordSource	v_purchase	We point the grid to the view of our purchase information.
ScrollBars	2	We only show a vertical scrollbar. We set up the grid so that all columns are always visible, and don't allow the grid to scroll right and left.

Four of the grid's methods are specialized as well.

```
*-- grdPurchases.Init()
*-- Set all grid columns to read only if the grid is readonly
IF this.ReadOnly
   this.SetAll("ReadOnly", .T., "Column")
ENDIF
```

The Init() method checks to see if the grid is marked as ReadOnly, and if so, it marks every column as ReadOnly as well.

```
*-- grdPurchases.AfterRowColChange()
LPARAMETERS nColIndex
*-- Calls to LockScreen() are necessary to work-around refresh
*-- problems with the grid
=LockScreen(.T.)
this.Parent.cboTitleMusician.Refresh()
this.Parent.spnQuantity.Refresh()
this.Refresh()
=LockScreen(.F.)
```

When we move to a new row of the grid, we want to automatically refresh the "fast entry" controls (the combobox and spinner) as well.

```
*-- grdPurchases.Valid()
IF TYPE("goApp.oMenu.oInvoicePad") == "O"
   goApp.oMenu.oInvoicePad.Enabled = .F.
   *-- Force the menu to refresh
```

```
    ACTIVATE MENU _MSYSMENU NOWAIT
ENDIF
```

As we leave the grid, we disable the Invoice menu pad.

```
*-- grdPurchases.When()
IF TYPE("goApp.oMenu.oInvoicePad") == "O"
    goApp.oMenu.oInvoicePad.Enabled = .T.
    *-- Force the menu to refresh
    ACTIVATE MENU _MSYSMENU NOWAIT
ENDIF
```

As we enter the grid, we enable the Invoice menu pad.

There is one more method that is associated with the grid that is specialized. That method is the When() of the Extension columns textbox. We RETURN a false from this method in order to keep the user out of this field.

"Fast Entry" Controls—Add CommandButton

This button allows the user to add invoice line items. We set the caption property to Add, and set the Click() method to tell the business object to add. To do this, we use one line of code:

```
this.Parent.New()
```

"Fast Entry" Controls—Delete CommandButton

This button allows the user to delete invoice line items. We set the caption property to Delete, and set the Click() method to tell the business object to delete. To do this, we use one line of code:

```
this.Parent.Delete()
```

"Fast Entry" Controls—CD ComboBox

This drop-down combobox allows the quick selection of existing compact discs. This combobox has three specialized methods.

```
*--cboTitleMusician.Init()
CComboBox::Init()
this.RowSource = ;
    "select compactdisc.ctitle, musician.cname, " + ;
    " compactdisc.yprice, compactdisc.cid " + ;
    " from compactdisc, musician " + ;
```

```
        " where compactdisc.cmusicianid = musician.cid " + ;
        " order by compactdisc.ctitle, musician.cname " + ;
        " into cursor cTitles "
    this.BoundColumn = 4
    this.ColumnCount = 2
    this.ColumnWidths = STR(FSIZE("cTitle", "cTitles") * ;
        FONTMETRIC(TM_AVECHARWIDTH, this.FontName, this.FontSize)) + ;
        ", " + ;
        STR(FSIZE("cName", "cTitles") * ;
        FONTMETRIC(TM_AVECHARWIDTH, this.FontName, this.FontSize))
```

The Init() method of the combobox calls up to its superclass and then sets the various properties of the combobox that bind data to the box. The BoundColumn property tells the combobox to put the cID of the selected compact disc in the .Value property. The ColumnCount property tells the combobox to show the first two columns of the SQL SELECT. The ColumnWidths property is set to the correct size to show the two columns nicely.

```
*--cboTitleMusician.InteractiveChange()
LOCAL loSelect

loSelect = CREATEOBJECT("CSelect", this.Parent.GetAlias())

*-- Get the current extension for the current line
lyCurrentExtension = icdquantity * ycdamount

this.Parent.txtTotal.Value = ;
    this.Parent.txtTotal.Value - lyCurrentExtension

REPLACE ctitle WITH this.GetColumnValue(1), ;
    cname WITH this.GetColumnValue(2), ;
    icdquantity WITH 1, ;
    ycdamount WITH NTOM(VAL(this.GetColumnValue(3))), ;
    ccdid WITH this.GetColumnValue(4)

this.Parent.txtTotal.Value = this.Parent.txtTotal.Value + ;
    icdquantity * ycdamount

=LockScreen(.T.)
this.Parent.grdPurchases.Refresh()
this.Parent.spnQuantity.Refresh()
this.Parent.txtTotal.Refresh()
=LockScreen(.F.)
```

The InteractiveChange() method subtracts the current line item amount from the textbox that displays the total, does a REPLACE statement to place the new selection into the view, and adds the new line to the total textbox. It then refreshes all of the appropriate controls.

Note the use of the GetColumnValue() method of the combobox. This is a custom method that we have added to all multi-column controls (see the chapter on CCONTROLS.VCX). It returns the value of whatever column number we pass it.

```
*-- cboTitleMusician.Destroy()
IF USED("cTitles")
   USE IN cTitles
ENDIF
```

The destroy method simply closes the cursor that drives the combobox.

"Fast Entry" Controls—Quantity Spinner

This drop-down combobox allows the quick selection of existing compact discs. This combobox has three specialized methods.

```
*-- spnQuantity.KeyPress()
LPARAMETERS nKeyCode, nShiftAltCtrl
DO CASE
   CASE INLIST(nKeyCode, KEY_ENTER, KEY_TAB)
      this.Parent.cmdAdd.SetFocus()
      NODEFAULT
   CASE nKeyCode = KEY_DASH
      *-- Do not allow negative entries in the spinner
      ?? CHR(7)
      NODEFAULT
ENDCASE
```

We specialize the Keypress() method to speed up data entry for the user. If the user presses the Enter or Tab key while in the spinner, we automatically set the focus to the Add command button. If the user presses the dash, the program will beep and do nothing, keeping the user from entering a negative number.

```
*-- spnQuantity.InteractiveChange()
LOCAL lyCurrentExtension, ;
        lyDifference, ;
        loSelect
```

```
loSelect = CREATEOBJECT("CSelect", this.Parent.GetAlias())

*-- Get the current extension for the current line
lyCurrentExtension = icdquantity * ycdamount

*-- Force the icdquantity field to be updated with the
*-- value of this control
REPLACE icdquantity WITH this.Value

*-- Now calculate the difference
lyDifference = this.Value * ycdamount - lyCurrentExtension

*-- Update the total and the grid
=LockScreen(.T.)
this.Parent.txtTotal.Value = this.Parent.txtTotal.Value + lyDifference
this.Parent.txtTotal.Refresh()
this.Parent.grdPurchases.Refresh()
=LockScreen(.F.)
```

The InteractiveChange() method updates the quantity field as the user changes a value in the spinner, keeps the Total textbox updated, and updates the grid as well.

PurchaseObj—A Summary

As you can see from the above code and description, we look at the default behavior for this business object, and code in the specific behavior that is required by the users of the application.

Class Name: InvoiceObj

Superclass:	conetomanybizobj (..\..\common30\libs\cbizness.vcx)
Description:	The invoice business object.
Base Class:	container

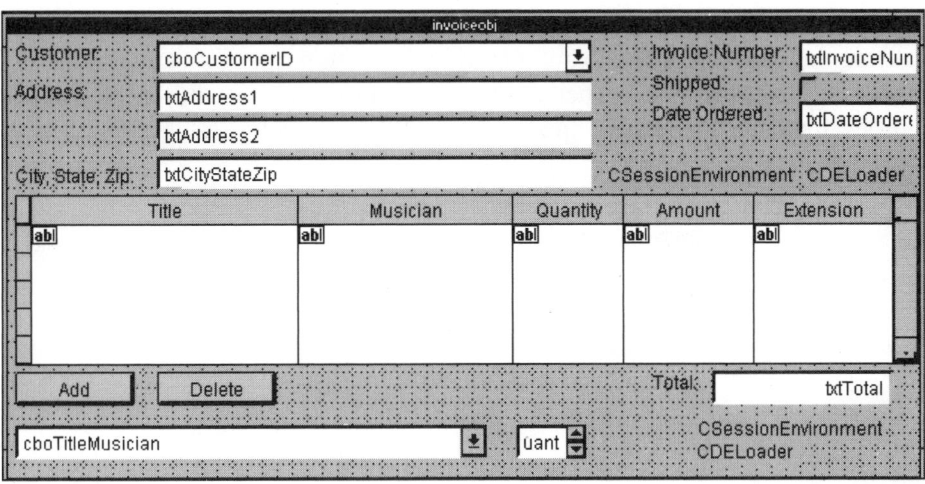

The InvoiceObj in design view

InvoiceObj is an example of a one-to-many business object. It is subclassed from COneToManyBizObj, and has many specializations. The InvoiceObj is made up of an Invoice Header with a PurchaseObj instance dropped in, giving us all the capabilities of the purchase object without requiring us to code it again. The only code that we focus on is the code that provides the unique capabilities of an invoice. The line items take care of themselves. As developers, it allows us to focus our efforts, providing for tighter code, with less chances of introducing bugs. It also allows us to reimplement the purchase object (if, for example, you wanted to display the line items in a listbox instead of a grid) with minimal impact on the rest of the system.

The container's cDeleteTriggerMsg property has been overridden to say, "Cannot delete invoices that have been shipped." This is the message users will get whenever they try to delete an invoice that has been shipped. The invoice object's delete trigger fails and causes this message to display. The cInsert-TriggerMsg property has been overridden to say, "Cannot add record. Customer may have been deleted!" The cUpdateTriggerMsg property has been overridden to say, "Cannot save record. Changes are not permitted to invoices that have been shipped."

As with all CBIZOBJ subclasses, this business class includes instances of CSessionEnvironment and CDELoader. CSessionEnvironment is not touched because we don't have to change the default settings of any of our SET commands.

CDELoader has the cDataEnvironment property set to InvoiceEnvironment, causing this business object to automatically load the proper data environment whenever it is instantiated (whether that is on a form or is instantiated directly).

Seven methods have been specialized for the InvoiceObj class.

```
*-- InvoiceObj.Init()
LOCAL llRetVal
llRetVal = COneToManyBizObj::Init()
IF llRetVal
    this.cboCustomerID.ListIndex = 1
    this.cboCustomerID.Valid()
ENDIF

RETURN llRetVal
```

The Init() method calls up to the superclass, and if all is okay, it sets the customer combobox to the first customer, and calls the Valid() method of the combobox, causing the customer's address to be displayed.

```
*-- InvoiceObj.Cancel()
LPARAMETERS tlAllRows
LOCAL lnRetVal, ;
          loSelect

loSelect = CREATEOBJECT("CSelect", this.GetAlias())

*-- If there are no records, then there is nothing to cancel
lnRetVal = IIF(RECCOUNT() > 0, FILE_OK, FILE_CANCEL)
IF lnRetVal = FILE_OK
    *-- If the saved field is .F., then we
    *-- are canceling an add operation.
    *-- Since transactions do not work with local views, we need
    *-- to delete the header record.
    IF !lsaved
       this.oChildBizObj.Cancel(.T.)
       this.Delete()
    ELSE
       lnRetVal = COneToManyBizObj::Cancel()
    ENDIF
ENDIF

RETURN lnRetVal
```

The cancel is specialized to cancel all pending edits for the children (by passing the Cancel message to the purchase object) and then it deletes itself.

```
*-- InvoiceObj.New()
LOCAL lnRetVal, ;
        loSelect

*-- Insert the customer ID into the new record
loSelect = CREATEOBJECT("CSelect", this.GetAlias())
=LockScreen(.T.)
lnRetVal = COneToManyBizObj::New()
IF lnRetVal = FILE_OK
   *-- Since customer is pre-selected, we have to update the
   *-- value in the cursor manually
   REPLACE ccustomerid WITH this.cboCustomerID.Value

   *-- Default to today's date for date ordered
   this.txtDateOrdered.Value = DATE()
   this.txtDateOrdered.Enabled = .T.

   *-- Make sure the child business object is enabled
   this.oChildBizObj.Enabled = .T.

ENDIF
=LockScreen(.F.)

RETURN lnRetVal
```

The New() method selects the proper work area, calls up to its superclass, and then we update the invoice's customer with the current customer that is selected in the pulldown. We also set any necessary default values and enable the purchaseobj instance.

```
*-- InvoiceObj.OnNew()
COneToManyBizObj::OnNew()
REPLACE cinvoicenumber WITH NewID("cinvoicenumber")
```

When a new invoice is being added, we grab an invoice number to show the customer service representative who is entering the order.

```
*-- InvoiceObj.OnSaveNew()
COneToManyBizObj::OnSaveNew()

*-- Replace the update flag with .T. indicating that this
*-- record was saved. Note that this field has no corresponding
*-- field on the "back-end",
*-- so we use SETFLDSTATE() to mark it as not being changed.
```

```
IF CURSORGETPROP("SOURCETYPE") <> DB_SRCTABLE
   REPLACE lsaved WITH .T.
   =SETFLDSTATE("lsaved", 1)
ENDIF
```

When we are saving a new invoice object, we set a flag field called lSaved to true, and use the Visual FoxPro SETFLDSTATE() function so that the setting of that flag won't affect our check to see if anything was modified.

```
*-- InvoiceObj.Requery()
PRIVATE vp_CustomerID
LOCAL lnRetVal, ;
        loSelect, ;
        llEnabled

loSelect = CREATEOBJECT("CSelect", this.GetAlias())
vp_cCustomerID = this.cboCustomerID.Value
loMsg = CREATEOBJECT(GetMessageClass(), REFRESHING_LOC)

this.cboCustomerID.Requery()
lnRetVal = REQUERY("v_CustomerInvoice")
IF lnRetVal = REQUERY_SUCCESS
   lnRetVal = COneToManyBizObj::Requery()
   llEnabled = RECCOUNT() <> 0
   this.txtDateOrdered.Enabled = llEnabled
   this.oChildBizObj.Enabled = llEnabled
   this.Refresh()
ENDIF

RETURN lnRetVal
```

The Requery() method is used to tie the combobox to the v_purchase view parameter. As we select a customer, it uses the value to refresh our view of the data.

```
*-- InvoiceObj.Save()
LPARAMETERS tlAllRows, tlForce
LOCAL loSelect
loSelect = CREATEOBJECT("CSelect", this.GetAlias())

IF CURSORGETPROP("SOURCETYPE") <> DB_SRCTABLE
   *-- Update the view's nInvoiceTotal field. This is field
   *-- is a calculated field in the view, so no updates will
   *-- be done to the back end.
   REPLACE ninvoicetotal with this.oChildBizObj.GetTotal()
```

```
ENDIF

RETURN COneToManyBizObj::Save(tlAllRows, tlForce)
```

When we save an invoice, we REPLACE the invoice total with the total of the purchase object. To do this, we "ask" the purchase object for its total. We then call up to the superclass to handle the actual save.

Now, let's look at the default interface for our business object. The invoice header is made up of a combobox that controls our view into our data. When the combobox is selected, we requery() the view and refresh the customer address information. The header also contains an invoice number, a checkbox that displays whether the order was shipped, and the date of the order.

One interesting thing to note is that txtDateOrdered is subclassed from our CDateTextBox customer control, allowing the user to quickly change the date by hitting the plus or minus keys, as well as other hot keys (see the chapter on CCUSTCTL.VCX).

The Customer ComboBox

cboCustomerID is a combobox that allows the user to select a customer, to call up the previous orders for a particular customer, and to add new orders or change existing ones. The RowSource of the combobox is set to the following SQL SELECT.

```
SELECT ALLTRIM(Customer.cLastName) + ", " + ;
   Customer.cFirstName as Name, Customer.cID ;
 FROM Customer ;
 ORDER BY Name ;
 INTO CURSOR cCustomer
```

We set the following properties on the combobox.

Property	Value	Description
BoundColumn	2	This is the column of the RowSource that we want returned into the .Value property of the combobox. In this case, it places the customer ID.
RowSourceType	3	The RowSource comes from a SQL statement.

We also specialize three methods of cboCustomerID.

```
*-- cboCustomerID.Valid()
*-- Check if any changes were made and prompt user to save
*-- if necessary before changing customer
IF this.Parent.IsChanged()
   IF TYPE("thisform") == "O" AND thisform.AskToSave() = IDCANCEL
      this.Value = OLDVAL("v_invoice.ccustomerid")
      RETURN
   ENDIF
ENDIF

=LockScreen(.T.)
IF TYPE("thisform") == "O"
   thisform.Requery()
ELSE
   this.Parent.Requery()
   this.Refresh()
ENDIF
=LockScreen(.F.)
```

When the user changes a customer, we are going to requery the parameters on our view. Therefore, we check if InvoiceBizObj has changed, and if so, we ask if we should save the changes and act acccordingly. We then refresh the business object if we end up moving to a new customer.

```
*-- cboCustomerID.Refresh()
*-- We need to disable the combo box when adding a new invoice.
this.Enabled = !IsAdding(this.Parent.GetAlias())
IF !this.Enabled
   this.Parent.txtDateOrdered.SetFocus()
ENDIF
```

When adding a new invoice (the business object has received a "New" message), we want to disable the combobox, forcing entry for the currently selected customer. The Refresh() method does this, and sets the focus to the Date Ordered textbox.

```
*-- cboCustomerID.Destroy()
IF USED("cCustomer")
   USE IN cCustomer
ENDIF
```

The Destroy() method of the combobox simply cleans up after itself by closing the cCustomer cursor that it uses.

Class Name: MarkInvoiceObj

Superclass: cbizobj (..\..\common30\libs\cbizness.vcx)

Description: The mark invoice business object.

Base Class: container

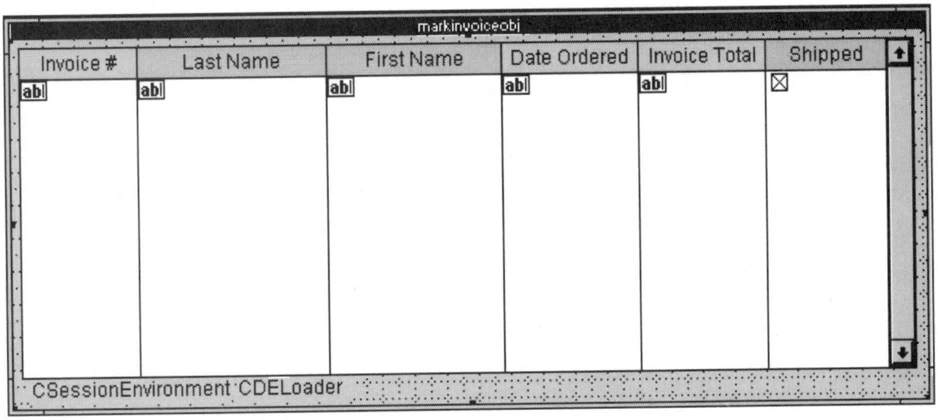

The MarkInvoiceObj in design view

MarkInvoiceObj is an example of a fairly straightforward business object that looks very complex. It is subclassed from CBizObj and allows a user to directly manipulate a checkbox that is placed in a grid.

This business object handles the process of marking shipped orders. It is easiest in this case to show the orders in a row, clicking on the ones that are shipped.

No properties of the MarkInvoiceObj have been specialized. They all use the defaults.

Some of the business object's methods have been specialized, mostly to handle the fact that we're working with multiple rows at a time.

```
*-- MarkInvoiceObj.Cancel()
LPARAMETERS tlAllRows
RETURN CBizObj::Cancel(.T.)
```

When cancel is selected by the user, we want to cancel all of the changes made in all of the rows, and therefore force a True to be sent back to the Cancel method of the CBizObj superclass. This sets tlAllRows to true, forcing a cancel of all the changes.

```
*-- MarkInvoiceObj.Save()
LPARAMETERS tlAllRows, tlForce
RETURN CBizObj::Save(.T., tlForce)
```

Like the Cancel() method, the Save() method sends a true to the CBizObj superclass telling it to do the save on all rows.

```
*-- MarkInvoiceObj.IsChanged()
RETURN (GETNEXTMODIFIED(0, this.GetAlias()) <> 0)
```

Since this is a multi-row business object, we check to see if any changes were made by using the Visual FoxPro 3 GETNEXTMODIFIED() function to see if we are returned the information that any rows were modified.

CDELoader has the cDataEnvironment property set to MarkInvoiceEnvironment, causing this business object to automatically load the proper data environment whenever it is instantiated (whether that is on a form or is instantiated directly).

The Mark Invoice Grid Control

The main user interface element in the default "view" into the business object is a grid whose elements are read only with the exception of a checkbox that has been set as the currentcontrol in the last column. The overridden methods of the grid are used to provide for this functionality.

We set the following properties on the grid.

Property	Value	Description
ColumnCount	6	This is the number of columns that we want in the grid.
DeleteMark	.F.	We don't show the delete mark area on the left of the grid.
GridLines	2	We only show vertical grid lines.
ReadOnly	.T.	We want the grid to be read only by default.
RecordMark	.F.	We don't want to show the record mark area on the left of the grid.
ScrollBars	2	We only show a vertical scrollbar.

By turning off the DeleteMark and RecordMark, and setting the grid-to-vertical-grid lines and scroll bars, we make it look like and emulate a listbox.

The grid has one changed method, Init(), which works as follows:

```
*-- grdInvoices.Init()
LOCAL lnShippedColumn
CGrid::Init()
lnShippedColumn = this.GetColumnNumber("Shipped")
this.Columns(lnShippedColumn).ReadOnly = .F.
this.ActivateCell(this.ActiveRow, lnShippedColumn)
```

The Init() method first calls up to its superclass, then it uses the custom GetColumnNumber method to get the column number of the "Shipped" column (this allows the method code to work even if we change the number of columns, or the user moves the column). We set that column's ReadOnly property to false, allowing for entry, and we place the cursor in the current row's "Shipped" column.

To the users, this means that when the grid comes up, they are ready to enter the first order as shipped.

Conclusion

These business objects make up the core functionality of the system. We subclass a class of the CBIZOBJ class library, and decide on the default "view" into the business object, writing code and setting properties that make the business object work appropriately.

We made the decision to have the business object provide a default "view" into itself because of the "Visual" in Visual FoxPro. Visual FoxPro has a wonderful set of robust visual development tools, and it makes sense to have a framework for the product take advantage of the tools and capabilities of that product.

Note that the business object classes have a base class of "container" which will allow us, as developers, to change the "view" into the object for each form we tie it to, should we need to.

As we'll see in the next chapter, for this sample application we won't often need to.

Chapter 39

CLASSLIB: AFORMS.VCX

Introduction

AFORMS.VCX contains our application-specific forms. They are subclassed from form classes that are stored in the CFORMS.VCX class library. They demonstrate a number of capabilities of the Codebook Foundation Classes including the use of a business object on multiple forms (allowing you to show it different ways, with the business object handling itself), reading and writing from and to an external storage source (in this case the Windows NT and '95 Registry or an .INI file), and the capability of changing the external appearance of a stock form class.

Class Name: MusicianForm

Superclass: cbizobjmaintform (..\..\common30\libs\cforms.vcx)

Description: The form class that supports the musician business object (musicianobj).

Base Class: form

MusicianForm is the standard maintenance form for the musician business object. As such, it is subclassed from CBizObjMaintForm, providing us with a three-tabbed dialog box. The first tab allows entry of selection criteria for the business object, the second tab allows data entry for the business object, and the third tab shows a list view of their data, allowing the user to select another row quickly and easily.

This is a simple form to implement, as we will see. There is no code in any method in this form. The form's superclass and the business object instance that is embedded in the form know how to handle themselves.

The Selection Criteria Tab

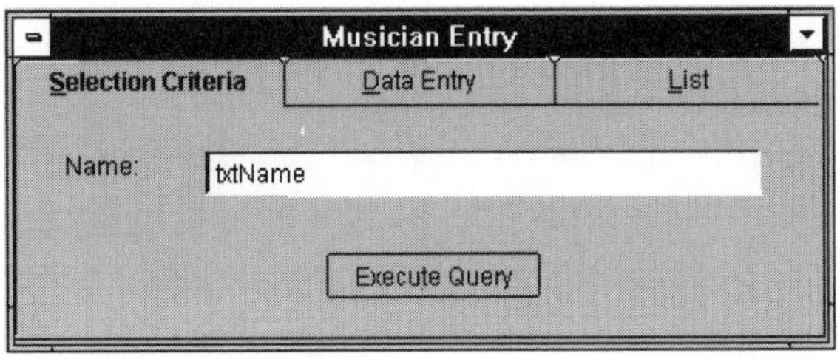

The MusicianForm's Selection Criteria tab in Design mode

The objects in this tab are created very easily. When we subclass the CBizObj-MaintForm, we are provided with this tab, and the "Execute Query" button. We simply drop the label and textbox onto the form (using our CCONTROLS class library, of course), and set the cViewParameter of the textbox to vp_cName. This automatically binds anything that the user types into this textbox to the parameter in the parameterized view that we use to access our customer data.

That's all there is to it! We now have a form that can send parameters to its view, whether the data is coming from Visual FoxPro DBFs, SQL Server, Oracle, or any server product.

The Data Entry Tab

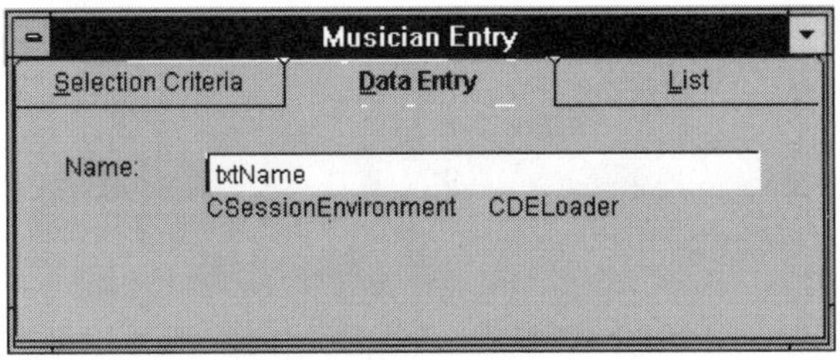

The MusicianForm's Data Entry tab in Design mode

The Data Entry tab is quite easy to put together as well. We select this page, and drop an instance of the MusicianObj onto it. Done!

Note that we could drill down into the MusicianObj and specialize any of its default behaviors for this form. There is rarely a need to do that, however.

The List Tab

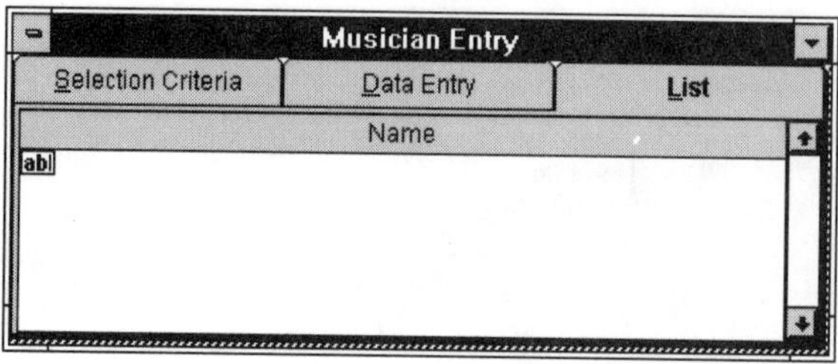

The MusicianForm's List tab in Design mode

When we subclass CBizObjMaintForm, we are given a grid in the List tab that defaults to all columns in the business object's view. We simply set how many columns we would like to display, and which ones, and we are done.

We focus on the *visual* issues involved in displaying the business object, that's it.

Class Name: MusicianAddForm

Superclass:	cbizobjaddform (..\..\common30\libs\cforms.vcx)
Description:	The form class that allows the user to add one musician business object.
Base Class:	form

The MusicianAddForm in Design mode

MusicianAddForm is subclassed from CBizObjAddForm, and allows the addition of one business object to a modal form. All we do is drop the business object onto this type of form and add the following to the Init() method:

```
*-- MusicianAddForm.Init()
LPARAMETERS tcName
CBizObjAddForm::Init()
this.oBizObj.txtName.Value = tcName
```

This code accepts a parameter, calls up to the Init() of the superclass, and then sets the txtName textbox's Value property to the passed parameter.

This form is used in the CompactDiscForm by the Intellifind ComboBox that is used for musician names. If a non-existent musician is typed in by the user, it automatically calls this form and passes what the user typed. For more information on how this works, see the last chapter's discussion of the CompactDiscObj.

As always, we could drill down into the business object should we want to specialize it for this form.

Class Name: CompactDiscForm

Superclass: cbizobjmaintform (..\..\common30\libs\cforms.vcx)

Description: The form class that supports the compact disc business object (compactdiscobj).

Base Class: form

CompactDiscForm is the standard maintenance form for the compact disc business object. As such, it is subclassed from CBizObjMaintForm, providing us with a three-tabbed dialog box. The first tab allows entry of selection criteria for the business object, the second tab allows data entry for the business object, and the third tab shows a list view of their data, allowing the user to select another row quickly and easily.

This is a simple form to implement, as we will see. There is no code in any method in this form. The form's superclass and the business object instance that is embedded in the form know how to handle themselves.

The Selection Criteria Tab

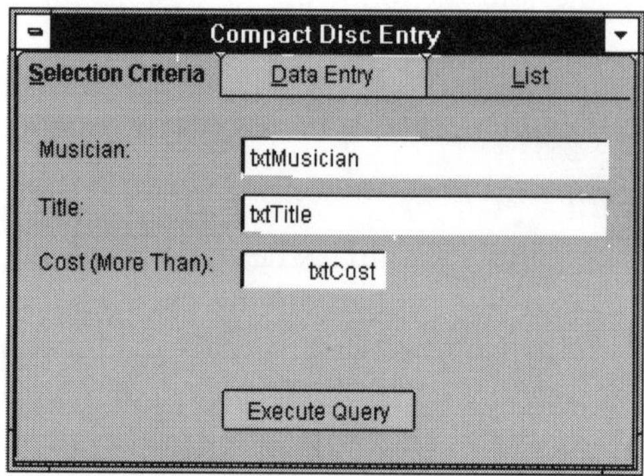

The CompactDiscForm's Selection Criteria tab in Design mode

The objects in this tab are created very easily. When we subclass the CBizObjMaintForm, we are provided with this tab and the Execute Query button. We simply drop the three labels and three textboxes onto the form (using our CCONTROLS class library, of course), and set the cViewParameter of the textboxes to the correct parameters (vp_cMusician, vp_cTitle, vp_yCost). This automatically binds anything that the user types into this textbox to the parameter in the parameterized view that we use to access our customer data. Note that the view uses a "greater than" as the comparison to vp_yCost, so we can limit our results to those compact discs that cost more than an amount entered by the user.

That's all there is to it! We now have a form that can send parameters to its view, whether the data is coming from Visual FoxPro DBFs, SQL Server, Oracle, or any server product.

The Data Entry Tab

Compact Disc Entry
Selection Criteria | Data Entry | List
Musician: cboMusician
Title: txtTitle
Cost: txtCost CSessionEnvironment
Price: txtPrice CDELoader
Description: edtDescription

The CompactDiscForm's Data Entry tab in Design mode

The Data Entry tab is quite easy to put together as well. We select this page, and drop an instance of the CompactDiscObj onto it. Done!

Note that we could drill down into the CompactDiscObj and specialize any of its default behaviors for this form. There is rarely a need to do that, however.

The List Tab

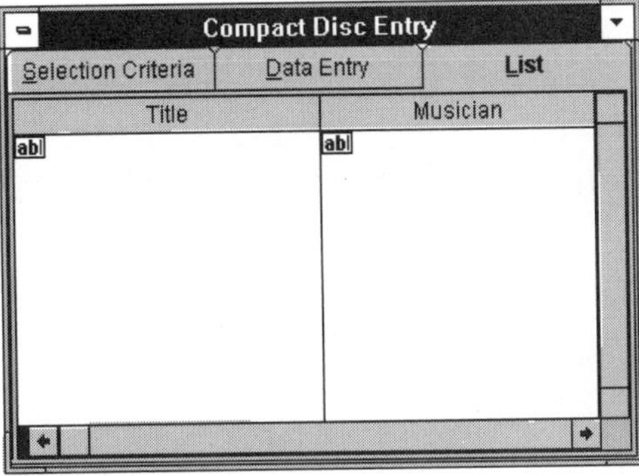

The CompactDiscForm's List tab in Design mode

When we subclass CBizObjMaintForm, we are given a grid in the List tab that defaults to all columns in the business object's view. We simply set the number of columns we would like to display and which ones, and we are done.

We focus on the *visual* issues involved in displaying the business object, and that's it.

Class Name: CustomerForm

Superclass:	cbizobjmaintform (..\..\common30\libs\cforms.vcx)
Description:	The form class that supports the customer business object (customerobj).
Base Class:	form

CustomerForm is the standard maintenance form for the customer business object. As such, it is subclassed from CBizObjMaintForm, providing us with a three-tabbed dialog box. The first tab allows entry of selection criteria for the business object. The second tab allows data entry for the business object, and the third tab shows a list view of their data, allowing the user to select another row quickly and easily.

This is a simple form to implement, as we will see. There is no code in any method in this form. The form's superclass and the business object instance that is embedded in the form know how to handle themselves.

The Selection Criteria Tab

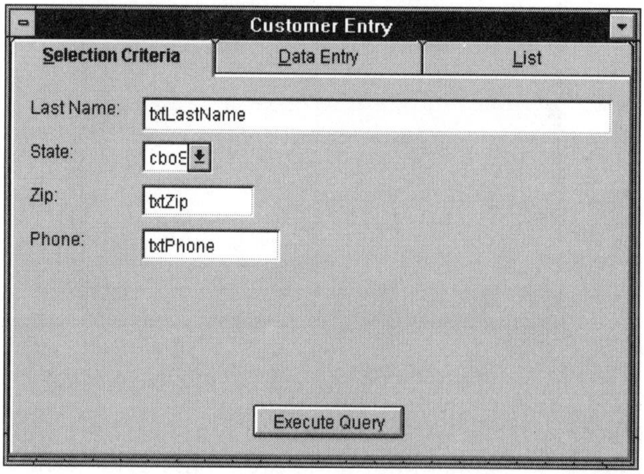

The CustomerForm's Selection Criteria tab in Design mode

The objects in this tab are created very easily. When we subclass the CBizObj-MaintForm, we are provided with this tab and the Execute Query button. We simply drop the four labels and three textboxes onto the form (using our CCONTROLS class library, of course), drop the custom control CStateComboBox (from the CCUSTCTL.VCX class library) and set the cViewParameter of the text-boxes and combobox to the correct parameters of the view. This automatically binds anything that the user types into these controls to the parameter in the parameterized view that we use to access our customer data.

That's all there is to it! We now have a form that can send parameters to its view, whether the data is coming from Visual FoxPro DBFs, SQL Server, Oracle, or any server product.

The Data Entry Tab

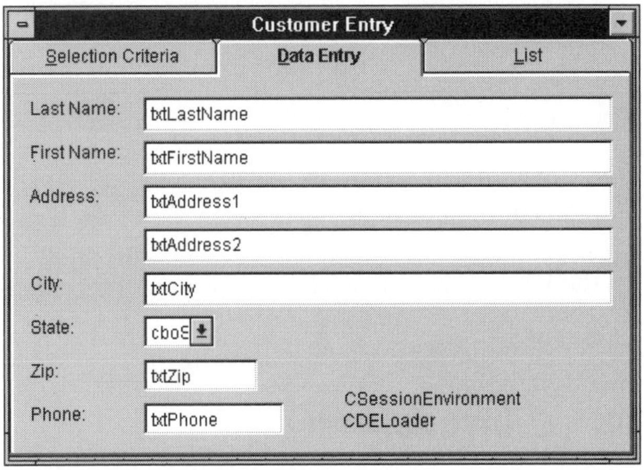

The CustomerForm's Data Entry tab in Design mode

The Data Entry tab is quite easy to put together as well. We select this page, and drop an instance of the CustomerObj onto it. Done!

Note that we could drill down into the CustomerObj and specialize any of its default behaviors for this form. There is rarely a need to do that, however.

The List Tab

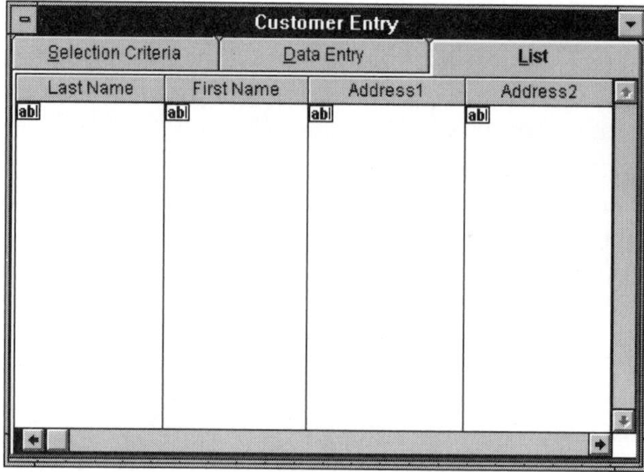

The CustomerForm's List tab in Design mode

When we subclass CBizObjMaintForm, we are given a grid in the List tab that defaults to all columns in the business object's view. We simply set the number of columns we would like to display, and which ones, and we are done.

We focus on the *visual* issues involved in displaying the business object, and that's it.

Class Name: InvoiceForm

Superclass: cbizobjmaintform (..\..\common30\libs\cforms.vcx)

Description: The form class that supports the invoice business object (invoiceobj).

Base Class: form

Invoiceform is the standard form for the invoice business object. It is subclassed from CBizObjMaintForm, which is modified at runtime to remove the selection criteria tab—the customer dropdown will do the entry of the selection criteria for us. We retain the tab that allows data entry for the business object and the tab that shows a list view of their data, allowing the user to select another row quickly and easily.

Despite these changes, this is a simple form to implement, as we will see. There is very little code in this form. The form's superclass and the business object instance that is embedded in the form know how to handle themselves, so we simply worry about the appearance of the form.

The Selection Criteria Tab

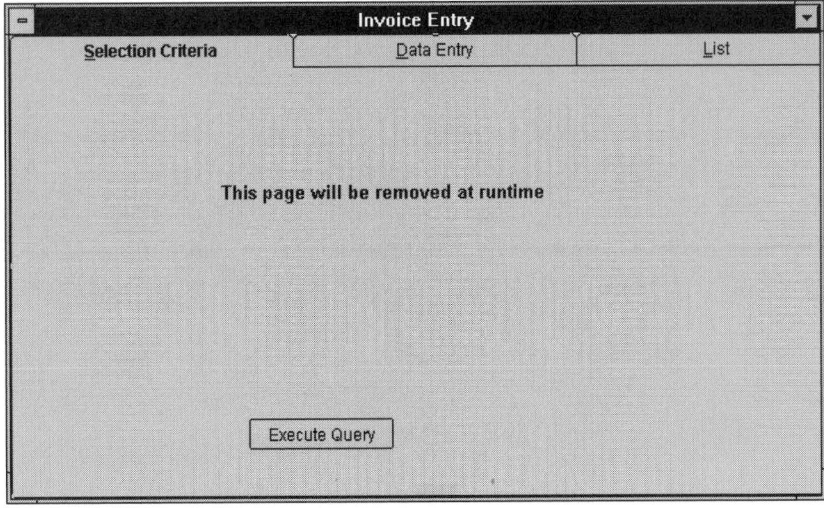

The InvoiceForm's Selection Criteria tab in Design mode

We are going to be removing this tab at runtime, so we simply place a textbox here to remind us of the fact. No "real" controls are dropped onto this page.

The Data Entry Tab

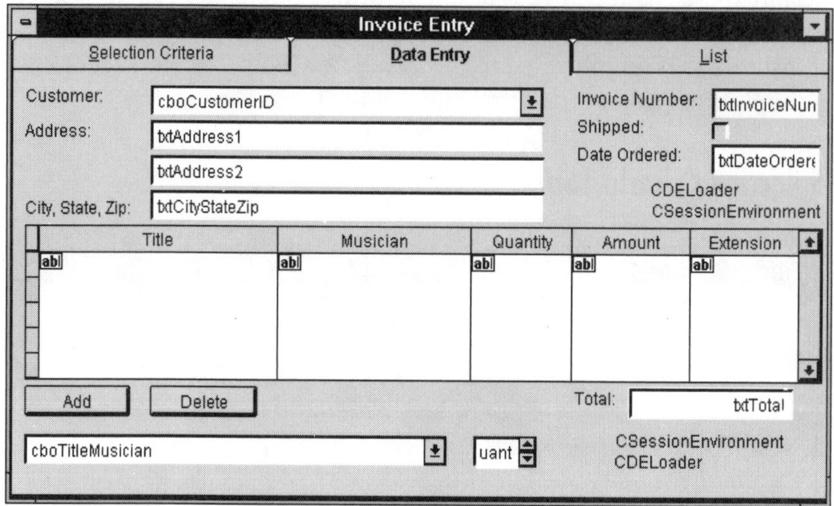

The InvoiceForm's Data Entry tab in Design mode

The Data Entry tab is quite easy to put together. We select this page, and drop an instance of the InvoiceObj onto it. Done!

Note that we could drill down into the InvoiceObj (and even into its contained PurchaseObj) and specialize any of the default behaviors for this form. There is rarely a need to do that, however.

The List Tab

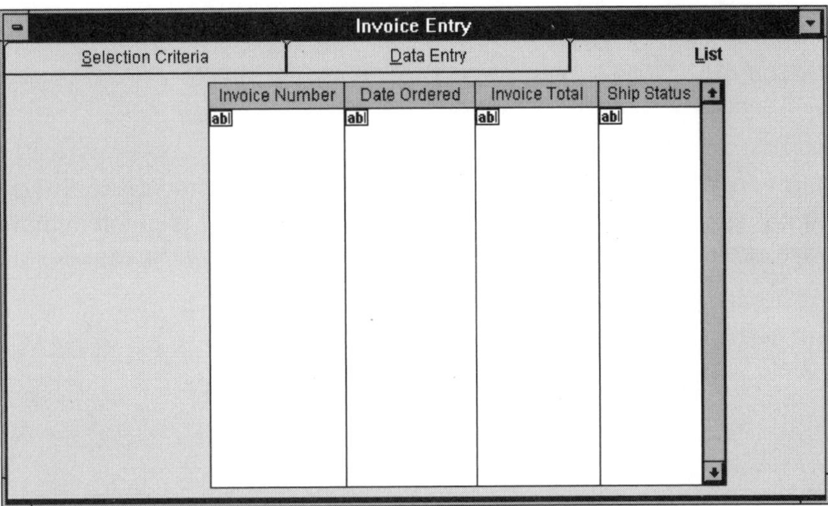

The InvoiceForm's List tab in Design mode

When we subclass CBizObjMaintForm, we are given a grid in the List tab that defaults to all columns in the business object's view. We simply set how many columns we would like to display, and which ones, and we are done.

In this form, we've set the Shipped column to display as a textbox (it's a logical field in the database) with the word "shipped" appearing if the order has shipped, otherwise it is blank.

As always, we focus on the *visual* issues involved in displaying the business object, and that's it.

Code Changes

Let's take a look at the changed methods and the added property of this form, and see what was done and why.

```
*--InvoiceForm.OnCancelFirstRecord()
CBizObjMaintForm::OnCancelFirstRecord(PAGE_DATAENTRY)
this.oBizObj.oChildBizObj.Enabled = .F.
```

When an event occurs that causes us to want to disable the current business object, we also disable the child business object, and have the pageframe set to the Data Entry tab.

```
*--pgfBizObj.Init()
CBizObjMaintForm.pgfBizObj::Init()
*-- Remove the Selection Criteria page
this.RemoveObject("Page1")
```

This form does not require the criteria page—the criteria is automatically set by selecting a new customer from the customer dropdown. We therefore remove the first page of the pageframe.

```
*--Page2.Activate()
*-- Performance enhancement
LOCAL llIsFirstActivate

llIsFirstActivate = this.Parent.lFirstActivate
CBizObjMaintForm.pgfBizObj.Page2::Activate()
IF llIsFirstActivate
   this.Parent.lFirstActivate = .F.
   RETURN
ENDIF

=LockScreen(.T.)
IF !thisform.oBizObj.IsChanged()
   IF thisform.nRecNo <> RECNO()
      this.cntInvoiceObj.oChildBizObj.Requery()
      thisform.nRecNo = RECNO()
   ENDIF
ENDIF
=LockScreen(.F.)
```

When using a pageframe, there are often times where you will want to perform a Refresh() or a Requery() when a certain page is selected. Sometimes this can conflict with initialization of the form when the form is being displayed for the first time. In other words, there may not be a need to perform this Refresh() or Requery() action if the page is being activated for the first time, since this may have already been handled by the form. The lFirstActivate property is initially set to .T. in CPageFrame, and allows the developer to bracket code in various page Activate event methods that he or she does not want to execute the first time the form is displayed. This property exists purely for performance reasons. If you use it, be sure to set its Value to .F. when appropriate.

```
*--Page2.Deactivate()
CBizObjMaintForm.pgfBizObj.Page2::Deactivate()
thisform.nRecNo = RECNO()
```

When we leave the Data Entry tab, we save the current record number. We can then check to see if the user has changed the row, allowing us to only refresh the form (issuing the Requery() method) when we have to.

Property	Description
nrecno	Holds the current record number so that the form will only be refreshed if the user has moved the record pointer in the List page. This property is used exclusively for performance reasons.

Class Name: MarkInvoiceForm

Superclass: cbizobjmaintform (..\..\common30\libs\cforms.vcx)

Description: The form class that supports the markinvoice business object (markinvoiceobj).

Base Class: form

MarkInvoiceForm is used in the shipping department to mark an order as shipped. It is subclassed from CBizObjMaintForm, and is modified at runtime to remove the Selection List tab—to speed up work, the data entry will take place in a list view.

Despite these changes, this is a simple form to implement, as we will see. There is very little code in this form. The form's superclass and the business object instance that is embedded in the form know how to handle themselves, so we simply worry about the appearance of the form.

The Selection Criteria Tab

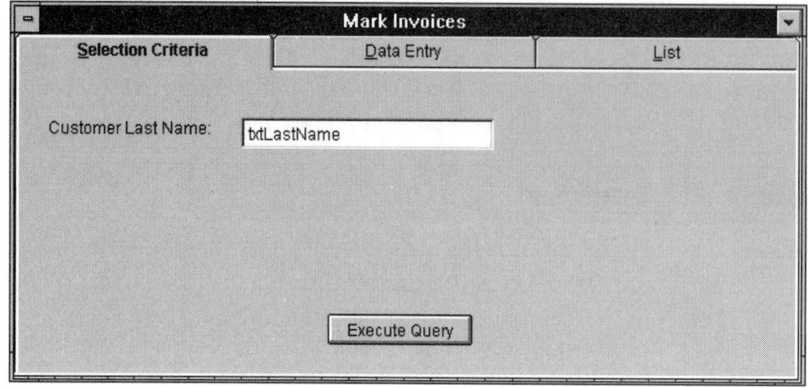

The MarkInvoiceForm's Selection Criteria tab in Design mode

The objects in this tab are created very easily. When we subclass the CBizObj-MaintForm, we are provided with this tab and the Execute Query button. We simply drop the label and textbox onto the form (using our CCONTROLS class library, of course), and set the cViewParameter of the textbox to vp_cLastName. This automatically binds anything that the user types into this textbox to the parameter in the parameterized view that we use to access our customer data.

That's all there is to it! We now have a form that can send parameters to its view, whether the data is coming from Visual FoxPro DBFs, SQL Server, Oracle, or any server product.

The Data Entry Tab

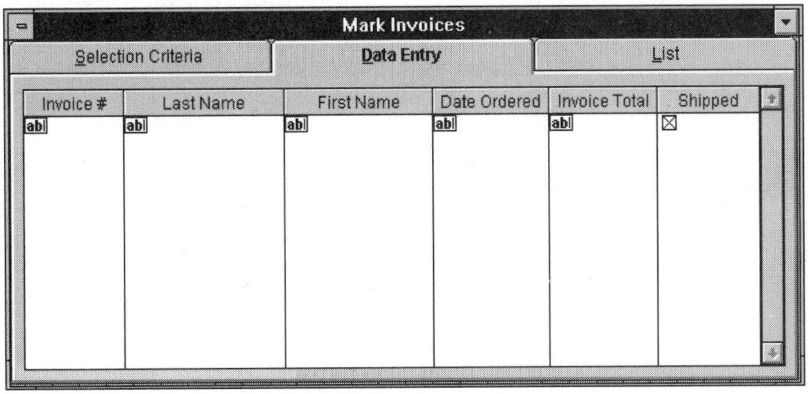

The MarkInvoiceForm's Data Entry tab in Design mode

The Data Entry tab is quite easy to put together. We select this page and drop an instance of the MarkInvoiceObj onto it. Done!

Note that we could drill down into the MarkInvoiceObj and specialize any of the default behaviors for this form. There is rarely a need to do that, however.

The List Tab

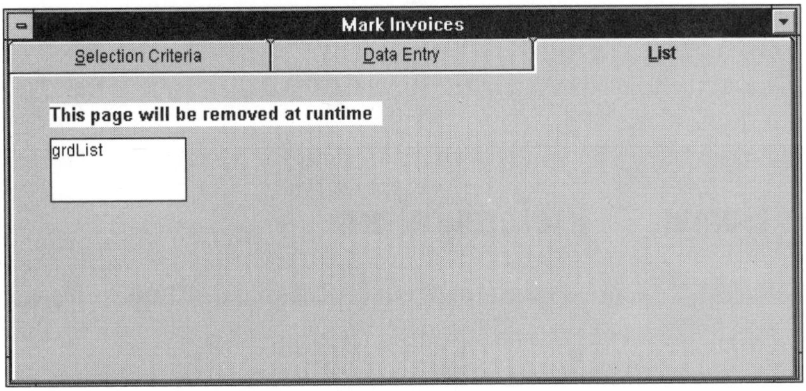

The MarkInvoiceForm's List tab in Design mode

We are going to be removing this tab at runtime, so we simply place a textbox here to remind us of that fact. No "real" controls are dropped onto this page. The grdList that shows in design mode is carried over from the CBizObjMaintForm superclass, and will automatically be removed when this tab is removed.

As always, we focus on the *visual* issues involved in displaying the business object, and that's it.

Code Changes

Let's take a look at the changed methods and the added property of this form, and see what was done and why.

```
*--MarkInvoiceForm.Save()
LOCAL lnRetVal
lnRetVal = CBizObjMaintForm::Save()
IF lnRetVal = FILE_OK
   this.Requery()
ENDIF

RETURN lnRetVal
```

When the user wants to save the changes to this form, we call up to the superclass to perform the save, and then issue a Requery() method to refresh the information from the server.

```
*--pgfBizObj.Init()
CBizObjMaintForm.pgfBizObj::Init()
*-- Remove the list page
this.RemoveObject("Page3")
```

We call up to the Init() method of the superclass and then remove the List page from our form.

Class Name: PreferenceForm

Superclass:	cpreferencemodalform (..\..\common30\libs\cforms.vcx)
Description:	The form where all Codebook user preferences are maintained.
Base Class:	form

PreferenceForm is a modal dialog that allows the user to set various preferences for the application. These preferences are saved in either an .INI file (for 16-bit Windows platforms) or in the Registry (for 32-bit Windows platforms). As such, all controls are subclassed from the CUserPref set of classes.

The form provides many useful functions and capabilities to the user (and the developer), and yet is quite easy to put together. Let's take a look at each tab in the dialog box and some of the controls in the tabs.

The Data Tab

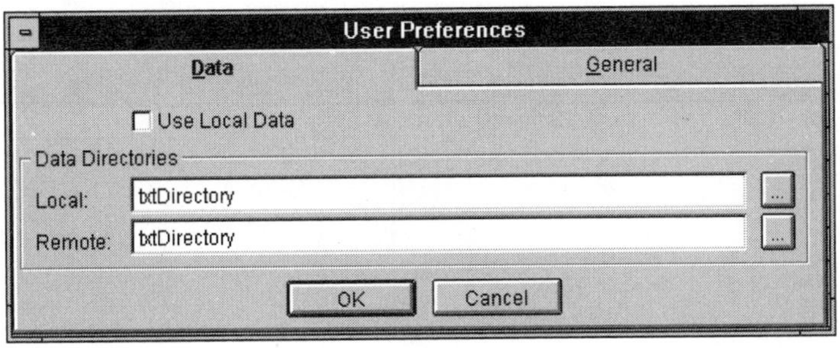

The PreferenceForm's Data tab in Design Mode

The Data tab allows the user to select whether they want to work off local views or remote views, and allows them to select separate DBCs that contain those views. Note that both sets of views could be in the same DBC, and that this same approach can be used to allow for multiple company subdirectories if that should be required by your application. We can easily switch directories or DBCs on the fly!

Let's look at how this page was created. We subclassed CPreferenceModalForm, which gave us the two-tab pageframe with the OK and Cancel buttons. We then dropped a shape and some labels on our form to describe what it does. Then we added the controls that give the form its functionality. We dropped a checkbox (subclassed from COnOffPref) and two custom controls subclassed from the CDirectoryPref control.

The COnOffPref has the following preferences set:

Property	Setting
cPreferenceName	Use Local Data
cPreferenceSection	Data Settings
cPreferenceValue	Yes

This causes the setting of the checkbox to be saved in the Data Settings section of our .INI file or Registry, under the Use Local Data preference. Here's a picture of the Windows NT registry after this setting is checked:

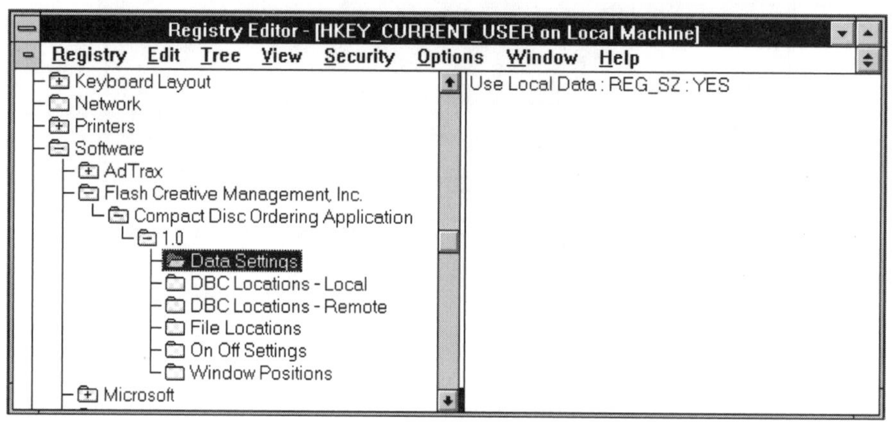

The Use Local Data preference

The two directory controls were created in a similar manner. The Init() method of the controls are used to fill in the cPreferenceValue because #DEFINE constants must appear in code for VFP to substitute the value at compile time.

The General Tab

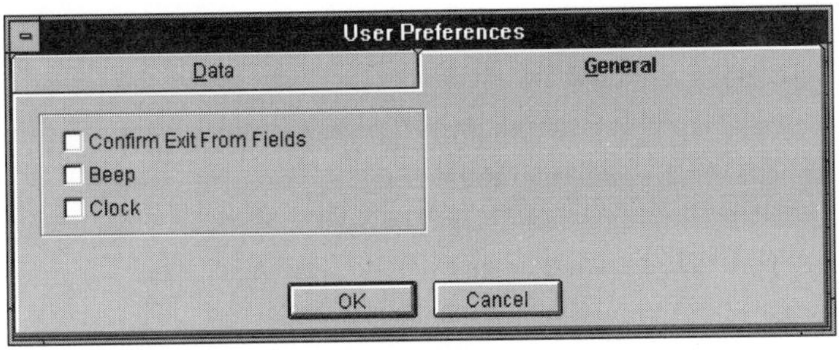

The PreferenceForm's General tab in Design mode

The general tab allows the user to change various SET settings for our system. This page is created in the same way that we created the first tab. There is one difference, however. The COnOffPref class knows how to handle ON/OFF-type SET commands, so we fill in the cSetCommand property, which is used to create and run the SET command that is tied to the checkbox.

We change some code in the SetPreferenceValue method for the clock checkbox to equate the checked state with the status bar.

```
*-- oClock.SetPreferenceValue
LOCAL lcCommand, ;
        lcSetting
IF !EMPTY(this.cSetCommand)
   lcSetting = IIF(this.cPreferenceValue = "ON", ;
      "STATUS", this.cPreferenceValue)
   lcCommand = ALLT(this.cSetCommand) + " " + lcSetting
   &lcCommand
ENDIF
```

That's all there is to it. When the user changes one of these checkboxes and clicks on OK, the form's superclass will iterate through it, setting all of the proper commands as we want them.

Appendix A

Bibliography

Introduction

This appendix contains a list of books and magazines that are mentioned in this book, or that you may find worthwhile in your own development efforts. I have included a brief description of the books as well.

Object Orientation

Jacobson, Ivar. *Object-Oriented Software Engineering*. Reading, Mass.: Addison-Wesley, 1992. Jacobson's book introduces the concept of the *Use Case* which is used in this book for analysis. The approach takes a global view of system development and focuses on minimizing the system's life cycle cost. Highly recommended.

Taylor, David A., Ph.D. *Business Engineering with Object Technology*. New York: John Wiley & Sons, Inc., 1995. An excellent practical guide to applying object technology to business engineering. Taylor covers the historical need for having software mirror business and suggests that object technology is the perfect vehicle for doing so.

Taylor, David A., Ph.D. *Object-Oriented Technology: A Manager's Guide*. Reading, Mass.: Addison-Wesley, 1990. A very good introduction to object-oriented concepts. Written in a very lucid and straightforward manner. Highly recommended.

Wirfs-Brock, Rebecca, Brian Wilkerson, and Lauren Wiener. *Designing Object-Oriented Software*. Englewood Cliffs, N.J.: P T R Prentice-Hall, 1990. This book walks through the use of *Class-Responsibility-Collaboration (CRC) Cards* which are extensively used in *The Visual FoxPro 3 Codebook* for class hierarchy creation. Highly recommended.

Object Magazine
Publisher: Sigs Publications

JOOP (Journal of Object-Oriented Programming)
Publisher: Sigs Publications

General Software Development

Maguire, Steve. *Debugging the Development Process*. Redmond, Wash.: Microsoft Press, 1994. Discusses good practices for managing a software development team. Excellent.

McConnell, Steve. *Code Complete*. Redmond, Wash.: Microsoft Press, 1993. A "must have" book for software developers. Discusses the theory and practicality behind good software design.

Business Process Reengineering and Client-Server

Bruce, Thomas A. *Designing Quality Databases with IDEF1X Information Models*. New York: Dorset House Publishing, 1992. A very good book on data modeling, it discusses the Zachman Framework (used in our business analysis).

Hammer, Michael and James Champy. *Reengineering the Corporation*. New York: HarperCollins, 1993. The seminal work on reengineering. Focuses on why a company should look at processes instead of tasks.

Treacy, Michael and Fred Wiersema. *The Discipline of Market Leaders*. Reading, Mass.: Addison-Wesley, 1994. Discusses how to choose customers, narrow a company's focus, and dominate a market. Very interesting discussion of business strategies.

Vaskevitch, David. *Client/Server Strategies*. San Mateo, Calif.: IDG Books Worldwide, 1993. Discusses a strategy for application development that enables BPR by focusing on distributed data delivery.

Visual FoxPro Development

FoxPro Advisor Magazine
Publisher: Advisor Publications

Foxtalk
Publisher: Pinnacle Publishing

Cobb FoxPro Journal
Publisher: The Cobb Group

Appendix B

OLE Controls with Visual FoxPro 3

Introduction

OLE brings a new world of opportunities to Windows system development. OLE 2.0 presents a standard for creating components that can be used across multiple development environments. These components, known as OCXs or OLE Controls, provide additional controls for our use in Visual FoxPro.

This document discusses three controls that ship with Visual FoxPro 3: the Outline Control and the two MAPI (Mail API) Controls.

The Outline Control

The Outline Control is a special listbox-type control that shows list information in hierarchical order. It is useful for showing a myriad of information from files and directories (much like File Manager in Windows) to sales by territory and much more. Basically, any information based on ownership or containership can be shown in hierarchical order with the Outline Control.

A good example of this is the Class Browser which is based on the Outline Control. The Class Browser is shown here.

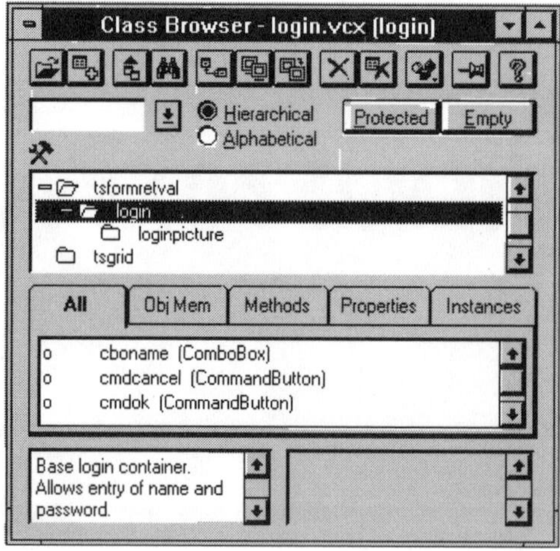

Class Browser

Note how the classes are shown in hierarchical order. This is a very useful way to present this information because it provides a clear picture of the class tree.

Registering OLE Controls

OLE controls can be used like any other control, provided they have been *registered* with Visual FoxPro. This is accomplished using the *tools/options* dialog box as shown below.

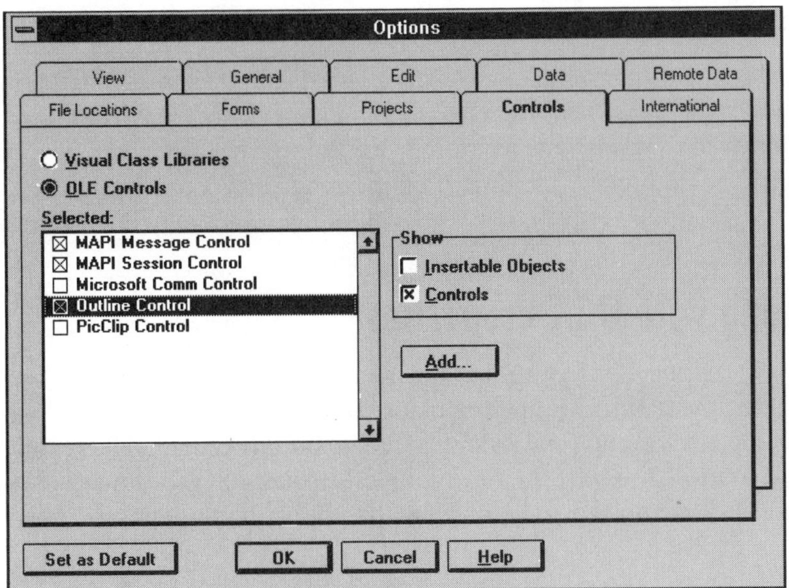

Tools/Options dialog box

In order to see the list of OLE controls available on your system, you will have to select the OLE Controls option button and make sure that the Controls checkbox is checked. In this case, the Insertable Objects checkbox (which refers to OLE 2.0 applications such as Microsoft Word for Windows) is not checked to keep the list more readable and manageable.

In this example, note the five controls shown. All these controls ship with Visual FoxPro 3 and are installed with the full installation (you can, of course, opt not to install these. If you do not see these controls on your list, you can install them from the Visual FoxPro 3 installation diskettes. See the Visual FoxPro 3 manual for more information on this).

In order to permanently register a control with Visual FoxPro 3 (so that it is always available in the design surfaces), check those controls you are interested in and then click on Set as Default and the controls will always show up in the list of OLE controls in the design surfaces.

If you acquire additional OCX controls and install them, you will then have to use this dialog box to register them for use with Visual FoxPro 3.

Using the Controls

Once the controls are registered, they are accessed with the Form Controls toolbar. To show the registered controls, click on the View Classes button on the toolbar and select OLE Controls. The registered OLE controls will show on the toolbar. Click on the object to use and drop it on the container (Form, PageFrame, Grid, etc.). From that point on, you can work with it like almost any other control.

Working with OCX Properties

The properties of an OLE control can be accessed in one of two ways. The first way is using the standard Properties dialog box. This will show the control's PEMs (properties, events, and methods) much like any other FoxPro control.

OLE controls also have their own properties dialog which can be accessed via the RightClick menu (shown here). Note that the properties option is now at the bottom of the list.

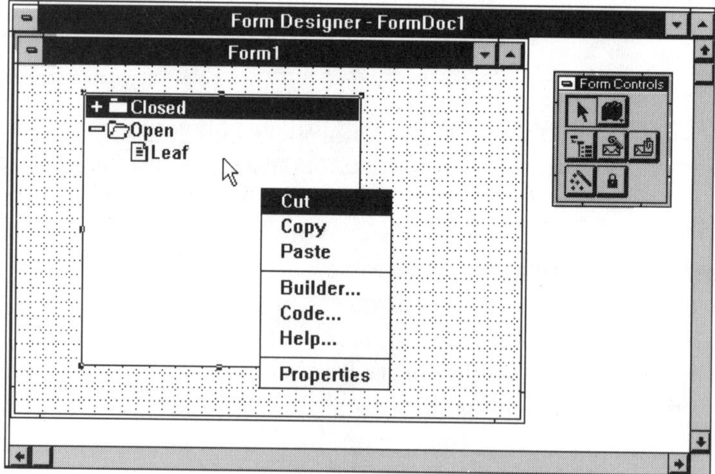

OLE Control RightClick menu

The properties dialog box brought up by selecting the Properties option from this menu shows *only those properties programmed into the control*. The figure below shows the Properties dialog box for the Outline Control.

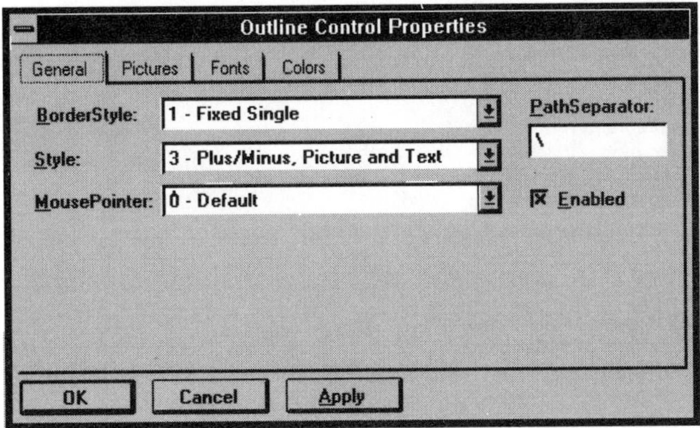

Outline Control Property dialog box

Note that this dialog only allows access to *properties* of the control; events and methods are not accessible. The standard Properties dialog box, on the other hand, allows access to all of Visual FoxPro's standard properties, events, and methods, as well as the properties specific to the control. The reason for this is interesting. Visual FoxPro wraps the .OCX in an OLE container that allows the developer access to the standard PEMs as well as the properties specific to the .OCX control. This means that you can subclass OLE Controls. This feature is *unique* to Visual FoxPro 3.

Now that we have discussed the issues related to working with OLE controls in general, the next step is to discuss the particulars of the Outline Control.

An Outline Example

The following is an example of a form using the Outline Control. It shows customers and the products they have ordered (the data for this example comes from the TESTDATA database that ships with Visual FoxPro 3.

Here's what the form looks like:

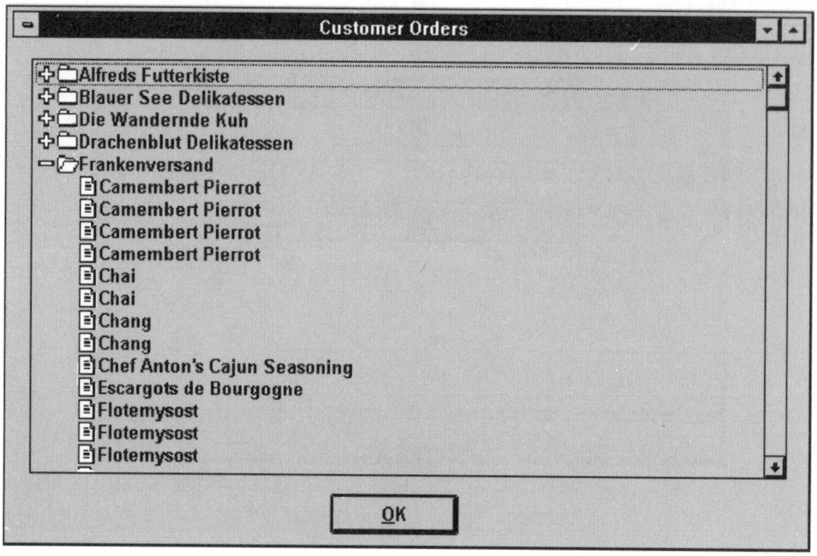

Customer Orders form

As can be seen, this is a powerful way of looking at data. Only the detail for the companies the user specifically expands are shown. This allows the user the ability to limit the information he or she sees on the form.

Here's the code for this form:

```
*  Class............: Frmcustord
*  Notes............: Exported code from Class Browser.

**************************************************
*-- Form:         frmcustord
*-- ParentClass:  form
*-- BaseClass:    form
*
DEFINE CLASS frmcustord AS form


   DataSession = 2
   Height = 358
   Width = 588
   DoCreate = .T.
```

```
AutoCenter = .T.
BackColor = RGB(192,192,192)
BorderStyle = 2
Caption = "Customer Orders"
Name = "frmcustord"


ADD OBJECT oleoutline AS olecontrol WITH ;
   Top = 12, ;
   Left = 12, ;
   Height = 301, ;
   Width = 565, ;
   Name = "oleOutline"


ADD OBJECT cmdok AS commandbutton WITH ;
   Top = 324, ;
   Left = 240, ;
   Height = 29, ;
   Width = 94, ;
   Cancel = .T., ;
   Caption = "\<OK", ;
   Default = .T., ;
   Name = "cmdOK"


*-- Loads the customer orders into the Outline Control
PROCEDURE loaddata
   SET TALK OFF
   WAIT WINDOW NOWAIT "Loading information. Please stand by..."
   SELECT _cCustOrders
   GO TOP

   LOCAL lcCompany
   SCAN
      lcCompany = _cCustOrders.Company
      thisform.OleOutline.AddItem(lcCompany)

      DO WHILE lcCompany == _cCustOrders.Company
         IF !EMPTY(_cCustOrders.Product)
         this.OleOutline.AddItem(Product)
         this.OleOutline.Indent(this.OleOutline.listcount-1) = 2
         this.oleOutline.PictureType(this.OleOutline.listcount-1) = 2
```

```
         ENDIF
         SKIP
      ENDDO
   ENDSCAN
ENDPROC


PROCEDURE Init
   thisform.LoadData()
ENDPROC


PROCEDURE Load
   OPEN DATABASE home()+"samples\data\testdata"

   SELECT Customer.company, ;
          Products.prod_name AS Product;
     FROM testdata!customer, ;
          testdata!orders, ;
          testdata!orditems, ;
          testdata!products ;
    WHERE Customer.cust_id = Orders.cust_id ;
      AND Orders.order_id = Orditems.order_id ;
      AND Products.product_id = Orditems.product_id ;
      AND Customer.Country = "Germany" ;
    UNION ALL ;
          SELECT Customer.company, ;
                 "" ;
            FROM testdata!customer ;
           WHERE Customer.cust_id NOT IN ;
               (SELECT Orders.cust_id FROM testdata!orders) ;
             AND Customer.Country = "Germany" ;
    ORDER BY 1,2 ;
     INTO CURSOR _cCustOrders

   GO TOP

ENDPROC


PROCEDURE oleoutline.Collapse
   *** OLE Control Event ***
```

```
      LPARAMETERS listindex
      IF this.hassubitems(listindex)
         this.picturetype(listindex) = 0
      ENDIF
   ENDPROC


   PROCEDURE oleoutline.Expand
      *** OLE Control Event ***
      LPARAMETERS listindex
      IF this.hassubitems(listindex)
         this.picturetype(listindex) = 1
      ENDIF
   ENDPROC


   PROCEDURE cmdok.Click
      RELEASE thisform
   ENDPROC


ENDDEFINE
*
*-- EndDefine: frmcustord
**************************************************
```

The LOAD event runs a SQL Select off the information from the TESTDATA database to extract the names of customers in Germany, and the products they have purchased. The list is ordered by company name and then by product name.

The list is populated in the Loaddata method which is a custom method to this form. All this method does is scan through the result set. Customers are added at the default indent level (level 1) whereas the products they ordered are added at level 2. Indenting items to level 2 makes them subitems of the immediately prior level 1 item. Products are also set to have the Document icon by setting the picturetype for that element to 2.

When the list is expanded and contracted, the picture for the main item has to be changed from the Closed Folder to the Open Folder icon. This is accomplished in the Expand and Collapse event methods which are part of the outline control.

As you can see, the amount of code needed to work with Outline Control lists is minimal.

Outline Control—A Final Word

The Outline Control is a wonderful example of how an OLE Control can enhance a system. The ability to translate data into a visual, hierarchical display is a powerful way to allow users to view and work with data. However, OCXs can add much more than display features to an application. The two MAPI controls that ship with Visual FoxPro provide an example of how OCX controls can add functionality to your applications.

Mail-Enabling Applications with the MAPI Controls

Visual FoxPro ships with two controls designed to enable applications to interact with MAPI-compliant mail systems. These two controls, the MAPI Session Control and the MAPI Messages Control, work in tandem and allow an application to send, respond, and reply to messages in addition to managing the e-mail system.

Mail-enabling applications are becoming a requirement in many business applications. The MAPI Controls make this easy to accomplish.

Managing Sessions

Before you can work with e-mail, you have to establish a *session* with the e-mail system. You can think of a session in e-mail in the same manner as you might think of working with an Automated Teller Machine. In order to work with the ATM, you first have to establish a session. Part of establishing a session includes logging into the system. Once you have a session established, you can initiate and complete many transactions. The same is true of a mail system.

Establishing the Session

Establishing a session with the MAPI Session Control is a simple matter. All you need to do is to drop the control on a form and put the following code in its Init() event:

```
THIS.LogonUI = .t.
THIS.SignOn()
```

The Signon() method accesses the mail system and attempts to establish a mail session. Since the LogonUI property is set to .t., if the user is not logged in yet, a dialog box is displayed for the user to enter a user name and password.

The session is terminated with the SignOff() method.

Each MAPI session has an ID. The ID of the session is stored in the SessionId property of the Session control. The ID is important for the Message control to be able to communicate with the session.

Composing Messages

Composing messages with the MAPI Message is also simple. The control has a series of methods and properties that a developer may modify and work with in order to compose messages to be sent via the mail system. For example, the MsgNoteText property has the text of the message. Placing text in that property will put the text into the body of the message. The control also allows you to attach files, work with address books, and read messages, as well.

MAILME.SCX is a sample form that illustrates well how messages, with attachments, can be composed and sent using the MAPI Message control. The figure below shows the form in the designer followed by the code to the form.

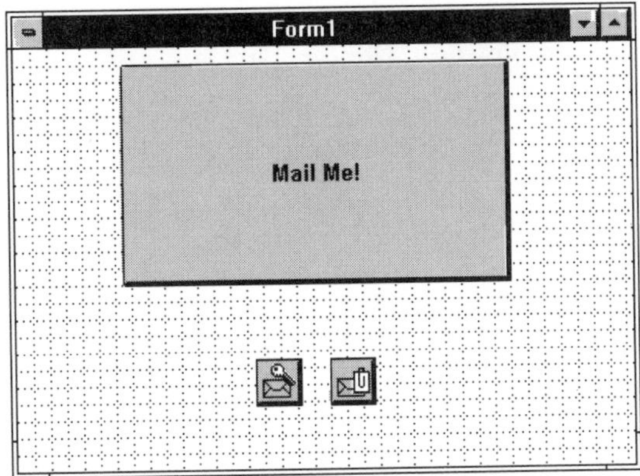

Form MAILME

```
*  Form..............: MAILME.SCX
*  Notes.............: Exported code from Class Browser.

**************************************************
*-- Form:          form1
*-- ParentClass:   form
*-- BaseClass:     form
*
DEFINE CLASS form1 AS form
```

```
DoCreate = .T.
Caption = "Form1"
Name = "Form1"

ADD OBJECT olesession AS olecontrol WITH ;
   Top = 204, ;
   Left = 120, ;
   Height = 100, ;
   Width = 100, ;
   Name = "oleSession"


ADD OBJECT olemessage AS olecontrol WITH ;
   Top = 204, ;
   Left = 180, ;
   Height = 100, ;
   Width = 100, ;
   AddressModifiable = .T., ;
   AddressResolveUI = .T., ;
   Name = "oleMessage"


ADD OBJECT cmdmailme AS commandbutton WITH ;
   Top = 36, ;
   Left = 36, ;
   Height = 133, ;
   Width = 253, ;
   Caption = "Mail Me!", ;
   Name = "cmdMailMe"

PROCEDURE olesession.Init
   *-- Establish a session

   THIS.LogonUI = .T.
   THIS.Signon()
ENDPROC


PROCEDURE olesession.Destroy
   this.signoff()
ENDPROC
```

```
PROCEDURE olemessage.Init
   THIS.SessionID = THISFORM.oleSession.SessionID
ENDPROC


PROCEDURE cmdmailme.Click
   *-- First, save this as a class to JUNKME.VCX

   LOCAL lcOldSafety
   lcOldSafety = SET("safety")
   SET SAFETY OFF

   thisform.SaveAsClass("JunkMe.VCX", "MailMe")

   *-- Set the address book caption
   thisform.oleMessage.AddressCaption = "Select Recipient(s)"

   *-- Clear the compose buffer.
   thisform.oleMessage.Compose()

   *-- Get the recipient's address.
   thisform.oleMessage.Show()

   *-- Set the message subject and the body text.
   thisform.oleMessage.msgNoteText = ;
      "Please see that these files get into the class libraries " ;
      +  REPL(chr(13)+chr(10), 3) +  "   "
   thisform.oleMessage.msgSubject  = "Attached Files"

   *-- Add first attachment
   thisform.oleMessage.AttachmentIndex = ;
      thisform.oleMessage.AttachmentCount
   thisform.oleMessage.AttachmentType = 0
   thisform.oleMessage.AttachmentPathName = "JUNKME.VCX"
   thisform.oleMessage.AttachmentPosition = ;
      LEN(thisform.oleMessage.msgNoteText)-2
```

```
      *-- Now the second attachment
      thisform.oleMessage.AttachmentIndex = ;
         thisform.oleMessage.AttachmentCount
      thisform.oleMessage.AttachmentType = 0
      thisform.oleMessage.AttachmentPathName = "JUNKME.VCT"
      thisform.oleMessage.AttachmentPosition = ;
         LEN(thisform.oleMessage.msgNoteText)-1

      *-- Diplay the Send dialog before sending
      thisform.oleMessage.Send(.T.)

      *-- Reset SET SAFE and go on home
      SET SAFETY &lcOldSafety
   ENDPROC


ENDDEFINE
*
*-- EndDefine: form1
**************************************************
```

This form contains both a session and a message control on it.

The Init() of the message control sets the SessionId property of the Message Control to the SessionId of the Session Control. In this way, our messages are linked to the current open session of Microsoft Mail.

Most of the work takes place in the Click() method of cmdMailMe CommandButton. Basically, here's what it does:

- The form is saved to a .VCX using the SaveAsClass() method. This gives us a couple of files to attach to the message.
- The AddressCaption property is set. When the address book is displayed with the Show() method later on, this will be the caption on the dialog box window.
- The Compose() method is called. This basically clears everything in the current compose buffer and allows us to work with a clean buffer.
- The user is presented with the list of addresses so that he or she can select a recipient.

- The message body and subject are set using the msgNoteText and msgSubject properties, respectively.
- The attachments are added. The process of adding the attachments work as follows:
    1. The AttachmentIndex property is set to a value equal to or greater than the AttachmentCount property. Attachments are numbered 0-n in the MAPI MessageControl. If the AttachmentIndex property is set to 0, you are working with the FIRST attachment in the message. When the AttachmentIndex property is set to 0, for example, the AttachmentCount property is automatically set to 1 (because there is one attachment in the message).
    2. The type of attachment is specified. Type 0 is a plain data file.
    3. The name of the file is specified (JUNKME.VCX/T).
    4. The position of the attachment in the message is specified. The attachment shows as an icon in the message. The AttachmentPosition property, which refers to the currently indexed attachment, defines which character position in the message the attachment will show up in. It is very important to allocate text (in this case, we allocated a few spaces at the end of the message) for the attachment icons and to place the icons properly. If you do not, you may overwrite characters in the message or even get an error (if you did not specify enough characters in the msgNoteText property to allow for the attachment icons).
- The Send() method is called. By specifying a parameter of .T., a dialog box is displayed with the message allowing the user to edit it. If the logical parameter is not sent through, the message is sent without the dialog box.

And that's all there is to it. The following figure shows the message dialog box that appears at the end of this process.

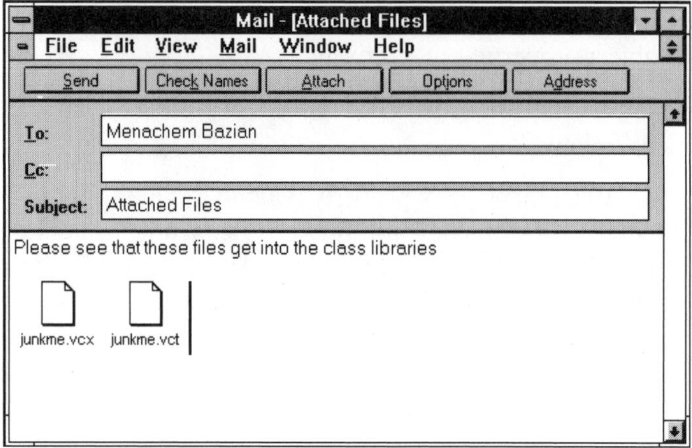

Composed message

MAPI Controls—Conclusion

The MAPI Controls show another side to working with OLE Controls. They provide a host of possible additions to the capabilities of Visual FoxPro 3 applications. These controls, although non-visual, reduce the complexity and tedium of mail-enabling applications to setting a few properties and calling a few methods. This is, in essence, what easy development is all about.

OLE Controls—Conclusion

Extensibility. Once it was an option in a development language. Today it's the key to success. As technology becomes more advanced, users expect more from their applications. No single software vendor can anticipate all the needs and desires of the user market. However, many vendors can address a much broader range of needs.

By adding OLE support to Visual FoxPro 3, Microsoft has opened the door to a flood of additional functionality. With support for this powerful feature, Visual FoxPro 3 has no limits on what it can do.

Appendix C

Codebook Step by Step

Introduction

This appendix discusses the steps that will usually be followed in creating a Codebook-style application, and answers a number of frequently asked questions that we've received from people attending our classes on the Codebook Framework.

Creating a Directory Structure

We have included a Visual FoxPro 3 version of our QuickStart utility with this book which will create a base Codebook-style application for you.

When you run QSTART.APP, you will see the following dialog:

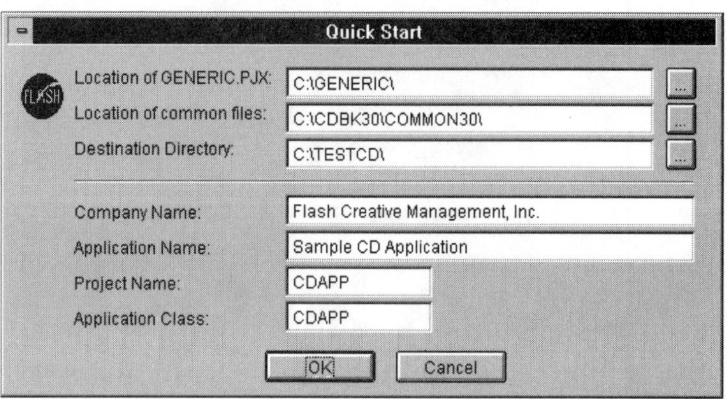

The QuickStart dialog

Fill in all of the text boxes. Codebook ships with a GENERIC subdirectory that contains all of the generic parts of an application that need to be moved to the new location. It also contains the subdirectory structure that Codebook uses. QuickStart does the following things:

1. Creates the directory structure, and copies over any application-specific files, renaming them as necessary.
2. Auto subclasses the CApplicationClass, and auto fills in the appropriate properties.
3. Creates a shell ADATAENV.PRG for you with templates for your data environment classes.

4. Creates a default database for you (with the same name as the project) and adds the necessary stored procedures and ID table.

Once this is done, you have an application that will start up, and put up a menu and an empty Application toolbar. The functionality for print setup, the about screen, and the debugging tools will be available.

Creating Your Data Environments

Your next step is to create your application-specific tables, views, and stored procedures.

Once that is done, open the ADATAENV.PRG library and customize the data environment to your requirements. The file has a template for your convenience. Fill in your LocalTablesEnvironment with all of the local tables that you want your users to be able to reindex and pack.

Create subclasses of CCursor and CDynamicViewCursor as necessary for your tables and views.

Creating Your Business Objects

When that is done, it's time to create application-specific business objects. Simply subclass CBizObj or COneToManyBizObj and add the default look that you would like for your business object. Make sure to fill in the cDataEnvironment property of the CDELoader instance with the correct data environment for this business object.

Note that QuickStart will give you an ABIZOBJ.VCX to store your business objects in, but you don't have to use it, feel free to store your business objects in whatever class library or class libraries you wish.

Creating Your Forms

Creating a form is simple. Simply select the CBizObjForm subclass that you wish to use to display your business object. Drop a business object onto the form. Make any customizations that you require.

Note that QuickStart will give you an AFORMS.VCX to store your business object forms in, but you don't have to use it, feel free to store your forms in whatever class library or class libraries you wish.

Creating Your Menus

We have provided a menu builder that eases the creation of menus for you. From the command window, DO COMMON30\UTILS\BUILDERB, and the builder will be installed for you (don't worry, it will not remove any existing builders). Select the AMENUS.VCX class library, and open MainMenu. Right-click on the container and select "Builder...."

You will see something like this:

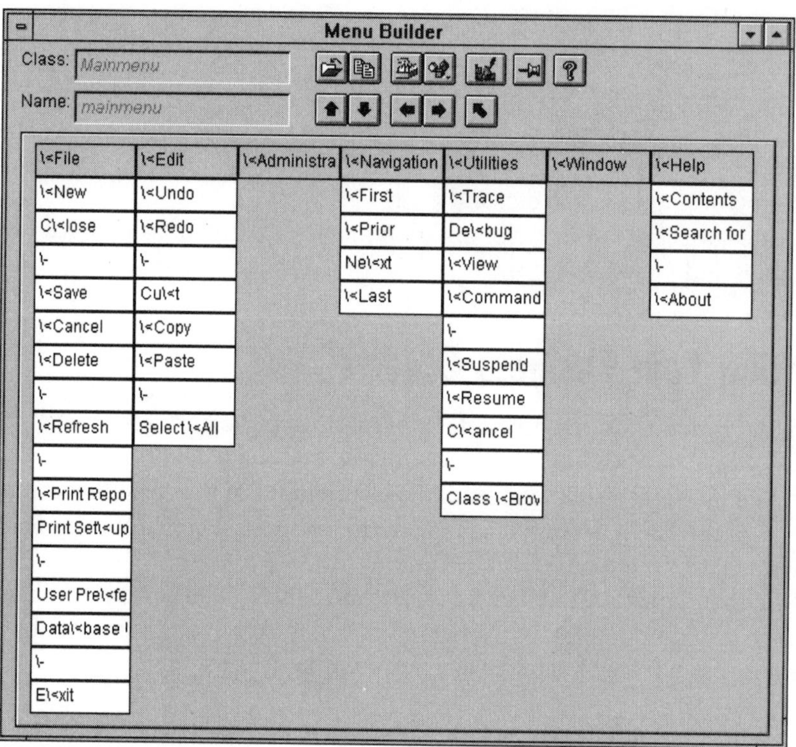

The menu builder with a template menu

In order to add a bar to the Administration pad, select that pad and right-click. Choose "Add Bar..." from the menu, and you will be placed in a menu bar item builder. This builder allows you to create a new class, or subclass an existing menu bar.

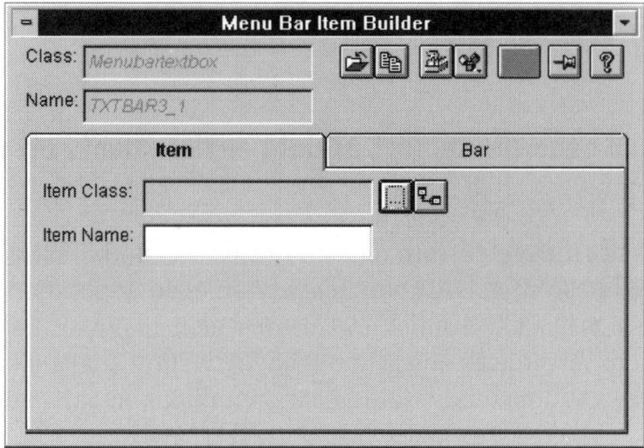

The menu bar item builder

When you select either of the Item Class buttons, you are first prompted for a class library in which to store the menu bar that you are creating, and then you are brought into the standard VFP subclassing dialog.

The Bar tab allows you to type in Click() method code for your bar, should your application require it.

When you close this window, you will see a new bar added to your main menu. Type in the caption for the bar. You are now done!

If you need to, you can right-click on the bar to run the bar builder which allows you to modify other properties including the shortcut key, message clause, and skip for clause.

You can move bars and pads by using right-mouse drag-and-drop functions.

Creating Your Application Toolbar

Simply open the MainToolbar class in the AToolbar class library and drop in instances of CAdminToolbarButton, filling in the cForm property with the form that you wish to call, and any other properties that you wish to customize (typically these will be ToolTipText, cMenuBar, cMenuPad, and Picture).

Frequently Asked Questions

Why don't you generate cursors or data environments off a DBF to data drive it?

The capability of creating custom data environments and cursors in Visual FoxPro 3 caused us to decide to code this portion of an application. Note how we've added things like CDynamicViewCursor which allows a cursor to change from local data to server back end without any recoding. The ability to create custom properties and methods would be more difficult in a data-driven environment.

Why is there a DEBUG.TXT file in my application's root directory?

DEBUG.TXT is the default value of DEBUGMODEFILE in APPINCL.H. When DEBUGMODEFILE is found in the application root directory, a Codebook Framework-based application goes into DEBUG mode, forcing the creation of METADATA.DBF and adding a Utilities menu option so that the developer can use the trace, debug, command, or class browser windows.

What's up with the menus? By using your classes, you've thrown out one of the VFP tools. I realize the menu builder is virtually unchanged and therefore has no object-oriented capabilities, but this approach really seems to add an unnecessary level of complexity.

Internal complexity, yes. But it actually makes development with VFP much simpler, since you can now treat menus using an interface similar to the rest of the product. Suspend Codebook, and in the command window type:

```
goApp.oMenu.oUtilitiesPad.Hide()
goApp.oMenu.oNavigationPad.Hide()
goApp.oMenu.oUtilitiesPad.Show()
goApp.oMenu.oNavigationPad.Show()
```

In design mode, look how easy it is to bind a toolbar button to a menu bar. For the toolbar button, just specify the name of the pad and the name of the bar. For the bar, just specify the action to take in the cToolbarCommand property as if you had a reference to the toolbar for the active form. Note how the SetEnabled method of CToolbarButton automatically sets the Enabled property of its associated menu bar to dim a menu item! Now think of all the possible ways to customize this behavior with custom properties, methods, and the ability to subclass menu items.

As far as the tools go, we had two options:

- Create a new menu builder that is designed to work with the menu objects.
- Create a custom GENMENU to generate the menu code.

We felt that the first option made the most sense, and have therefore included a builder for the various menu classes.

Why are all of the forms stored in a class? From what I can tell about how forms are being called in the application, there doesn't seem to be a practical advantage to this.

This is an excellent question that will be asked again and again. The primary reason is to achieve maximum flexibility of data environment design:

- A DE can be created independently of a form.
- A DE can be reused and subclassed as necessary.
- It is now very easy to switch between local or remote data. (Or for that matter, between local views and local tables.)

Since the DE is not bound to a form, we can now use a DE just about anywhere we want. For example, note that each business object has its own DE. Business objects are designed to be instantiated outside of any form. Because of this, you can drop the business object on just about any type of form without having to set up its data environment each time.

Additionally, class members declared as PROTECTED in a form class become PRIVATE (C++ private, not FoxPro PRIVATE) in a form (SCX) based on that class. In other words, if you have a form class with a protected property called cOldName, and you create a form (SCX) from that class, you cannot access that property anywhere in the form! This leads to poor designs, and essentially renders protected properties useless.

Also, using a form class instead of a form offers more control over when the form is displayed. There may be a situation where you want to load a form but not show it right away. Since a DO FORM executes an implicit Show(), this is not possible. There may be a way to do this with a NODEFAULT in the form's Show() method, but that approach seems kludgy.

Last but not least, using the form class approach results in a design that is much cleaner, easier to understand, and easier to reuse. It allows you to see your entire application's hierarchy in the class browser at once if necessary, and also allows you to live in that tool full-time if you prefer.

What is the reasoning behind the DoForm() method residing in the utility program rather than in a class?

I think a developer should be able to create a form and show it in the "simplest" way possible. Nine out of 10 times, the form class will be created with CREATEOBJECT(), then shown with <objname>.Show(). DoForm() simply automates this process, nothing more, nothing less. It will never change. If necessary, it is perfectly acceptable to circumvent DoForm() by manually creating the form and showing it yourself. The form is responsible for adding itself to the oForms collection, so there is nothing else for the developer to worry about.

I feel that functions like this belong in a PRG, where they can be accessed from everywhere very easily. In fact, every function in Utility.prg follows this principle. Since VFP is not a pure OOP environment like Smalltalk, we should take advantage of this where it "makes sense" to do so. (Much as C++ programmers do.)

We like the approach you've taken with placing record selection criteria in the first page frame of each form—for client-server applications. This really doesn't make a lot of sense for local data access, though. Is this type of form going to be a "Codebook" standard or can we deviate from it? We think Codebook should probably at least include one single table form that doesn't use this approach.

There is no single "Codebook" standard form; there are many. Since we have separated the business object from the form, you can create whatever "look" you need for your forms. For handling business objects, you can create as many subclasses of CBizObjForm as you like. CBizObjMaintForm is just one implementation. Note that the Invoice form is a subclass of CBizObjMaintForm, but it does not have a Selection Criteria page.

One of the things that nobody seems to like in Tastrade is the list pageframe. We were kind of surprised to see it in Codebook. Will the list pageframe also be considered part of a "Standard Codebook Form" or will it be an option?

Nobody likes it? Really? I have to admit that I'm bit surprised by this. It's really no different than the list in Codebook 2.6, only you can't resize it. In 2.6 you clicked a list button, in 3 you click a list tab.

In any case, this is an option. Simply use a different superclass for your maintenance forms, if you wish.

The Visual Codebook in some ways does not offer as much flexibility for finding records as the 2.6 implementation, primarily because it does not allow searching on all fields. This is probably a client-server issue more than anything else, but do you envision adding anything like the AppSearch screen that is in Codebook 2.6?

Codebook 2.6 did not allow searching for all fields, only those that are indexed. In some ways, Codebook 3 is more flexible than 2.6 in that it allows you to search on criteria that are not directly stored in one table. For example, what if you wanted to see only those customers whose total sales are greater than $1000.00? This information is derived from the invoice and purchase tables. With the current Codebook, the view is created with parameters, and all the developer has to do is drop controls on the Selection Criteria page, and link each control to a view parameter by way of the cViewParameter property.

Glossary of Terms

Abstract Data Type

A data type defined by the programmer which is not supported by the language. These data types are generally high-level definitions within a program that correspond to real world objects.

Abstraction

The benefit of ignoring irrelevant details of software components and focusing on only those details required to interface, send messages, etc. Some of the concepts of abstraction include information hiding and black box routines. Since most real world objects include abstract details, objects allow an improved representation of real world objects as compared to functions.

Business Process Reengineering

A business term popularized by the book *Reengineering the Corporation* by Hammer and Champy. According to them, reengineering is defined as "the fundamental rethinking and radical redesign of business processes to achieve dramatic improvement in critical, contemporary measures of performance such as cost, quality, service and speed."

Reengineering is a change in the way we approach evaluating what needs to be reviewed. We no longer look at tasks but at processes. Processes are a collection of activities that take one or more kinds of inputs and create an output that is of value to the customer.

Class

A blueprint, or template, for defining methods and properties of a particular type of object. Classes are defined at design time and are not executed at runtime. Objects are created based on class blueprints at runtime. Multiple objects can be created (instantiated) from a single class at runtime.

Class Hierarchy

A tree structure of classes which represents the relationship between a set of classes of similar type. The top node of a class hierarchy is known as the base class while related classes below it are known as subclasses. Although any number of levels of subclasses can be created, most methodologies state that well-defined class hierarchies should not exceed about five levels in depth.

Composite Object

An object that contains one or more objects. This occurs when at least one instance variable of an object is of type "O" (object). Composite objects, along with delegation, are typical techniques to eliminate the unwanted side effects of multiple inheritance (see inheritance below).

Delegation

Delegation occurs when an object receives a message and passes it on to another object. Delegation is useful when responsibilities of objects are passed on to other objects. Non-OOP languages can also support delegation simply by defining a UDF to simply pass any parameter(s) on to another UDF. The interface to the developer sending the message does not have to know about the internal details.

Encapsulation

The concept of methods (procedures or functions) and properties (data memory variables) packaged together. The result of this packaging is the object. Objects contain both methods and properties. The methods are referred to as the object's behaviors and the properties are referred to as the object's attributes.

Enterprise Modeling

A method of doing business analysis that helps us to understand the processes the business performs and where they are performed. This analysis gives us a "road map" that we can use when implementing an information infrastructure to help enable those processes.

Foundation Classes

Foundation classes are typically a set of classes that help to automate the development of an application. A set of Foundation Classes typically provides interface and control classes, which manage the interface and interactions between pieces of an application. This allows the developer, who is familiar with the problem set that causes the development effort, to focus on the entity classes that make up the business solution.

Inheritance

When a class is derived based on another existing class, the existing methods and properties are referenced for reuse with the new class. A subclass uses all of the methods and properties defined in the superclasses above it within the class hierarchy. Inheritance can be broken for individual methods and properties when creating a subclass. This is known as specialization.

Generally the term *inheritance* implies single inheritance. In some languages such as C++, *multiple inheritance* is supported. In multiple inheritance, a single subclass can be derived from more than one superclass. Along with the problems of naming conflicts within the union of methods and properties of the superclasses, multiple inheritance is usually considered an improper class hierarchy design solution. The combination of composite objects and delegation is superior to multiple inheritance.

Instance

A term which describes a runtime occurrence of an object belonging to a particular class. Classes are defined at design time, while object instances are created from defined classes at runtime.

Message

An instruction from one object (the sender) to another object (the receiver) to execute one of the receiver's methods. The three parts of a message are defined by the receiver object name, the method name, and any parameters the method may require. Messages can also be two way, which occurs when the receiver object's method returns a value to the sender.

Object

A software collection of related methods (functions) and data (memory variables). Generally the methods act on the associated data. Generally an object refers to an instance of a class.

Polymorphism

The ability to send the same message to various objects while each object is responsible for acting on the common message. Polymorphism allows a common interface to be created for objects sending messages. For example, sending the message "Draw" to both a box object and a circle object would be an example of polymorphism since the message that was sent to each object had the same name while each object contained its own Draw method. A Draw method would be defined in both the Box class and the Circle class and each may have similar or completely different behaviors. Polymorphism is supported by allowing the same method name to be defined within different classes.

SQL Pass Through

SQL Pass Through is a Visual FoxPro 3 capability that gives you low-level access to the back-end data source. SPT requires us to write code that opens the connections, passes commands, checks for errors, and more. These things are handled through a group of functions that start with the three letters SQL. Visual FoxPro also supports updateable views, which provide higher level access to back-end data.

Index

NOTE: Page numbers in *italics* refer to locations of code; page numbers in **bold** refer to primary discussion of a topic.

Symbols

A

B

C

D

E

G

H

I

J

M

N

P

Q

R

S

T

U

V

W

X

Z

[1648] The Visual FoxPro® 3 Codebook

GET A FREE CATALOG JUST FOR EXPRESSING YOUR OPINION.

Help us improve our books and get a ***FREE*** full-color catalog in the bargain. Please complete this form, pull out this page and send it in today. The address is on the reverse side.

Name ______________________________ **Company** ______________________________

Address ______________________________ **City** __________ **State** ___ **Zip** _______

Phone ( ) __________________

1. How would you rate the overall quality of this book?

- ❑ Excellent
- ❑ Very Good
- ❑ Good
- ❑ Fair
- ❑ Below Average
- ❑ Poor

2. What were the things you liked most about the book? (Check all that apply)

- ❑ Pace
- ❑ Format
- ❑ Writing Style
- ❑ Examples
- ❑ Table of Contents
- ❑ Index
- ❑ Price
- ❑ Illustrations
- ❑ Type Style
- ❑ Cover
- ❑ Depth of Coverage
- ❑ Fast Track Notes

3. What were the things you liked *least* about the book? (Check all that apply)

- ❑ Pace
- ❑ Format
- ❑ Writing Style
- ❑ Examples
- ❑ Table of Contents
- ❑ Index
- ❑ Price
- ❑ Illustrations
- ❑ Type Style
- ❑ Cover
- ❑ Depth of Coverage
- ❑ Fast Track Notes

4. Where did you buy this book?

- ❑ Bookstore chain
- ❑ Small independent bookstore
- ❑ Computer store
- ❑ Wholesale club
- ❑ College bookstore
- ❑ Technical bookstore
- ❑ Other __________________

5. How did you decide to buy this particular book?

- ❑ Recommended by friend
- ❑ Recommended by store personnel
- ❑ Author's reputation
- ❑ Sybex's reputation
- ❑ Read book review in __________
- ❑ Other __________________

6. How did you pay for this book?

- ❑ Used own funds
- ❑ Reimbursed by company
- ❑ Received book as a gift

7. What is your level of experience with the subject covered in this book?

- ❑ Beginner
- ❑ Intermediate
- ❑ Advanced

8. How long have you been using a computer?

years __________________

months __________________

9. Where do you most often use your computer?

- ❑ Home
- ❑ Work
- ❑ Both
- ❑ Other __________________

10. What kind of computer equipment do you have? (Check all that apply)

- ❑ PC Compatible Desktop Computer
- ❑ PC Compatible Laptop Computer
- ❑ Apple/Mac Computer
- ❑ Apple/Mac Laptop Computer
- ❑ CD ROM
- ❑ Fax Modem
- ❑ Data Modem
- ❑ Scanner
- ❑ Sound Card
- ❑ Other __________________

11. What other kinds of software packages do you ordinarily use?

- ❑ Accounting
- ❑ Databases
- ❑ Networks
- ❑ Apple/Mac
- ❑ Desktop Publishing
- ❑ Spreadsheets
- ❑ CAD
- ❑ Games
- ❑ Word Processing
- ❑ Communications
- ❑ Money Management
- ❑ Other __________________

12. What operating systems do you ordinarily use?

- ❑ DOS
- ❑ OS/2
- ❑ Windows
- ❑ Apple/Mac
- ❑ Windows NT
- ❑ Other __________________

13. **On what computer-related subject(s) would you like to see more books?**

14. **Do you have any other comments about this book? (Please feel free to use a separate piece of paper if you need more room)**

PLEASE FOLD, SEAL, AND MAIL TO SYBEX

SYBEX INC.
Department M
2021 Challenger Drive
Alameda, CA
94501